DATE DUE

JUN 0 7 1994		
SEP 2 2 1994		
NOV 2 8 1994		
DEC 16 1994		
DEC 16 1994		
DEC 0 5 1996		

DEMCO 38-297

A TOWER IN BABEL

A HISTORY OF BROADCASTING IN THE UNITED STATES

VOLUME I — A TOWER IN BABEL

VOLUMES II AND III — IN PREPARATION

A TOWER IN BABEL

A History of Broadcasting
in the United States

Volume I—to 1933

ERIK BARNOUW

New York OXFORD UNIVERSITY PRESS 1966

CONTENTS

A TOWER IN BABEL

INTRODUCTION

And they said . . . "Let us build us a city and a
tower, whose top may reach unto heaven; and let us
make us a name . . ."   Genesis 11, 4

Every medium of information has made names—and meanwhile, values.
New media have meant new values. Since the dawn of history, each new
medium has tended to undermine an old monopoly, shift the definitions of
goodness and greatness, and alter the climate of men's lives.

In ancient Egypt the transition from stone—as in the pyramids—to papyrus as transmitter of truth, prestige, and doctrine seems to have brought
on or encouraged many other changes. Because papyrus was portable, it
helped rulers exercise authority over wide areas. But the power now had
to be shared with armies of copyists, and the literate became a privileged
class. Because papyrus was scarce, control of its production became crucial, and again this meant a sharing of royal power, in this case with man-
agers of productivity. All this meant a shift away from absolute monarchy,
a dispersal of authority, that is said to have penetrated deeply into Egyp-
tian life.[1] Papyrus begat bureaucracy.

Toward the end of the Middle Ages, the arrival of paper in Europe
began to undermine a church monopoly of knowledge, which had been
based on the scarcity of parchment and on the skills of monastery copyists.
Ample supplies of paper now encouraged the development of printing,
and spread written communication to new fields and ideas. It became an
instrument in the growth of trade, the rise of the vernacular, and the
spread of heretical ideas via tract, story, and image. It reinforced the rise
of merchant, lawyer, explorer, scientist. The chain reactions echoed
through centuries.

1. Innis, *Empire and Communications*, pp. 17-19, 118.

3

After World War I, broadcasting began to play a prominent role in our lives. Men had for some years been erecting towers that could send out signals, words, and music, but these had—in spite of the evangelism of a few—been put to limited use. During the war period they had been devoted to naval and military purposes, largely as instruments of point-to-point communication. Now released from war duty, the men and mechanisms of radio began to address the population as a whole—with reverberating results. "We have witnessed in the last four or five months," said Secretary of Commerce Herbert Hoover early in 1922, "one of the most astonishing things that have come under my observation of American life." [2] In 1920 just one station, KDKA, Pittsburgh, was licensed to render a regular *broadcasting* service. In 1921 it was joined by a few others. Then, in 1922, more than five hundred broadcasting stations went on the air. So widespread was the feeling that broadcasting was a key to influence and power, that the rush was joined by many different interests. They included, not surprisingly, telephone and telegraph companies and the makers and sellers of electrical equipment. But educational institutions also took a prominent role. Scores of universities had long been active in radio experimentation and felt especially ready for this moment. By January 1923, broadcasting licenses had been obtained by 72 universities, colleges and schools, while many others prepared to follow. Newspapers were only slightly less numerous; in the same period 69 newspapers became broadcasting licensees, along with 29 department stores, 12 religious organizations, several city governments, and a sprinkling of automobile dealers, theaters, and banks.[3] A many-sided struggle for dominance began.

It is ironic that the starting signal for this rush, comparable to the Oklahoma land rush or California gold rush, was a broadcast of a presidential election in which the two major contestants, Warren G. Harding and James M. Cox, were newspaper publishers. Their nomination had symbolized the long-held place of the press in the constellation of power, and also marked its zenith. The glory would soon begin to dim—a dislocation was being set in motion, leading to decades of unbalance and shift, whose ramifications may only have begun.

It is far too early to attempt an assessment of the impact on our civilization of the shift from printed words, as carriers of information and pres-

2. *Radio Broadcast*, May 1922.
3. *Radio Service Bulletin*, February 1, 1923.

tige, to the ever-present broadcast word, sound, and image. But it is not too early to chronicle how the broadcast media have grown, both as instruments of expression and as industries; who has risen to leadership in them, and how; what these media have told us, and not told us, about ourselves and our world; what struggles have been fought, open and hidden, for their control. In this volume and those that follow, our focus will be on what has been broadcast, by whom, and why. The "why" will require us at times to look behind the scenes, as well as we are able, with full awareness that accumulating evidence may amend the picture.

Our chronicle will involve statesmen, mountebanks, teachers, salesmen, artists, wheeler-dealers, soldiers, saints, reporters, propagandists—and others. The tower-builders reached for heaven, each in his way.

Daily Graphic, New York, March 15, 1877

Terrors of the Telephone: an 1877 prophecy

1 / VOICES

broadcast . . . act or process of scattering seeds
New National Dictionary, 1901

broadcast . . . to scatter or disseminate . . . specif.,
radio messages, speeches, etc.
New Century Dictionary, 1927

The age of broadcasting was foreseen, at least by some, almost from the moment that Alexander Graham Bell demonstrated his telephone. His revelation in 1876 stirred astonishing visions of things to come. An artist for the New York *Daily Graphic,* in the issue of March 15, 1877, depicted what he called "Terrors of the Telephone." He showed an orator at a microphone heard by groups of people throughout the world.

In the same year a popular song, "The Wondrous Telephone," published in St. Louis, described the glories of the invention in these terms:

> You stay at home and listen
> To the lecture in the hall,
> Or hear the strains of music
> From a fashionable ball! [1]

In 1879, in *Punch,* the artist George Dumaurier took a further forward leap—into the age of television. He showed two people by a fireplace, watching a sporting match on a screen above the mantel. Sounds were transmitted by a telephone.

Bell himself visualized diverse uses for the telephone, which his patent application called "a method of, and apparatus for, transmitting vocal and other sounds telegraphically." Starting that spring, he gave lecture-demonstrations in which he always included music as well as speech. The Boston *Evening Transcript* described him as demonstrating "telephony, or

1. Quoted, Banning, *Commercial Broadcasting Pioneer,* p. 3.

7

the telegraphing of musical sounds."[2] On one occasion a band playing "The Star-Spangled Banner" in Boston was heard by an audience of 2000 in Providence. On another, a singer performing selections from *The Marriage of Figaro* in Providence was heard by an audience in Boston. Another program included an exhortation by the evangelist Dwight L. Moody with a gospel hymn sung and played by Ira David Sanky. When Bell exhibited his invention at the Philadelphia Centennial Exposition during the summer of 1876 he included a reading of "To be or not to be." The following summer his demonstrations for Queen Victoria at Windsor Castle offered transmissions from various points and included bugle calls, organ music, and a young lady singing "Kathleen Mavourneen." Her Majesty and royal household "evinced the greatest interest."[3]

During the following years such possibilities were not developed in a significant way but were not forgotten. In the summer of 1890, at the Grand Union Hotel in Saratoga, eight hundred people were provided with a concert by telephone wire from Madison Square Garden, as well as entertainment from other points, including dance music and a recitation of "The Charge of the Light Brigade." The program was also heard by a gathering at the home of a telephone executive in New Jersey, where guests danced "with perfect ease" to the music. Both here and at Saratoga regular telephone receivers were used—with an improvised addition:

> The orchestral music was listened to at Saratoga by means of sets of hand telephones, and every note was heard distinctly, even to the applause of the audience gathered at Madison Square Garden. Some of the songs and solos and the recitation were heard all over the room at Saratoga by means of a single loud-speaking receiver provided with a large funnel-shaped resonator to magnify the sound.

Significantly, the magazine which reported this event, *Electrical Engineer*, felt that the American Telephone and Telegraph Company was not doing enough to exploit the possibilities of "furnishing of musical and other entertainments by wire at the fireside."[4]

The truth was, the telephone company was finding it profitable to concentrate on what had become its special function, a link for two-way talk. It saw for the moment little reason for digressing into what must have

2. Rhodes, *Beginnings of Telephony*, pp. 26-30.
3. Harlow, *Old Wires and New Waves*, pp. 265, 372.
4. Quoted, Banning, *Commercial Broadcasting Pioneer*, pp. 4-5.

seemed, at best, side-show possibilities. But when the wireless age dawned, such dreams stirred again.

The inventions that marked the road to radio and television have often been traced and are not our main concern. But almost every invention became the property of a company, and eventually a weapon in titanic struggles, deals, and mergers, bearing on control of the broadcasting media. These maneuvers, in which the stakes were high, were to have a profound effect on the shape of broadcasting in the United States, and must be reviewed to lay the groundwork for our story.

There is a direct line of descent from the youth Marconi, who received a patent at the age of twenty-three, to the Radio Corporation of America and its subsidiary the National Broadcasting Company. This and other lines must now be followed.

THE BLACK BOX

By the early 1890's the waves we call radio waves were already a subject of intense speculation and experiment. Because it was Heinrich Hertz of Germany who, during the years 1886-89, had clearly demonstrated their nature, they were at the moment called "Hertzian waves." He had shown how to set them in motion and how to detect them.

The fact that some of these waves could pass through fog and solid objects was especially provocative. Sir William Crookes, in a widely read article in the London *Fortnightly Review* in 1892, discussed the implications:

> Here is unfolded to us a new and astonishing world. . . . Rays of light will not pierce through a wall, nor, as we know only too well, through a London fog. But the electrical vibrations of a yard or more in wave length . . . will easily pierce such mediums, which to them will be transparent. Here, then, is revealed the bewildering possibility of telegraph without wires, posts, cables or any of our present costly appliances. Granted a few reasonable postulates, the whole thing comes well within the realms of possible fulfillment. . . .
>
> This is no mere dream of a visionary philosopher. All the requisites needed to bring it within the grasp of daily life are well within the possibilities of discovery, and are so reasonable and so clearly in the path of researches which are now being actively prosecuted in every capital of Europe that we may any day expect to hear that they have emerged from the realms of speculation into those of sober fact.[1]

1. *Fortnightly Review*, February 1, 1892.

Among the many pursuing these reasonable, bewildering, astonishing possibilities were Oliver Lodge in England, Alexander Popov in Russia, Adolphus Slaby in Germany, Edouard Branly in France. Alternative avenues to wireless communication were also being explored, both in Europe and America.

Guglielmo Marconi was at this time a youth in his late teens, living with his family in a villa near Bologna. His mother was an Irish girl who, before she was of age, had fallen in love with an Italian gentleman, older and already a widower and a father. Her parents forbade an engagement. Biding her time until she was twenty-one, she crossed the Channel and married him, and they went to Italy and settled at the Villa Grifone; in due time she bore two sons, Alfonso and Guglielmo. For years she did not see her homeland.

Guglielmo became a thin, intense youth, who read all the scientific books at the villa and revered Benjamin Franklin and other giants of electricity. Much of his education was provided by tutors. Even at mealtimes he often got lost in thought. The elder Marconi, who believed in instructive discourse during meals, found this irksome, especially when Guglielmo would suddenly ask a question having nothing to do with the topic at hand. In the summer of 1894, Guglielmo and his half-brother Luigi took a vacation trip to the Italian Alps, where Guglielmo picked up a periodical with an article on Hertzian waves. From that moment on, he was like someone possessed. His brother found him constantly sketching strange diagrams, making calculations. On returning to the Villa Grifone, he practically confined himself in a third-floor room that had become his workshop. For long stretches the door stayed locked. His mother, worried about his thinness, took to carrying trays upstairs and leaving them on the landing outside the locked door. His father fumed: the boy was wasting irreplaceable years.[2] The first experiments were clearly failures, but experimenting continued. In due time the family was allowed a look. Guglielmo had reached a point at which, via Hertzian waves, he could ring a bell across the room, or even downstairs. He knew he was only beginning. He hardly dared open an electrical journal lest he read that the goal, so clearly defined by Sir William Crookes, had been reached. Was it possible that those famous men in all the capitals of Europe had not yet found it? Guglielmo introduced a Morse key into his circuit. "From the beginning 1 aimed at . . . breaking the emission up into long and short periods so

2. Degna Marconi, *My Father Marconi,* p. 12.

that Morse dots and dashes could be transmitted." [3] The tests now extended to the outdoors; his older brother Alfonso became his helper.

To actuate his waves, Guglielmo used the method Hertz had used: a spark leaping across a gap. His receiver was a device developed by Lodge, from an idea by Branly. Branly had found that certain metal filings would *cohere* when Hertzian waves struck them. Filings in a glass tube could thus be used as a detector. A tap was needed to loosen the filings for the next dot or dash. Morse key, spark, coherer, tapper: to these essential elements young Marconi now made crucial additions: something he called an *antenna,* and a grounding at each end of the operation.

Young Marconi knew that success required distance, and clear demonstration that the waves would overcome obstacles such as hills and mountains. During 1895 the tests moved forward. Family tradition described them as follows:

> The handkerchief was adequate to signal success from the fields in front of the Villa Grifone. It would not be seen if Alfonso went to the far side of the hill behind the house. For this he was armed with a hunting rifle and he marched sturdily off, up the narrow path past the farm buildings. It was the end of September now and the vines were heavy with purple grapes, the air golden. The walk over the rim of the hill took twenty minutes. Alfonso led, followed by the farmer Mignani and the carpenter Vornelli, lugging the antenna. Finally, Guglielmo, watching tensely from a window, lost sight of the small procession as it dropped over the horizon.

Marconi himself has told the rest of the story. "After some minutes I started to send, manipulating the Morse key . . . In the distance a shot echoed down the valley." [4]

The elder Marconi for the first time began to take the events seriously. The parish priest and family doctor were consulted. The priest listened to the whole story, nodding thoughtfully. Finally a letter was dispatched to the Italian Minister of Post and Telegraph. When the reply came, saying the government was not interested, his mother made a prompt, resolute decision: she and Guglielmo would go to England with the invention. Perhaps she was homesick; perhaps she was protecting her son against the hurt of rejection. But she could not have made a sounder decision. The British empire, held together by thin lines of ships and threads of ocean cable, could use such a means of communication better than any other

3. Quoted, Dunlap, *Marconi,* p. 18.
4. Quoted, Degna Marconi, *My Father Marconi,* p. 30.

world power. Her virtual control of ocean cables, important as it was, was of uncertain military value; what would become of them in war was not yet known.

Young Marconi himself carefully packed, locked, and carried the black box that held the invention. In February 1896 they set sail for England: the mother, beautiful and aglow with anticipation; he, thin and primly dressed in dark suit and a high-collared shirt. To offset his youth, he "drew a cloak of dignity around himself." The black box at once aroused the suspicion of British customs officials. Only two years earlier, the French President had been killed by an Italian anarchist. In the box were wires, batteries, dials; smashing it seemed the wisest policy, and this the officials did. On arrival in London, Marconi had to begin by rebuilding it. But meanwhile a relative, to whom his mother had written ahead, was putting them in touch with one of London's best patent attorneys. While the patent procedure went forward, they were also calling on Sir William Preece, chief engineer of telegraphs in the British Post Office system. In all this they were fortunate. Preece had himself experimented in wireless—with success, but without achieving a useful distance. He was able to appreciate what Marconi had done. Tests began in rooms of the London Post Office, then moved onto Salisbury plain, reaching a hundred yards, then one mile; then six miles, nine miles. Marconi later recalled: "The calm of my life ended then." [5]

Marconi received his patent July 2, 1897, and in that same month a small, powerful British group joined with him to form Wireless Telegraph and Signal Company, Ltd., later renamed Marconi's Wireless Telegraph Company, Ltd. It was capitalized at £100,000 and acquired Marconi's patents everywhere except in Italy and dependencies. Marconi received half the stock and £15,000 in cash. He became one of six directors, in charge of development. He was twenty-three.

For years the pace of events was not to slacken. As soon as the company was formed, Marconi moved to the coast. Setting up equipment on the Isle of Wight, he communicated with the mainland 14 miles away, then with a ship 18 miles away, penetrating fog and rain. The tests caused international excitement. Newspapers throughout the world carried accounts. Foreign observers arrived, especially naval and military observers. In 1898 the new company received its first revenue: wireless equipment was ordered for several lighthouses. In a comic-opera development, Queen Vic-

5. *Ibid.* pp. 36-46.

toria entered the wireless story—as she had the telephone story. The Prince of Wales had wrenched his knee and was recuperating on a yacht, perhaps to get away from his anxious mother. The Queen's entourage contrived a countermove—wireless. Marconi was enlisted to keep her informed. He fitted the ship with an antenna and built a land station at Osborn House, where the Queen was staying. Marconi, wandering about the garden to find the best location for his antenna, was stopped by a gardener. He had apparently intruded where servants were not to go. Marconi ignored his warning and the incident was reported to the Queen, who was affronted by Marconi's behavior. "Get another electrician," she instructed, but was told that alas, England had no Marconi. Before long, however, bulletins began to arrive from the yacht: "H. R. H. the Prince of Wales has passed another excellent night . . . the knee is most satisfactory." [6]

Meanwhile, Marconi had undertaken another assignment as ephemeral in content, and as certain to thrust him onto the international scene. The Dublin *Daily Express* requested a minute-by-minute wireless account of the Kingstown Regatta. A steamer, chartered to follow the racing yachts, was fitted with a 75-foot antenna. The details of the race, received at a shore station, were telephoned to the newspaper and were in print before the ships had returned to port.[7] The feat was dazzling and brought an invitation from the New York *Herald* to report the *America's* Cup Race in the United States in October 1899. Marconi and his associates saw the invitation as a timely opportunity for overtures to the American navy.

During 1899 Marconi equipment was being installed on three British battleships and was used during naval maneuvers. Demonstrations were also made across the English Channel, and these brought Marconi his first contact with French officials. Now the Marconi directors were thinking about the United States. To exploit the possibilities there, they planned to form an American subsidiary. All this was part of the plan, as Guglielmo Marconi accepted the invitation of the New York *Herald*.

Large-scale international rivalry and intrigue were already afoot. We have mentioned Adolphus Slaby of Germany and Alexander Popov of Russia as early experimenters in wireless communication. These and many others—on both sides of the Atlantic—were now involved in efforts to catch up with and surpass the achievements of Marconi.

6. *Ibid.* pp. 66-7.
7. Schubert, *The Electric Word*, p. 24.

Slaby, who had studied with Heinrich Hertz, had actually witnessed some of the Marconi demonstrations in Britain. In the April 1898 issue of *Century*, he wrote:

> . . . when the news of Marconi's first successes ran through the newspapers, I myself was earnestly occupied with similar problems. . . . Quickly making up my mind, I traveled to England, where the Bureau of Telegraphs was undertaking experiments on a large scale. Mr. Preece, the celebrated engineer-in-chief of the General Post Office, in the most courteous and hospitable way, permitted me to take part in these; and in truth what I there saw was something quite new.

Slaby presently returned to Germany, continued his research, and was soon awarded several patents. In collaboration with Count Arco he developed the Slaby-Arco system, the foundation of Telefunken. Soon Slaby-Arco representatives would be submitting equipment and bids to the U. S. Navy Department, with considerable success.

Alexander Popov's interest in electromagnetic theory had already taken him to the United States. In 1893, representing Russia's Torpedo School at Kronstadt, he had gone to Chicago to see the World's Columbian Exposition, and also to attend an electrical congress presided over by Helmholtz, in which there was intense discussion of Hertzian waves. Popov was caught up in the same excitement that had possessed Marconi. Returning to Russia, he pursued similar experiments at the Torpedo School, which was destined to become Russia's "cradle of radio." He too used the spark transmitter with a coherer. On May 7, 1895, he read a paper reporting on the ringing of a bell by these means.[8] Popov subsequently developed equipment which was used by the Russian navy and to some extent by the French navy. Soon other French experimenters were demonstrating equipment for the French navy, as well as for the American navy. The Italian navy was by now dealing with Marconi. The rivalry was international.

It was, in various ways, the perfect moment to approach the United States armed forces on the subject of wireless. When Guglielmo Marconi arrived in New York City on September 11, 1899, aboard the *Aurania*, the city was preparing a spectacular welcome not for him but for the hero

8. For this reason May 7 is celebrated as Radio Day in the U.S.S.R. See Radovsky, *Alexander Popov*, p. 50.

of Manila Bay, Admiral George Dewey. Overshadowed too were Sir Thomas Lipton and his *Shamrock,* arriving for the *America's* Cup Race. It was an hour bursting with manifest destiny. The American republic had suddenly turned empire, with overseas possessions. There were protests, like those of the Anti-Imperialist League; one of its spokesmen, William Jennings Bryan, would soon be campaigning for the presidency as an anti-imperialist. But he was already being reviled as wanting a "small" instead of a "big" America. The prevailing mood was more muscular and arrogant. The building of frenzy and newspaper circulation had gone hand in hand; aided by these, navy and army appropriations slid swiftly through Congress. Those with overseas interests were not averse: protected bases, harbors, coaling stations, were needed by a great and expanding power. Such a nation would also, like the British empire, have to think about communication. In the "splendid little war," as John Hay had named it, there had been some difficulties in communication. According to navy annals, it had been splendid within naval squadrons but unsatisfactory between army and navy, and between the field forces and Washington. In fact, to inform Washington of his victory and subsequent actions at Manila, Admiral Dewey had had to send dispatch boats to Hong Kong, whence the news was telegraphed westward, going over British-controlled cables via the Indian Ocean, the Red Sea, the Mediterranean, and the Atlantic Ocean.[9] Somehow, it didn't fit with the new world posture. At this juncture Guglielmo Marconi arrived in America.

Beginning October 16, 1899, the races between the *Shamrock* and *Columbia* were duly reported by wireless and acclaim was distributed—to the *Herald* for vision, to Marconi for genius, to America for seamanship, to Sir Thomas for sportsmanship. Army and navy officials watched with interest and excitement. Remembering Guantanamo, a navy observer wrote: "If we could only have had this last year, what a great thing it would have been." After the races there were special tests for the navy; off the New Jersey coast messages were sent and received by ships and a shore installation. Along with this there was historic legal business: on November 22, 1899, the Marconi Wireless Company of America was incorporated under the laws of New Jersey, to exploit Marconi patents in the United States and various possessions including Cuba. Authorized capital of $10,000,000 was covered by two million shares with a par value of $5. Many of these shares went back to England, 365,000 being held by the parent firm, and

9. *History of Communications-Electronics in the United States Navy,* p. 13.

600,000 assigned to Marconi.[10] Two decades later, in a new incarnation, this company would become the Radio Corporation of America.

As the new century dawned, the equipping of ships with wireless proceeded at a rapid and quickening pace. The parent Marconi company and subsidiaries organized themselves to supply the need, while building shore stations to communicate with the ships. Other companies labored to the same end. Marine disasters anywhere speeded the process. The life-saving aspects of wireless were constantly discussed, but its adoption also dovetailed with the needs of trade, the zeal for empire, the burgeoning of military budgets. The new medium would grow on those budgets, and they would shape its youth.

The spirit of the time was symbolized by the hasty departure of Marconi for England before the naval demonstrations were even finished. It was explained that England had requested his return to prepare apparatus for use in the Boer War.[11]

In spite of the enthusiasm that surrounded the navy tests, official reports had a restrained tone befitting seasoned officials. It was recommended that the navy give the invention a trial, but reservations were mentioned. The drama of the bluish spark, crashing noisily across its gap, had left afterthoughts. "The shock from the sending coil," said the report, "may be quite severe and even dangerous to a person with a weak heart." However, "no fatal accidents have been recorded." But the effects of rolling and pitching were not yet known. And the apparatus might "injuriously affect the compass if placed near it." Behind such objections appear to have been fears of some officers that their authority at sea would be undermined by the new invention. But the navy hierarchy had other objections. They had asked Marconi and his associates about senders interfering with each other, and had found the answers evasive. Here Marconi had, in fact, reason to be guarded. He was hard at work on the principle of tuning to different wave lengths. Need for such a provision had already been foreseen by Sir William Crookes in 1892. Without it the air would become chaos. Marconi felt he had solved the problem, but he did not receive a patent until later—in April 1900. Meanwhile the U. S. Navy was nettled by his answers, which one officer thought were "intended to mislead." [12]

10. *Ibid.* pp. 27, 35.
11. The Boers also sought and obtained wireless equipment. The British captured equipment apparently made in Germany, similar in design to Marconi equipment. New York *Herald*, December 31, 1899.
12. *History of Communications-Electronics in the United States Navy*, pp. 28, 34.

A more serious cause of friction was coming between the navy and Marconi—with far-ranging results. Marconi's first income had involved outright sale of equipment, but a new policy was evolving. It paralleled the policy pursued by telephone companies: the Marconi companies would not sell equipment but *communication*. In dealings with commercial shipping companies, the policy worked in this way. A Marconi company would install equipment on a ship and furnish a man to maintain and operate it. The equipment would remain Marconi property, and the man a Marconi employee. An annual fee to the Marconi company would cover use of the equipment and the services of the operator.

Aboard ship Marconi operators would transmit "marconigrams" to and from passengers at rates to be established; company and officers would be served at a much reduced rate. Meanwhile Marconi shore stations would be maintained at various points to provide the Marconi-equipped ships with shore communication. For a time these shore stations communicated freely with wireless operators on any ship, but in reaction to growing competition, this practice was abandoned. Why should the Marconi companies maintain shore stations for the convenience of ships equipped by rival companies? It became the policy of Marconi shore stations—except in emergencies—to communicate only with Marconi-equipped ships; communications from non-Marconi operators and equipment were, by and large, to be ignored.

While such a plan could not apply to naval forces, a variation was worked out for them. In proposals made to the U. S. Navy Department at the end of 1899 the Marconi representatives offered to equip twenty vessels for a lump sum of $10,000 plus a royalty of $10,000 per year. Navy personnel would be permitted to operate the equipment, but it must be agreed that they would not communicate with non-Marconi shore stations except in emergencies. The navy was offered special low rates at Marconi stations so that it would not need to build shore stations of its own.

The navy reacted to these terms with indignation. It considered the royalty plan illegal and the other proposals a high-handed attempt to establish a world monopoly over wireless.

The Marconi policy became ammunition for rival companies. That the Marconi companies were instruments of "British monopoly," an attempt to extend to wireless the control already exercised by the British over cables, became a favorite theme among the rival companies and among navy officials. It had an important effect: it briefly slowed the surge of the Marconi companies, at least in their relations with the United States government. Turning away from Marconi, the navy would establish its own shore stations, and buy equipment from other experimenters. This, incidentally, would precipitate years of patent disputes. But meanwhile the spotlight would turn to these other experimenters—including many in the United States.

ON NATIVE SOIL

Before Marconi seized world attention, native experimenters in wireless communication had generally worked in obscurity, getting newspaper attention only as items of the bizarre, like the finding of dinosaur eggs. Later years brought to light that there had been a number of such experimenters; just what they had done was by that time difficult to determine.

There was a Dr. Mahlon Loomis, who had experimented in the Blue Ridge Mountains in Virginia. Raising kites from two mountain peaks 14 miles apart, he is said to have sent "intelligible messages" between them in October 1866.[1] In 1872 he obtained U. S. Patent No. 129,971 for an "improvement in telegraphing."

There was Professor Amos Dolbear of Tufts College, who had been a telephone experimenter before Bell and later became an early wireless experimenter. In 1886 he obtained U. S. Patent No. 350,299 for an "induction" system of wireless telegraphy. It apparently did not achieve notable distances, but on the basis of the patent he threatened for a time to restrain Marconi from reporting the America's Cup races by wireless. He later changed his mind.[2]

There was the mysterious figure of Nathan B. Stubblefield, whose gravestone in Murray, Ky., names him the Father of Radio Broadcasting. He is said to have transmitted voice as early as 1892 and made public demonstrations in 1902, including one in Philadelphia and another near Washington. His U. S. Patent No. 887,357, obtained in 1908, was the subject of long litigation, which won him victories but no revenue. He died of starvation in 1928 in a shack in Kentucky.[3]

These were early starters, pre-Marconi. Now, with wireless a center of attention, there would be experimenters by hundreds and by thousands.

1. Young, The Real Beginning of Radio," Saturday Review, March 7, 1964.
2. History of Communications-Electronics in the United States Navy, p. 26.
3. Johnson, Address to Kentucky Broadcasters Association, 1961.

For a number of these the dream would be different: speech and music. With them a new era began, associated with the terms *wireless telephone . . . radio telephone . . . radiophone . . . radio.* On the heels of Marconi's recall to England it began.

VOICES IN THE NIGHT

One of its first leaders was Reginald Aubrey Fessenden, a Canadian, who had worked for Thomas Edison at his New Jersey laboratory and for the Westinghouse company in Pittsburgh. In 1893 he had become professor of electrical engineering at Western University—later renamed University of Pittsburgh—where he had experimented with Hertzian waves. In 1900 the Weather Bureau of the U. S. Department of Agriculture, stirred by the Marconi excitement, employed him at $3000 a year to test the idea of disseminating weather information by wireless.[1]

Already Fessenden had his mind on voice transmission. To accomplish this, he proposed a heresy. The wave sent out must *not* be—as in the Marconi system—an interrupted wave or series of bursts. Instead it must be a *continuous* wave, on which voice would be superimposed as variations or modulations. This heresy became the foundation of radio.

In 1901, using a telephone microphone, Fessenden superimposed a voice on such a wave. Now he needed a detector more sensitive than the primitive coherer. By 1902 he had one, an "electrolytic" detector. This and similar detectors soon came into fairly wide use.

Fessenden's ideas went beyond the aims and funds of the Weather Bureau; and, moreover, Fessenden was nettled by a government tendency to consider all his findings its property. But two Pittsburgh financiers, T. H. Given and Hay Walker, Jr., now decided to back his experiments. The National Electric Signaling Company was formed, to which they contributed cash—eventually almost $1,000,000[2]—and Fessenden his patents and services. He moved to the shore, first to Chesapeake Bay, then to Brant Rock, Mass. He turned to General Electric in Schenectady to construct for him the kind of alternating-current generator he felt was needed for his transmission. At General Electric the regular designers considered his ideas absurd, and they gave the task to a recent immigrant, Swedish-born Ernst F. W. Alexanderson, who had studied with Professor Slaby

1. Helen M. Fessenden, *Fessenden,* pp. 76-7.
2. *Ibid.* p. 116.

in Germany; the newcomer was "crazy enough to undertake it." [3] After many difficulties the needed "alternator" was installed at Brant Rock.

A climax to these events came on Christmas Eve, 1906. Over a wide area ship operators, with earphones to head, alert to the crackle of distant messages, were snapped to attention by a "CQ, CQ" in Morse code. After a moment they heard

> a human voice coming from their instruments—someone speaking! Then a woman's voice rose in song. It was uncanny! Many of them called their officers to come and listen; soon the wireless rooms were crowded. Next someone was heard reading a poem. Then there was a violin solo; then a man made a speech, and they could catch most of the words. [4]

They were hearing a Christmas Eve broadcast. The violin solo was played by Fessenden himself (Gounod's "O, Holy Night") and he also sang a few bars and read verses from Luke. The woman's voice came from a phonograph recording of Handel's "Largo." At the end Fessenden wished his audience a Merry Christmas and promised another broadcast on New Year's Eve. Those listening were asked to write to R. A. Fessenden at Brant Rock, and many seem to have done so. The New Year's Eve program, of similar pattern, was heard by ships as far away as the West Indies, including banana boats of the United Fruit Company. [5]

All this had an immediate result. The United Fruit Company was already experimenting with wireless, by which perishable cargoes could be directed to profitable markets, and scattered plantations could be coordinated. Spurred by the Fessenden successes, it now bought a quantity of his equipment and assumed a pioneering role throughout the Caribbean—first in dot-and-dash wireless, eventually in voice transmission.

But meanwhile the big wireless push took other directions. For many experimenters, including Marconi, the obsession was not voice but *distance*—especially the crossing of oceans. In 1901 the letter S, sent from Cornwall by Morse code, had been received in Newfoundland via a kite antenna and heard by Marconi on an earphone. On the strength of this, transatlantic stations were built. On January 19, 1903, a greeting from President Theodore Roosevelt to King Edward VII was hurled out in noisy dots and dashes by a Marconi station at South Wellfleet on Cape

3. Alexanderson, *Reminiscences*, p. 16.
4. Harlow, *Old Wires and New Waves*, p. 455.
5. Helen M. Fessenden, *Fessenden*, p. 153.

Cod, and a reply was received. These stations were erratic, unreliable; often, for hours, not an intelligible signal came through. Yet they could be seen as eventual competitors to the lucrative cables. Fessenden too worked in this direction, with successes followed by exasperating failures. But his great goal was to include speech and music. Why? To many it seemed a frill, economically unpromising. But Fessenden was stubborn and continued. Others followed.

MISSION IN THE ETHER

Lee de Forest was born in 1873 in a parsonage in frontier Council Bluffs, Iowa, where his father, a minister, had married the young choir leader. They soon moved to Alabama, his father to head Talladega College, which had been founded by missionaries after the Civil War to educate the "freedmen." Resented as northern meddlers, the De Forests found themselves ostracized by the white citizens of Talladega. Their life revolved around the Negro college, where young Lee spent hours in the library, poring over the *Patent Office Gazette,* fascinated by its mechanical drawings. At home he read the Bible from cover to cover. But the unforgettable times were the parlor musicales arranged by his mother, a soprano and pianist. Lee himself took cornet lessons.

The Talladega atmosphere never left De Forest. Throughout life he had a sense of isolation, and at the same time addressed the world in statements with a biblical ring. In his diary, begun when he was seventeen, he constantly seemed to see himself as a figure in an epic pilgrimage, struggling up a steep and difficult road; in many an entry he exhorted himself to sterner effort. Though he rejected his father's pleas to become a minister, the mission he found among Hertzian waves seemed to become for him a new evangelism, in which he, like his father, constantly had a soprano at his side.

Though his school preparation was biblical and agricultural, he passed examinations which admitted him, in 1893, to the Sheffield Scientific School of Yale University. Before starting his studies he headed for Chicago and its World's Columbian Exposition, getting a job as chair pusher at $8 per week and sleeping at a farm for fifty cents a night.[1] Whenever his customers agreed, he steered them to Machinery Hall, where he saw the electrical exhibits again and again.

1. De Forest, *Father of Radio,* pp. 62-3.

He owed his job to a strike of the Amalgamated Order of Chair Pushers, which meant that he was a strike breaker; this troubled him, a diary entry tells us, but to leave would have been like "leaving heaven." [2] Among the innumerable customers he wheeled to Machinery Hall may have been the man who became Russia's "Father of Radio," Alexander Popov, sent as observer from Kronstadt.

At Yale, Lee was a lonely figure. He could spend only fifteen cents per meal and often got up at 4 A.M. to mow lawns. When he lost time, he reprimanded himself in his diary. "The morning wasted, bitterly will its hours be craved, but no tears of remorse avail to bring back one golden moment." When other students scattered for Christmas he stayed, working ceaselessly on a design for an underground trolley, for a $50,000 prize offered by *Scientific American*. When he finished, he could not conceive of the possibility of not winning the prize. "I felt so supremely happy I could have shouted . . . I vowed to give $5,000 to the Lord if I won . . ." He did not win. Nothing he did at Yale quite worked out. Meanwhile his readings in Darwin made him anxious, undermining the faith of his upbringing; he tried consciously to find a religious dimension in his study of science. He won his undergraduate degree in three years. His classmates voted him Nerviest and also Homeliest.[3] Perhaps his dedication to great ends invited retaliation.

De Forest stayed on for his Ph.D., earned in 1899 with a dissertation on *Reflection of Hertzian Waves from the Ends of Parallel Wires*. Then he headed back for the Chicago area, where he held several jobs over a two-year period. One was with Western Electric, where he managed to be transferred to the telephone department, "goal of my hopes." In his diary he wrote: "What finer task than to transfer the sound of a voice of song to one a thousand miles away. If I could do that tonight!" His one indulgence in Chicago was an occasional twenty-five-cent balcony ticket for the Castle Square Opera Company; he gloried in its music. Most of his evenings were spent experimenting in his rented room. He had decided, along with many others, that the coherer was the weak link in the Marconi system, and he was developing an alternative which he called a "responder." The work that went into it diverted cash from food and clothing. When his employers gave him a $10 a week raise he was ecstatic. "Never again

2. Carneal, *A Conqueror of Space*, p. 3.
3. De Forest, *Father of Radio*, pp. 67-82.

shall I . . . wear the same collar longer than three days." With two other experimenters he tested his responder from rooftop to rooftop. De Forest stood in the rain on top of the Lakota Hotel with his heart pounding. The results were so good that he felt his hour had come. That year, 1901, there would be a new international yacht race off Sandy Hook. They must go to New York and report it by wireless. "Emboldened . . . I forced the hands of my confreres." [4] After the trip to New York by day coach, De Forest was taken aback to learn that the New York *Herald* and the Associated Press had already contracted with Marconi to report the races. But De Forest managed to obtain a commission from the lesser Publishers Press Association. On the strength of this contract, he raised $1000 to prepare equipment. De Forest and his associates had endless difficulties but worked day and night, hardly eating. Before they were ready, Lee de Forest collapsed and was taken to a hospital. They were saved from disaster by a grisly event. The assassination of President McKinley resulted in postponement of the yacht races; the extra time allowed De Forest to recover and prepare the equipment. Meanwhile, still another wireless entrepreneur, though without sponsor, announced that he would report the events by wireless.

The races began. From three transmitters along the route the reports crackled into the air, producing chaos. Navy observers were on hand; not a signal was intelligible. Each transmitter completely blotted the others. The fiasco could not have been more total.[5] But the enterprising, competitive spirit of the press saved the day for De Forest. Newspapers, which had taken the precaution to get results by semaphore, blandly announced that they had the news "by wireless." De Forest's name was in the paper; he was being mentioned along with Marconi; people began to pay attention. De Forest met a promoter, a "very personable Wall Street character," Abraham White, who in one afternoon became extremely interested and said he would back De Forest. Before leaving him that day, White slipped him a $100 bill, because the young man would need pocket money.[6]

Early in 1902 they incorporated the De Forest Wireless Telegraph Company, with capitalization of $3,000,000. De Forest received a block of stock, a salary of twenty dollars a week, and a chance to continue experi-

4. *Ibid.* pp. 104-23.
5. *History of Communications-Electronics in the United States Navy*, p. 38.
6. De Forest, *Father of Radio*, pp. 126-9. Carneal, *A Conqueror of Space*, p. 144.

menting. Almost immediately, through a demonstration for the Signal
Corps, the company made a sale to the War Department. And the navy
decided on a small purchase for testing purposes.

But White, unlike Fessenden's backers, wanted to sell stock to the public: this was his main intention. One of De Forest's functions was to help
him do it by staging demonstrations, dramatizing the new era. De Forest
entered enthusiastically into all this. With the flamboyance of White and
the technical skill of De Forest, the company became known for dazzling
salesmanship. Paul Schubert, in *The Electric Word,* writes:

> A "latest model" 1902 automobile ran about the streets of New York
> carrying a demonstration De Forest apparatus; its spark gap crackled
> daily before gaping crowds, and every afternoon it invaded Wall
> Street and stopped before the Stock Exchange to telegraph the "clos-
> ing prices" to mythical listeners. At Coney Island, the city's amuse-
> ment resort, a high mast went up and there, too, hundreds were in-
> troduced to the new telegraphy.[7]

The public was buying the stock. White decided that $3,000,000 wasn't
enough. In a reorganization, the capitalization was set at $15,000,000[8] and
the pace of stock-selling stepped up. White was living in a splendid style
and shopping for a Long Island mansion. The company put out grandiose
brochures, envisaging a world-wide chain of De Forest stations. Through
these the Caribbean would be firmly welded; the Pacific would become
"an American lake." [9]

At the 1904 St. Louis world's fair—the "Louisiana Purchase Exposition"
—Lee de Forest and his wireless tower became a star attraction. In a glass
house the chair pusher of yesterday was on view to thousands. "The stac-
cato crackle of our spark, when purposely unmuffled, brought them
swarming." [10]

No doubt such occasions had, for De Forest, a quality of evangelism. He
was a prophet pointing to a promised land. To some people the circus
promotion, coupled with the financial manipulations of White, were giving the company an air of chicanery. But De Forest allowed himself to
feel that things were going well. At the company plant in Newark equipment was being made and sold. Shore stations were being built. In ship-to-

7. Schubert, *The Electric Word,* p. 51.
8. *Success Magazine,* June 1907. Quoted in *History of Communications-Electronics
in the United States Navy,* p. 48.
9. Schubert, *The Electric Word,* p. 51.
10. De Forest, *Father of Radio,* p. 165.

shore communication, especially in coastal shipping, the company was competing successfully with American Marconi. In 1903 it merged with another company, increasing its shore stations. Best of all, De Forest was getting the chance to continue research, aiming at his real goal: transmission of speech and music. In this, momentous things were about to happen.

In 1904 in England, Professor John Ambrose Fleming, utilizing an observation made by Edison years earlier during work on the incandescent lamp, developed a glass-bulb detector. Fleming was working for the Marconi company, which obtained the patents—in 1904 in England, in 1905 in the United States. That same year De Forest carried this work an historic step forward. He added a third element or "grid" in the vacuum tube, enormously increasing its effectiveness as detector and amplifier. The "Audion," as he called it, was patented in 1906. Here was one of the key elements on which radio, and the whole electronics industry, were to grow. "Unwittingly then," wrote De Forest in his diary, "had I discovered an Invisible Empire of the Air." [11]

Early in 1907 he formed the De Forest Radio Telephone Company; in New York he began intensive tests to demonstrate his Audion. It was used in receiving, and later also in sending. On March 5, 1907, he wrote in his diary:

> My present task (happy one) is to distribute sweet melody broadcast over the city and sea so that in time even the mariner far out across the silent waves may hear the music of his homeland . . .

At first Columbia phonograph records supplied the music, but De Forest now began to invite singers to his laboratory. Leading the way was a Miss Van Boos, who sang "I Love You Truly" and was heard by two operators at the Brooklyn Navy Yard.[12]

Most of these experimental broadcasts were done from the top floor of the Parker Building, on Fourth Avenue at 19th Street. Among De Forest's listeners, growing in numbers, were two inventors working nearby. In the Metropolitan Life Building was Miller Reese Hutchinson, who was trying to improve the klaxon; in Madison Square Tower, Peter Cooper Hewitt, inventor of a mercury-vapor light. Both were wireless enthusiasts and experimenters. De Forest often alerted them by phone when ready to test;

11. *Ibid.* p. 4.
12. *Ibid.* pp. 225-33.

they would signal results. People in the streets below were sometimes puzzled to see a man waving a towel from a high window of the Metropolitan Life Building.[13]

People often asked De Forest, what was the use of all this? In the New York *World*, De Forest answered with rhetorical questions.

> What is the use . . . of attuning a new Aeolian harp and having it vibrate . . . to the rhapsodies of master musicians played in some far-distant auditorium? [14]

The broadcasting idea became a grand obsession, marred only by a growing stench from the manipulations of Abraham White. White and others formed a new corporation, United Wireless Telegraph Company—capitalized at $20,000,000—which took over the activities of the De Forest Wireless Telegraph Company. White, controlling both companies, arranged this in a way that was completely to the advantage of the new company, and left nothing to the stockholders of the older company, including De Forest.[15] The inventor found himself powerless, with a block of almost worthless stock. Dismayed and infuriated, he had seen a paper fortune vanish. Fortunately he had hung onto his Audion and radio telephony, and these became his means to rebound. In the navy a number of officers were rallying enthusiastically to the radio telephone. Most early navy orders had gone to Slaby-Arco; the navy had usually shied away from De Forest, for reasons that included excessive stock promotion and untidy management. But now, for a proposed round-the-world cruise of an American squadron—a bid for world prestige—the radio telephone seemed essential. An order for twenty-six sets of De Forest equipment was placed.[16] For De Forest disaster was averted, but his De Forest Radio Telephone Company was still on thin ice. The panic of 1907 created unpromising prospects. What was needed, De Forest felt sure, was promotion—and sale of stock to finance further development.

He was falling in love with a lady pianist living in the apartment next to his. He had admired her playing through the wall, even before meeting her. "Propinquity led to acquaintance." Nora Blatch soon shared his excitement over the quixotic idea of broadcasting. She married him, and early in 1908 joined him in one of the most spectacular of De Forest pro-

13. Carneal, *A Conqueror of Space*, p. 206.
14. New York *World*, April 7, 1907.
15. De Forest, *Father of Radio*, p. 217.
16. *History of Communications-Electronics in the United States Navy*, p. 136.

motions. They went to Paris and secured permission to broadcast from the Eiffel Tower. All one night they shared the work of feeding discs to a Pathé phonograph. Later they learned they had been heard 500 miles from Paris. De Forest returned to New York in an aura of celebrity, which helped to dispel somewhat the United Wireless scandals. The messy affairs of that company would in time be aired in the courts. Meanwhile De Forest pursued tenaciously his broadcasting ideas, which now included more than "sweet melody." In 1909 Mrs. Harriet Blatch, his mother-in-law, was invited to send into the ether a plea for woman suffrage, marking a broadcasting milestone of a sort.[17]

The following year came a more astonishing achievement: a broadcast with Enrico Caruso direct from the stage of the Metropolitan Opera House—January 13, 1910. It was a double bill of *Cavalleria Rusticana* and *Pagliacci*. Two microphones were used, one on stage, the other in the wings. A 500-watt transmitter was installed in a room at the top of the Opera House. The antenna, suspended from two bamboo fishpoles, led to an attic room off the ballet rehearsal room.

Groups of listeners, passing earphones around, were assembled at the Newark plant and at several points in New York City, including De Forest's laboratory and the Metropolitan Life Building. The broadcast was also heard by ship operators and amateurs.[18]

Excitement prevailed, but scoffers were also heard. Interference from other stations, including code transmissions and snatches of ribald talk between unidentified operators, caused some difficulty. And there was fading. The "homeless song waves," as the New York *Times* put it, kept losing their way. According to its report, one listener, when asked if he heard the singing, replied that he could occasionally "catch the ecstasy." [19]

What did it all amount to? The importance of this, as of other De Forest experiments, was only partly in the technical study involved. Equally important was the bond it provided for a growing brotherhood, scattered far and wide, that already numbered thousands; a host of experimenters, of every age and status; of listeners who didn't merely listen but communicated feverishly with each other; of enthusiasts who, for want of better terminology, were called amateurs. Their importance, at this juncture of the broadcasting story, must be made clear.

17. De Forest, *Father of Radio*, pp. 222-49.
18. Carneal, *A Conqueror of Space*, p. 232.
19. New York *Times*, January 14, 1910.

THE GREATEST BUNCH OF JUNK

In the wake of Marconi, zealous followers sprang up everywhere. They were of all ages, but mostly young. Marconi's youth acted as a spark. The fact that he had used materials available to anyone was additional incentive. Some experimenters worked alone, others jointly. At schools and colleges, groups in electricity clubs defected and formed wireless clubs, and later radio clubs. Some assisted, and also prodded, faculty experimentation. Boys—and men—were constantly filing down nickels to make coherers, or winding wires around round objects—broken baseball bats or, later on, Quaker Oats boxes. In attics, barns, garages, woodsheds, apparatus took shape. Because of the noise and other menaces and hazards, real or imagined, the activity was for a long time banned from living quarters. Some people were drawn by the drama that awaited them in the airwaves, others by technical fascination. Most started with a receiver, with transmission as the next step. For each one who was already transmitting there were always many who had not yet reached this stage.

These experimenters, in city and country, were not only the beginning of what became the radio audience; they were also the cadre from which many broadcasters were to spring. Many of those who started and directed radio broadcasting stations in the 1920's—and, in many cases, television stations later—were "amateurs" in the fertile time before World War I.

Edgar Felix, who in 1922 was to become a staff member of WEAF, New York—a station playing a pivotal role in broadcasting history—got acquainted with wireless in 1904 when he paid a visit to an amateur's "table-top spark coil radio transmitting and receiving station." He would never forget "the Leyden jars which lighted up" when the key was pressed, and the "brilliant flash of the spark." [1] Soon afterwards he built his own first receiver, following directions in a Boy Scout manual.

About 1910 he visited "that great emporium of the amateur world, Hugo Gernsback's Electro Importing Company, under the 'El' at Fulton Street," in New York. Here he bought headphones. In this he differed from others; many an amateur got his from a phone booth. Felix also visited Eimer & Amend, on Third Avenue in New York, and for about half a dollar bought an assortment of crystals—galena, silicon, iron pyrites,

1. Felix, *Reminiscences*, p. 1.

perikon.[2] It had been found—at about the time that De Forest was developing the Audion—that each of these crystals could likewise, in some mysterious way, "detect" radio waves, and transform them into electric current if touched in the right spot with a thin wire (or "cat's whisker," as the amateur called it). The received current was feeble but could be made audible with the help of headphones. The crystal thus became the poor man's Audion, more limited in range, erratic, but nonetheless a thing of miracles. Because of low cost its use spread rapidly, especially among amateurs.[3]

Summering in the still sparsely settled area of Greenwich, Conn., Felix found he could pick up navy stations at Portsmouth, Boston, New London, Brooklyn, Philadelphia—and at times even Charleston, Guantanamo, Colon. Rolling a newspaper into a cone, he made a loudspeaker; at noon all members of the household were summoned to set their watches by the daily time signals from navy station NAA at Arlington. He also listened to the Marconi station at South Wellfleet on Cape Cod, which broadcast news to ships several times a day and produced an extraordinary "musical roar . . . rhythmic and beautiful." Distress signals were a collector's item. In 1909 the few boys at school who had heard the distress signals from the S. S. *Republic,* when it was rammed by the *Florida,* were local heroes, winning new converts to amateur radio. Since all but two aboard the *Republic*—which sank—were rescued, the event was also a strong boost for ship wireless.[4]

Drama awaited the amateur along the coast. Stanley R. Manning, who was to play a pioneer role in Detroit during the broadcasting boom of the 1920's, grew up in Irvington, N.Y. Here he built his first receiver in 1909. He soon received a letter from the Brooklyn Navy Yard, complaining that he was blanketing out its operators when they were trying to talk to ships at sea.

> They wanted me to lay off when they were on the air. I wasn't perturbed about it because there weren't any laws, rules, or regulations in those days. All they could do was ask me to be careful about it, which naturally I was, too.

2. *Ibid.* p. 3.
3. One of the developers of the crystal detector, J. G. Pickard, formed the Wireless Specialty Apparatus Company to exploit it; in 1912 the company was bought by United Fruit and became its radio-equipment subsidiary.
4. Felix, *Reminiscences,* pp. 3-5.

Manning, like Felix, made a pilgrimage to the Electro Importing Company run by Hugo Gernsback, who sold "the biggest bunch of junk you ever saw." Manning did not buy his headphones there. "Where I got the headphones I'd rather not say." In 1912 his father gave him $15 to buy a De Forest Audion, a fabulous treasure.[5]

The appearance of speech in the ether generated enormous excitement. Listeners had long used headphones because they made it possible to catch weak signals. An operator expecting dots and dashes would occasionally hear on his phones a voice or fragment of music. Such episodes were reported in the newspaper and not quite believed. Then one day, it happened to oneself. Manning caught a test by Fessenden—some talk and music.

> When I heard it I thought I was going crazy . . . I had never heard anything like it. I was living in a rooming house up on 72d Street—I believe—at the time and I called in several people, and they heard it, so it was real.[6]

John A. Fetzer, who was to become a midwestern broadcasting pioneer and, during World War II, chief radio censor in the U. S. Office of Censorship, had a similar boyhood experience in Lafayette, Ind. His brother-in-law, a dispatcher on the Wabash Railroad, had interested him in telegraphy and in 1913 helped him start in wireless. They built a 70-foot antenna, which could pull in the time signals from NAA, Arlington. "Every night . . . we would set our clocks with great satisfaction, always marveling at the ability of man to conquer distance." Then, on a night in November 1913,

> we were suddenly startled to hear violin music bursting forth from the headphones . . . as far as we were concerned, a miracle never to be explained. This phenomenon occurred for fully twenty minutes. The headphones were passed around . . . We called in the neighbors, all of whom agreed that not a single one of us was having daydreams.[7]

Such experiences gradually, very gradually, became more frequent. They also had their variations. Everett L. Bragdon, who was to become radio editor of the New York *Globe* in 1921—one of the first on a daily newspaper—began wireless experimentation in 1907 in Westbrook, Me.

5. Manning, *Reminiscences*, pp. 2-5.
6. *Ibid.* pp. 5-6.
7. *Ibid.* pp. 2-3.

He was the only amateur in town. Two brass spheres from an old bed-stead were his spark gap. The 250 watts jumping across this gap made thunderous noises. He listened on headphones for hours every day. One stormy day, the first sound he heard was not code but a woman's voice. Struck with the proper amazement, he then recognized the voice as that of the lady across the street, apparently in a phone conversation. The wet-ness of phone wires and insulators may have created a leak, which never recurred.[8]

The relation of amateur to governmental authority was a topic of grow-ing interest during the years 1907-12, when Bragdon was experimenting in Maine. Ship traffic off the Maine coast was heavy, and included navy ships moving in and out of Portland. Every amateur "felt that the world was his to explore," and that he had the right to talk with anyone he could reach. Bragdon in Westbrook and two or three experimenters in Portland spent night after night "going up and down the dial" trying to talk to the steam-ship *Belfast* on her way east along the coast or the *North Star* out of Portland en route to New York. For a time there seemed no limit to the readiness of ship operators to converse. But so many official messages were blotted out that naval authorities became increasingly testy, and then in-dignant, about amateur interference. Most amateur transmitters were not sharply tuned, and this added to the problem.

> We might think we were on 200 meters but we were probably just as powerful on 300 meters, possibly on 500 meters. Thus, no matter how selective the Navy equipment, they still couldn't escape us.[9]

According to Alvin F. Harlow, in *Old Wires and New Waves*, the fleet returning from its world trip under Admiral Evans was unable to commu-nicate with Portsmouth Navy Yard "because of amateur clamor." In some cases, amateurs are said to have broadcast fake orders to naval vessels, purportedly from admirals.[10]

It was perhaps not surprising that the armed forces—and especially the navy, which had the larger stake in radio, and was given the leading role in it as a matter of government policy—began to demand regulation. The amateurs rose in righteous anger, but to no avail. In 1912 the first radio licensing law was passed by Congress and signed by President Taft.[11] It

8. Bragdon, *Reminiscences*, p. 4.
9. *Ibid*. pp. 5-6.
10. Harlow, *Old Wires and New Waves*, p. 469.
11. See Appendix B. Earlier radio laws, passed in 1910 and 1912, had the purpose

remained the basic radio law of the land until 1927. Although written and passed without thought of the possibilities of broadcasting, it was to be the law under which the first years of the broadcasting era would be governed.

To many in the scattered brotherhood, it seemed the end of freedom. But in practice the law introduced only minor restraints. For transmission a station license was now required; it was available on application from the Secretary of Commerce and Labor. It was also now required that transmission be done or supervised by someone with an operator's license; this license would be awarded on the basis of an examination.

In granting station licenses the Secretary of Commerce and Labor—after 1913 the Secretary of Commerce—could assign wave lengths and time limits, but he apparently could not refuse a license. Such details would in time cause difficulties—in fact, chaos.

A person had to be an American citizen to obtain a station license. However, a company incorporated under the laws of any state could also obtain a license, and this meant that subsidiaries of foreign corporations could get licenses. This too would become an issue.

The new law began an attempt to divide the spectrum by function. Ship, amateur, and government transmissions were to be kept apart. Amateurs were to stay at 200 meters or above. The law also contemplated special "experimental" allocations.

The enactment of the law was quickly followed by the licensing of almost a thousand existing transmitters. These included transmitters at a number of schools, colleges, and universities, some of which already had years of experience behind them.[12]

In addition to those licensed under the new law, we can assume there were a number who continued to send without a license. Among them was Edgar S. Love, an amateur near Pittsburgh, who eventually became head engineer of WWJ, Detroit. He knew there was some sort of law, but felt it

---

of requiring ships of specified types to carry wireless equipment and adequate operating personnel.

12. Among them were the University of Arkansas, Cornell, Dartmouth, University of Iowa, Loyola (New Orleans), University of Nebraska, Ohio State, Pennsylvania State College, Philadelphia School of Wireless Telegraphy, St. Joseph's College (Philadelphia), St. Louis University, Tulane, Villanova, University of Wisconsin, Wittenberg. Many additional licenses were issued subsequently. See Frost, *Education's Own Stations.*

wasn't meant for him. Among his friends "nobody . . . knew anything about licensing." [13] And nothing happened.

We can also assume that the number receiving but not sending—therefore not needing a license—far exceeded the licensed senders. The non-sending listeners may have numbered many thousands.

In spite of the cries of doom with which amateur experimenters greeted the new law, they continued to grow rapidly in number. By 1917 they held 8562 transmitting licenses.[14] In many instances, amateur activity developed into professional work that, in one way or another, built foundations for the broadcasting age.

BUILDERS

In Detroit, Thomas E. Clark, who ran an electrical appliance store, began about 1899 to experiment with wireless. He put an antenna on the Banner Laundry building on Michigan Avenue opposite the old Cadillac Hotel, and another on the Chamber of Commerce building at Griswold and State streets,[1] and began to amaze his friends and acquaintances with demonstrations. Before long he was equipping lake steamers—the *Garland,* the *Sappho,* the *Promise*—and launching a wireless service for the Great Lakes under the name Clark Wireless. By 1903 he was calling this company the Thomas E. Clark Wireless Telegraph and Telephone Company[2] and beginning experiments with voice transmission.

In 1902 James E. Scripps, founder and owner of the Detroit *News,* visited the Banner Laundry station with his nineteen-year-old son William. With flashing of sparks, a message was wirelessed by Clark to the Chamber of Commerce building, and the inconclusive answer came back in Morse code: "We received your message by wireless." The younger Scripps hardly knew what to make of it, and peered behind a curtain, which hid more equipment. The elder Scripps made no comment but asked Clark to stop at the house some evening. When he came, Mr. Scripps wrote out a check for $1000, saying he merely wanted to help the experiments.[3]

Clark built transmitters in a number of port cities on the Great Lakes,

13. Love, *Reminiscences,* p. 6.
14. *Wireless Age,* February 1919.

1. Clark, *Reminiscences,* p. 5.
2. *Western Electrician,* May 1, 1903 (advertisement).
3. William Scripps, *Reminiscences,* pp. 19-20.

equipped more steamers, and in 1906 contracted to broadcast election returns to them.[4]

He later began to broadcast phonograph music; on the steamers four or five people could listen on a telephone receiver.[5] He had expansion plans, but in 1911 another company, blanketing his transmissions, put him out of business. Meanwhile young William E. Scripps, on the death of his father, had become publisher of the Detroit *News,* and developed an increasing interest in radio. Some years later he sought out Clark for advice on the starting of a Detroit *News* station, which began under an amateur license but became WWJ—a historic Detroit station.

In San Jose, Cal., "Professor" Charles D. Herrold or "Doc" Herrold, a genius without formal qualifications, started in 1909 a College of Engineering in which radio became the main attraction. He began transmitting from the Garden City Bank building in San Jose in that same year, and promptly took up voice experiments. Wireless students assisted, and of course learned from the activity. Some twenty amateurs in the Santa Clara Valley became a faithful following; Herrold had helped many of these install crystal detectors for voice reception. They would often call on the phone to ask when he would be on the air again. One of the followers, Ray Newby, a seasoned experimenter—his first antenna had been knocked down by the San Francisco earthquake in 1906—became an assistant to Herrold.[6] Schoolteachers from the area brought classes to see the station in operation; some of the children later became students of Herrold. The voice experiments grew into weekly programs—each Wednesday evening, with news bulletins, and phonograph records provided by a San Jose music store, which received a mention. It became "almost a religion" with Herrold to be ready on Wednesdays, with his records laid out. Occasionally a singer was brought in. According to a listener of 1912—Joseph Cappa— the quality was always fine at the start of a program, but got "mushy" as Herrold's carbon microphone "burned up on him . . . it would be so mushy and so bad that he'd shut down and be off the air." Next Wednesday he would apologize for the way it had ended. "Then he would say he would try to give a program if his microphone would hold out," but it would often end the same way. As time went on, the programs gathered

4. Letter of agreement, Detroit and Cleveland Navigation Company, October 9, 1906 (see Plate 2). Clark, *Papers.*
5. Clark, *Reminiscences,* p. 21.
6. Newby, *Interview,* pp. 1–11. The interviews here cited were recorded by Gordon B. Greb in 1959.

listeners far beyond the valley. A group of experimenters at the Fairmont Hotel in San Francisco, some forty miles away, heard them and conversed with Herrold. In 1913 Herrold married a young lady who acquired virtuosity in Morse code, and began teaching the introductory course in code transmission—in the dining room at home. Around the dining table eight Morse keys and eight receiving headsets were arranged. Sybil Herrold had never before seen a house with an aerial, but Herrold told her all homes "would have these poles." When their first child was born in 1914, she held it up before the microphone so that friends in the Fairmont Hotel could hear the cries. In 1915 the Panama Pacific Exposition at San Francisco featured radio exhibits by the federal government and by Lee de Forest. At both exhibits listeners heard, on headphones, programs from the Herrold station, which gave daily broadcasts during the fair for this purpose. For New Year's Eve that year Herrold announced a stunt: at midnight he would shoot a gun before his microphone—"the shot heard round the world." He used a blank cartridge in a 45-caliber army pistol. Listeners heard a *whsst*, and Doc Herrold was off the air again.[7]

Herrold would do anything for his station and school. During the night, for long-distance tests, he began to appropriate power at 600 volts from the Street Railway Company, tying onto trolley lines from the roof of the bank building by means of a long bamboo pole with a hook at the end. He also strung an antenna between two mountain tops and took his students, "his boys," into the hills to test reception at a radio-equipped shack with four bunks. The war stopped Herrold's operation. He tried to revive it after the war but couldn't manage, and sold the station to the Second Avenue Baptist Church, which ran it as KQW. The church later turned it over to a commercial operator, who sold it to another, who sold it to the Columbia Broadcasting System, which made it KCBS, San Francisco— 50,000-watt descendant of a 15-watt school station of 1909.[8]

Harold J. Power, a student at Tufts College, near Boston, was an avid wireless experimenter in the early 1910's and organized the campus radio club. In the summer of 1913 and again in 1914, after graduation, he had a job as wireless operator on J. P. Morgan's yacht, *Corsair*. This led to a long talk with J. P. Morgan; Power told him he believed in *broadcasting:* eventually everyone should have a receiver. The financier shrugged his shoul-

7. *Interviews* with Cappa, Newby, De Forest, True. The last-mentioned is with Mrs. Herrold—Sybil True by a later marriage.
8. Interviews with Newby, Cappa. See also Greb, "The Golden Anniversary of Broadcasting," *Journal of Broadcasting*, Winter 1958-59.

ders. How could an ordinary person run a radio set? "You've got to be an engineer." Not so, Power told him. As with automobiles, this would be a passing phase. Simple, complete sets could be built. As Power explained his views, Morgan began to show interest. Power said he hoped to go to Harvard for a year of graduate work, study the idea, and draw up a plan. "How much do you need?" Morgan asked. For a year at Harvard, said Power, just $500. Morgan said, "You can't do anything with $500." Power explained that he could attend Harvard for that, if he also gave lessons in radio. Morgan opened his wallet and gave him a $500 bill. A year later Power returned with a complete plan. He wanted to start a station. He had developed a saying: "To get broadcasting started, you have to start broadcasting." Along with that, there must be a laboratory to develop equipment. Power had a budget prepared: the whole thing could be started for $25,000. Morgan said, "I don't think you can do much with that." But Power said he could start it with that, so the financier said, "See my lawyers and organize the corporation." [9] They built a great antenna tower, on land made available by Tufts, and in 1915 organized AMRAD, the American Radio and Research Corporation. The station began a schedule of news bulletins and phonograph records, "for the entertainment of ships at sea." All members of the Tufts Radio Club worked at the station. But the war diverted the plans. Instead of receivers, they were enlisted to make cart transmitters and trench transmitters for the Signal Corps—barbed wire could be used as an antenna.[10] Broadcasting was halted. After the war they started up again; in 1922 the station became WGI, Medford Hillside, Mass. But the laboratory, expanded for war work, was in financial trouble as the work ended. J. P. Morgan kept tiding them over, but presently they sold out to Crosley, and became part of the manufacturing and broadcasting empire of the Crosley Radio Corporation.

These capsule chronologies will suggest how amateur ventures became professional pursuits that led by circuitous routes toward something new. What the new might be, none on the way could be sure. Some had a destination in mind, without knowing how to reach it. Meanwhile they shared the excitement of the journey.

On the eve of World War I the air crackled with code, with people

9. Dunham, *This Is the AMRAD Story*, pp. 2-20; this paper includes the texts of interviews with Power and various associates recorded by Dunham in 1964.
10. *Standard Book of Reference*, Section 9A, pp. 11-12.

here and there—for one reason or another—talking, playing a phonograph record, reading a poem, singing a solo, making a speech, giving a time signal, predicting the weather. Almost everything that became "broadcasting" was being done or had been done. The experimenters talked about the broadcasting idea, some with a sense of mission. The periodicals they read—such as *Wireless Age,* launched in 1913 by American Marconi—discussed it occasionally. But while the broadcasting devotees excited themselves and each other, they had so far made little impact on the general public. Many people looked on broadcasting as a slightly eccentric activity. The pronouncements made by De Forest and others seemed merely impractical. The devotees themselves must sometimes have wondered whether the idea wasn't irrelevant. Events of the day seemed to proclaim its irrelevancy. As war grew imminent, military uses usurped attention. When war came, everything changed.

We have mentioned that Edgar Felix, experimenter in the countryside near Greenwich, Conn., used to listen to the Marconi station at South Wellfleet, with its beautiful, rhythmic roar, as it wirelessed news to ships at sea. That is how he learned one day that war had begun in Europe. He told neighbors, who seemed unsure whether to believe him. Half a day later a boy on a bicycle, carrying an "extra," brought confirmation.[11] The episode must have been duplicated in hundreds of wireless-equipped households.

From that moment the amateur experimenters knew their days were numbered. A clause in the 1912 law provided that "in time of war or public peril or disaster" the President might close or seize any radio apparatus.[12] For a while the amateurs continued to send and listen; in many ways, these were the most exciting months. Then, on April 6, 1917, the blow came. A state of war existed with Germany. That same day, all amateur radio apparatus was ordered shut, dismantled, sealed. Next day commercial wireless stations such as ship-to-shore stations were taken over by the navy. Almost all stations still in operation were now under navy or army control.

A number of campus radio units had already been taken over for training, and others were reopened for similar use. Trainees began to pour into such units on the Arkansas, Harvard, Loyola, Ohio, Wisconsin and other campuses. Broadcasting was forgotten.

11. Felix, *Reminiscences,* p. 5.
12. Public Law No. 264, 62nd Congress, Sec. 2.

Two or three years later it would be said that broadcasting had been tried by De Forest and others but "nothing came of it." [13] It would seem a discredited notion, belonging to yesterday.

The amateur experimenters gave little thought to this change of direction. There was suddenly a great deal for them to do. The armed forces were seeking them out. Their special knowledge was in demand. Some were being sent overseas. Others would follow.

13. Allen, *Only Yesterday*, p. 13.

"We asked the cyclone to go around our barn but it
didn't hear us."   CARL SANDBURG, *The People Yes*

What World War I meant for the radio enthusiasts can be suggested by
the chronicle of Malcolm P. Hanson. He had entered the University of
Wisconsin in 1914 and became a student of Professor Earle M. Terry, a
confirmed wireless experimenter. Hanson, who sent letters to his mother
regularly, wrote on May 20, 1915,[1]

> We have all kinds of military parades and other competitions these
> days.   . . . I am now in the Radio Detachment, that is a wireless
> division of Cadets.   . . . Next Saturday there is a big sham battle, the
> University regiments pretend being at war with each other and they
> shoot blank cartridges and use wireless.

February 6, 1916:

> I have built one in my room, with iron wire out of the window and
> I practice codes with the amateurs around here.   . . . I believe that
> the wireless is more than a hobby for me.

January 20, 1917:

> The work at the radio station is wonderful.

April 3, 1917:

> If war is declared, I do not know what will be done with us.

April 15, 1917:

> I am at Mackinac Island up in Michigan alone with Bill Lewis and
> run the radio station which the Navy has taken over. I am in charge
> of it for the moment, and believe me, it is interesting. I have orders

1. Hanson, *Papers*. The original letters are in Danish.

39

to open it for the government, and we arrived yesterday noon here at the island. It is still cold, a lot of ice on the lake so that the boats still have trouble getting through . . . We have a little wood stove and oil stove, so that we can keep it warm . . . we are not afraid because Bill has his big revolver and we carry that always around with us . . . it is best to be sure in this time of war, and a Navy station . . . Tonight I sit here with my phones on my ears.

April 18, 1917:

We have not had too much to do . . . the main thing is to be on watch so that one can answer if someone should call, and watch the security of the ships on the Great Lakes, if they should call for help.

April 21, 1917:

I have found two dogs, wonderful animals, half starved to death, in the woods. . . . We are going to adopt them. . . . It is wonderful to have them here, and it is more secure at night. . . . We call them Radio and Sparks.

May 15, 1917:

I have been reading . . . that the University wireless station has special permission to operate. . . . it will be wonderful to hear our station again. . . . Professor Terry is doing research with a new invention in the field of wireless for the Navy, that is why he got the permission to open the station.

June 8, 1917:

We are getting along fine with our money. . . . Since we expect a rise in prices we have bought a whole case of Van Camp's baked beans.

December 17, 1917:

It is fun to hear all the ships on the Atlantic Ocean. . . . Some fellows have been sent from the Great Lakes to land stations in France and England to work with U. S. ships and stations. That would not be too bad.

October 3, 1918, from Norfolk, Va.:

What I have seen the last 24 hours has opened my eyes, everything seems like a fairy tale. Hundreds of huge auto trucks for the Army, many of them camouflaged in all rainbow colors. Large soldier camps, dozens of Army airplanes doing somersaults in the air. Hundreds of merchants ships and transports are in the port.

While waiting for shipment overseas, he was assigned to air patrol along the Atlantic coast, looking for mines; he was put in charge of wireless communication for all the patrol planes. When he finally got to Europe, the war was over, but he stayed for many months. In France he was dismayed by what he found. On January 31, 1920, he wrote:

> The French and English do not care for Americans, and it does not seem that they recognize how much we have helped them during the war and that they would have been beaten without us. . . . It does not take a lot of imagination to believe that our whole civilization has gone to the dogs because we have had it too comfortable.

August 1920 found him back at the University of Wisconsin, registering as a junior and working with Professor Terry, who was experimenting with voice, and determined to broadcast speech and music. This called for vacuum tubes, but they couldn't be bought; there was a big problem about patents. So Professor Terry had taken up glass-blowing and was making his own tubes, large transmitter tubes. Hanson worked with him for "advanced credit." On February 21, 1921, he wrote home:

> Are getting along fine with the wireless telephone, our concerts are heard in Boston, Texas, North Dakota, and a lot of places.

Without knowing it, they had reached the starting line for what would be a stampede, an upheaval, a delirium. Toward this starting line many others were moving into position.

THE BIG ONES

Until now our story has been one of individuals and the small enterprises they started. Experimenters in bedrooms, attics, shacks, and rooftop laboratories had started the story and carried it forward. But shortly before the war several giant corporations, with resources developed in other fields, began to step in. During the war they strengthened their position. By the end of the war period they controlled all principal patents, which put them in position to dominate later developments. They made the broadcasting story in the United States different from that of any other country. More and more, the story would become one of large corporations, sometimes working together, sometimes in mortal conflict. To many people in the radio world these titanic struggles would seem as remote as those of the gods on Mt. Olympus; but, like the struggles and jealousies on Olympus, they would sometimes have a fateful impact on the lives of men.

We must now begin to introduce these new, corporate dramatis personae. First, however, we should bring up to date the stories of smaller enterprises already mentioned that sprang up within radio.

The National Electric Signaling Company, founded by Fessenden in 1902, survived until 1912. It had had its moments of glory. It had been an early supplier of equipment to the United Fruit Company and also to the U. S. Navy. But United Fruit later decided to make its own equipment, acquiring a subsidiary for the purpose—the Wireless Specialty Apparatus Company. As for the navy, it seems to have found Fessenden troublesome. When it placed large orders with Slaby-Arco or others, the "irascible" Fessenden would belabor the Secretary of the Navy with letters of protest.[1] Fessenden had made historic contributions to radio but did not succeed in translating his patents into steady revenue. He eventually quarreled with his backers; by 1912 the company was in a state of collapse.

The De Forest Radio Telephone Company, built on the Audion patent, also received harsh blows in 1912. De Forest and several other officers were indicted for using the mails for fraudulent stock promotion. De Forest himself was eventually exonerated—others were convicted—but the effect on his prestige was damaging. And with legal costs weighing heavily, De Forest was desperate for funds. To add to his troubles, the Marconi interests were challenging his Audion patent; further court struggles lay ahead. For De Forest it was a time of crisis.

For the United Wireless Company, the Abraham White creation built on earlier work of De Forest, 1912 was also a crushing year. Several of its officers had, during the previous year, been convicted of fraud in the sale of stock. Now the Marconi interests sued for patent infringement. United Wireless pleaded guilty, went into bankruptcy, and gave up. Its far-flung assets were promptly bought by Marconi.

American Marconi had grown slowly but solidly. The policy that had won it ill will—the boycotting of non-Marconi installations—had been abandoned. Now the acquisition of the United Wireless facilities, including 17 land stations and 400 ship installations,[2] and the collapse of competition gave American Marconi for the first time the look of bigness. It had a virtual monopoly of marine communication in the United States.

1. *History of Communications-Electronics in the United States Navy*, pp. 55-9, 89, 99.
2. Dunlap, *Radio and Television Almanac*, p. 48.

About this time the company also became the center of attention through the *Titanic* disaster. It was through a lone Marconi operator in New York, young David Sarnoff, that the United States learned of the sinking and of its toll. The tragedy spurred new attention to wireless. From 1912 on, American Marconi would rise in power, and the name Sarnoff would more and more often be associated with it.

The sudden emergence of American Marconi was among the factors that brought the first of the giant corporations onto the scene. In 1912 there were rumors that American Marconi, now supreme in wireless telegraphy in the United States, would move into wireless telephony, including transoceanic telephony. Here it touched the nerves and domain of the American Telephone and Telegraph Company, and the giant stirred.

It was perhaps strange that AT&T had waited so long. Its own rise to power had, in another day, been made possible by the aloofness of another giant, Western Union. When the telephone appeared in 1876, Western Union was considered all-powerful; among monopolies it was one of the most feared, most hated, most avidly courted. The small firm launched by Bell in 1877—the Bell Telephone Company—was almost at once in financial straits; a delegation therefore called on President Orton of Western Union and offered him the whole Bell Telephone Company and its patent for $100,000. President Orton is said merely to have smiled. The telephone, a toy for hobbyists, was not taken seriously. Within months Western Union realized its error. It then acquired some Edison and Dolbear patents relating to their pre-telephone experiments; claiming priority on the basis of these, it went into the telephone business, organized a rapid promotion, and launched a patent war against Bell. A year later, as the legal dispute moved toward a decision, fortunes were clearly at stake. At this point attorneys for Western Union warned their client that the case would be lost, that Bell's patent would prevail. A settlement was urged, and sought, and a peace treaty signed. Under this 1879 agreement Western Union withdrew from the telephone business. The sensational Bell victory sent the price of its stock skyrocketing. From $50 a share in the spring of 1879 it edged up to $200 as signs of victory appeared; after the settlement it shot to $995.[3]

As part of the peace treaty, the Bell Company agreed to stay out of telegraphy, but this pledge was circumvented in 1885 by formation of a new corporation, the American Telephone and Telegraph Company. Or-

3. Harlow, *Old Wires and New Waves*, pp. 372-83.

ganized to provide long lines to link the local companies, it soon became the central power in the Bell System. The wording of its certificate of incorporation gives some sense of the staggering potential of this company, and its ultimate bearing on broadcasting. AT&T, said the certificate, would connect every city, town, and place in New York State with

> one or more points in each and every other city, town or place in said state, and in each and every other of the United States, and in Canada and Mexico; and each and every other of said cities, towns and places is to be connected with each and every other city, town or place in said states and countries, and also by cable and other appropriate means with the rest of the known world, as may hereafter become necessary or desirable in conducting the business of this association.[4]

The web, as planned, spread westward. Long distance telephone service reached Chicago ahead of the 1893 world's fair, and pushed on. By 1909 AT&T was so wealthy that it was able, for a $30,000,000 check, to buy control of Western Union.[5] Theodore B. Vail, president of AT&T, became president of Western Union also. At this juncture the federal government slowed the surge with antitrust action, forcing separation of the companies. Possibly these readjustments had kept AT&T busy during the rise of American Marconi. A reorganization of AT&T had been in progress. But by 1912 it was ready to move again.

It had two immediate objectives. One was transatlantic telephony. The other—which seemed more urgent to many of the executives—was to inaugurate coast-to-coast telephone service for the 1915 San Francisco world's fair. Available amplification systems were not yet adequate to cover the distance. But a solution came from an unexpected quarter.

On October 30 and 31, 1912, Lee de Forest demonstrated for AT&T executives the use of his Audion as a line amplifier. According to an AT&T research worker, they were "amazed" at its capabilities, and at once began extensive tests under research director H. P. Arnold. They tested, among other things, the effects of a more perfect vacuum, and for this they imported from Germany the latest form of vacuum pump.[6] The result was so good that they resolved to buy line amplification rights from De Forest. The inventor, desperate for funds, wanted to sell.

4. Rhodes, *Beginnings of Telephony*, p. 197.
5. Casson, *The History of the Telephone*, p. 276.
6. Espenschied, *Recollections of the Radio Industry*, pp. 19-20.

The telephone executives kept him waiting for months. When they were ready to act, they went about it in dime-novel fashion.

According to De Forest, he was approached during the summer of 1913 by one Sidney Meyers, a pleasant and dapper attorney, who said he represented a client interested in purchasing certain rights under the Audion patent. He could offer $50,000. He stated "on his word of honor as a gentleman" that he did not represent the telephone company, but would not say who his client was. More than half a year had passed since the demonstrations, and for many months there had been no word from the phone executives; De Forest had virtually given up hope. His plight seems to have been critical. He later wrote, "Just how we managed to exist through the balance of that summer I cannot now say." He had been divorced and had by now married Mary Mayo, a soprano of "birdlike purity." But their finances were so precarious that she pawned her ring, and he his watch, so that they could rent a piano. Under such pressure he resolved on the sale to Meyers, and it pulled him through the crisis.[7]

According to De Forest's account he learned later that Meyers did represent the telephone company, and that the company had been prepared to pay as much as $500,000 for the wire rights. However, within two years AT&T decided to purchase additional rights—radio telephone rights—under De Forest's Audion patent, and this time De Forest managed to obtain $90,000. Later he decided to sell all his remaining patents, which included valuable circuits, and AT&T paid him $250,000. In these transactions De Forest made only one reservation: he retained the right to sell his equipment to amateurs.[8]

With these negotiations AT&T moved into the new world of radio, in which its role would be far-reaching. Meanwhile De Forest, characteristically a lone experimenter, stepped to the sidelines. He had already turned to another idea, which seemed to many as visionary as broadcasting—talking pictures. He would reappear on the radio scene from time to time. To sell equipment to amateurs, as he was entitled to do under the rights he had reserved, he returned to the air in New York City in 1916, with a regular schedule of "radio telephone" entertainment interspersed with his own discussions of De Forest equipment. The entertainment included Columbia phonograph records and an occasional live singer. Vaughn de Leath, later a radio celebrity, made her appearance at this time. In No-

7. De Forest, *Father of Radio*, pp. 301-8.
8. *Ibid.* p. 327.

vember De Forest anticipated history in a curious way: with the help of a special line from the New York *American,* he broadcast the presidential election returns of 1916, and personally announced to his audience that Charles Evans Hughes had been elected President.[9] Thirty-two years later H. V. Kaltenborn was to do the same for Thomas E. Dewey.

During these months of 1916, the New York City air presented an ironic rivalry. While De Forest was broadcasting, there were also experimental transmissions by Western Electric, subsidiary of AT&T, now the owner of the De Forest patents. These patents had helped AT&T reach San Francisco on schedule, and had also put it in position for lucrative navy and army contracts. Western Electric was hard at work developing electronic equipment for war use.

Hearing De Forest's broadcasts, the Western Electric experimenters could not resist twitting him over the air, sometimes injecting a few words into his sales talks. This brought angry protest from De Forest:

November 21, 1916

Charles Scribner
Chief Engineer, Western Electric Company
463 West Street
City

Dear Mr. Scribner:
It seems wise to call your attention to the practice of some of the Western Electric radio engineers, in their wireless telephone conversations, to "josh" or make unnecessary remarks to our men or to the Brooklyn Navy Yard. For example, last night one talking to the Navy Yard prefaced his remarks, "We have no amplifiers to sell."

My company has amplifiers to sell, and we have announced the fact several times on our nightly wireless concerts. Such remarks seem rather uncalled for . . .

Very respectfully yours,
Lee de Forest.

The culprit at Western Electric, Raymond A. Heising, was promptly reprimanded by Scribner in a memo:

We may not think it seemly to advertise on the radio, but it is not for us to censor De Forest. This sort of thing must stop.[10]

9. Archer, *History of Radio,* pp. 132-4.
10. Espenschied, *Recollections of the Radio Industry,* pp. 29-30.

The irony is that AT&T would soon become the leading proponent—and De Forest a leading critic—of the commercialization of radio.

The fall of 1916 brought a further crucial event in the history of the vacuum tube—a fateful decision. On September 20, 1916, the U. S. District Court in New York City ruled that De Forest's Audion, as a detector, infringed on Fleming's original glass-bulb detector, owned by the Marconi interests. Thus the Audion could not be marketed in the United States as a radio detector without the consent of American Marconi. However, the innovation introduced by De Forest—the third element or "grid"—was properly protected by his patent, now owned by AT&T; the Marconi company would have no right to use this without consent of AT&T.[11] Each company was thus the owner of something it could not use in its own right. The two companies found their fortunes intertwined.

To complicate things further, Edwin H. Armstrong, an undergraduate at Columbia University, had developed a new circuit—the "feedback" circuit—that greatly increased the value of the Audion as a detector. He showed that part of the received current could be fed back through the Audion to reinforce itself many times. In 1914 a patent was awarded to him. Effective use of the Audion in radio reception now called for use of this patented circuit. A new factor was thus added to the patent tangle.

In addition, it was being found that the Audion could *generate* radio waves as well as detect and amplify them. It thus became important in voice transmission. This development involved still another dispute, with priority claimed by several inventors including De Forest and Armstrong.

This patent stalemate came precisely at the time when the army and navy, impelled by the war in Europe and backed by mounting appropriations, were beginning to demand mass production of electronic equipment. They wanted transmitters and receivers of range and sensitivity—for ships, airplanes, automobiles. They wanted mobile "trench transmitters," "pack transmitters," and compact receivers. They wanted submarine detectors, radio direction finders, and equipment for the recording and study of code transmissions. All required vacuum tubes. The patent log jam must not be allowed to obstruct.

Under wartime powers the disputes were put on ice. Contractors were to make the equipment needed. Claims under patent rights could later be filed with the government and adjudicated. A letter from Franklin D. Roosevelt as Assistant Secretary of the Navy guaranteed each contractor

11. *Marconi* v. *De Forest*, 236 Fed. 942.

"against claims of any and all kinds" in the carrying out of government contracts, and each was told to use "any patented invention necessarily required." [12] The log jam was broken. Development and production forged ahead.

Such means made possible a vast co-ordinated development of radio technology during World War I. While serving war problems, it set the stage for things unforeseen. It was a development financed by government, co-ordinated largely by the navy. This was its hour. With few restrictions as to funds, it became the inspirer and guiding patron of diverse assembly lines and research laboratories, from huge ones like Western Electric to fledglings like the AMRAD unit at Tufts.

Because a central need was vacuum tubes, the work soon included two great lamp-bulb manufacturers, General Electric and Westinghouse. It would not have occurred to anyone a few years earlier that lamp-bulb factories—like the GE plants at Harrison, N.J., and Cleveland, O.—would soon be war assets. Now they were that. Thus, two more industrial giants entered the world of radio, to play roles not less momentous than that of AT&T. The tube made them radio manufacturers and would eventually make them broadcasters.

The General Electric Company—a product of Edison's work on the electric light and of later mergers—had begun study of De Forest's Audion as early as 1912, at about the same time that AT&T showed interest in it. GE had at that time no right to market the tube, but its research laboratory was dedicated to the notion that its scientists should pursue any mystery that stirred their curiosity. "Are you having any fun?" was the question with which Dr. Willis R. Whitney, director of the laboratory, greeted researchers on his laboratory rounds.[13] This attitude toward research was to pay vast dividends. One of the researchers, Dr. Irving S. Langmuir, had decided to have fun with the Audion. He wanted—like Arnold at AT&T— to study the effects of a more perfect vacuum. (Fleming and De Forest had thought the residual gas was essential.) Within a short time GE had developed a tube that could be used in transmission with far higher voltages than the De Forest Audion. By 1914 daily on-the-air tests were being made between the Schenectady laboratory and the GE plant at Pittsfield, Mass. In these tests the high-vacuum tubes were used in conjunction with the Alexanderson alternator—descendant of the one made for Fessenden,

12. Archer, *History of Radio,* p. 138.
13. Hull, *Reminiscences,* p. 5.

which GE had patented. In the course of the tests the scientists exchanged comments on the research; amateurs within range wrote letters, contributing their own comments and providing needed information. The results were increasingly brilliant. When the war orders began to pour in, GE was ready.

While furthering the high-vacuum tube, the GE tests also focused new attention on the Alexanderson alternator, which gradually placed GE in a position of strategic importance. When Guglielmo Marconi came to the United States in 1915, he went to Schenectady for a look at the alternator. The visit came to have significance for two reasons: first, because it involved a man who had risen to the position of general counsel to GE, and who would make this a step toward a dazzling career in communications diplomacy—Owen D. Young; and second, because the discussions took a prophetic turn.

Marconi was apparently convinced that the alternator was the key to the still unsolved problem of reliable transoceanic communication. A huge deal was discussed: GE to retain exclusive manufacturing rights, the Marconi companies to have exclusive use. To obtain this, the Marconi companies would order a substantial number of alternators, for a purchase price of millions of dollars.

The discussions were cut short by the urgencies of war. As on a previous Marconi visit, he was suddenly needed in Europe, this time by the Italian government. The huge deal was set aside, at least for the moment. But one part went forward: a 50,000-watt Alexanderson alternator was delivered to the Marconi installation at New Brunswick, N. J.—and promptly taken over by the navy. Under navy sponsorship, researchers of GE and American Marconi continued to study and improve it, and marvel at its range.

As the needs of war mounted, GE's involvement grew. In the prewar period, at the GE research laboratory, vacuum tubes had been made one at a time by a glassblower, with other experimenters looking over his shoulder and making suggestions.[14] Not long afterwards they were in mass production. At one point the Signal Corps placed a single order for 80,000 tubes. All were made to exact government specifications, so that identical tubes could be made by other companies, and used with equipment designed and made by various companies—AT&T, GE, Westinghouse, American Marconi. More and more, their fortunes became interlocked by war.

14. White, *Reminiscences*, pp. 15-16.

CLOAK AND DAGGER WIRELESS

Meanwhile high drama usurped the air waves and surrounded the men of radio.

As Marconi sailed back to Europe, elaborate precautions shielded him, lest he fall into German hands. Labels were removed from his clothing and luggage, and a hiding place assigned in the bowels of his ship. He was given clothes suitable to his disguise as a crew member. His presence aboard, rumored among passengers, was flatly denied. Those who knew the facts agreed to "lie like gentlemen." [1]

Radio became important in intelligence work. Because the British had cut cable connections with Germany, the Germans necessarily took to the air to communicate with neutrals and their own ships and overseas agents. The air crackled with occult codes; everywhere the recording and studying of coded material went on day and night.

In 1915 an amateur in Westfield, N.J.—Charles E. Apgar—recording coded messages sent out by a Telefunken-owned station in Sayville, Long Island, gathered evidence that it was sending information on neutral ship movements—presumably for submarines. The navy promptly took control of the station.[2]

Halfway across the world a German cruiser sunk by Russia was visited by divers, and yielded a treasure: in the cruiser's safe was a code manual, which subseqently enabled the Allies to decode many wireless orders coming out of Germany. Other ships, sunk or crippled, were to provide similar information, keeping code information up to date. The British, maintaining radio silence, listened and decoded.[3]

After the United States became a combatant, study of captured German equipment became part of the work of various war contractors. A worker at the Marconi plant at Roselle Park, N.J., Gustave Bosler, was given a German trench transmitter.

> It was a miniature affair, but it was a real job, it kicked out. It was about six inches wide, about eight inches high, and about a foot long. It was captured . . . by one of the American boys who struck the German who was working on the transmitter over the head. Blood spattered all over it. That is how I received it.

1. New York *Tribune*, June 2, 1915.
2. Dunlap, *Radio and Television Almanac*, p. 56.
3. Schubert, *The Electric Word*, pp. 138-9.

Bosler's job was to develop a similar, improved transmitter for American troops, which he did. "It was a peculiar feeling, though, to handle this thing with blood all over it." [4]

As the war approached a climax, the Alexanderson alternator played a role in propaganda and intrigue. The equipment installed at New Brunswick and taken over by the navy had amazing results. The call letters were NFF. Throughout Europe, NFF was loud and clear.

On January 8, 1918, operators everywhere were asked by NFF to stand by for an important message from President Wilson. Soon afterwards it began: the Fourteen Points, which the President had just delivered to Congress. "Open covenants of peace, openly arrived at . . . opportunity of autonomous development . . . general association of nations." [5] Words of extraordinary hope, darting across the world into earphones in remote cities and villages, and on ships and battlefields.

A short time later the 50,000-watt alternator was replaced by a 200,000-watt alternator, and the barrage of hope continued. From ships on every ocean, stations on every continent, even from soldiers with field receivers in France, came the reports: NFF was booming in.

Then, later in the year, NFF took the world by surprise. It was heard addressing the German station POZ, at Nauen, near Berlin. For years operators of the Allies had kept an ear to POZ but never talked to it; it might have been considered treason. Now NFF was calling, "POZ—POZ—POZ."

Startling as the call itself was the promptness of the reply—and its wording. The reply was: "Your signals are fine, old man." [6] NFF proceeded with its message, again from President Wilson. It was nothing less than an appeal to the German people to remove their Kaiser, or to the Kaiser to remove himself. It was an astute thrust, aptly timed. By-passing the round-about peace feelers in progress via Switzerland, it seemed to dramatize Wilson's condemnation of secret diplomacy, his call for "open" negotiation.

At the transmitter at New Brunswick, as it sent the President's words, was Ernst Alexanderson himself [7]—born in Sweden, pupil of Professor Slaby of Germany (co-founder of Telefunken), immigrant to the United States, researcher for General Electric, who had developed an idea of the Canadian Fessenden and had now built a station for Marconi, operated by

4. Bosler, *Reminiscences*, pp. 6-7. He later became an NBC staff member.
5. New York *Times*, January 9, 1918.
6. *Wireless* Age, July 1919.
7. Alexanderson, *Reminiscences*, p. 25.

the U. S. Navy. Alexanderson had reached the goal of many: world com-munication.

When President Wilson sailed for Europe for the peace conference, the Alexanderson alternator was his link with the world. He wanted, while en route on the S.S. *George Washington,* to be kept informed by his aides at home via radio telephone. To be ready to serve him, NFF researchers made continual voice transmission tests, and in the process grew tired of talking. Other experimenters had solved this with phonograph records, but on this occasion a telephone with the receiver off the hook was placed near the orchestra pit in a New Brunswick movie house, three miles away. For tests this line was switched on.[8] Over oceans and continents into dis-tant earphones, NFF sent "hurry themes," "chase themes," "agitatos," "misteriosos"—being played for films of Mary Pickford, William S. Hart, and Theda Bara. From operators far away came letters of appreciation. The men at NFF called it "testing," but they were broadcasting.

GOLDEN SUNSET

In the official *History of Communications-Electronics in the United States Navy,* the section on the years 1914-18—the time of greatest human slaughter yet known—is entitled "The Golden Age." [1] Curious as the title may seem, it conveys something of the pride the navy felt in its achieve-ments of that period. With firm hand it had guided a technological revolu-tion. It had created from quarrelsome enterprises a co-ordinated industry. At the heart of this industry lay the new science of electronics, which already gave promise of developments far beyond radio. The navy's achievement also had international meaning: while the war had made the United States a world power, radio had given it a transoceanic voice.

Even before the war was over, there were suggestions from the navy that this productive era, made possible by navy control, should be carried on into the peace. Immediately after the armistice a bill to this effect (H. R. 13159) was introduced in the House of Representatives. Because of the maritime environment in which radio had grown up, proposals on radio were almost automatically referred to the House committee on merchant marine and fisheries, which also studied such matters as "An Act To Pro-mote the Welfare of American Seamen," "Protection of the Lobster," "Pro-

8. W. W. Brown, *Reminiscences,* p. 12.
1. *History of Communications-Electronics in the United States Navy,* pp. 207-394.

tection of the Sponge Industry," and "A Bill to Prohibit Shanghaiing and Peonage." The customary procedure was followed, and the committee held hearings December 12-19, 1918.

Among high navy officials who testified for the bill, Secretary of the Navy Josephus Daniels led off:

> . . . the passage of this bill will secure for all time to the Navy Department the control of radio in the United States, and will enable the Navy to continue the splendid work it has carried on during the war.[2]

A return to the free-for-all of the prewar years seemed unthinkable to Secretary Daniels:

> . . . we would lose very much by dissipating it and opening the use of radio communication again to rival companies.[3]

He did not shrink, under questioning, from the thought that the navy plan meant a monopoly:

> . . . it is my profound conviction and is the conviction of every person I have talked with in this country and abroad who had studied this question that it must be a monopoly. It is up to the Congress to say whether it is a monopoly for the government or a monopoly for a company . . .[4]

Some proponents argued that monopoly in radio was an inevitable development that might as well, as a practical matter, be supported. Others spoke of radio as a "natural monopoly," with the apparent implication that the natural was good. In this vein Commander S. C. Hooper argued that radio

> is a natural monopoly; either the government must exercise that monopoly by owning the stations or it must place the ownership of these stations in the hands of some one commercial concern and let the government keep out of it.[5]

The bill contemplated continued transmissions for experimentation and technical instruction in radio, but under navy control. "Amateurs" were not specifically mentioned. Any transmission would require the approval of the navy, which might impose restrictions it thought proper.

2. *Government Control of Radio Communication*, pp. 10-11.
3. *Ibid.* p. 5.
4. *Ibid.* p. 37.
5. *Ibid.* p. 86.

Because Secretary Daniels was close to President Wilson, it was assumed that the President approved the bill. Its passage was strongly recommended by the Department of State, which expressed its "entire
approval of the bill as drawn." [6] In governmental circles, the only inhar-
monious note came from the army. It by no means disapproved of government ownership but felt that army use of radio should not be under navy
control.[7]

The views expressed at this hearing were to have echoes elsewhere in
the world. In almost every country similar views were urged and accepted. No doubt the European countries, many living at close quarters
with recent enemies, and a Russia in revolution and turmoil, were far
more conscious of radio as a weapon of intrigue and propaganda, and a
possible threat to security. Ravaged by war, many were also turning, in
varying degrees, toward publicly financed enterprises. In this context, arguments for government operation of radio were readily accepted. Not so
in the United States.

The House hearings produced some passionate and even eloquent arguments against the navy measure. An interesting aspect of these protests is
that not one of them was based on a clear vision of things to come. All
seemed to sense that radio had a future, but none could define it. John W.
Griggs, president of American Marconi, said:

> Just when the farmer has planted his seed, plowed his field, and har-
> rowed it, and cultivated his crop, and the corn is ready to husk, the
> government comes in and says, "We want that crop." [8]

What sort of crop did Mr. Griggs foresee? Did he mean revenue from
marine communication, international communication? Sale of equipment
to amateurs? If he had thoughts beyond these, he did not reveal them.

Hiram Percy Maxim, president of the American Radio Relay League,
always a battler for the amateur experimenters, spoke in their interest.
The achievements of the navy, he pointed out, had been made possible by
those amateurs, who by tens of thousands had poured into war communication. Now those same men were leaving the armed forces. The navy's
expectations of continued glory were therefore illusory, he argued. The

6. *Ibid.* p. 121.
7. Letter from Newton D. Baker, Secretary of War, in *Government Control of Radio
Communication*, Addenda, p. 3.
8. *Government Control of Radio Communication*, p. 224.

men needed for the work would not be there. They would be back home, looking for new ways to apply their special knowledge. "We block the ambition of over 100,000 of the best brains we possess to apply their efforts in that field in which they most want to work." [9] Maxim estimated that in 1917, when 8562 were licensed to transmit, 125,000 possessed receiving equipment.[10]

It was Congressman William S. Greene of Massachusetts who took up the monopoly challenge. By what right did the proponents of the bill so cavalierly flout the aims of the antitrust laws? Besides, "I have never heard before that it was necessary for one person to own all the air in order to breathe." After praising the navy for its wartime achievements, he commented: "I do not believe all wisdom is contained there." Finally he hit hard: "Having just won a fight against autocracy, we would start an autocratic movement with this bill." [11]

Such words may well have seemed a stinging outrage to navy spokesmen. In the words of Paul Schubert, excellent chronicler of the navy's work in radio, "they believed in the beneficence of their guidance" in the nation's hour of need, and could not well comprehend the sudden and violent repudiation of things military in the weeks after November 11, 1918.[12]

The saluting was over. The committee tabled the bill.

As the committee was winding up its hearings, President Wilson was arriving in Europe. Before the peace talks—scheduled to start January 12, 1919—he made a triumphal tour of Allied countries. Everywhere the frenzied cheering for Wilson exceeded anything ever known before. Never had so many Frenchmen, so many Englishmen, so many Italians, gathered to pay homage to one man. Many people trembled at the roar of the crowds. But the ecstasy went far beyond its fringes.

> In the area of the Allied intervention in northern Russia his picture was almost as common in the peasant huts as the ever-present icon, and from Egypt an American wrote that the natives held him to be the Mahdi, the Mohammedan Messiah calling for revolt that would drive out the English so that he might send Americans to help govern the country. His name was recited as an incantation by the effendis,

9. *Ibid.* p. 244.
10. *Wireless Age*, February 1919.
11. *Government Control of Radio Communication*, pp. 11, 29.
12. Schubert, *The Electric Word*, p. 160.

the harem women, the imams and mullahs; with tomtoms beating and
pipes shrilling, crowds in the East cried for hour after hour, "Yahia
Dr. Wilson." ("Long Live Dr. Wilson.") In the mountains of the Bal-
kans the villagers settled petty disputes by saying, "President Wilson
would have it so." [13]

To what extent the sending of the Fourteen Points via NFF and other
stations had contributed to the delirium, we cannot know. It may well be
that the war tension had conferred extraordinary authority on those few in
every embattled land who sat with headphones, and to the words of hope
they plucked from the air, over vast distances from a fabled land.

After the delirium came the conference: the bargaining, bickering, trading, compromise, fury, despair, deflation. Wilson fell ill. Drawn and ashen,
he sat in bed and conferred, and kept fighting. He said: "We are running a
race with Bolshevism and the world is on fire. Let us wind up this work
here . . ." He had agonizing headaches, which he blamed on the impossible demands of Lloyd George.[14]

Meanwhile men in uniform were starting back, including the 100,000
mentioned by Hiram Percy Maxim. The radio enthusiasts had been boy
wonders throughout the war, pampered by generals and admirals. Now
they brought back their know-how, and looked about at home. Everything
seemed to have come to a halt. Government contracts for radio equipment
had been canceled. Almost all experimentation had stopped. Shore stations and ship installations were to stay in government hands till a peace
treaty was signed. What else was happening? Apparently nothing. Production of vacuum tubes had almost stopped, since they could not be sold
because of patent conflicts.

In mid-1919 the ban on amateurs was lifted. The experimenters began
to break the seals and unpack equipment. They knew a lot more than
when they had left, and the old transmitters and receivers were now
largely obsolete. But some men had brought a tube or two from army or
navy supply stocks. They began tinkering again—listening and sending—
and meanwhile looking around intently. There must be some way their
knowledge could be used. Within a few months thousands were in operation again. They were scattered in cities and towns throughout the United
States. They were determined; perhaps a little angry; above all, restless.
They would make themselves felt.

13. Smith, *When the Cheering Stopped,* p. 42.
14. *Ibid.* p. 46.

WATCHING THE RAMPARTS

In the navy the top men of radio had not given up. Commander S. C. Hooper, whose curious title was "executive officer of the radio division of the bureau of steam engineering," had urged a navy monopoly, but even then had mentioned an alternative which seemed to him acceptable—to put radio "in the hands of some one commercial concern and let the government keep out of it." Secretary Daniels was also mentioning this as a possibility.[1] The navy found an opportunity to press for this alternative. It was brought on by a move from the Marconi companies.

It will be recalled that in 1915, Guglielmo Marconi and Owen D. Young had discussed a deal under which the Marconi companies would acquire exclusive world-wide use of the Alexanderson alternator. This idea, brushed aside by war, was now revived by an offer.

The Marconi companies proposed to buy from General Electric twenty-four complete transmitters for use in the United States and abroad. An over-all price of $4,048,000 was negotiated. The Marconi companies would buy additional alternators from time to time from GE, which retained exclusive manufacturing right, while Marconi would have exclusive use.

To General Electric officials the proposal appeared a shift in fortune: a possible chance to use war-developed capacity, idled by the peace. But in the hands of Owen D. Young, the offer became a key to developments which had vast ramifications. In a letter to acting Secretary of the Navy Franklin D. Roosevelt, dated March 29, 1919, he explained all the details of the proposed Marconi deal. Roosevelt sent the letter to Commander Hooper, who reacted with alarm, which he communicated to Secretary of the Navy Daniels, who was in Paris. A series of swift actions followed, which probably fitted Young's expectations perfectly. Rear Admiral W. H. G. Bullard, just back from Paris, was enlisted to "direct the fight against British monopoly." Meanwhile a letter from Roosevelt to Young, dated April 4, asked that General Electric, "before reaching any final agreement with the Marconi companies,"[2] confer with navy representatives. Three days later Admiral Bullard and Commander Hooper met privately with Owen D. Young, and the next day with the board of directors of General Electric.

1. *History of Communications-Electronics in the United States Navy*, p. 317.
2. *Ibid.* p. 353.

In the course of these meetings Admiral Bullard gave the impression, in off-the-record fashion,[3] that he had come under instructions from President Wilson. There is no clear evidence of what President Wilson may have said to Admiral Bullard in Paris. They could not have discussed the letter from Young to Roosevelt; Bullard had left Paris before this was written. But President Wilson had reason to prize the Alexanderson alternator, and they may have discussed its value. He knew it had accomplished effective communication with Germany, which had been disrupted when the British cut the cables in 1914. He knew the role that dominance of ocean cables played in British power. And increasingly exasperated with the British, especially Lloyd George, he was becoming pathologically suspicious of their intentions. The Bullard intimations fitted the picture.[4]

In any case, Owen D. Young later helped the impression of presidential backing to take firm root, and in his hands it became a diplomatic trump card. In the following months and years, with extraordinary skill, he used it to create and protect a new instrument of power.

COVENANTS QUIETLY ARRIVED AT

During the remainder of 1919, while radio lay suspended between war and peace, and paralyzed by a patent stalemate, Young made a series of swift moves.

It was during these same months that President Wilson, completing his work in Paris, came home to face a hostile Senate and, threatened with possible rejection of the League of Nations, began an agonizing tour: an appeal, over the heads of the legislators, to the people themselves. Later Presidents would make such an appeal from a White House desk by way of nation-wide broadcasting chains. With no such means available, Wilson made his plea from train platforms and lecterns in jammed arenas and stifling halls. He was urged to stop—to accept the "reservations" proposed by Senator Henry Cabot Lodge. But Wilson would not hear of it, and was felled by a series of thromboses.

Meanwhile Owen D. Young was fashioning the organization that would within a few years make network broadcasting a fixture in American life. Curiously enough, he had no such aim in view. Broadcasting does not

3. Archer, *History of Radio*, p. 163, footnote.
4. Baker, *Woodrow Wilson and World Settlement*, III, 425-8. Smith, *When the Cheering Stopped*, pp. 102-3.

PROPHECY

Marconi and his black box, *c.* 1896.

Fessenden and co-workers at Brant Rock, *c.* 1907.

De Forest broadcasting from Parker building, New York, *c.* 1907.

De Forest Audion patent, 1907.

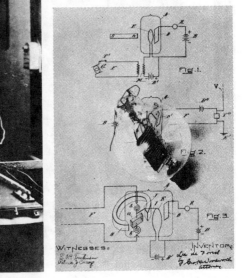

Detroit Historical Museum

C. 1902: Thomas Clark antenna on Banner Laundry building, Detroit.

1906: Clark arranges to broadcast election returns to Great Lakes steamers.

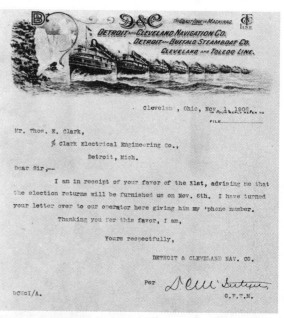

Cleveland, Ohio, Nov. 1, 1906

FILE

Mr. Thos. E. Clark,

% Clark Electrical Engineering Co.,

Detroit, Mich.

Dear Sir,—

I am in receipt of your favor of the 31st, advising me that the election returns will be furnished us on Nov. 6th. I have turned your letter over to our operator here giving him my 'phone number.

Thanking you for this favor, I am,

Yours respectfully,

DETROIT & CLEVELAND NAV. CO.

Per

O.F.T.M.

DCMCI/A.

KCBS

C. 1913: Charles Herrold station in San Jose. In doorway, "Doc" Herrold.

seem to have been discussed. He was working for an American-dominated system of world communication.

This objective could be viewed in a variety of ways: in idealistic terms—*let nation speak to nation;* in isolationist terms—*end the British monopoly;* in business terms—*we can undersell the cables;* in patriotic terms—*give America a voice;* in military terms—*we need it.* With such a background of forces working for him, Young negotiated deftly and with mounting success.

When his plans had been approved by his board of directors, Young went to Washington to review them with Secretary of the Navy Daniels, who suggested he check them with Senator Henry Cabot Lodge, who promptly approved. Young also discussed with Daniels the idea of a government charter, specifically authorizing a monopoly in radio communication, but Daniels felt doubtful that Congress could be persuaded to approve it. The charter idea was therefore dropped.[1]

On October 17, 1919, the Radio Corporation of America was formed. Its articles of incorporation provided that only United States citizens might be directors or officers. It was also stipulated that not more than 20 per cent of the stock might be held by foreigners. Provision was made for a government representative with "the right of discussion and presentation in the board of the Government's views and interests concerning matters coming before the board." [2]

For the moment the new organization was an empty receptacle. Now American Marconi was invited to transfer its assets and operations to it. Individual stockholders would be asked to accept RCA shares in place of American Marconi shares. GE proposed to purchase the 364,826 shares held by British Marconi.

For the Marconi interests, there was virtually no alternative but to accept the entire plan. Almost all land stations of American Marconi were still in government hands. The attitude of the Navy Department—with apparent presidential backing—seemed to make it clear that they would not be returned to a British-dominated company. And if they were, such a company could not expect government co-operation and contracts. On the other hand, a navy-sponsored RCA could expect to be a government favorite. To individual stockholders in American Marconi this would be

1. Clark, *The Formation of RCA,* pp. 53-60; *History of Communications-Electronics in the United States Navy,* pp. 356-8.
2. *Ibid.* p. 181.

important. In addition, a strong RCA might in the long run be a more valuable ally to British Marconi than a weak American Marconi. On November 20, 1919, with the approval of the stockholders, American Marconi transferred all its assets and operations to RCA.

Owen D. Young became chairman of the board, Edward J. Nally of American Marconi became RCA president. In January 1920, to no one's surprise, Rear Admiral W. H. G. Bullard was named the government representative who was to sit with the board.

On February 29 the government-held land stations and ship installations formerly owned by American Marconi were turned over to RCA. International wireless telegraphy on a commercial basis was begun by RCA the next day. Messages would go to England at 17 cents a word, in competition with cable rates of 25 cents a word.[3]

Thus RCA from its infancy virtually controlled radio telegraphy in the United States. Now it was ready to face radio telephony—and the deadlock of the vacuum tube.

Within a few months General Electric and the Radio Corporation formed an alliance with the American Telephone and Telegraph Company and its subsidiary, Western Electric. The patents of all would be available to each. These companies staked out areas of interest so that the world of electronic communication, as the conferees viewed it in the early months of 1920, might be developed co-operatively rather than in competition. AT&T, like GE, became owner of a block of RCA stock.

Meanwhile Owen D. Young was already making international moves. English, French, and German wireless interests had won concessions in South America, looking toward development there. Again Young moved with extraordinary rapidity, capitalizing on existing rivalries. There might not be enough business to go around; competition might be destructive to all. A "consortium" was therefore arranged; each would share equally in development costs—and in profits. In the final arrangements it was agreed that an American would be chairman, with important veto rights. This crucial edge, providing a lever of power in South America, was described by Young as an extension of the Monroe Doctrine.[4] Construction of stations began. Meanwhile RCA was already building 200,000-watt alterna-

3. Subsequently cable rates were lowered and RCA rates raised; in 1923 both became 20 cents a word. *Report of the Federal Trade Commission on the Radio Industry,* p. 36.
4. Tarbell, *Owen D. Young,* p. 136.

tors in California and Hawaii and negotiating for rights in China.[5] The general public was scarcely aware of the existence of RCA, but it was already a world force. During 1920 and 1921 the vision was taking shape —and at the same time expanding.

Almost all employees of American Marconi had continued with RCA. Among them was David Sarnoff, who became commercial manager for the new company. If Young had given no thought to broadcasting, Sarnoff had. He had once written an office memorandum about its possibilities; this had been ignored. Now Sarnoff mentioned it to his new boss, Owen D. Young. But by now, others were moving along similar paths.

FERMENT

After restrictions on amateurs were lifted in 1919 many experimenters— amateur and otherwise—became busy again. We have noted that Charles Herrold of San Jose, and Harold Power of Medford Hillside, were among those who prepared to go back on the air.

Similarly in Madison, at the University of Wisconsin, Professor Earle M. Terry was busy with station 9XM. In 1917 this station had started sending by Morse code daily weather bulletins supplied by the Weather Bureau, and several hundred listeners in farm areas around Madison seemed to value the service. The daily weather bulletins were resumed in 1919— again in code. But Professor Terry was anxious to shift to voice, which he had experimented with during the war. With vacuum tubes made in the university laboratory—none were on the market—he began voice tests in 1919 and continued throughout 1920. That fall occasional musical pro- grams were heard over wide areas. During this period, a campus tradition tells us, the experimenters decided that Hawaiian music was especially suitable for radio, because it twanged anyway.[1] Professor Terry was sur- rounded by an ardent group that once again included Malcolm P. Hanson, back from overseas. By the end of the year, test broadcasts by 9XM were being heard in Texas. Beginning January 3, 1921, weather forecasts were given by voice every day, still supplemented by Morse code bulletins.[2]

In Detroit, publisher William E. Scripps of the Detroit *News* thought it

5. *Report of the Federal Trade Commission on the Radio Industry*, pp. 60-67.
1. McCarty, "WHA, Wisconsin's Radio Pioneer," *Wisconsin Blue Book 1937.*
2. Hanson, *Papers.* See especially letter to Professor Andrew W. Hopkins, November 12, 1923, reviewing the development of the station.

was time to introduce his son to the mysteries of radio. They bought receiver parts and assembled them at home, and one night plucked voices from the air. Amid the excitement the father began to think the Detroit *News* should be involved in this. He sensed a new interest stirring. To many young people radio was unknown, an activity suppressed by government since 1917, and now carrying an aura of wartime mystery. When the father saw an advertisement for a De Forest "radiophone" transmitter, he promptly bought it and had it installed at the *News*. The hobby left home and went to the office. With call letters 8MK, testing of the apparatus began early in 1920.[3]

Elton M. Plant, from Ontario, had joined the Detroit *News* in 1919 at the age of sixteen as an office boy. During lunch one day he was heard singing, which resulted in Mr. Scripps assigning him to work on the radiophone with a Mr. Francis Edwards, who was getting the equipment in shape. The apparatus was in the file room where the bound volumes of the *News* were kept. The transmitting equipment took up part of a regular desk. There was a telephone mouthpiece, to which someone had attached a huge Edison gramophone horn about three feet in diameter. Plant's task would be to put his head inside the horn and speak or sing. He was annoyed with the whole business and afraid it might interfere with his dream of becoming a writer. He asked if it would and was told: "For goodness sakes, no! This is after hours." [4] Later he was allowed to write news items for the paper about the radiophone activity.

For a long time the work was tiresome beyond imagining. Night after night, Plant kept saying into the huge horn: "Testing, one, two, three, four. If you are hearing this, will you please call?" He gave a phone number but on many nights no one called. In the hope that music would bring more results, Plant sometimes sang and one night brought a friend to play the ukulele; to Plant's chagrin, no one phoned. Mr. Edwards kept fiddling with gadgets, which showed they were "broadcasting," he always insisted. Most *News* staff members did not take it seriously, but Mr. Scripps remained boyishly enthusiastic. "He used to drop in at night . . . and ask if we were getting out on the air." One night came a great thrill: a phone call from Lansing, Mich. The calls began to increase.[5]

On August 20, a formal period of testing began; this was announced in

3. Plant, *Reminiscences*, pp. 3-4.
4. *Ibid.* p. 3.
5. *Ibid.* pp. 5-6, 15.

the Detroit *News*. By this time the equipment had been moved to the conference room, and use was being made of phonograph records. The tests culminated in a dramatic announcement in a box on the front page of the *News* on primary election day—August 31, 1920.

RADIO OPERATORS! ATTENTION!

Here is the necessary data by use of which you may listen in tonight and get election returns and hear a concert sent out by the Detroit News Radiophone:

FOR LISTENING: Use wave length of 200 meters.
FOR CALLING THE NEWS TO REPORT RESULTS: Use call "8MK."
TRANSMITTING BEGINS 8 O'CLOCK TONIGHT.
MISCELLANEOUS NEWS and music will be transmitted from 5 until 9 o'clock that operators may adjust instruments . . .[6]

There were at this time about fifty licensed radio operators in the Detroit area. The newspaper estimated there were perhaps five hundred amateurs with receiving equipment only.[7]

The Detroit *News* reported in florid style on the primary election broadcast:

The sending of the election returns by the Detroit *News* radiophone on Tuesday night was fraught with romance and must go down in the history of man's conquest of the elements as a gigantic step in his progress. In the four hours that the apparatus, set up in an out-of-the-way corner of the *News* building, was hissing and whirring its message into space, few realized that a dream and a prediction had come true. The news of the world was being given forth through this invisible trumpet to the unseen crowds in the unseen marketplace.[8]

It was announced that the presidential returns in November would also be broadcast by 8MK.

The station became the subject of constant bulletins in the *News*. On September 5 the social page told of a radio dance at the home of an amateur. He was quoted as saying: "We had some of our girl friends up to hear the concert and the news bulletins, and when 'The Naughty Waltz' came in we started to dance. It was great fun." One girl thought it was eerie. "It was just like a séance." [9]

6. Detroit *News*, August 31, 1920.
7. *Ibid.* September 1 and 19, 1920.
8. *Ibid.* September 1, 1920.
9. *Ibid.* September 5, 1920.

On November 2, as announced, the Harding-Cox presidential returns were broadcast by 8MK. Elton Plant, the office boy, rushed back and forth between the editorial department, where the returns were received by telegraph wire, and the conference room "studio," where he handed the information to someone else or, if he found no one available, read it himself. Outside, as it had for decades, the Detroit *News* was projecting the returns by lantern slide and making announcements by megaphone. The megaphone on that day may have reached more people than the radiophone—but for the last time.

Everywhere the radio experimenters who were back in action were finding themselves a center of interest. In Hollywood during 1920, Fred Christian, an electrical engineer, built a 5-watt transmitter in a back bedroom of his home and began entertaining the neighborhood with concerts, with call letters 6ADZ.[10] At the same time near Stevensville, Mont., Ashley Clayton Dixon, a young man from Chicago, having built a home just north of Three Mile Trading Post, started broadcasting from it; he talked or had friends in for a pickup orchestra.[11] At the same time in Charlotte, N.C., a contractor named Fred M. Laxton, whose former employment with General Electric had enabled him to acquire a vacuum tube, was joined by two friends in building a transmitter in a chicken house behind his home; with call letters 4XD they broadcast phonograph records via a wire relay from the house.[12] Similar activity was erupting in many cities and towns. There was a ferment of interest, but without sense of direction—until something happened in Pittsburgh.

DECISION IN PITTSBURGH

To the Westinghouse Electric and Manufacturing Company the years 1918-20 brought a succession of frustrations and defeats.

First the war contracts stopped. Westinghouse had adapted to large production of radio equipment and now it was over. Then it saw its huge rival, General Electric, executing maneuvers by which—through an ingenious subsidiary called Radio Corporation of America—it won virtual control of marine and transoceanic communication.

10. It became KNX. *KNX-CBS Radio*, p. 2.
11. Richards, "Montana's Pioneer Radio Stations," *Montana Journalism Review*. Spring 1963.
12. It became WBT. Wallace, *The Development of Broadcasting in North Carolina*, pp. 59-60.

Next Westinghouse watched the formation of a GE-RCA-AT&T alliance that seemed to take control of the destiny of the vacuum tube and its multiplying uses. The new combination appeared to have a stranglehold on valuable patents.

Especially dismaying to Westinghouse was the situation with respect to international communication. The final days of the war had dramatized transoceanic wireless and radio; as effective competitors to cables, they held obvious promise. Transoceanic traffic in messages was increasing so sharply that cables could not keep up with the demand, sometimes falling days behind, especially in the Pacific area. "Confirmation sent by mail" had been known to arrive before the cable it confirmed.[1] There was business for the taking, through the use of radio. For this purpose Westinghouse moved to acquire a group of patents not swallowed by the GE-RCA-AT&T alliance—those of Reginald Fessenden, controlled in Pittsburgh by the heirs of one of the Fessenden backers. Armed with these patents, a Westinghouse envoy journeyed abroad in 1920 to attempt to negotiate agreements with European radio companies, only to find that Owen D. Young had moved too swiftly, having acquired exclusive agreements that blocked Westinghouse at almost every point. Westinghouse seemed completely stymied.

In its search for useful patents Westinghouse made one investment that turned out to have crucial value. Among the returning men in uniform was Signal Corps Major Edwin H. Armstrong, the young man who, as an undergraduate, had developed a "feedback" circuit. It had been used in war production and proved valuable. However, it was involved in patent disputes and Armstrong had so far earned virtually nothing from his invention. Meanwhile he had developed and patented, while in France, a "superheterodyne" circuit that accomplished an even more astonishing amplification than the feedback circuit. As he returned to the United States—in debt to lawyers and glad to accept a faculty appointment at Columbia University—Westinghouse offered to buy both his feedback and superheterodyne patents for $335,000, payable over a ten-year period, plus additional sums if litigation over the feedback patent was won by Armstrong. Immediately after this offer General Electric expressed interest in buying the same patents.

The inventor debated: should he hold off, and try to get the companies bidding against each other? No, his attorney warned—the companies

1. Jome, *Economics of the Radio Industry*, p. 45.

might get together and beat down his price.[2] Armstrong took his advice and on October 5, 1920, made the sale to Westinghouse. Some patents owned by Michael Pupin, under whom Armstrong had worked at Columbia, were purchased by Westinghouse at the same time. In this sale Armstrong, following the example of De Forest, managed to reserve experimental and amateur rights in his patents.

Throughout these months Westinghouse had been searching with some desperation for ways to use production capacity idled by the peace. It even staged demonstrations for the New York, New Haven & Hartford Railroad to persuade it to put radio equipment on its tugboats in New York harbor. Nothing came of this. Demonstrations for the Fall River Line were likewise a failure.[3] During 1919 one of the Westinghouse researchers, Vladimir K. Zworykin, who had been a communication specialist in the Czarist army and also done television experiments in Russia, asked for permission to pursue these. The permission was given reluctantly because the possibilities seemed so remote.[4]

Meanwhile the men who had guided the wartime radio development at Westinghouse were being shifted to other duties. Frank Conrad, a leader in the work, was busy with electric switches. Donald G. Little, who had worked with him, was put in the lightning arrester section.

Donald Little, an ex-amateur who had built his first transmitter in the ninth grade and had later studied electrical engineering at the University of Michigan, had gone from those studies into the Signal Corps. Later in the same year—1917—the Signal Corps contracted with Westinghouse for the production of some 75 transmitters and 150 receivers of light weight and compact design—SCR-69 and SCR-70—and sent Little to Pittsburgh to watch over their development. Thus he began a close association with Conrad, who had charge of the work for Westinghouse, and who was also a prewar amateur. Much of the testing of SCR-69 and SCR-70 was done at Conrad's home workshop over his garage in Wilkinsburg.[5]

The college-trained Little acquired an almost worshipful admiration for Conrad, who had left school after the seventh grade and done most of his learning as a Westinghouse bench-hand. Conrad, in spite of this beginning, held some 200 patents. His mind leaped to solutions of technical problems; according to engineers he "could usually guess closer than they

2. Lessing, *Man of High Fidelity*, p. 131.
3. Little, *Reminiscences*, pp. 16-17.
4. Zworykin, "The Early Days," *Television Quarterly*, November 1962.
5. Little, *Reminiscences*, pp. 9-10.

could figure." He was thin, wiry, with a suggestion of frailness but constantly working. Even Saturdays and Sundays would find him busy in his garage workshop. In addition to the SCR-69 and SCR-70, Conrad developed for the armed forces a wind-driven generator to be attached to the fuselage or wing of an airplane to power its radio transmitter. Such generators were sold to both the army and the navy. The directing of artillery by voice from airplanes became important in the final days of the war. Conrad also developed an improved hand grenade.[6]

After the war Donald Little joined Westinghouse, hoping to stay in radio with Conrad. Although he soon found himself in lightning arresters—considered "the nearest available thing"—he continued his friendship with Conrad and often dropped in at the garage workshop, where Conrad now resumed his amateur activity with his old call letters 8XK. Before the war he had not had vacuum tubes but did now as by-products of his war work. He experimented, talked with other amateurs, and played phonograph records. Letters began to arrive from other amateurs, praising the quality of his transmissions and requesting particular numbers.

Early in 1920 a coterie began to develop around the garage activity; Donald Little was often there. "There was usually a crowd of interested people . . . I believe the first announcer, aside from Conrad himself, was a brother-in-law of Conrad's." [7] The Hamilton Music Store in Wilkinsburg provided records and in return was mentioned on the air. The two Conrad sons, Francis and Crawford, began to take part in the planning and announcing. The "concerts" were at first intermittent but were soon given every Saturday evening; later, weekday performances were added. Newspapers began to take note. A newspaper item of May 2, 1920, mentioned a piano solo by Francis Conrad, for which a line was run from the home to the garage "to be sent out into the ether by the radiophone apparatus located there." [8] The same story promised future saxophone solos by a friend of the Conrad family.

Until this moment the activity in the Conrad garage was not markedly different from that in the home of Ashley Clayton Dixon near Three Mile Trading Post in Montana, or in other homes, garages or chicken coops housing amateur stations. But in September 1920 a small new ingredient was added.

6. *Ibid.* pp. 11-12.
7. *Ibid.* p. 20.
8. Quoted by Shurick, *The First Quarter Century of American Broadcasting,* p. 17.

In the Pittsburgh *Sun* the Joseph Horne department store ran an advertisement which included the following items:[9]

AIR CONCERT "PICKED UP" BY RADIO HERE

Victrola music, played into the air over a wireless telephone, was "picked up" by listeners on the wireless receiving station which was recently installed here for patrons interested in wireless experiments. The concert was heard Thursday night about 10 o'clock, and continued 20 minutes. Two orchestra numbers, a soprano solo—which rang particularly high and clear through the air—and a juvenile "talking piece" constituted the program.

The music was from a Victrola pulled up close to the transmitter of a wireless telephone in the home of Frank Conrad, Penn and Peebles avenues, Wilkinsburg. Mr. Conrad is a wireless enthusiast and "puts on" the wireless concerts periodically for the entertainment of the many people in this district who have wireless sets.

Amateur Wireless Sets, made by the maker of the Set which is in operation in our store, are on sale here $10.00 up.

—West Basement

The advertisement was seen by Harry P. Davis, Westinghouse vice president and Conrad's superior, and it gave him pause. Davis knew of Conrad's amateur activity and had never given it much thought, even when it received newspaper attention. But the advertisement, presumably reflecting a judgment on a merchandising value, had an entirely different effect on him.

The few hundred amateurs thought to be listening to Conrad's concerts in the Pittsburgh area were all technical-minded individuals who had themselves assembled their receivers. Since the turn of the century, receiving had been for those with technical knowledge. But during the war, Westinghouse had made receivers like the SCR-70, complete in one unit, easy to operate. What dawned on Mr. Davis was the vision of a market— not of electrical wizards but, simply, of everyone. "Here was an idea," Mr. Davis recounted later in an address to the Graduate School of Business Administration at Harvard, "of limitless opportunity." [10]

On the very next day he held an office conference with Conrad and others. He proposed that Conrad be invited to build a new and stronger

9. Pittsburgh *Sun*, September 29, 1920.
10. Davis, "The Early History of Broadcasting in the United States," *The Radio Industry*, p. 194.

transmitter at the Westinghouse plant. It would broadcast on a regular daily schedule, always advertised in advance, to give buyers of receivers assurance of continuing service. If the market for receivers was as "limitless" as Mr. Davis thought, Westinghouse would get its return through the sale of sets as well as through publicity for the Westinghouse name. The service must be launched as dramatically as possible. Could they be ready for the presidential election on November 2? Conrad said they could.

Events in Pittsburgh now followed the pattern of events in Detroit, but with important differences.

As in Detroit, a hobby moved into the business. On the roof of one of the taller buildings of the East Pittsburgh Westinghouse works a shack was built, and a 100-watt transmitter assembled. The antenna ran from a steel pole on the roof to one of the powerhouse smokestacks. Frank Conrad and Donald Little did most of the work. On October 16, Westinghouse applied to the Department of Commerce for a special license to launch a broadcasting service. A week or so later, by telephone, the Department assigned the amateur call letters 8ZZ for use in case the license did not arrive in time.[11] On October 27 the Department assigned the letters KDKA—commercial shore-station call letters—and authorized use of 360 meters, a channel away from amateurs and comparatively free of interference.

The antenna and transmitter were completed only a few days before election. Arrangements were made with the Pittsburgh *Post* to telephone results to the station as they came into the wire services room at the newspaper. At the shack a hand-wound phonograph was installed to fill periods between returns.

Because the time available for testing was inadequate, Frank Conrad decided to stand by at his amateur transmitter in Wilkinsburg in case trouble developed at the East Pittsburgh plant. On the roof in East Pittsburgh Donald Little was the engineer. John Frazier, supervisor of the plant telephone system, was in charge. Leo H. Rosenberg of the publicity department read the bulletins. The broadcast started at 8 P.M. and ran until after midnight.[12]

By then it was clear that Warren G. Harding, U. S. Senator from Ohio, had been elected President. The nation, in rejecting James M. Cox, Governor of Ohio, had also in effect said "no" to the League of Nations. It was

11. Little, *Reminiscences*, p. 23.
12. *Ibid.* pp. 23-5.

shaking off the internationalism of another hour, the Wilsonian call to duty, and the glorious phrases that went with it. It was expressing an urge to get on to something else—a job, an angle, some fun. The KDKA venture marked the transitional moment, and also reflected its mood.

Among listeners to KDKA was a jubilant group at the Edgewood Club outside Pittsburgh. A receiver and a loudspeaker system—two horns borrowed from the navy—had been installed there and a number of people gathered to listen. A member of the group phoned the rooftop shack from time to time to report on the reception. They wanted more returns, less music.[13] Various company officials also had listening groups at their homes. Sets for this purpose had been made up specially at the Westinghouse plant.

Although no sets were yet on the market, Westinghouse focused from the start on the aim of developing a demand for them. For this reason its publicity emphasis was quite different from that of the Detroit *News;* this may help to account for the vast difference in impact. The nation was hardly aware of the Detroit election broadcasts; the excitement radiating from KDKA set off a national mania.

The Detroit *News,* which had no special interest in selling equipment, depicted its radio listeners as technical prodigies, referring to them as "radio operators," who could be expected to report back by wireless on the quality of the 8MK transmission. Their installations were sometimes called "receiving stations." They were pictured in their traditional setting. "But up in their attic rooms or in shed loft," said one story, they "tuned up their receivers and listened to the fate of the candidates being settled long before the office-seekers themselves could know the results."[14] The broadcasting of the returns was thus seen as a project shared by a brotherhood of initiates.

Westinghouse, on the contrary, presented the activity as something for everyone, a social delight for home or country club. References to the equipment were fairly casual, suggesting ease of operation rather than need for mysterious knowledge and ritual.

The Detroit *News,* intent on publicizing itself, could perhaps not expect extensive publicity in rival papers. The Westinghouse bulletins, on the other hand, came to newspapers not from a rival but from a large-scale

13. *Ibid.* p. 26.
14. Detroit *News,* September 1, 1920.

advertiser, launching a nation-wide merchandising campaign. It readily won wide publicity.

As election day faded, Westinghouse hardly paused for self-congratulation. In accordance with its announced intention, it continued broadcasting daily, at first only an hour or so each evening—8:30-9:30 P.M.—but soon on an expanding schedule. It was a period of improvisation, sometimes bold, occasionally bizarre. A Westinghouse band was presented by wire from a hall, but the reverberation was unendurable on the air, giving an impression of chaos. So the next musical group was presented from the roof, where the acoustics were splendid. Rainy weather came, and a tent was built; the acoustics were still good. Then the tent blew down, and it was necessary to move indoors again. The acoustical problem was now solved by erecting the tent indoors. In time the tent gave way to burlap hangings, and the studio came to resemble "a burlap-lined casket." [15]

By January 2, 1921, KDKA was attempting a remote broadcast from the Pittsburgh Calvary Episcopal Church. Two Westinghouse engineers, one Jewish and one Catholic, were dressed in choir robes to handle the technical aspects of production, which involved three microphones. The Reverend Jan Van Etten felt all this symbolized the "universality of radio religion." [16] On January 15, Secretary of Commerce Herbert Hoover spoke over KDKA from the Duquesne Club, to be followed in March by three other cabinet members, in April by a prizefight broadcast, in May by a pickup from a Pittsburgh theater. [17]

Within weeks the 100-watt transmitter was replaced by a 500-watt transmitter. While building this, Little constructed several others almost identical to it—one to be sent to Newark, for the roof of the company's Newark plant; another to Chicago, for the roof of the Commonwealth Edison Building; another to Springfield, Mass., for the East Springfield plant. Here the first Westinghouse home receivers—crystal receivers— were to be manufactured.

The impact of this activity was immediate, and mounting. People were lining up at the counters of electrical shops. Department stores were starting radio departments. All over the country amateurs were assembling sets

15. Davis, "The Early History of Broadcasting in the United States," *The Radio Industry*, p. 200. Saudek, "Program Coming in Fine," *American Heritage*, August 1965.
16. Westinghouse brochure. Among the actual choir boys was Robert Saudek, who became vice president of the American Broadcasting Company.
17. Dunlap, *Radio and Television Almanac*, pp. 66-7.

for friends or relatives, or going into business by starting radio shops. The assembling of sets became a national preoccupation. Complete sets were promised for sale in the near future and impatiently awaited. Newspaper bulletins on the subject were frequent. In the press KDKA programs were continuously discussed; columns of radio news and comment appeared. Plans for new stations were widely publicized. The Department of Commerce began to receive a wave of applications for "broadcasting" licenses; within a year it would become a tidal wave. Many were from amateur stations which wished to convert to a regular, scheduled broadcasting operation and asked for new wave lengths and call letters.

One effect of KDKA occurred in a Pittsburgh suburb. Edgar S. Love, an amateur we have already mentioned, had been operating for years in a coal shed behind his house in Etna, Pa., often with frost-bitten fingers. In 1920 he began getting Frank Conrad from the Wilkinsburg garage. When KDKA started Edgar's father let him bring the set into the house "and actually put up a good antenna." [18] The family started listening with him. Radio had entered the home.

After KDKA, circumstances changed dramatically for Westinghouse. In mid-1920 it had seemed about to be left behind as the GE-RCA-AT&T alliance swept forward. Then, late in October, Westinghouse had acquired control of the Armstrong-Pupin patents; a week later came the KDKA debut, and each moment of its reverberating success dramatized the value of those patents. The future of radio suddenly looked quite different.

On June 30, 1921, the epic of high radio diplomacy reached a fitting climax. The cross-licensing empire fashioned by Owen D. Young took in a new partner—Westinghouse. It became a GE-RCA-AT&T-Westinghouse alliance; an additional company, United Fruit, had also been invited to join because it owned patents on crystal detectors and a loop antenna. Now about two thousand patents were in the pool.[19]

Each of the partners acquired representation on the RCA board of directors.

Thus, within eight months after the KDKA premiere, the Owen D. Young creation reached completion. The allied companies, all pre-eminent in their own spheres, had readjusted their division of the new world of radio. The details of that division would begin to come to light before long.

18. Love, *Reminiscences*, pp. 4-5.
19. *Report of the Federal Trade Commission on the Radio Industry*, p. 3.

The patent allies became owners of RCA stock in the following pro-
portions:[20]

	COMMON	PREFERRED	TOTAL	PER CENT
GE	2,364,826	620,800	2,985,626	30.1%
Westinghouse	1,000,000	1,000,000 (to be issued)	2,000,000	20.6%
AT&T	500,000	500,000	1,000,000	10.3%
United Fruit	200,000	200,000	400,000	4.1%
	4,064,826	2,320,800	6,385,626	65.1%
Others	1,667,174	1,635,174	3,302,348	34.9%
Total shares outstanding	5,732,000	3,955,974	9,687,974	100. %

Though designed for other ends, the alliance now seemed ready to take
control of the broadcasting boom. For the moment, the group seemed
powerful beyond challenge. Yet its very power made it a target—for competitors and government trustbusters. For although RCA and the alliance
behind it had been formed with the active prodding of a few highly
placed government officials, this could not exempt it from the watchfulness of those charged with responsibilities under the Sherman and Clayton
anti-trust acts. Anti-monopoly rumblings stirred again, and grew.

Owen D. Young, writing in a later period, when RCA and big business
in general were under sharp attack, expressed his views on the American
capitalist:

> He works less for luxury than for power. His aim is primarily achieve-
> ment. He will give away his money to universities and hospitals, but
> the power to embark on great enterprises he will not give away. And
> so I say to his critics, if this be materialism, make the most of it.[21]

Young had embarked on great enterprises and had achieved. He had created power. Power for what? He did not say. And the power would more
and more be exercised by others.

While the KDKA venture brought the alliance to completion, it had a
jolting effect on each of the allies. At the General Electric research laboratory William C. White found himself "amazed at our blindness . . . We

20. Archer, *Big Business and Radio*, p. 8.
21. *Saturday Evening Post*, November 15, 1929.

had everything except the idea." He and others began to agitate for a General Electric station at Schenectady.[22]

At the American Telephone and Telegraph Company, the KDKA success precipitated a turmoil of memo-writing and meetings. Here too there was strong pressure for a plunge into the broadcasting field.

At RCA the impact was similar, and more immediate in effect. While the company had been designed to exploit transoceanic and marine communication, it now seemed there might be a bonanza in the backyard. This brought to the foreground a man who had envisioned this possibility but received little encouragement—David Sarnoff. As transmitter towers went up all over America—landscape features of a new age—Sarnoff became a central figure. He too would be a symbol of the age.

22. William White, *Reminiscences*, p. 19; Baker, *Reminiscences*, p. 12.

3 / TOWERS

For out of olde feldes . . . cometh al this newe corn.
Chaucer, The Parlement of Foules

The village of Uzlian—a cluster of wood huts in southern Russia—was biblical-poor when David Sarnoff was born there in 1891.[1] When he was four, his father set out for a new home in a distant land and was to send word when it was time to follow. David went to live with a great uncle in another village, a rabbi. Here young David rose each day at dawn to learn two thousand words of the Talmud by the end of the day; his own training as a rabbi was beginning. After several years came a miracle: the father had sent instructions and money, and David was to join his mother and two brothers in the journey to America. They sailed from Libau and changed ships at Liverpool, with pickled kosher meat for a long journey. They landed in Montreal, took a train to Albany, a night boat to New York. It was 1900 and the harbor and streets were crowded with life, but the reunion was a shock. The father was a shadow of himself; for six years he had been a house painter, saving money for the family migration. Now he gasped for each breath and soon went to bed in the East Side tenement that would be their home, to be an invalid until death.[2]

David, a day or two after arrival, got a job as a delivery boy for a butcher and soon added a paper route. The neighborhood was alive with pushcarts and people, and he thrived. He went to school to learn English and within a year was assigned to debate the topic: "Resolved, that the

1. The following is based on *David Sarnoff: biographical sketch,* and other sources as noted.
2. Tebbel, *David Sarnoff,* pp. 42-5.

Philippines be given their independence." David impressed his neighbors, who lent him $200 to buy a newsstand of his own on Tenth Avenue. He had no childhood but did not seem to miss it. At ten he was the head of the family. He supplemented his patchwork of earnings by singing in a synagogue choir for $1.50 a week. When his voice broke, he had to give that up, and he decided to look for a full-time job. At fifteen, in his best suit, he went to the New York *Herald* Building. The first desk he saw was that of the Postal Telegraph office. There he was hired as messenger at $5 a week. The click of the telegraph instruments excited him, and he soon learned the Morse code. When the machines weren't busy he practised constantly at the office, carrying on Morse conversation with a man at another office whom he did not know, but who told him of an opening for a telegrapher at American Marconi. When David applied for it he was turned down as telegrapher but hired as office boy at $5.50 per week. Characteristically, he accepted this, while preparing relentlessly for a future move upward. As office boy he filed letters, reading each one. Before long he, only he, knew where everything was and who had promised what to whom. With special care he read letters from the president of the company and studied the presidential prose style. He carried a pocket dictionary and looked up every unfamiliar word. In spare moments he went to the library and read technical books. On weekends he hung around the company's experimental workshop downtown on Front Street. It was 1907 and American Marconi was still a struggling young company; the boy was part of the struggle, heart and soul. At an electrical show, where the company exhibited, he got his first chance as telegrapher. Soon he became a full-time operator and people said he had a great "fist." He was one of the fastest, and he loved competition. When Guglielmo Marconi came to the United States, telegrapher David Sarnoff got a chance to talk with him, run errands for him, and deliver flowers to young ladies for him. In 1908, at seventeen, Sarnoff became operator at the lonely Sciasconset station on Nantucket Island at $60 a month, soon raised to $70, of which he sent $40 to his mother while boarding at a farm for $25. In spare time he read technical books. After two years at the shore station he served as Marconi operator on several ships, including a sealing ship that went to the Arctic. Then he asked for, and got, the job of operator at the busiest of all American Marconi stations—Sea Gate in Brooklyn.[3]

In 1911 the Wanamaker stores in Philadelphia and New York con-

3. *Ibid.* pp. 50-63.

tracted with American Marconi to equip the stores with wireless; at each station a Marconi operator would be stationed. It was an unusual move on the part of the stores, giving them intercommunication and also publicity. Sarnoff asked for the New York assignment; it was a chance to take advanced night courses at Pratt Institute. On an April afternoon in 1912, while on duty at the store, he heard weak signals: "S. S. *Titanic* ran into iceberg. Sinking fast." Sarnoff gave the information to the press and sought further word from distant cracklings. He alerted ships he could reach; he kept at his key. He established very faint communication with the S. S. *Olympic*, 1400 miles away, which told him that the *Titanic* had sunk and the *Carpathia* was picking up survivors. Sarnoff relayed the news to the world and tried to reach the *Carpathia*. President Taft ordered all other stations in the United States off the air. Officials, press services, newspapers, relatives stood by. The twenty-one-year-old telegrapher at the Wanamaker store in New York became their one communication link with the scene of disaster. For seventy-two hours he was at it. Over the miles, through deafening atmospheric noises, names of survivors on the *Carpathia* began to come through. The Wanamaker store was overwhelmed with crowds: reporters, friends, relatives, curious people. Some were hysterical. A line of police tried to hold them back. A few anxious relatives—with well-known names like Astor, Strauss, and others—were allowed in the wireless room to look over the young man's shoulder as he wrote down names of survivors. As the *Carpathia* drew close he spent additional hours at the Sea Gate station until the lists of the living and dead were complete. Then he had a Turkish bath and went to bed. The name Sarnoff was known all over the country.

A new law, stiffening ship radio requirements,[4] was passed, and it meant a boom for American Marconi. Other companies were dropping by the wayside, but American Marconi became big business, and Sarnoff was its man. He would take any job, the harder the better. He became training instructor, equipment inspector, chief inspector, assistant traffic manager, assistant chief engineer, commercial manager—in rapid succession. He was indispensable. He understood businessmen and their problems, and could also deal with technical people. They believed in him, and when they had new ideas they looked to him to translate them into business terms. When young Edwin H. Armstrong invented a new circuit that was said to do wonders, it was Sarnoff who was delegated to evaluate it. In a

4. Public Law No. 238, 62nd Congress, approved July 23, 1912.

drafty shack in Belmar, N.J., in frigid weather in January 1914, Armstrong and Sarnoff sat together all one night pulling in Ireland, Germany, Hawaii—taking down messages to be checked later with the originating stations. "Well do I remember that memorable night," Sarnoff was to write Armstrong years later. "Whatever chills the air produced were more than extinguished by the warmth of the thrill which came to me at hearing for the first time signals from across the Atlantic and across the Pacific." [5] That meeting held the seeds of friendship—and of longer enmity. There was a gulf between them. For Armstrong was a lone experimenter, an inventor in a pattern that might be passing into oblivion, but Sarnoff was a company man.

Sarnoff kept in touch with everything going on in the wireless and radio world: its future was constantly before him. In November 1916 he wrote to his superior, Edward J. Nally, vice president and general manager of American Marconi, a memorandum outlining a plan. Its main ingredients were not new; Lee de Forest was at that very time broadcasting music and news bulletins—including election returns—in New York City. But Sarnoff translated the idea into a business plan and began with the consumer:

> I have in mind a plan of development which would make radio a "household utility" in the same sense as the piano or phonograph. . . .
>
> The receiver can be designed in the form of a simple "Radio Music Box" and arranged for several different wave lengths, which would be changeable with the throwing of a single switch or pressing of a single button.
>
> The "Radio Music Box" can be supplied with amplifying tubes and a loudspeaking telephone, all of which can be neatly mounted in one box. The box can be placed in the parlor or living room, the switch set accordingly and the transmitted music received. . . .
>
> The same principle can be extended to numerous other fields—as for example—receiving lectures at home which can be made perfectly audible. . . . This proposition would be especially interesting to farmers and others living in outlying districts removed from cities. By the purchase of a "Radio Music Box" they could enjoy concerts, lectures, music, recitals, etc., which may be going on in the nearest city within their radius. [6]

General manager Edward Nally seems to have considered the idea "harebrained." Sarnoff's reaction was characteristic. He put the memoran-

5. Lessing, *Man of High Fidelity*, p. 220.
6. Archer, *History of Radio*, pp. 112-13.

dum aside and bided his time. With the formation of RCA, he apparently felt his time had come. In January 1920 he spoke to Owen D. Young. Resubmitting his plan, he added details. It now included *Wireless Age,* the American Marconi periodical that RCA had taken over.

> Every purchaser of a "Radio Music Box" would be encouraged to become a subscriber of the *Wireless Age* which would announce in its columns an advance monthly schedule of all lectures, recitals, etc., to be given in various cities of the country. With this arrangement the owner of the "Radio Music Box" can learn from the columns of the *Wireless Age* what is going on in the air at any given time and throw the "Radio Music Box" switch to the point (wave length) corresponding with the music or lecture desired to be heard.
>
> If this plan is carried out the volume of paid advertising that can be obtained for the *Wireless Age* on the basis of such proposed increased circulation would in itself be a profitable venture. In other words, the *Wireless Age* would perform the same mission as is now being performed by the various motion picture magazines which enjoy so wide a circulation.[7]

In further paragraphs Sarnoff considered the plan from an investment point of view. He felt that manufacturing costs would allow sale of the radio music boxes at $75 each. If a million families responded, a revenue of $75,000,000 would result.

Again Sarnoff had to wait. Weeks later E. W. Rice, president of General Electric, asked for specific details, and Sarnoff quickly provided them. In that time of paralysis and restlessness before the AT&T alliance, his predictions must have seemed brash. But Sarnoff felt the pulse of the time. He estimated that Radio Music Boxes at $75 would sell as follows:

1st yr.	100,000	Radio Music Boxes	$ 7,500,000
2nd yr.	300,000	Radio Music Boxes	22,500,000
3rd yr.	600,000	Radio Music Boxes	45,000,000
		TOTAL	$75,000,000[8]

These estimates were to win for Sarnoff legendary repute as a prophet. In 1922, the first year in which RCA sold radio sets, its sales totaled about $11,000,000, or substantially more than the prediction. For the second year Sarnoff's prediction was exactly right. For the third, sales ran to $50,000,000, or more than predicted.

But in the spring of 1920 RCA officialdom, tangled in world-wide diplo-

---

7. Tebbel, *David Sarnoff,* pp. 99-106.
8. Archer, *History of Radio,* p. 189.

macy, was not ready to believe. Sarnoff was pushing something unrelated to their main preoccupation. They decided to appropriate $2000 so that he could produce a model of the kind of receiver he had in mind. This got the matter off the agenda momentarily. Then the success of KDKA put it right back on. RCA had, in effect, missed the boat. Within weeks the national excitement was boiling in a way that could not be ignored. Early in 1921 the reorientation within RCA was under way. In April, David Sarnoff, aged thirty, became general manager, and within months RCA president Edward Nally, confused by the new developments, began to talk to Owen D. Young about withdrawing from the leadership.

Sarnoff meanwhile kept on the move. Production plans for home radios were being hurried in the alliance group. Sarnoff felt that RCA must at the same time put itself dramatically into broadcasting. Among the most discussed coming events was the heavyweight championship prizefight scheduled for July 2 at Boyle's Thirty Acres in Jersey City, between champion Jack Dempsey, the "Manassa Mauler," and Georges Carpentier, champion of France. Sarnoff arranged to borrow a portable transmitter made by General Electric for the navy and not delivered. Submitting a license application, he recruited Major J. Andrew White, editor of *Wireless Age*, to organize the premiere. White with two electricians set out for New Jersey and persuaded the Lackawanna Railroad to let them use its property. An antenna was strung between railroad towers. Equipment was set up in a galvanized iron hut used by Pullman porters to change into their uniforms. Because the porters objected to the invasion, technician J. O. Smith slept in the hut to guard the equipment. A telephone line was run to the arena. There on July 2, with Sarnoff at his side, Major J. Andrew White did a blow-by-blow description that launched a new career for him but which, curiously enough, was not broadcast. In the railroad hut the information was jotted down and spoken into the microphone by technician J. O. Smith. Only Smith's voice reached the listener. Meanwhile the transmitter was operating at more than its intended power; shortly after Dempsey's victory by a fourth-round knockout, the overheated equipment became virtually a "molten mass." So went the debut—and temporary suspension—of WJY.[9]

For Sarnoff the entire venture, especially in its behind-the-scenes ramifications, was another triumph. He had won the co-operation of Tex Rickard, promoter of the fight, and they had arranged for radio sets and loud-

9. Goldsmith and Lescarboura, *This Thing Called Broadcasting*, pp. 210-11.

speakers to be set up at theaters, lodge halls, ballrooms, and barns throughout the eastern United States. About a hundred such gatherings had been organized as charity affairs, and an admission charge made for "aid to devastated France." Vigorous promotion had been provided under a sponsoring committee headed by Franklin D. Roosevelt. Also participating were the Elks, Masons, and Knights of Columbus. Amateur wireless groups had been enlisted to set up the equipment at the gatherings; the volunteer amateurs got certificates signed by Tex Rickard, Georges Carpentier, Anne Morgan, Franklin D. Roosevelt. Thus sports excitement, interest in radio, patriotism, and humanitarianism were all skillfully channeled into a formidable promotion for the age of broadcasting. As many as 300,000 people were estimated to have heard the broadcast.[10] The pot that KDKA had set cooking was kept boiling vigorously by RCA. Tubes and other parts carrying the RCA trademark were beginning to move into electrical stores; within a few months radio sets would follow. A demand was assured.

There was now no doubt who was in charge. David Sarnoff, the immigrant boy, the speed telegrapher with the great fist, the aggressive worker who would tackle the hard jobs, was running things. As he surveyed the scene for RCA and its allies, the outlook was brilliant. With two thousand patents, they were strong and well fortified.

Yet there were loopholes—totally unforeseen—that now came to plague the life of David Sarnoff.

One had to do with "amateurs."

Under the GE-RCA-AT&T-Westinghouse agreements, an effort had been made to allocate everything. The making of receivers and parts would be done by GE and Westinghouse; the marketing of these receivers and parts would be done through RCA under RCA trademarks. RCA would assign 60 per cent of all manufacturing to GE, 40 per cent to Westinghouse. The sale of transmitters would be mainly an AT&T concern. Telephony as a service, or involving any business aspect, belonged to AT&T, whether wired or wireless. RCA had limited rights in wireless telephony and the chief role in international communication. Government orders were exempted from the provisions of these agreements; any of the companies could fill government contracts in any field. There were innumerable additional provisos and reservations, but in general the radio world had been divided along these lines—*except for the amateurs.*

10. Archer, *History of Radio*, p. 215.

GE and Westinghouse could make—for sale via RCA—radio parts for the use of amateurs, for receiving or sending, and could transmit to them. But so could others. It will be recalled that De Forest and Armstrong had reserved certain rights in the amateur field. What did these rights amount to? And just who was an amateur?

All over the country amateurs—they now numbered tens of thousands —were buying parts and putting sets together. People wanted to buy these, so the amateurs sold them and got more parts and made more sets. Amateurs were also making transmitters, often using one or more parts sold by RCA. In many cases they then decided to use these transmitters for regular broadcasting and applied for new call letters and wave lengths. Thus 8MK became WWJ, Detroit; 9XM became WHA, Madison; 9CT became WDAP, Chicago; 1XZ became WCN, Worcester; 6ADZ became KNX, Hollywood; 9ZJ became WLK, Indianapolis; W9CNF became KWCR, Cedar Rapids. The amateur-made transmitters were leaving garages and attics and were, in many cases, appearing on the buildings of newspapers, department stores, hotels. AT&T was up in arms. These transmitters were not being used for amateur purposes but—said AT&T—for telephony as a service, in many cases with a business purpose. The terms of the alliance were being violated, said AT&T. GE and Westinghouse were also upset. All over the country sets were being assembled and sold, using parts covered by patents of the alliance. These companies likewise considered the terms of the alliance violated. The pressure was on Sarnoff to crack down on the "amateurs."

The upstart competition, though stemming from amateur beginnings, was rapidly turning into a sizable industry. Suddenly several hundred companies were at work. A number of entrepreneurs were turning out sets under Armstrong licenses, using his feedback circuit. Most were tube sets complete except for the tubes. Distributor or dealer or customer could insert the needed tube or tubes—generally RCA tubes sold for amateur use. Why not? Wasn't a radio listener an amateur?

The carefully built alliance of the titans, dividing the world, seemed to be crumbling. In the words of Lawrence Lessing, biographer of Armstrong, "A raggle-taggle mob of free enterprisers was running away with the business." The term "amateur" had come to cover "nearly everyone in the country." [11]

11. Lessing, *Man of High Fidelity*, pp. 132-4.

Herbert Hoover, Secretary of Commerce, discussing the boom that was inundating his office with paper, took note of the same phenomenon but in different terms. This boom, he said, had been created by "the genius of the American boy."[12] It was this genius that Sarnoff was now called on to chastise, and bring to book. It couldn't possibly be a popular move, but Sarnoff was a company man. The agreements had to be upheld. Patent rights must be respected. As RCA prepared to market radio sets it also girded for battle, while the mania mounted.

UP A LADDER IN NEWARK

Westinghouse had won a headstart in broadcasting and hoped to keep it. On the roof of the Westinghouse plant at Orange and Plane streets, Newark, a shack was being built. A transmitter had arrived from Pittsburgh— one of the duplicates of the KDKA transmitter. A staff was being assembled.

We come now to a time when broadcasting talent—producer and performer—began to develop as a separate entity. Heretofore the inventor had been impresario and often chief entertainer. Fessenden had played the violin, De Forest had read election returns, Conrad had introduced records. As broadcasting became corporate enterprise, specialization began.

Thomas H. Cowan—everyone called him "Tommy"—was a product of northern New Jersey. He got his first job with Thomas Edison in West Orange. From there he went to the Remington plant in Hoboken, which in 1916 was making ammunition for the armies of imperial Russia. The following year the Russian Revolution brought unemployment to Hoboken, but the Westinghouse plant in Newark was busy with United States war work so Tommy moved there and stayed on after the war. On a day in 1921 Tommy was told to go up to the roof, to the shack. They were going to try to "make this thing talk."[1]

Years before, staying with his aunt in New York at the age of fourteen, he had been an extra in the Metropolitan Opera, dressed as a child. The episode had clung to him and had now apparently caused his assignment

12. *Radio Broadcast*, May 1922.
1. Cowan, *Reminiscences*, pp. 1-10. He eventually became studio manager of WNYC, New York.

to the rooftop. Reaching the shack via an iron ladder and hatchway, he found engineer George Blitziotis at work on equipment. This included a telephone with the hook removed; Tommy's job would be to talk into it.

One evening soon afterward he began his *récitatif:* "This is WJZ, WJZ, WJZ, the radio telephone broadcasting station located at Newark, New Jersey. Please stand by to tune." (They said "tune" at this time, not "tune in.") As he gathered courage, he talked at random, on the plans and expectations of WJZ. Before they were even offering a program schedule they were getting appreciative letters, some from beyond the Mississippi.[2]

On Friday, September 30, 1921—the day before the formal opening— Tommy went down to the Edison laboratories to try to borrow a phonograph from the old inventor. He found that Edison had a sign on his door: I WILL NOT TALK RADIO TO ANYONE. Tommy gathered that Edison was chagrined because the radio vacuum tube, though descended from his incandescent lamp, had been developed by others. Nevertheless Edison lent him a phonograph for WJZ and added some records, including Anna Case singing "Annie Laurie." At Newark the phonograph turned out to be too big to go through the hatchway, so it had to be hoisted up outside the factory building. Some days later Edison phoned to ask them to stop using his phonograph. "If the phonograph sounded like that in any room, nobody would ever buy it." WJZ therefore bought another Edison phonograph and Tommy took the borrowed one back. He found the old man very critical. "Why do you give people a laboratory experiment? I give the public a finished product." Tommy explained that interest was very high, and asked Edison what he thought was wrong. Edison took a piece of paper and drew a circuit, an elaborate diagram. Tommy didn't understand it but nodded and put it in his pocket. Back at the shack he found two engineers tinkering with the equipment. He showed them the sketch and they studied it intently. Two days later Tommy was startled to learn that he was wanted for immediate assignment to Pittsburgh. "That drawing you turned in was a masterpiece." He desperately explained that Thomas Edison had made the drawing, and managed to avoid the transfer.[3]

Meanwhile WJZ had opened, but its big splash began October 5 with broadcasts of the World Series between the New York Giants and the New York Yankees at the Polo Grounds in Manhattan. This was to be for WJZ what election returns had been for KDKA.

2. *Ibid.* pp. 11-13.
3. *Ibid.* pp. 18-21.

The broadcast itself was equally simple and again relied on newspaper co-operation. Like the Dempsey-Carpentier fight it was really a relay. During the first game Tommy sat in the shack holding a telephone receiver to one ear; at the other end of the line, at the Polo Grounds, was a reporter from the Newark *Call*. When Tommy heard, "Strike one," he quickly repeated, "Strike one." After "Ball one," he said, "Ball one." The hand holding the receiver became bloodless, the shell of his ear raw. The thing seemed to go on for hours. At the end he did not know who had won. For the second game he was given a headset.[4]

For a short time the shack was the studio, and they relied mainly on the Edison phonograph. A Sunday schedule was reported as follows in the WJZ log:

7:55- 8:05—Two test records on Edison phonograph.
8:10- 8:15—Newark *Sunday Call* news read by Thomas Cowan.
8:15- 8:18—Stand by 3 minutes.
All quiet.
8:20   —Sacred selections on Edison phonograph.
8:35   —Sacred selections on Edison phonograph.
8:50   —Stand by 3 minutes. KZN and WNY.
8:55   —Sacred selections on Edison phonograph.
9:15   —End of concert.
WJZ signing off.
9:50   —Explain Arlington time signals.
9:55-10:00—NAA time signals.
10:05   —Weather forecast.
10:10   —WJZ signing off.
10:25   —Played an Edison record for Walton 2B2H, a local manager, the gentleman who installed Westinghouse receivers.[5]

A few performers actually came to the shack. It is said that a lady, invited to do a children's story, climbed the iron ladder, was pulled and pushed through the hatchway, but fainted.[6]

A studio was needed, so part of the ladies' dressing room—"cloak room," some called it—was curtained off for the purpose. Tommy bought some Canton flannel to drape it and had this dyed dark red. He thought it had distinction and wouldn't show dirt. At an auction in Halsey Street in Newark he bought two Oriental rugs to kill the resonance.[7] They tried

4. *Ibid.* p. 17.
5. Quoted in Robinson, *Radio Networks and the Federal Government*, p. 12.
6. Gross, *I Looked and Listened*, p. 58.
7. Cowan, *Reminiscences*, p. 24.

various microphones: one resembled a dishpan, another a tomato can suspended from a music stand. An upright piano was found. Charles Popenoe
became station manager and Raymond Guy joined as engineer. Now the
artists began coming.

Among the first was Eddie Janis, who had a vaudeville act with his wife.
He was playing in Newark at Proctor's Theater and was asked by the
theater manager, Mr. Goulding, to please go over to WJZ and broadcast.
He went, did some songs and played a violin solo. By the time he got back
to the theater there was a telegram from the manager of the Keith Theater
in Cincinnati. congratulating him on a fine performance. Janis found it an
astounding experience.[8] On November 1, Pathé Records sent over a quartet called the Shannon Four, who later became the Revelers. They were so
enthusiastic about their experience that Pathé sent another act—Billy
Jones and Ernie Hare. Someone phoned from Columbia University and
offered to send a student orchestra. Milton Cross, a member of a Paulist
choir, came to sing, in a plaintive tenor, songs like "Little Mother of
Mine." Vaughn de Leath, a girl singer who had broadcast for De Forest in
1916 came whenever Tommy said the word. He was always back and
forth to New York, and would drop in at her apartment on 38th Street off
Sixth Avenue and say, "Come on, you're going to Newark." [9] During November and December the Aeolian Company sent John Charles Thomas,
Johanna Gadski. Percy Grainger, and others. It was like a pilgrimage to a
shrine, known for certified miracles. Olga Petrova, who was appearing at
the Broad Street Theater in Newark, decided to come. Everyone was
nervous about this because she was a fanatic on birth control and always
making speeches about it. There was a sense of relief when she said she
just wanted to read some Mother Goose rhymes, her own versions. She
then broadcast:

> There was an old woman who lived in a shoe,
> She had so many children because she didn't know what to do.[10]

The staff was terrified; they were certain there would be trouble from
Washington. Westinghouse executives were already nervous about possibilities of this sort, and had wondered what to do if a "red" got on the air.
An emergency switch was provided for the engineer in the shack. At any
moment he could switch to a phonograph beside him—on his own judg-

8. Janis, *Reminiscences*, p. 2.
9. Cowan, *Reminiscences*, pp. 25-46.
10. *Ibid.* p. 34.

ment or on signal from the studio.[11] The Petrova episode meanwhile caused a careful eyeing of program plans. The producers of *Tangerine*, a musical comedy running on Broadway, had offered to send the whole cast to Newark for a Sunday broadcast of the full production, and this was scheduled. But perhaps there would be risqué jokes. On Saturday, Tommy Cowan was dispatched to New York to explain that all lewd jokes would have to be eliminated. The producers were offended at the imputation of lewdness; the whole venture was canceled.[12] This left a gap in next day's schedule. Tommy, discouraged, had dinner at the Hotel Pennsylvania. Never mind, said Vincent Lopez, whose orchestra was playing there; he would take the band over instead. Via Hudson tube they came the next day—November 27, 1921—to play for an hour and a half. That is how it went, and no one wanted a cent.

Soon came a move to a larger studio on the ground floor of the factory. The visits by artists were gratifying to the Westinghouse executives, and they began to appropriate money for things like flowers, and limousines to meet artists at the Hudson tube or the ferry. They hired a doorman—Alvin E. Simmons—to receive them at the studio and bring them glasses of water. Tommy Cowan, as announcer, always wore a tuxedo, or even white-tie-and-tails. The new studio was decorated with publicity pictures of stars. All this was necessary, because coming across the Hudson to a factory in an arid sector of Newark was really an ordeal.

It couldn't last. Other stations were getting ready to start in New York; newspapers were reporting plans for at least a dozen. All would be clamoring for talent and Newark would be forgotten. Within months it was decided to install a studio in the Waldorf-Astoria Hotel, then at Fifth Avenue and 34th Street in New York. A Western Union wire was run from there to the Newark transmitter. The new studio had a grand premiere, with an address by the president of Western Union, who, pleased to get into the radio spotlight, spoke of the miracle of modern communication, but the quality of the line was so bad that it was difficult to hear what he said.[13] However, WJZ was stuck with the line and somehow would have to make it work. Now, for some months, the station's history would be tied up with New York City and that Waldorf-Astoria studio. This began a

11. Goldsmith and Lescarboura, *This Thing Called Broadcasting*, p. 27. The authors state that the switch was used "time and again" while a speaker continued to "wax eloquent" with radical views.
12. Cowan, *Reminiscences*, p. 35.
13. Guy, *Reminiscences*, p. 22.

more aggressive, competitive, flamboyant chapter, and was the end of innocence.

CHICAGO, CITY OF OPERA

In Chicago it was not election returns or sports, it was Mary Garden. She was a beautiful opera star, who had become general director of the Chicago Civic Opera and whose name was being linked with that of Samuel Insull, legendary utility magnate. Perhaps for all these reasons Westinghouse, in opening KYW on November 11, 1921, chose Mary Garden and opera. In fact, the KYW schedule for the 1921-22 season was entirely Chicago Civic Opera. All performances, afternoon and evening, six days a week, were broadcast—and nothing else.

Would it prove as potent as election returns or World Series baseball? It was more so. At the beginning of the season there were thought to be 1300 receivers in the Chicago area. No sets were yet in the stores, but people began clamoring for them. The assembling of sets by amateurs and ex-amateurs became a round-the-clock occupation. It was a popular high school activity. By the end of the opera season 20,000 sets were reported in operation in Chicago. "The ears of the entire Midwest," according to one writer, had been in the opera house all that winter. "Crude homemade aerials are on one roof in ten along all the miles of bleak streets in the city's industrial zones." [1]

At KYW as at WJZ, there was of course the need to recruit a staff. Walter Chew Evans had become a wireless bug in his early teens, exchanging messages with a neighborhood buddy in Chicago. Licensed at sixteen, Walter worked summers and weekends during high school as wireless operator on lake steamers. After graduation he went to New Orleans and got similar work on oil and banana boats, including the United Fruit ship *Suriname*. When the war came, he took up study at the University of Illinois but then joined the navy and was assigned to teach code at Harvard in the naval radio course, then sent for radio duty on a submarine chaser.[2]

After the war, back in Illinois, he was glad to get a wire from United Fruit asking him to come back to the Caribbean. Later that year aboard

1. *Radio Broadcast*, October 1922.
2. Evans, *Reminiscences*, pp. 1-5. He eventually became president of Westinghouse Radio Stations.

the *Parismina*, testing his radio equipment, he was asked by an operator at Ceiba, Honduras, to put on "some kind of program." The ship was carrying a circus troop to Havana, so he brought the circus band to his microphone for a number or two. Evans didn't know that the Ceiba operator was hooked up with a long distance phone line and was providing entertainment for the presidential palace. It was Walter Evans's debut in showmanship.

He decided to go for a degree at Illinois, but lack of funds sent him back to the Great Lakes to earn tuition. As operator aboard the lake steamer *Alabama* in the fall of 1921 he listened to KDKA. Then he heard that Westinghouse was planning a similar station in Chicago, atop the Commonwealth Edison building; at the earliest possible moment he applied and was hired. All that winter, afternoons and evenings, he sat in a regular seat at the Chicago Civic Opera with switching equipment on his knee.[3]

Ten microphones were used. Technically it was the most elaborate programming yet undertaken. In an address over KDKA a Westinghouse executive, C. W. Horn, later discussed the matter. Walter Evans—with some exaggeration—was pictured as a musical genius:

> At Chicago our station KYW has ten microphones scattered about the auditorium where the Chicago Civic Opera Company renders its selection. An expert sits in the audience with a small switchboard in his lap and cuts in the proper microphone for whatever type of performance is being offered at that instant. He uses a different microphone for a solo than he does when the orchestra is playing, and he must make the change instantly . . . Needless to say this man knows all the operas by heart.[4]

As the opera season drew to a close, KYW reluctantly faced the fact that it would need a studio and studio equipment, including, of course, an emergency switch. A small room in the Commonwealth Edison building was hung with draperies. Salesmen for the Westinghouse company in Chicago became the first announcers. Through Western Union, plans were made for lines to stadiums. Arrangements were later made with International News Service to provide information for bulletins—for which INS would be mentioned. During this period Evans was often back and forth to Pittsburgh, checking arrangements with Harry P. Davis, who kept a

3. *Ibid.* pp. 6-11.
4. Horn, *Address*, January 3, 1923.

tight rein on policy matters. Davis by now had four stations under him. Besides KDKA, WJZ, and KYW, he had in October 1921 launched WBZ, Springfield, Mass. He felt he was making history; he concerned himself relentlessly about every detail. Evans found him to have no hobbies; rather, work was his hobby. When persuaded to play golf, he "practically trotted around the golf course to get back to work."[5]

At KYW as elsewhere, the parade of notables began: Rudolf Valentino, Madame Schumann-Heink, Tito Schipa, Al Jolson, and countless others of lesser fame. It was a journey that had to be made. But soon there would be competition. In Chicago, at the end of 1921, there were plans for almost a dozen stations.

That winter, observers noted, every school in Chicago felt the radio fever. Classes in electrical theory "doubled and redoubled." Shop classes "suddenly came to life" as boys began to make radio cabinets. Teachers "felt ashamed" when they couldn't answer student questions about radio. At the KYW studio a never-ending procession of visitors began. The older people just looked and nodded. But kids in short pants "staggered" the staff with questions that went straight to the heart of things. There were radio clubs in many schools. Marshall High School started such a club in May 1922, and by June 1 it had four hundred members.[6]

What else was happening in Chicago? As in other cities, the peace had brought problems. Organized crime was said to be on the rise. With Prohibition, gangs were getting interested in liquor and battling over territories. There was widespread unemployment; among Negroes it was catastrophic. Thousands had been drawn north for jobs in war production; with the peace, most of the jobs ended. In the crammed Negro ghettoes of Chicago the pressure mounted. There were race riots in which scores were killed. There was wide labor unrest. In Chicago, as elsewhere, officials had little patience with it. People who complained were probably reds and it was best to crack down. The Russian Revolution helped to create on American shores a billy-club era. Seldom were civil liberties at lower ebb. The mood of the day frowned on the critic and hailed the booster.

In this atmosphere broadcasting spent its first year. It was glorious. All was optimism. Hardly a hint of a turbulent world showed through the surface. In that way broadcasting was, in a sense, expressing the era.

5. Evans, *Reminiscences,* pp. 13, 38.
6. *Radio Broadcast,* October 1922.

1920: Making vacuum tubes for 9XM, University of Wisconsin. Malcolm P. Hanson and Professor Earle M. Terry.

WHA

1920: Staff of 8MK, Detroit *News,* testing. Center, Elton Plant—office boy, announcer, singer.

Detroit Historical Museum

1920: Society event, September 4. At home of Charles F. Hammond, dancing to music of 8MK, Detroit.

Detroit Historical Museum

DECISION

Frank Conrad home and garage in Wilkinsburg, Pa., where he operated 8XK, ancestor of KDKA.

NBC

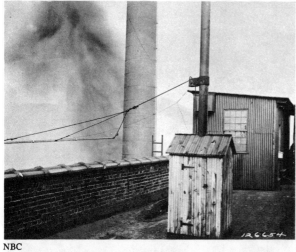

NBC

1920: Rooftop shack, KDKA.

NBC

1920: KDKA, interior of rooftop shack. Broadcasting the returns.

Along with mah-jongg and Florida real estate and the hip flask, radio was reflecting the nation's determination not to look at its problems.

THE EUPHORIA OF 1922

The year 1922 opened with exhilaration. Business was improving and radio zooming. In broadcasting, euphoria was at the controls. A new era in human history was surely beginning.

Along with radio parts, full sets were coming on the market: the Grebe, the Aeriola, the Radiola, and a flood of others—first crystal sets, then tube sets. Makers of sets and parts couldn't produce fast enough. The rate of increase among listeners seemed "almost incomprehensible" to one reporter, who tells of standing "in the fourth or fifth row at the radio counter." [1]

This boom fed another boom, that among broadcasters. This was more incomprehensible. In 1921 the Department of Commerce, in the wake of the KDKA success, formally adopted "broadcasting" as a separate class of station and began issuing licenses. From January through November of 1921 it issued five; in December, twenty-three. Then the deluge:[2]

	NEW STATIONS
1922	LICENSED
January	8
February	24
March	77
April	76
May	97
June	72
July	76

Astoundingly, all these stations were to be found at the same spot on the radio dial—360 meters (833.3 kc.), the wave length allocated to "news, lectures, entertainment, etc." [3]

The station had one apparent escape from this jam. The wave length of 485 meters (618.6 kc.) was allocated to government functions such as weather and crop reports. It was felt that a private station broadcasting a

1. *Radio Broadcast*, May, 1922.
2. Jome, *Economics of the Radio Industry*, p. 70.
3. *Radio Service Bulletin*, April 1, 1922.

government bulletin could—and should—use 485 meters for that one item. A Louisville journalist who went to Washington early in 1922 to get a broadcasting license for the *Courier-Journal*, relates: "In the Department of Commerce a young man stated that our call letters were WHAS, our wave length 360 meters, except when broadcasting weather reports when we would use 485 meters." [4]

Similarly the Detroit *News* station, by now called WWJ, was telling its audience in a 1922 promotion booklet: "Weather and all government reports are broadcast on 485 meters; everything else is on 360 meters." [5]

For bulletins the stations apparently swept back and forth across the dial, urging their listeners to tag along.

The confusion must have been immense. The Department of Commerce did not allocate time periods; it simply told each station to work out a division with others in its area. Unending local bargaining—or bickering —therefore followed.

For a time this was reasonably peaceful. When the Bamberger department store inaugurated WOR in Newark early in 1922, it quickly arrived at a treaty with WJZ. On one day WOR would have sunrise to sunset, and WJZ the remaining hours; on the following day the arrangement would be reversed, and so on. [6]

All this was sometimes done ceremoniously, becoming part of the mystique of broadcasting. On March 15, influenced by the Mary Garden triumphs in Chicago, WJZ decided to offer opera: a complete studio performance of Mozart's *The Impresario* by an opera touring company. A reporter described the event.

> The company arrives and is shown into the *sanctum sanctorum*. They take their places. The announcer explains that they are subject to certain radio traffic regulations, as other broadcasting stations are also operating and it would be discourteous to begin until the exact hour announced, when the air lanes are free. [7]

Sometimes at the exact hour the air lanes were not free, with harsh results.

The arrangement also invited skulduggery. WDAF, station of the Kansas City *Star*, regularly went off at 7 P.M. to let another Kansas City station, WHB, take over from 7 to 8 P.M. One day it was learned that a local

4. Harris, *Microphone Memoirs*, p. 22.
5. *WWJ—The Detroit News*, p. 25.
6. Barnett, *Reminiscences*, p. 7.
7. *Radio Broadcast*, August 1922.

politician was going to appear on WHB and "rake the Kansas City *Star* over the coals." The WDAF engineer was asked by a superior if he could do anything about it. He met the situation by staying on the air without speech "but with just a little heterodyne and tuning and detuning of the frequency, the 360 meters, and causing a very weird effect." [8]

As the stations in each community multiplied, the division of time became difficult and vexing. The schedule became a checkerboard of short time patches. Some stations had an hour or two during the week. In Los Angeles, twenty-three stations shared the channel.[9] New arrivals were increasingly resented by earlier stations.

There were still other hazards. As a holdover from the pre-broadcasting era, each station was expected to maintain an alert for distress signals, and leave the air for any SOS. At WGY, Schenectady, studio manager Kolin Hager once astonished a lady singer by announcing: "Miss ———— had just sung 'All Through the Night.' We will now stand by for distress signals." [10]

A further complication was added by an institution called Silent Night.

As each new set-owner joined the growing audience, he itched to experience personally KDKA, WJZ, KYW, WWJ, or other stations already a part of radio legend. This was impossible if a local station was broadcasting on the one wave length. To satisfy the yearning for far places the stations in some cities, by agreement, began a policy of silence for particular periods. In the fall of 1922, in a Silent Night poll conducted by the Chicago *Daily News*, votes ran 3700 for the idea, 320 against. Monday from 7 P.M. became Chicago's Silent Night.[11] In Kansas City, Saturday night was chosen. In Cincinnati, it was Thursday, 8-10 P.M. In Dallas, it was Wednesday from 3 P.M. or whenever the local baseball game ended. San Francisco chose a daily period, 7-7:30 P.M. A broadcaster of that area described Silent Night in these terms: "That's when a man would tell his neighbor, 'Last night on my crystal set I listened to the hoot owls up in Portland.'" [12] Silent Night was religiously observed for some years but was abandoned about 1927, amid recriminations. By then it meant a loss of revenue. In 1922, with all stations sharing one channel, Silent Night was merely one of the many factors limiting individual station time.

8. Patt, *Reminiscences*, p. 28.
9. *KNX-CBS*, p. 3.
10. Hager, *Reminiscences*, p. 7.
11. Caton, *Radio Station WMAQ*, p. 84.
12. Hart, *Interview*, p. 80.

For the listener, the patchwork schedule was especially jarring when a program from a 10-watt transmitter was immediately followed by one from a 500-watt transmitter.

Some stations tried to escape interference from other regions by operating slightly above or below the assigned frequency. The Department of Commerce for a time ignored these informalities. This hardly helped the situation. A tube set could sometimes pick up a number of stations simultaneously—from different regions—all clustered closely around 360 meters. Trying to disentangle them was an evening's occupation.

These were fascinating problems, to be discussed in impressive terms by any knowledgeable person, but at the moment they seemed to discourage no one. They were part of the wonder of it all; if there was a problem, science would solve it, or Mr. Hoover would. In fact, Herbert Hoover, appointed Secretary of Commerce by President Harding in 1921, by the end of that year sensed the approach of chaos. The correspondence and applications arriving at his department made it clear that pandemonium was on its way. He decided to convene a Washington Radio Conference, and an industry scarcely out of its swaddling clothes had its first national meeting.

It assembled on February 27, 1922, with representatives from various regions and industry interests. Among the invited were executives of the Radio Corporation of America, the American Telephone and Telegraph Company, General Electric Corporation, Westinghouse Electric and Manufacturing Corporation, and lesser companies. There were also representatives from various government agencies, a few inventors and engineers, and Hiram Percy Maxim representing the amateurs. They were welcomed by Secretary Hoover in these words:

> It is the purpose of this conference to inquire into the critical situation that has now arisen through the astonishing development of the wireless telephone; to advise the Department of Commerce as to the application of its present powers of regulation, and further to formulate such recommendations to Congress as to the legislation necessary.[13]

That Secretary Hoover should be asking leaders of the industry to advise him concerning his regulatory powers and how to use them, was characteristic. He was liked for this tendency and also came to be criticized for

13. Hoover, *Memoirs: The Cabinet and the Presidency,* p. 140.

it. Frederick Lewis Allen, for example, described Hoover as "helping business to help itself" by turning regulatory matters over to representatives of
the business to be regulated.[14] However, there was something else involved in Secretary Hoover's approach. He was painfully—and rightly—
uncertain about his powers under the 1912 radio law, which he was to call
"a very weak rudder to steer so powerful a development." [15] The law gave
him no discretion in the issuing of licenses—at least, not explicitly. If he
could not refuse licenses, chaos could hardly be avoided. The law also
gave him no power to make regulations to supplement those in the act
itself. It was ambiguous as to other matters, such as the right to limit
station power. Hoover wanted to recommend a new regulatory law under
which an orderly reallocation of stations could be accomplished, and
hoped to do it with backing from the industry. He got the hoped-for ammunition: the conferees told him, again and again, that the air was becoming "a mess," that the situation called for government action. Hoover
noted with satisfaction that "this is one of the few instances where the
country is unanimous in its desire for more regulation." [16] The conference
then passed a resolution recommending that the Secretary of Commerce
be given "adequate legal authority" for effective control. Representative
Wallace H. White, Jr., of Maine, who was attending the conference on
Hoover's invitation, proceeded to draft legislation along this line.

On this much the conference could agree. If they had tried to agree on
details, they would have fallen into angry dispute. A spokesman for Westinghouse, which already had four stations on the air, expressed the view
that fifteen stations could serve the whole country adequately. For him the
purpose of regulation would presumably be to stop in their tracks the
hundreds of new stations about to invade the air.

If the conference recommendations did not at once result in legislation,
still another factor was involved. The law drafted by Representative
White gave all licensing power—without review by the courts—to the
Secretary of Commerce. In Congress many felt that Herbert Hoover, already considered presidential material, had found in the unexpected
broadcasting boom an extraordinary plum. As broadcasting czar he would,
it was feared, become all-powerful. A countermove developed—with bi-

14. Allen, *Only Yesterday*, p. 184.
15. Hoover, *Memoirs: The Cabinet and the Presidency*, p. 139.
16. *Radio Broadcast*, May 1922.

partisan support that included many a presidential possibility—calling for an independent regulatory commission—an idea firmly rejected by others, and so a stalemate developed.

Such problems were not foreseen at the first Washington Radio Conference, at which everyone merely agreed that regulation was needed. As the future was scanned, intoxicating words were heard. Along with these, antique terminology persisted. Secretary Hoover still spoke of radio as the "wireless telephone" and referred to radio sets as "receiving stations," as when he said:

> The comparative cheapness with which receiving stations can be installed, and the fact that the genius of the American boy is equal to construction of such stations within the limits of his own savings, bids fair to make the possession of receiving sets almost universal in the American home.[17]

The conference produced a curious discussion on advertising—curious in the light of later developments. The idea of "ether advertising" was mentioned but with disfavor. One of those who did so was Secretary Hoover, who said: "It is inconceivable that we should allow so great a possibility for service to be drowned in advertising chatter." [18]

Since the danger of this particular drowning seemed remote—inconceivable, according to Hoover—his remark caused little comment at the time. The prevailing mood was, in any case, one of excitement and anticipation. Soon, very soon, a nation-wide audience would take shape, and the thought of this pulled them on. It was also what was bringing the hundreds of new stations to the air.

The conferees went home and the boom continued. Sets sped from workshop and factory. People lined up at radio counters. Station licensees rushed to the air—by the hundreds.

Who were these hundreds? How could they afford this? Such a question, if asked, was likely to be answered by further questions. With such an audience developing, how could one stand aside? Would one want to say to one's children, "It happened, but I was on the sidelines." The sense of history was part of the moment.

Dr. Levering Tyson, who was director of extension activities at Colum-

17. *Ibid.*
18. Hoover, *Memoirs: The Cabinet and the Presidency*, p. 140.

bia University, related how, on the morning after the Harding election, he had read in the New York *Times* about KDKA and the reaction to it. He could not contain his excitement. "I did not even finish my bacon and eggs that morning but hurried over to the University." At five minutes past nine he was in the anteroom of President Nicholas Murray Butler. The president himself arrived at a quarter to eleven; Tyson, with zeal undimmed, was still waiting. He spoke of what had happened and what it meant to university extension work. To his dismay President Butler waved it aside. "Tyson, don't bother about that. There are gadgets turning up every week in this country." [19] But Tyson continued to bother about it.

At some colleges the excitement came from above. An amateur experimenter of Lafayette, Indiana, John E. Fetzer, had a visit in 1922 from Dr. Frederick Griggs, President of Emmanuel College in Michigan. Griggs had journeyed to Lafayette to persuade young Fetzer—whose station 9FD had attracted regional attention—to establish a broadcasting station at the college in Berrien Springs. He saw it as a great educational force; also, as the key to his expansion plans for Emmanuel. So Fetzer packed his equipment in a truck, and established the station in a tower room at the college, where it opened in 1922 as 8AZ and a year later became KFGZ at 360 meters.[20] Such a sequence of events was duplicated at many colleges, large and small.

While some educators thought of broadcasting as a new arena for extension teaching and others as an aid to fund-raising, still others saw it as an adjunct to degree study in the home. The University of Nebraska, which had an experimental voice transmitter by 1921 and moved it to 360 meters as WFAV in 1922, began at once to give credit courses at $12.50 per student, for which the listener was offered textbook, examination, and two points of credit on satisfactory completion.[21] Many another college and university followed this example.

For one reason or another, the winter of 1921-22 saw a huge academic procession to the air. It moved at more than academic speed. In December 1921 one university, the Latter-Day Saints University of Salt Lake City, received a broadcasting license—for KFOO. Early in January the University of Wisconsin station became WHA. By the end of the spring

19. Tyson, "Looking Ahead," *Education on the Air* (1936), p. 58.
20. Fetzer, *Reminiscences*, p. 14.
21. Frost, *Education's Own Stations*, pp. 233-6.

term at least nineteen other institutions had joined them.[22] At the end of the year seventy-four colleges and universities were broadcasters.

At the same time newspapers were experiencing a related upheaval, which had many aspects. The Detroit *News*, first to launch a station, was apparently also first to start a radio column. Begun December 19, 1920, it continued without interruption. As the broadcasting fever spread, news about radio built circulation, and the column grew into pages. This had impact elsewhere. In 1921 the New York *Globe* decided to launch a radio *supplement;* to organize it Everett L. Bragdon, veteran amateur experimenter, was lured from the staff of *Popular Science Monthly.* The supplement began as a four-page tabloid but attracted so many readers, and so many advertisers, that expanded within weeks into a 16-page supplement. *Globe* circulation and revenue shot up, to the alarm of rival papers. The *Sun* solved this problem by buying and absorbing the *Globe,* whereupon Bragdon became radio editor of the *Sun.* The tabloid supplement continued in the *Sun* until the Depression.[23]

During the 1922 ecstasy the broadcasting supplement was put together in zesty, slapdash fashion. According to Bragdon, a profusion of diagrams was at first an essential ingredient. "While the diagrams each week *looked* different, they were often the same diagram with the tube in a different place." The theory was that people loved to take a set apart and then put it together again. "We catered to that desire. Sometimes we would add a part that hadn't been used before, implying that it would improve the reception. It did not always do so." [24]

The *Globe* radio section was followed by similar sections in the New York *Evening World* and *Evening Mail.* Their emphasis gradually shifted from technical to program matters.

There were also reverberations in other cities. In Chicago William S.

22. The University of Minnesota, Minneapolis, WLB; St. Martin's College, Lacey, Wash., KGY; University of Texas, Austin, WCM; Clark University, Worcester, Mass., WCN; St. Louis University, St. Louis, Mo., WEW; West Virginia University, Morgantown, WHD; Union College, Schenectady, N.Y., WRL; University of Illinois, Urbana, WRM; Loyola University, New Orleans, La., WWL; New Mexico College of Agriculture and Mechanic Arts, State College, KOB; Tulane University, New Orleans, La., WAAC; University of Missouri, Columbia, WAAN; Purdue University, Lafayette, Ind., WBAA; Bradley Polytechnic Institute, Peoria, Ill., WBAE; James Millikin University, Decatur, Ill., WBAO; Marietta College, Marietta, O., WBAW; Iowa State College, Ames, WOI; St. Joseph's College, Philadelphia, WPJ; Kansas State Agricultural College, Manhattan, WTG. For a full account see Frost, *Education's Own Stations.*
23. Bragdon, *Reminiscences,* p. 11.
24. *Ibid.* pp. 10-11.

Hedges, who had been University of Chicago campus correspondent for the Chicago *Daily News* and was hired as reporter after military service, was called in by the news editor, who tossed the *Globe* radio section at him. "Do you think we should have a section like that?" The young reporter considered it completely unnecessary. He said so, and was then told he was the radio editor. He was advised not to be unhappy; the thing might blow over like mah-jongg. No sooner had Hedges become involved in the work than he began wondering: why write about *other* people's stations? He learned of an available prewar transmitter owned by the Fair Store. He explored the matter; it led to negotiations between the Fair Store and the *Daily News*. Before long Hedges was ordering a Western Electric transmitter. On April 13, 1922, WGU went on the air—studios in the Fair Store, occasional bulletins from the *Daily News*. It soon became WMAQ.[25]

In city after city, newspapers followed a similar course. U. S. Department of Commerce lists of stations, published in its monthly *Radio Service Bulletin*, showed eleven newspaper-owned stations in May 1922.[26] At the end of the year there were sixty-nine.

It was a surging pilgrimage; the churches joined it. Transmitters began going up on church buildings and Bible institutes. Was it not fitting? The Word, it had been said, should be "proclaimed upon the housetops."

Radio was a crowd-maker, and the stores loved it. In many cities department stores began building studios which attracted visitors and increased store traffic and sales. Hotels became interested. Stations were also started by a stockyard (WAAF, Chicago), a marble company (KHD, Colorado Springs), a laundry (KUS, Los Angeles), a poultry farm (WPG, New Lebanon). Several were started by rich men as hobbies.

At hundreds of stations people were hired in the most casual manner. In April 1922 Joseph Barnett, a young man in New Jersey who was studying singing, thought he would let his mother hear how he sounded on radio. So he dropped in at WOR, just opened in the Bamberger department store in Newark. Outside the studio, near the music department of the store, he found a Miss Koewing. She was expecting a singer from New York, but he

25. Hedges, *Reminiscences*, p. 9. He eventually became vice president of the National Broadcasting Company.
26. In addition to the Detroit *News* and Chicago *Daily News* stations, they were: Rochester *Times Union*, WHQ; Atlanta *Journal*, WSB; St. Louis *Post Dispatch*, KSD; Des Moines *Register and Tribune*, WGF; Fort Worth *Record*, WPA; Spokane *Chronicle*, KOE; Los Angeles *Examiner*, KWH; New Orleans *Times Picayune*, WAAB; Richmond *Times Dispatch*, WBAZ. *Radio Service Bulletin*, May 1, 1922.

hadn't arrived. "Can you really sing?" she asked. Barnett did not have time to notify his mother. He sang over the air for an hour and ten minutes, with piano, announcing his own numbers. Meanwhile a messenger rushed to and from the music counter with sheets of music and held them up, while Barnett sang, so that he could indicate with nods and shakes whether he knew the song and whether the key was right. After it was all over Miss Koewing told him he would make a marvelous announcer and offered him a full-time announcing job; in emergencies, she noted, he could sing. He accepted and three months later, at 22, became manager of WOR.[27]

City after city saw new stations racing for the air. Three stores in Philadelphia got licenses in the same month: March, 1922. Gimbel's was licensed to start WIP; Strawbridge & Clothier, WFI; John Wanamaker, WOO. The first two began a scramble for pioneer honors. They picked the same day for their openings: Saturday, March 18. Both worked furiously to be ready. Gimbel's invited the mayor, J. Hampton Moore, to take part; Strawbridge & Clothier countered with the governor, William C. Sproul. Both stations scheduled a formal "inaugural"; then, to get on the air first, each arranged programs to *precede* the formal inaugural. WIP scheduled its inaugural ceremony for 11 A.M., so WFI put on a broadcast 10:45-11 A.M. but WIP, apparently anticipating the move, had presented some programs the day before. Its advertisement that Saturday morning said: "Yesterday's broadcasting was most successful." [28]

During the spring of 1922 the Department of Commerce ran out of three-letter combinations and began assigning four-letter combinations. Then that summer, it took an action that seemed momentarily to ease the congestion. In addition to 360 meters, 400 meters (750 kc.) was made available for broadcasting. The Department decided that 400-meter stations—class "B" stations, they came to be called—would have to operate on 500-1000 watts and would not be allowed to use phonograph records.[29] Stations not able to meet these requirements could not apply for a 400-meter license and would have to remain in the heavily populated 360-meter spot. The rule tended to create an aristocracy of well-financed stations at 400 and a *hoi polloi* aggregation at 360. The move was liked by listeners and by those who, like Westinghouse, GE, and RCA, favored the

27. Barnett, *Reminiscences*, pp. 3-4.
28. Davies and Tisdale, *Philadelphia's Pioneer Voice*, pp. 2-5.
29. *Radio Service Bulletin*, September 1, 1922.

idea of a small group of powerful stations. Secretary Hoover, though still unsure of his powers, had apparently decided that some start toward regulation was essential. His hope for early legislation was dimming, and new stations kept coming. So the action was taken. The "B" stations were, for the moment, relatively free of chaos. But at 360 meters the congestion grew.

To stations everywhere, people, famous and not so famous, came in a stream. It seemed unending. For months it wasn't a matter of recruiting performers but keeping them out. Most stations started with only one studio and a staff of five or six, and this created problems.

At WWJ, Detroit, the processing of talent during 1922 became the job of Edwin "Pappy" Tyson, who had studied forestry at Pennsylvania State College but somehow got diverted into the radio boom. He handled things with dispatch. "The talent would come over to the office and tell us what they could do . . . We didn't rehearse them, we took their word for it." He would put them down for an allotment of time. Outside the studio was a reception area where people waited their turn. It had a loudspeaker. Tyson, having put a performer at the microphone in the studio, would return to the reception room to hear him on the loudspeaker—the only available monitor. If he seemed too loud or soft, Tyson would go in again to move the artist.[30]

Lawrence Holland, a former Penn State football player working at a Detroit gas station, used to come every evening to help Pappy. He wasn't paid but liked to hang around. "I would line up the talent . . . and the minute that they were through in there, Pappy would open the door and I would rush them in and rush the other ones out." Holland was a good bouncer when necessary. He stuck around without pay for months; then Pappy and he began to do football games, and Holland got a small fee as spotter. Pappy Tyson was a small man with an unexpectedly large, resonant voice; Holland was a huge man with no particular voice. People were always surprised that it was the small man they had heard on the air. At the stadium the two sat in regular seats; Holland listed the players on a piece of laundry board and pointed to the names of the players in the action. He kept a rolled copy of the Detroit *News* handy. "So if these fellows would jump up in front of us so we couldn't see, I would hit them over the head." Some took offense but, after a look at Holland, would not pursue the argument. Pappy Tyson also did an early man-on-the-street

30. Tyson, *Reminiscences*, p. 4.

interview program and Holland helped. "My duty was to get the people up in front of the microphone and if they were not right, or would speak out of turn, I would . . . just sort of push them away in a nice way . . . it would be a little crude." [31]

The fear that someone might "speak out of turn" was always present. Olga Petrova, who had worried WJZ with her birth-control enthusiasm, also arranged a visit to WOR, Newark, at the Bamberger store; again she said she merely wanted to read a poem. Mr. Edgar Bamberger came to welcome the famous lady. Normally a "retiring gentleman," he sat smiling in the studio as the program began. Suddenly he became aware that she was talking about—prostitution! He froze. He need not have worried, however. His alert station manager, Joseph Barnett, was onto her tricks. Before she had completed the first syllable of the forbidden word, "I gave her the button." [32] It apparently never occurred to staff members of the time that a subject like birth control or prostitution should have any treatment other than "the button." It was applied with untroubled zeal.

Of course the button was not invincible, as Walter Evans learned at KYW, Chicago. A gentleman wanted to do a talk on Americanism and even submitted a script. It seemed a standard treatment of the subject, and he was scheduled. But he was a potentate of the Ku Klux Klan and brought bodyguards, who dispersed through the premises and watched all buttons. Digressing from the script, the visitor extolled the glory of the Klan and of white supremacy. [33]

All this was, in a way, a tribute to the new deity of broadcasting and the power men ascribed to it. A new age was beginning. In the trade press, growing fast during 1922, page after page predicted startling things to come. *Radio World* and *Radio Dealer* were launched in April, *Radio Broadcast* in May. The first issue of *Radio Broadcast*—published by Doubleday Page—crackled with prophecies:

> . . . some day in the future the popularity of a political party in office may hinge entirely upon the quality of broadcasting service . . .

> . . . the government will be a living thing to its citizens instead of an abstract and unseen force . . .

31. Holland, *Reminiscences*, pp. 4-11.
32. Barnett, *Reminiscences*, p. 11.
33. Evans, *Reminiscences*, p. 32.

. . . it will elicit a new national loyalty and produce a more contented citizenry . . .

, . . at last we may have covenants literally openly arrived at . . .

. . . elected representatives will not be able to evade their responsibility to those who put them in office . . .

. . . the people's University of the Air will have a greater student body than all of our universities put together . . .[34]

Former Secretary of the Navy Josephus Daniels, in opening Station WLAC at North Carolina State College of Agriculture and Engineering on October 16, 1922, got into the spirit with his own tribute to radio and a prediction: "Nobody now fears that a Japanese fleet could deal an unexpected blow on our Pacific possessions . . . Radio makes surprises impossible." [35]

Radio was also blamed for things—dizzy spells, changes in weather, creaky floorboards. A farmer came to WHAS in Louisville with a stern warning. "Yesterday afternoon I took a walk across my farm. A flock of blackbirds passed over. Suddenly one of them dropped dead. Your radio wave must have struck it. (PAUSE) Suppose that wave had struck me?" [36]

Broadcasting was on everyone's tongue and in every periodical. The 1919-21 edition of *Readers' Guide to Periodical Literature* had listed no articles on radio broadcasting, although there was the entry: "Radio Telephony. See Wireless Telephony." The 1922-24 edition listed a cataract of radio articles, going on for ten pages: "How radio is remaking the world." "Are women undesirable over the radio?" "Removing the last objection to living in the country." "Telepathy and radio." "How ten concerns are putting radio to practical use." "Shall we advertise by radio?" "Church's new voice." "Is radio hurting the church?" "Broadcasting Browning." "Broadcasting health." "Broadcasting Wagner." "Ether waves vs. crime waves." "Teaching the Chinese radio." "What German listeners-in are up against." "When the bug bit Samoa." "Does radio rob the song writers?" "Fight for freedom of the air." "Urgent need for radio legislation." "Decorating the radio room." "Radio, the modern peace dove." [37]

The subject of broadcasting was calling forth some grand rhetoric, espe-

34. *Radio Broadcast*, May 1922.
35. Quoted in Wallace, *The Development of Broadcasting in North Carolina*, p. 54.
36. Harris, *Microphone Memoirs*, p. 99.
37. *Readers' Guide to Periodical Literature*, 1922-24, pp. 1417-27.

cially from broadcasters themselves. After an opera broadcast one of its producers wrote: "Music is no longer confined within the four walls of concert halls and opera houses. Radio-telephony has freed the captive bird from its prison, and it is now at liberty to soar." [38]

In a broadcast over KDKA on December 20, 1922, Westinghouse executive S. H. Kintner began:

> Fellow patrons of KDKA: Now that we are assembled again in KDKA's unlimited theater, where rear seats are hundreds of miles from the stage and where the audience, all occupying private boxes, can come late or leave early without embarrassing the speaker, or annnoying the rest of the audience—let us consider for a few minutes. . . .[39]

Perhaps the most arresting testimony to the impact of the radio boom was the simpler message put up by a minister in front of his church in Louisville, Ky.: GOD IS ALWAYS BROADCASTING.[40]

Of the 670 stations licensed by the end of 1922, the year of ecstasy, 576 were alive at the end of the year.[41] Ninety-four stations—14 per cent—had met an early death. Among the 72 stations licensed to educational institutions, the death rate was lower than average: seven stations—10 per cent —had expired.[42]

Who were the fallen? Few case histories are available, but that of KDYS, launched May 19, 1922, by the *Tribune* of Great Falls, Mont., may be typical. The transmitter had been assembled by a local auto mechanic. For the opening broadcast, in which the mayor spoke, 800 people crowded around a receiving set in a local dry goods store a block and a half from the *Tribune* office. A lady sang. The horn speaker vibrated badly in response to her soprano tones. Then mechanical failure at the transmitter ended the broadcast. An informal survey by the station just before the

38. G. E. Le Messena in *Radio Broadcast*, August 1922.
39. Kintner, *Address*, December 20, 1922.
40. Harris, *Microphone Memoirs*, p. 51.
41. Jome, *Economics of the Radio Industry*, table, p. 70, based on U. S. Department of Commerce data.
42. Frost, *Education's Own Stations*, p. 4. There are small discrepancies between various sets of statistics concerning this period. On the basis of files in Salt Lake City, Frost includes station KFOO of Latter-Day Saints University, licensed by the Department of Commerce in 1921. However, the Department of Commerce files provide no information on this license and it is not included in departmental statistics. (*Ibid.* p. 3.) Such discrepancies do not affect the percentages given.

opening revealed fifteen receiving sets in Great Falls. The station persisted, but in its second year closed for repairs and never reopened.[43]

What investment was involved in such ventures? To most broadcasting entrepreneurs, the costs didn't seem alarming—at first. Hiram L. Jome, who sent questionnaires to stations two years later and got replies from 106, found that 51 of these stations, or almost half, had been built for $3000 or less. At the other end of the scale were eight stations that had cost more than $50,000 each.[44] These had presumably included Western Electric transmitters, which in 1922 cost about $8500 for a 100-watt transmitter, $10,500 for a 500-watt transmitter.[45] As for operating costs—those were another matter, and hard to foresee.

WWJ, which the Detroit *News* had started in 1920 (as 8MK), cost the newspaper only $3606 in the first year of operation, according to Herbert Ponting, Detroit *News* business manager. That figure included a depreciation allowance for capital investment. For the second year the cost was $5760. Then, for 1922, costs shot up to $80,000.[46] Could the newspaper afford this?

The 690 stations licensed by the end of 1922 had almost all been intended to reap indirect values, not direct revenue. The precise form of the expected values—future sales, donations, prestige, enrollments—was seldom exactly defined. The costs to be weighed against those values were totally unpredictable. And in the euphoria of 1922 there was little possibility of thinking through such problems.

But one company had thought intently about them, and had reached decisions that now began to influence, in many and complex ways, the course of events.

PHONE BOOTH OF THE AIR

The American Telephone and Telegraph Company was cautious and slow-moving, but it had resources to back its decisions. It had long been hesitant about radio for a persuasive reason. Excitement over radio, AT&T feared, might bring a sudden decline in the value of telephone stock.

43. Richards, "Montana's Pioneer Radio Stations," *Montana Journalism Review*, Spring 1963.
44. Jome, *Economics of the Radio Industry*, p. 175.
45. Banning, *Commercial Broadcasting Pioneer*, p. 74.
46. Ponting, *Reminiscences*, p. 2.

AT&T did not want to contribute to such an excitement, but at the same time felt it had to keep a hand in radio, for self-protection. The conflicting motives caused a good deal of vacillation.

The cross-licensing alliance had a number of attractions for AT&T. To begin with, the agreements fortified AT&T in its special sphere, telephony. Within that sphere the company acquired access to numerous valuable patents. Immediate advantages followed: in July 1920 telephone service was extended to Catalina Island, thirty miles off the California coast, via a radio link.[1] Other such links were planned.

Meanwhile, at AT&T as elsewhere, there was earnest discussion about future possibilities. A schism developed between "radio people," who wanted the company to move further into radio, and "wire people," who wanted to revive the idea of disseminating entertainment through telephone wires. Use of wires would make possible a subscription system. In an intra-company memorandum dated December 18, 1919, Lloyd Espenschied outlined such a system, "permitting the subscriber to select at will his own type of amusement merely by pushing the proper button."[2]

The debut of KDKA and events that followed seemed to obliterate the wire idea, but AT&T continued to be hesitant about radio. It did not have the same incentive as its allies to plunge into broadcasting, because it had no receivers to sell.

When AT&T finally decided, at an executive meeting held in New York City on January 12, 1922, that it would take up "public radiotelephone broadcasting," it did so in a way all its own. The decision was framed wholly in telephone terms. Lloyd Espenschied, who was present, described the original conception:

> We, the telephone company, were to provide no programs. The public was to come in. Anyone who had a message for the world or wished to entertain was to come in and pay their money as they would upon coming into a telephone booth, address the world, and go out.[3]

In keeping with the telephony imagery, AT&T called this "toll broadcasting." It also continued to speak of "radio telephony," partly out of habit, but also for a strategic reason. Under the alliance agreements, telephony on a commercial basis was the exclusive province of AT&T. The new ven-

---

1. Banning, *Commercial Broadcasting Pioneer*, p. 41.
2. *Ibid.* p. 45. Also Espenschied, *Recollections of the Radio Industry*, p. 35.
3. Espenschied, *Recollections of the Radio Industry*, p. 41.

ture, AT&T was saying through its choice of words, was a form of commercial telephony and therefore reserved for AT&T and not open to GE, Westinghouse, or RCA, which could engage in radio telephony for their own purposes and sell equipment to amateurs, but who could not provide the public with telephone service on a commercial basis.

For the moment there was no argument about this, since none of the other allies was considering "toll broadcasting." But AT&T had laid a foundation for its argument, in case it should be needed.

The AT&T plan as envisioned in 1922 called for a network of thirty-eight AT&T "radiotelephone" stations linked by the company's long lines, all stations operating on a "toll" basis. A New York City station would be launched first—at the earliest possible date.

On February 11 the plan was made public. "The American Telephone and Telegraph Company," the announcement said, "will provide no program of its own, but provide the channels through which anyone with whom it makes a contract can send out their own programs. . . . There have been many requests for such a service. . . ." [4]

When the first Washington Radio Conference, meeting in that same month, expressed unfriendly views on "ether advertising," it must have irked AT&T officials, but the company took the situation in stride. Its position was described as follows in *Radio Broadcast:*

> The company is completing a broadcasting station for the purpose in New York. It is frankly an experiment . . .
> The conference under Secretary Hoover's chairmanship agreed that it was against public interest to broadcast pure advertising matter. The American Telephone and Telegraph officials agreed with this point of view. Their experiment is to see whether there are people who desire to buy the right to talk to the public and at the same time tell the public something it would like to hear.
> If this experiment succeeds, a commercial basis for broadcasting will have been established.[5]

In spite of long planning, the toll broadcasting idea got off to a shaky start. Published reactions were lukewarm, and in some cases indignant. *Radio Dealer* condemned its "mercenary advertising purposes"; it expected a "man-sized vocal rebellion." [6] *Printers' Ink* felt that use of radio as an advertising medium would prove "positively offensive to great num-

4. Banning, *Commercial Broadcasting Pioneer*, p. 68.
5. *Radio Broadcast*, May 1922.
6. *Radio Dealer*, April 1922.

bers of people." [7] Some writers were willing to see what would come of it, without finding much promise in the plan.

Then there was engineering trouble. AT&T had pride in its technical standards and was determined that its transmission should be the finest. No expense was spared in this respect. The 500-watt transmitter for WBAY—first radio telephone toll station—was erected atop a tall AT&T building at 24 Walker Street in lower Manhattan, the building where the company's long lines converged. On July 25 the station was ready for its debut. To the dismay of telephone officials, its effective range was lamentable. The metal framework of the tall building was apparently absorbing the radiation. President Harry B. Thayer of AT&T, at his home in New Canaan, Conn., could barely hear WBAY, while WJZ came booming in. He felt humiliated. In haste it was decided that the WBAY programs should be conveyed to Mr. Thayer's home by long distance telephone lines, and this was done. The "wire people" were vastly amused and the "radio people" discomfited.[8]

Fortunately a transmitter at the Western Electric building at 463 West Street was giving fine test results. On August 16 this transmitter, with call letters WEAF, was put into service in place of WBAY, and became the standard bearer for toll broadcasting. Thus an historic station—in later years called WRCA and WNBC—made its bow. Programs continued to originate in the Walker Street building but went into the air from West Street.

Other troubles, however, were on their way. AT&T had claimed to have "many requests for such a service," but this statement had not been a precise one. What AT&T had, at its manufacturing subsidiary the Western Electric Company, was a deluge of orders for transmitters. According to Edgar Felix, these included orders for more than a hundred broadcast transmitters intended for use in or near New York City.[9] Aware of the chaos the transmitters would bring, the company began telling customers that it would be months or years before they could have their transmitters but that WBAY—later WEAF—had been created to serve them. Thus AT&T hoped to divert them from one-time transmitter purchases to continuing time purchases. This turned out to be uphill work. Many had their

7. *Printers' Ink*, July 1922.
8. Espenschied, *Recollections of the Radio Industry*, p. 41.
9. Felix, *Reminiscences*, p. 24.

hearts set on transmitters. Decisions had been reached, appropriations made.

For example, there was the City of New York. In March 1922 a proposal for a municipal broadcasting station came before the Board of Estimate, and a study committee was appointed. Its chairman was Rodman Wanamaker of the Wanamaker stores, a radio enthusiast. Also on the committee was Grover Whalen, former Wanamaker executive and now holder of various city positions, including that of chairman of the Board of Purchase; he too was a radio enthusiast. The committee promptly recommended an appropriation of $50,000 to establish and equip a city station.[10] It was seen as having many values—to police and fire departments as well as to education. The appropriation was made.

However, in trying to buy a transmitter from Western Electric, Mr. Whalen found AT&T, the parent company, trying to head him off. Mr. A. H. Griswold of the telephone company, accompanied by engineer Lloyd Espenschied, called on him. Rather than build a station, they argued, the city should save its investment and buy time on the AT&T station. According to Espenschied, Whalen grew indignant at these arguments and pounded the table. "What! The great City of New York subsidiary to a commercial company? Decidedly no!"[11] Whalen persisted but could get no transmitter from Western Electric. More than a year later he finally succeeded in importing from Brazil a used Western Electric transmitter.[12]

AT&T encountered similar resistance elsewhere. In spite of the "many requests for such a service," more than a month went by before toll broadcasting found a single customer.

Meanwhile it had become clear that a key part of the original plan had to be abandoned. AT&T had at first been determined *not* to produce programs. It wanted no more responsibility over content than it had in the case of phone calls. But sale of time to address the public was hardly feasible unless people were listening. So elements began to be added to the plan. Reluctantly the company began to look for someone "with experience in broadcasting and phonograph work."[13] A Mr. Samuel Ross was hired to supervise programs.

Here too there were troubles. While attention and funds had been lav-

10. Whalen, *Reminiscences*, p. 3.
11. Espenschied, *Recollections of the Radio Industry*, p. 47.
12. Whalen, *Reminiscences*, p. 8.
13. Banning, *Commercial Broadcasting Pioneer*, p. 83.

ished on the transmitter, little thought had been given to the studio. The phone booth conception seemed to call merely for a simple room in which to address "the public." The building in which space had been allocated, the Walker Street building, was in a shabby section of Manhattan, surrounded by old warehouses, and badly lit at night. The space allocated for a studio adjoined the telephone operators' locker room, in which artists were to await their turn. The studio itself was originally a tiled room. To absorb echoes the walls had been so heavily draped with monkscloth, and the floor so padded and covered with rugs, that singers said they could not hear themselves. One basso said he could not sing unless something hard were found for him to stand on, so that he might feel vibrations. Someone went out and came back with a cast-iron manhole cover.[14]

The programs emanating from this Walker Street building, the "long lines" building, were at first limited in number. Sharing time with others at 360 meters, WBAY began with daily weekday programs from 11 A.M. to 12 noon and 4:30 to 5:30 P.M., and a Thursday evening program from 7:30 to midnight. It had no other evening hours.[15] WEAF began on a similarly limited schedule.

The first evening program, broadcast on August 3, was largely amateur. Helen Graves of the Long Lines Plant Department sang "Just a Song at Twilight" and other "vocal selections"; Joseph Koznick of the AT&T Drafting Department played "Träumerei" and other selections on his violin; Edna Cunningham of the Long Lines Traffic Department recited James Whitcomb Riley's "An Old Sweetheart of Mine" and spoke on the value of effective speech. In following weeks the spotlight shifted to professional talent, but Helen Hann of Long Lines remained as hostess-accompanist and sometimes announced; Vischer A. Randall of Long Lines remained as announcer and became a director. Albert V. Llufrio, who could sing or play piano in any emergency and for any required length of time, was his assistant.[16]

On August 28, 1922, 5-5:30 P.M., WEAF broadcast its first income-producing program: a ten-minute message to the public from the Queensboro Corporation to promote the sale of apartments in Jackson Heights. The sponsors paid $50 for the broadcast. An executive of the Queens-

14. Harkness, *Reminiscences*, p. 28.
15. Banning, *Commercial Broadcasting Pioneer*, p. 77. Time was being shared with nine New York and New Jersey stations.
16. *Ibid.* p. 97.

boro Corporation was the speaker. Vischer Randall opened the program:

> This afternoon the radio audience is to be addressed by Mr. Black-
> well of the Queensboro Corporation, who through arrangements made
> by the Griffin Radio Service, Inc., will say a few words concerning
> Nathaniel Hawthorne and the desirability of fostering the helpful
> community spirit and the healthful, unconfined home life that were
> Hawthorne ideals. Ladies and Gentlemen: Mr. Blackwell.

Mr. Blackwell followed:

> It is fifty-eight years since Nathaniel Hawthorne, the greatest of
> American fictionists, passed away. To honor his memory the Queens-
> boro Corporation, creator and operator of the tenant-owned system
> of apartment homes at Jackson Heights, New York City, has named
> its latest group of high-grade dwellings "Hawthorne Court."
>   I wish to thank those within sound of my voice for the broadcasting
> opportunity afforded me to urge this vast radio audience to seek the
> recreation and the daily comfort of the home removed from the con-
> gested part of the city, right at the boundaries of God's great out-
> doors, and within a few minutes by subway from the business section
> of Manhattan. This sort of residential environment strongly influ-
> enced Hawthorne, America's greatest writer of fiction. He analyzed
> with charming keenness the social spirit of those who had thus hap-
> pily selected their homes, and he painted the people inhabiting those
> homes with good-natured relish.
>   There should be more Hawthorne sermons preached about the
> utter inadequacy and the general hopelessness of the congested city
> home. The cry of the heart is for more living room, more chance to
> unfold, more opportunity to get near the Mother Earth, to play, to
> romp, to plant and to dig.
>   Let me enjoin upon you as you value your health and your hopes
> and your home happiness, get away from the solid masses of brick,
> where the meagre opening admitting a slant of sunlight is mockingly
> called a light shaft, and where children grow up starved for a run
> over a patch of grass and the sight of a tree.
>   Apartments in congested parts of the city have proven failures.
> The word neighbor is an expression of peculiar irony—a daily
> joke. . . .
>   The fact is, however, that apartment homes on the tenant-owner-
> ship plan can be secured by . . .[17]

During the following weeks the Queensboro Corporation broadcast four
additional afternoon talks at $50 each and an evening talk at $100. Sales of

17. Archer, *History of Radio*, pp. 397-8.

apartments are said to have resulted. In September two other companies rented the phone booth: Tidewater Oil and the American Express Company. Total station revenues for the first two months were $550.[18]

Until this time the toll venture had been the responsibility of the Long Lines Division of AT&T. However, the Long Lines people, seeing no future in it, asked to be relieved, and so in October WEAF was transferred to By-Products Services and came under the supervision of William E. Harkness. He had a background in fire-alarm systems using phone lines —another "by-product."

The three salesmen on loan from Long Lines seemed to Harkness so uninterested that he sent them back to Long Lines. He began to build a staff from the ground up, and also to make demands on AT&T for the support he needed.

A U. S. Commerce Department action now came to his aid. In its communications with government officials, AT&T had persistently used an ingenious argument on behalf of its venture. All other broadcasters, AT&T kept saying, used their stations for their own purposes, whereas a toll station was for "everyone," "the public in general," and should have special standing. In fact, there should be a special channel for AT&T toll stations, away from the clamor of those self-serving voices. The company did not get quite what it asked, but almost. In September WEAF was given the 400-meter wave length, along with a limited number of other stations of 500-1000 watts. This meant less interference and more time on the air—including four evenings each week. It also meant WEAF had to forsake the phonograph and expand its live entertainment schedule. This meant, Mr. Harkness told AT&T, that new studios must be built, with style, and in a good neighborhood so that artists could be attracted. Mr. W. S. Gifford, vice president, concluded: "There's no reason to do anything about broadcasting at all unless we do it right." [19] The reluctant showmen were being propelled further into showmanship and perhaps acquiring a taste for it. They began building studios at 195 Broadway—AT&T headquarters. Plans filtered out to the industry. An interior decorator had been enlisted. These studios would have an unprecedented air of distinction and at the same time be homelike, with easy chairs and "appropriate oil paintings." From a reception room hung with tapestries the studio would be seen through leaded pane windows—a Nathaniel Hawthorne touch. New salesmen were

18. Banning, *Commercial Broadcasting Pioneer*, p. 5.
19. *Ibid.* pp. 70-96.

enlisted, including George F. McClelland, who turned out to be a super-salesman. There was also Mark Woods, who came from the accounting department to work on financial problems. He had previously been with Thomas Edison, but Edison was in a state of decline and Woods had moved to the telephone business and now, late in 1922, into broadcasting.

For months every dollar of income was a struggle. "When Mr. McClelland or Mr. Harry Smith succeeded in bringing in an account it was almost like a Christmas holiday." [20] The approach of Christmas helped. The Macy, Gimbel, and Hearn department stores bought ten-minute periods. A. H. Grebe bought time for a talk about his radios. William H. Rankin of the Rankin advertising agency, approached by McClelland, decided to test the medium himself before recommending it to any of his clients; in December he bought a ten-minute evening period for $100, using it for a talk on advertising. He got twenty-five letters and phone calls, which wasn't impressive except that one was from a prospective client and led to an advertising contract.[21] The client was Mineralava, and by January the Rankin agency had this company on the air with a ten-minute talk by Marion Davies on "How I Make Up for the Movies." This was followed by an offer of a free autographed photo of the actress. For WEAF this was an injection of adrenalin. The mail came suddenly in the hundreds, and George McClelland gleefully rushed to spread the news, while the Rankin agency began proselyting others of its clients, among them the Goodrich Company. On the ledger WEAF was still a disaster, but the spirit was changing. Most important, AT&T was putting its resources on the line.

While income was edging up painfully, WEAF was beginning to make spectacular use of telephone lines. On October 28, 1922, it broadcast a description of a football game between Princeton and the University of Chicago, which came via long-distance lines from Stagg Field in Chicago to WEAF in New York. Four weeks later a broadcast of the Harvard-Yale game was likewise done with the aid of long-distance lines. Phone links were also used for an opera broadcast from an armory; a series of organ recitals from the College of the City of New York; and a series from the stage of the Capitol Theater—inaugurating the radio career of S. L. Rothapfel or "Roxy." [22]

Meanwhile requests from other stations for similar uses of telephone

20. Woods, *Reminiscences*, p. 10. Woods eventually became president of the American Broadcasting Company.
21. Gross, *I Looked and Listened*, p. 62.
22. Banning, *Commercial Broadcasting Pioneer*, pp. 112-13.

lines were being rejected. WJZ, asking for phone lines to broadcast the 1922 World Series—the New York Giants and the New York Yankees were again involved—received a flat refusal. In earlier days the Westinghouse stations had sometimes found the telephone people co-operative; in 1921 KDKA had broadcast a speech by Secretary Hoover from Pittsburgh's Duquesne Club via lines of the local company. But later AT&T instructed its local affiliates to discontinue co-operation of this sort and told Westinghouse that the alliance agreements ruled out pickups of this sort by Westinghouse.[23] RCA and GE received similar pronouncements. That is why their stations—and others—were struggling with lower-quality Western Union and Postal Telegraph lines, never intended for voice transmission. In time AT&T would introduce exceptions into this policy, but in 1922-23 applied it rigidly to give advantage to WEAF, New York, and presently to WCAP, Washington—second station in the toll system, launched in 1923.

As 1923 began, few other stations had thoughts of following in WEAF's footsteps. The Westinghouse stations—KDKA, Pittsburgh; WJZ, New York; KYW, Chicago: WBZ, Springfield—were not selling time nor planning to. Nor was WLW, Cincinnati, the already potent station started by Powel Crosley, Jr., to promote his Crosley radios. Nor were the leading newspaper-owned stations such as WWJ, Detroit; WMAQ, Chicago; WDAF, Kansas City.

But as whispers of success issued from the phone booth, as WEAF set new standards in technical excellence, especially in remote broadcasts, and as AT&T stepped up its investments in staff, programming, and promotion, all stations would feel the pressure.

The year 1923 therefore opened on a different note. A question about the financial structure of broadcasting had been raised. The discussion was on. A dispute was in the air.

Suddenly it was one of many.

DISCORD

The exuberance of 1922 carried into 1923 and beyond, and the boom went on. Sales of radio sets and parts had reached $60,000,000 in 1922 and went up to $136,000,000 in 1923.[1] The building of stations continued. Radio

23. *Ibid.* p. 58.
1. *Broadcasting*, 1939 Yearbook, p. 11.

columns, supplements, magazines expanded. Technical advances were made. New program ideas enlivened station schedules. Important subject matter was added. Professionalism developed.

But the excitement of 1923 was less child-like, and now there was a counterpoint of other sounds. Of some of the developing disputes the public was scarcely aware. Some would not reach a climax for decades. Yet a number of conflicts were already generating anger and bitterness. The dominance of the patent allies was a main source of conflict. It centered largely upon RCA and AT&T.

Of the $60,000,000 spent by Americans on receiving equipment in 1922, $11,000,000 was taken in by RCA as sales agent for General Electric and Westinghouse equipment.[2] It was a smashing sum and made the broadcasting field the chief source of RCA income, far exceeding marine and transoceanic communication. It strengthened David Sarnoff's position in the company.

But Sarnoff himself—and the allies generally—felt that the group had not obtained a sufficient share of the $60,000,000 total. They felt patent rights had been grossly violated. They were determined to improve their position.

Among the thousands of companies that were by now participating in the making of equipment, some two hundred were selling tube sets which were complete except for the tubes. Almost all these sets were eventually operated with RCA tubes—which had an effective monopoly.

During 1922 RCA sold 1,583,021 tubes. The company *had* to sell separate tubes to replace worn tubes in RCA sets, and also to serve amateur needs. But apparently most of the tubes sold were not going to these uses but were finding their way, through one channel or another, into sets assembled for sale by the two hundred companies.[3] These set-makers were thus boosting sales of RCA tubes, which might have been considered helpful to RCA and its suppliers, GE and Westinghouse. On the other hand, they were also taking the major share of the receiving-set market away from RCA, GE, and Westinghouse. The set-makers in question were of the opinion that they were not violating patent rights in making tube sets complete except for the tubes. RCA and its allies, however, insisted they were.

2. *Ibid.*
3. *Report of the Federal Trade Commission on the Radio Industry*, pp. 6, 82.

Undoubtedly the companies accused of infringement found safety in the large number of companies so accused. But, in spite of the numbers, RCA and its allies were determined to do battle.

In August 1922 an RCA patent policy committee, in a meeting attended by Sarnoff as general manager, recommended:

> That suits be brought . . . but that great pains be taken not to have a multiplicity of suits. Pains should, however, be taken to bring enough suits so that if one defendant goes out of business, time will not be lost.[4]

RCA also began to put increasing pressure on its distributors. It dropped distributors who ordered only tubes and favored those who pushed "the entire Radio Corporation line." Sometimes it allocated tubes to them in proportion to the number of complete sets ordered. For a time it required distributors to send, with an order for certain new tubes, an equal supply of burned-out tubes.[5]

At the same time the tube buyer was warned by a message on the tube carton that he was not authorized to use it "as an element or part of any combination" except as set forth in the RCA catalogue. This catalogue—if he found a copy and read it—told him that he was not to use an RCA tube with non-RCA components, "assembled or partially assembled." [6]

To the numerous set-makers the RCA moves were ominous and meant that the allies were determined to translate their tube monopoly into a monopoly in set manufacture and sale. The set-makers began to go to their congressmen. The "radio trust" became a burning issue on Capitol Hill.

A number of congressmen regarded concentrations of power—always a cause for watchfulness—as especially troublesome where the flow of information was involved. They were aware that the makers and sellers of equipment dominated the air. The large ones had been the first to enter broadcasting and had later won favored channels. Many other set-makers, including comparatively small firms, were also going on the air. They included, for example, A. H. Grebe, one of the first to place a set on the market, who had recently launched WAHG, New York.[7] This same A. H. Grebe had been chosen by RCA as one of the first targets for litigation.

4. *Ibid.* p. 90.
5. *Ibid.* pp. 83-5.
6. *Ibid.* pp. 72-3. Also *Radio Enters the Home*, title page.
7. Later named WABC and WCBS.

If RCA and its allies drove such competitors out of set manufacture, it would presumably also drive them off the air. The situation was therefore seen as more than a merchandising conflict.

On March 3, 1923, Congress requested the Federal Trade Commission to investigate the radio industry to ascertain whether patents were being used to gain control over "reception and transmission," and whether there was a possible violation of anti-trust laws. The FTC was not asked to make a judgment but to report all relevant facts. Thus an industry scarcely a year old had its first monopoly inquiry. Through months to come this would hover in the background.

While RCA was claiming infringement of patents by numerous set-makers, AT&T was making similarly sweeping claims about transmitters. During 1922 it asked all regional telephone companies of the Bell System to keep the parent company abreast of local radio matters. It told the regional affiliates that transmitters not made by Western Electric represented "in practically every case . . . an infringement of our patent rights." [8]

In February 1923, AT&T held a policy meeting to map action against infringers. Although almost six hundred stations were on the air, only thirty-five had bought Western Electric ($8500-$10,500) transmitters.[9] Another six stations had been equipped by AT&T's patent allies, who under the agreements were conceded the right to make transmitters for their own use but not for sale. Of the remaining five hundred-odd stations, virtually all were regarded by AT&T as violators of its patent rights.

William Peck Banning, AT&T executive who later wrote a company-sponsored history of the birth of toll broadcasting, explains that the wide sale of vacuum tubes "for amateur experimentation" made it easy for "local radio enthusiasts" to assemble transmitters. "If, however, such assembled transmitters were then used for broadcasts of entertainment and news, there was," Banning tells us, "an infringement of the American Company's patent rights." [10]

That AT&T regarded them as patent infringers was a surprise to several hundred stations. They had been so unaware of the problem that they had, in increasing numbers, been asking the Bell System for wires for remote pickups.

8. Banning, *Commercial Broadcasting Pioneer*, pp. 74-5.
9. *Ibid.* p. 134.
10. *Ibid.* p. 136.

AT&T, for its part, realized that its stand involved public-relations hazards. Therefore, at its policy meeting of February 1923 it adopted a plan put forward as a peace move. It offered to forgive any station its past infringements if it would pay a license fee—in most cases, from $500 to $2000—to AT&T for the privilege of continuing to broadcast. The fee was shortly changed to $4 per watt, with a minimum of $500 and a maximum of $3000.[11]

The problem of college and university stations was put aside for further study. AT&T asked its affiliates to supply information on just what these stations were doing.

The required license fee, AT&T decided, could be paid in monthly installments. The company also offered a special inducement. Once licensed by AT&T, a station would occasionally be permitted to lease telephone lines for remote pickups.

AT&T announced the entire plan in magnanimous tones. Without one hint of conscious humor, it informed its operating affiliates:

> The procedure for the licensing of unlicensed broadcasting stations is established not as a basis of revenue to the Bell System but in order that the broadcaster may be in position to obtain advantages which he could not otherwise secure.[12]

In other words, it was for the good of the stations, and in spite of their wayward ways.

The hundreds of stations did not rush to comply. Some were struggling with Western Union and Postal Telegraph lines and continued to do so. A few, as we shall see, experimented with alternative solutions. The stations had licenses from the Department of Commerce and felt that these entitled them to broadcast. The new "license" was considered an effrontery.

WHN, New York, for example, which had been started in 1922, did not have a Western Electric transmitter.[13] But its transmitter assembly included some parts—such as tubes bought in an electrical store—covered by patents of the patent group. Having used these in an unauthorized way, WHN was held an infringer.

Like hundreds of others, WHN sat tight. In the course of 1923 AT&T lost patience with the "widespread infringements." It spoke of the need for

11. *Ibid.* p. 139.
12. *Ibid.* p. 137.
13. Jome, *Economics of the Radio Industry,* p. 215.

protecting patent rights, and of its own large investments in patents and research. It decided on litigation, and WHN was selected as a target—partly for magnanimous reasons. "We decided to select a nearby station so as to minimize the costs to both parties concerned." [14]

Not surprisingly, the AT&T views and actions fed the talk about the "radio trust."

While the allies complained of violation of property rights in patents, other complaints were based on another kind of property—copyrights. Radio broadcasters had from the start used copyright material without permission. The matter had hardly been considered. The writers and publishers of songs, through the American Society of Composers, Authors and Publishers, were the first to make a demand for royalties. During 1922 ASCAP raised the issue in various ways, including a message to the Washington Radio Conference. ASCAP began to urge an annual license fee by each station. Broadcasters were, at first, incredulous. Could the song writers be serious? Wasn't radio helping to popularize their music? As ASCAP persisted, the broadcasters became indignant. To many it seemed a rapacious demand, profaning the idealism with which broadcasting had begun. The song writers, however, seemed to be serious. As 1923 dawned, broadcasters were confronted with two "license fee" demands—AT&T's and ASCAP's.

Under the copyright law of 1909 a music copyright holder controls the right to perform "publicly for profit." [15] Were broadcasting stations using songs "publicly for profit?" Indeed they were, said ASCAP. But most stations said they did not even have an income, much less a profit.

ASCAP had some precedents to cite. Among them was *Herbert* v. *Shanley*, a case decided in 1917. This was an action against Shanley's Restaurant, in New York City, where diners were entertained by musicians. (It stood on the site later occupied by the Paramount Theater.) The music included, on one occasion, Victor Herbert's "Sweethearts." When Herbert asked for an injunction against such use of his music without royalty payment, a lower court ruled against him—it pointed out that no admission was charged—but the U. S. Supreme Court reversed the decision. Its opinion, written by Justice Oliver Wendell Holmes, said: "The defendant's performances are not eleemosynary. They are part of a total for which the public pays." The court considered it unimportant whether the use of

14. Banning, *Commercial Broadcasting Pioneer*, p. 209.
15. Copyright Law, Sec. 1 (e).

music actually did, or did not, result in profit. "The purpose of employing it is profit and that is enough." [16]

The broadcasters saw no relevance in this. Many apparently felt their performances were eleemosynary. They began to hold meetings and exhibit a solid front. ASCAP decided to address its efforts to a particular station, and early in 1923 picked WEAF, New York. It was a shrewd choice. The station obviously had ample resources behind it; and it could hardly disclaim profit as its purpose. Also, AT&T's own demands for license fees and pronouncements on property rights made it, in a public-relations sense, vulnerable. When E. C. Mills of ASCAP called on William E. Harkness at WEAF to discuss the matter, negotiations seem to have moved rapidly. Mills suggested $1000 as a one-year license fee for WEAF to use ASCAP-controlled music. Harkness suggested $500. Mills promptly agreed.[17] With this behind him, Mills renewed his demands on other stations. They continued to be outraged. WJZ, Newark, said it would use no more ASCAP music. The broadcasting trade press applauded. *Radio Broadcast* condemned ASCAP for "grasping after revenues." [18] ASCAP began monitoring WOR, Newark. On its program schedule, presented by "L. Bamberger and Company, one of America's great stores," the song "Mother Machree" was heard. It sufficed. The case of *Witmark* v. *Bamberger* was concluded in August 1923, with the decision that the performance had not been eleemosynary.[19]

Stations operated for publicity by private companies now began in rapid order to settle for license fees of $250 and up. But the struggle was only starting. Efforts to reverse the precedent were begun through the courts. In Chicago angry broadcasters held more meetings; "and in our indignation we . . . decided we would form an organization. That led to the founding of the National Association of Broadcasters." It chose as its first managing director Paul Klugh, veteran of battles against ASCAP by the piano-roll industry.[20]

By midsummer the NAB group was discussing, according to *Radio Broadcast*, an alluring plan under which NAB would persuade song writers to turn their songs over to broadcasters free of charge. The broadcasters would get behind these songs and, by repeated performances, make

16. *Herbert* v. *Shanley*, 242 U.S. 591 (1917).
17. Harkness, *Reminiscences*, p. 73.
18. *Radio Broadcast*, August 1923.
19. *Witmark* v. *Bamberger*, 291 Fed. 776 (1923).
20. Hedges, *Reminiscences*, pp. 13-14.

them hits. Thus song writers would get immediate publication and rich rewards through sales of sheet music. Meanwhile the NAB, "as its reward for putting the music before the public, is to get the mechanical royalties —those reaped from phonograph records and roll music." *Radio Broadcast* applauded the plan and noted with satisfaction: "Societies like ASCAP . . . will have to look elsewhere for funds to pay their eminent counsel." [21]

The NAB would become a standard bearer in many battles—against ASCAP and others.

Besides patent and copyright battles, still others rumbled in the air as 1923 began. One was a growing tension between "have" and "have not" stations.

Early in 1923 Secretary Hoover, finding the chaos in the air "simply intolerable," [22] decided to call a second Washington Radio Conference, which was convened in March. He had concluded that no early legislation was likely. Representative White had offered his proposed law but others were also before the Congress; in fact, twenty measures relating to broadcasting were put before the 67th Congress in the sessions of 1921-23. They offered, among other proposals, various forms of government control (H.R. 4132 and others), nationalization (H.R. 14169), operation of government broadcasting stations (H.J. Res. 7), broadcasting of the proceedings of Congress (H.J. Res. 278), monopoly investigation (H. Res. 314).[23] Except for the last, all were regarded as doomed. Secretary Hoover turned to the industry for the mandate he felt was needed. In response, the Conference went on record as believing he had authority "to regulate hours and wave lengths of operation of stations when such action is necessary to prevent interference detrimental to the public good." [24]

Clearly Hoover himself doubted he had such authority; not finding it in the radio law of 1912, he had been asking Congress to give it to him. He was besieged, however, with demands for action; and now, with the resolution of the convened leaders behind him, he proceeded as though the matter were settled, and quickly put through a major reallocation. Announced April 4, it went into effect on May 15. The broadcast band now began to assume the pattern it would have in later years.

Stations were divided into three groups.

The first would be the high-powered stations of 500-1000 watts—or

21. *Radio Broadcast,* August 1923.
22. *Ibid.* January 1923.
23. *Congressional Record,* Vols. 61 and 62.
24. New York *Times,* March 25, 1923.

higher power, as the rules changed—serving large areas and having no interference within those areas. There would be some time-sharing if necessary. These stations would no longer be on the same channel but on various channels between 300 and 545 meters, largely near the center of the dial. They would not use phonograph records.

Another group would have power of not more than 500 watts. They would serve smaller regions and have no interference within those regions. They would operate at various channels between 222 and 300 meters. Some time-sharing might be needed.

This left, as the third group, a conglomeration of low-powered stations. Some industry leaders urged Hoover to abolish these altogether. Instead he left them all at one dial position—360 meters—all serving limited local areas, sharing time as required, and in many cases restricted to daytime hours to minimize the chronic interference.

The over-all reallocation was unquestionably welcomed by the public: it offered most listeners a scattering of stations which could be tuned in with reasonable clarity, especially on a tube set. But aside from the favored stations, many were still crammed into what had become an inferno of the unfavored, an underworld of 360, a place of howls and squeals and eternal misery, from which escape seemed difficult. How justify additional investment in such a channel?

The dwellers of this region noted that the patent allies were well represented among the favored channels. Hardly a listener doubted that they should be, since they provided varied programs and clear, strong transmission. At the same time there was restiveness among the unfavored. Almost all educational and religious broadcasters were squeezed into the 360-meter assignment, along with countless others, often in mutual resentment born of mutual interference. They eyed "the trust" with uneasiness and were wary of the course of events. The reallocation seemed to reflect a value judgment in which educational and religious interests were low on the scale.

Just as clearly, the allies of "the trust" were on the rise. On May 15, 1923, the very day the Hoover reallocations took effect, AT&T moved its WEAF to new and grandiose headquarters; and on the same day—it all seemed interrelated—Westinghouse turned WJZ over to RCA to be run in mid-New York from Aeolian Hall, along with the revived WJY. RCA meanwhile was building its Washington station, WRC. Westinghouse was continuing with its KDKA, KYW, and WBZ, while General Electric was planning KGO, San Francisco, and KOA, Denver, to add to its WGY, Schenectady. An understanding had developed among GE, Westinghouse, and RCA under which each would operate three high-powered stations, jointly achieving almost national coverage and stimulating set sales coast to coast.[25] And AT&T was going ahead with its Washington toll station, WCAP.

The impression given by "the trust" was one of assurance and unity. The impression was, however, misleading. Still another conflict was stirring in 1923. At the moment few knew it. The press seemed unaware of it. Government probers had no inkling of it. There were occasional rumblings from above that might have suggested the truth. AT&T was selling its RCA stock and withdrawing its representatives from the RCA board of directors. What did it mean? AT&T explained that it had found such representation unnecessary. But this explained nothing. The dispute remained hidden.

Almost all the developing struggles concerned RCA in one way or another.

As the lines of battle formed, Owen D. Young pursued his problem of hand-picking a new RCA president. Edward Nally was being shifted to supervise foreign relations. Domestically, David Sarnoff was boss. But a president—that was something quite different.

Exploring new worlds, RCA perhaps had no choice but to look to other fields for administrative talent. It became an RCA tradition to do so, often plucking executives from totally unrelated areas—not always with glittering results.

Young wrote down what was required in an RCA president.

> . . . known nationally and internationally . . . speak with authority either to foreign Governments or to our own Government . . . should not have been previously identified with politics . . . should not have been identified with Wall Street . . . no one should be able to question his Americanism, such as they have done in several instances in the case of our international bankers. . . . should be a man of public position whom to attack would be bad politics rather than good politics.[26]

25. Lang, *Reminiscences*, p. 13.
26. Archer, *History of Radio*, pp. 246-7.

Young—with his list—seems to have consulted many people. It was like a search for a prince. David Sarnoff, risen from immigrant boy to general manager, may have learned in this way that he was not ready for the big step. He would have understood, bided his time, and prepared.

Young's quest ended with someone he had never met. Major General James G. Harbord was suggested by Newton D. Baker, former Secretary of War, who said that General Pershing, as Chief of Staff in World War I, had relied heavily on Harbord. As co-ordinator of supplies, Harbord had been found a good administrator. He had been a Rough Rider in the Spanish-American War; his Americanism was unassailable. Young negotiated, and in January 1923 Harbord became president of RCA.

His experience was irrelevant to the developing arts of broadcasting, and there is no sign that he contributed to them; but that was not his task. Artists seldom saw him, and when they did, they had the impression he was still fighting World War I. On a ceremonial visit to a WJZ studio, he was clearly nettled. "Why is that woman singing German?" he asked Tommy Cowan, who explained that she was singing a German song.[27]

In the course of the 1920's General Harbord became dismayed at the rise of American anti-militarism and pacifism, and on one occasion was quoted as unburdening himself:

> War represents a permanent factor in human life and a very noble one. It is the school of heroism from which a nation's noblest sons graduated into highest manhood. Individual preparation for national defense is necessary for the peacetime benefits that come to the people who prepare themselves for the efficiency that will come when your streets will again echo to the tread of marching soldiers, your railways and your waterways again teem with men and implements of war assembling to protect the flag.[28]

The appointment of Major General Harbord represented a continuation of the military influence under which radio had grown; it was also a move to retain the shield of quasi-governmental sponsorship. His ability to speak with authority to those in government may have been crucial as disputes swirled about RCA. Meanwhile, as though in another world, thousands of artists in hundreds of studios, in scores of cities from coast to coast, were putting on programs.

27. Cowan, *Reminiscences*, p. 58.
28. Quoted in Tyler (ed.), *Radio as a Cultural Agency*, p. 120.

SHADE OF THE POTTED PALM

Through 1923 and 1924 the boom continued and, in spite of problems, showed no signs of slackening. People kept buying radio parts and sets; the emphasis shifted to complete sets. The public investment in equipment zoomed:[1]

1922	$ 60,000,000
1923	136,000,000
1924	358,000,000

Lured by the growing audience, new stations sprang up. A growing number failed, but others took their place. They ranged from the well-financed to the quaint and primitive. Some were launched for curious and transitory reasons. In 1923 in Wilmington, N.C., two partners in an electrical shop started to sell radios. But during the day, when the shop was open, no stations could be heard in Wilmington, which made demonstration impossible. The partners therefore wrote to the Department of Commerce and became licensees for WBBN, Wilmington, which they meanwhile put together over the store with a 10-watt transmitter. Now, when a customer came to the store, one partner slipped upstairs, turned on the transmitter and put on a phonograph record; the other handled the demonstration. After the customer left, the transmitter was turned off and normal business resumed. By the spring of 1924 other stations began to reach Wilmington with sufficient strength for demonstration purposes, so WBBN was allowed to die.[2]

Other stations were emerging from attics and shacks and putting on a front. In a number of cities, studios became an object of pride. "A visit to station WMAQ," said *Radio Digest* in February 1923, "is like entering a music conservatory. You enter a reception room . . . then on into the studio . . . artistically furnished in brown tones . . . here and there, a large fern . . . and a Mason and Hamlin grand piano."[3] Station WFAA in Dallas, like Chicago's WMAQ, referred to its one studio as "the conservatory," and felt it was so attractive that "even the most fastidious should welcome the opportunity to perform for WFAA."[4]

1. *Broadcasting*, 1939 Yearbook, p. 11.
2. Wallace, *The Development of Broadcasting in North Carolina*, pp. 82-3.
3. *Radio Digest*, February 17, 1923.
4. Dallas *Daily News*, June 25, 1922. Quoted in Stokes, *A Public Service Program History of Radio Station WFAA-820*, p. 29.

A leader in the prideful atmosphere was of course WEAF, so draped and cushioned that one artist quipped that it lacked only "a red light over the door." [5] Actually it had a red light, which went on when the studio was on the air. By 1923 many stations had this feature.

What came from these studios was almost entirely music, with here and there a talk or reading. The performers were mainly individuals or small groups. The tendency was to alternate vocalist and instrumentalist: a singer—a pianist—a singer—a violinist—a singer—a talk. Among singers, sopranos seem to have filled more air time than baritones, tenors, or contraltos.[6]

As to the music, it was almost all conservatory music; one program director dubbed it "potted palm music." It was the music played at tea time by hotel orchestras. It was recital music. European in origin, it was "culture" to many Americans. It was part of the heritage that thousands of musicians, amateur and professional, had brought with them from the old world, and was to this extent a typical feature of new-world experience. Seeking the new, the immigrant clung to symbols of the old. This music completely dominated radio in its first years and retained a leading role throughout the 1920's.

The program log of WFAA, Dallas, for Tuesday evening, October 10, 1922, might have been duplicated in almost any American city, on countless stations.

> Baritone solo
> (a) "Vision Fugitive" from *Herodiade* . . . Massenet
> (b) Recitative, "I Rage, I Melt, I Burn"; "Air Ruddier Than the Cherry," from *Acis and Galatea* . . . G. F. Handel
> (c) "Blow, Blow, Thou Winter Wind," words from *As You Like It* . . . J. Sarjeant
> Edward Lisman. Accompanist Miss Whitaker.
>
> Piano Concerto
> (a) "Bourree" . . . Louis Duillemin
> (b) "Pavane" . . .   "   "
> (c) "Gigue" . . .   "   "
> Mr. and Mrs. Paul Van Katwijk.
>
> Vocal Solo
> (a) "The Birthday" . . . Woodman

5. Harkness, *Reminiscences*, p. 34.
6. Goldsmith and Lescarboura, *This Thing Called Broadcasting*, p. 100.

(b) "Mi Chiamano Mimi," from *La Bohème* . . . Puccini
Mrs. R. H. Morton, lyric soprano.[7]

Folk music and hillbilly music were still unknown in Dallas radio offerings. As late as 1928, less than 4 per cent of the WFAA schedule could be classified under such headings, and this consisted of "old-time fiddler" items.[8]

The WFAA schedule was typical in its alternation of vocal and instrumental numbers. At WOR, Newark, which followed a similar pattern, the schedule tended at first to fall into twenty-minute segments, each consisting of four or five numbers. The segments gradually shortened and by the end of 1923 the schedule was being planned in fifteen-minute segments.[9]

WJZ saw a similar evolution. Sometimes an artist stayed for two segments separated by a breathing spell. The WJZ log for Tuesday afternoon, May 29, 1923—shortly after the station became a New York City station under RCA—showed such an alignment. In the neatly penciled logs the artist's address and telephone were usually entered.

3:00-3:20	Henry Palmer, pianist West Long Branch, N.J.
3:20-3:40	Marie Stapleton Murray, Sop. 476 W. 144, NYC Aud 5631
3:40-4:00	Henry Palmer, pianist
4:00-4:20	Marie Stapleton Murray Louise Baker Phillips accom.
4:35-5:00	Daisy Miller, Negro Dialect Stories 134 East 19 NYC Stuy 6078[10]

In this pre-network era, in which hundreds of stations were mounting their own programs—eked out by phonograph and player piano on low-powered stations—extraordinary numbers of musicians were involved. They ranged from established professionals to amateurs. For the moment,

7. Stokes, *A Public Service Program History of Radio Station WFAA-820*, p. 40.
8. *Ibid.* p. 162.
9. Barnett, *Reminiscences*, p. 9.
10. WJZ Log, May 29, 1923.

the boom gave encouragement to students. Chicago radio regularly featured recitals by the American Conservatory, Glenn Dillard Gunn School of Music, Cosmopolitan School of Music, Lyceum Arts Conservatory, and Bush Conservatory.[11] As top artists became elusive, conservatories found themselves all the more welcome.

It is ironic that the years dominated in radio by potted-palm music coincided with a period of rich growth in American music. These years saw an explosion of genius—the advent of jazz—that had not only musical but also social and racial ramifications. That scarcely an echo stirred the ferns and draperies of the radio conservatories is significant, and in many ways characteristic of the role of broadcasting at this time.

Yet the broadcasting boom, even in rejecting and ignoring jazz, was playing a role in its history. In strange fashion it was influencing the chain explosion that would, in due time, bring changes to broadcasting itself.

That chain explosion had been sparked by World War I. The wartime migrations of Negroes to northern industry had brought to many American cities their first experience of the swinging music of New Orleans. Those same years had given it the name "jazz." Already known in Memphis, Kansas City, St. Louis, it erupted in isolated night spots of New York, Chicago, Los Angeles, and elsewhere. In Europe some servicemen heard it. White musicians took it up. In 1917, Victor made its first notable jazz recording, featuring the white "Original Dixieland Jazz Band." The young Jimmy Durante, an early convert, said of this band: "It wasn't only an innovation, it was a revolution!" [12] This and subsequent jazz recordings —by white and Negro talent—began to be studied and imitated by musicians throughout the country.

Victor now began to develop "race" recordings as a separate category, promoted through a separate catalogue and sold mainly through stores in Negro districts. In other stores the knowledgeable might order them specially.

The year 1917, when jazz made its breakthrough into the recording field, was also the year the Navy protected American boys by closing brothels in New Orleans. That action brought unemployment to leading jazz musicians and resulted in their joining the northward trek. Before long forty of the best Negro musicians are said to have landed in Chicago —not many, but apparently enough for a revolution. By the end of the

11. Caton, *Radio Station WMAQ*, pp. 76, 88.
12. Stearns, *The Story of Jazz*, p. 113.

war it was Chicago, rather than New Orleans, from which the greatest excitement radiated. It was a cry in the street, a hammering at the door, a shout of exuberant vitality from those whom a white society seemed determined to ignore. It frightened the placid: it didn't belong in a conservatory.

Within months of the start of the broadcasting boom, the bottom dropped out of the phonograph business. But "race" records held their own. Millions of people were turning to the radio music box, but evidently the buyers of "race" records were scarce among them.

We have no information on how many Negroes in Chicago did, or did not, assemble radio sets to listen to Mary Garden. But we are told that when a new record by Bessie Smith came to a South Side record shop, Negroes "would form a line twice around the block . . . nobody ever asked for Paul Whiteman." [13] Personal appearances by Bessie Smith brought riots. Bessie Smith records are said to have kept Columbia Records afloat.

Columbia, Victor, Brunswick—inevitably, each began to expand its race catalogue and even to issue jazz under the "popular" labels. Radio in its success—while hardly aware of it—was forcing the record industry into an important step. Just as film was making theater change its role, so radio, putting pressure on records, was edging them firmly into a new world, with results no one could foresee.

Memoirs written in a later day would reveal that in the early 1920's in Spokane, the boy Bing Crosby was listening over and over to records of the Mound City Blue Blowers, studying and copying their tricks.[14] In Bloomington, Hoagy Carmichael was doing the same with records of the Wolverines, with Bix Beiderbecke.[15] Records were becoming the great school for a rising generation of musicians.

Potted-palm music was still the established order, but another world was beating at the door.

In 1921, the year of Mary Garden, two teen-aged boys, Jack and David Kapp—they would some day launch Decca Records—started a record shop in a seamy part of Chicago. They had grown up in the record business; their father had joined the Columbia Phonograph Record Company in 1905 as door-to-door salesman, and the boys had watched every step in

13. *Ibid.* p. 122. The passage quotes Clarence Williams, pianist-composer.
14. Crosby, *Call Me Lucky*, pp. 72, 80.
15. Carmichael, *The Stardust Road*, p. 42.

the growth of the industry. At first the father had the title of "canvasser" and peddled phonographs and records in Chicago. He would always be welcome in saloons—he would set up, play a few records, get a bite of free lunch. With rising prosperity he became a "franchised dealer," a title acquired by buying $75 worth of merchandise. In a horse and buggy he covered an assigned territory, and the boys would help him load. Many customers bought phonographs on time, and the father would go to collect the $2 monthly payment and, while there, play the new monthly releases and maybe sell a record or two. Eventually the father opened a music store in Chicago and the boys worked there. Records were their life. It was hard to think of any other career. When Jack was nineteen and David sixteen—and just out of high school—they bought a small store of their own. It was in a deteriorating neighborhood, close to the advancing line of the Negro ghetto. The record industry, at this time, was going through changes. Columbia patents were expiring, and the field was becoming more competitive. Record shops, instead of representing a single company, carried various labels. The Kapps expanded more and more into folk music, jazz, "race" records. Negroes were the first to buy these, but soon white boys and girls came, and listened by the hour. It was a glimpse into another world. The store was like an outpost on a mysterious, perhaps dangerous, frontier. Among those who came often, staying long, was Carl Sandburg. White musicians, music students, came to listen.[16]

The radio "conservatories" took little heed of all this. Yet change was in the air. Among the score of stations launched in Chicago by 1924 there was one—regarded as a rich-man hobby station—that was started by two brothers, Ralph and H. Leslie Atlass, in the basement of their home on Sheridan Road. To the horror of some, the brothers specialized in jazz,[17] which seemed a desecration of the air. The station, WBBM, later moved to the Broadmoor Hotel.

Feelings against jazz seemed often to have an almost pathological dimension. William W. Hinshaw, preparing the WJZ audience for Mozart's *Impresario*, went out of his way to denounce jazz as "unhealthy" and "immoral." [18] Another broadcaster called it an "abomination" that should be "absolutely eliminated." [19] Some centered their anger on particular instruments. According to the recollection of Walter Evans of KYW, Chicago,

16. David Kapp, *Reminiscences*, pp. 1-4.
17. Linton, *A History of Chicago Radio Station Programming 1921-1931*, p. 60.
18. *Radio Broadcast*, August 1922.
19. *Ibid.* September 1922.

some stations forbade saxophones, which were assumed to have "an immoral influence." [20]

But the jazz and "race" recordings were being heard and studied. Sometimes the results were a compromise. Vincent Lopez felt the pulse; he heeded it and made it polite. It was a decaffeinated jazz he sent to WJZ via Western Union lines from the Hotel Pennsylvania. A distant echo of New Orleans, yet it spoke to listeners. Paul Whiteman too was making jazz respectable, with large instrumentation and classical devices.

When WJZ moved to New York City in 1923 under the RCA banner, it was to studios in Aeolian Hall, temple of established culture on 42d Street near Fifth Avenue. In that same Aeolian Hall a few months later—February 12, 1924—Paul Whiteman gave a concert. Sponsored by such figures as Damrosch, Rachmaninoff, and Stokowski, it was a highlight of the social season and presented to an audience of the elite the possibilities of jazz. The program included George Gershwin playing "A Rhapsody in Blue," written for the occasion. Critical reaction to the concert was mixed, but its symbolic value gave it added meaning. Ripples emanating from slums of Chicago and other cities were reaching the mighty in Aeolian Hall. Paul Whiteman was winning wide bookings and beginning to make a fortune, and others followed; now and then they were heard on the air. The radio audience would begin slowly to become familiar with this music, especially through late-evening broadcasts from night clubs. The infiltration was progressing. In due time, in the wake of their music, Negroes would follow.

But not yet. In 1922, 1923, 1924, 1925, the potted palm ruled supreme.

The artists who brought their conservatory music to the radio studios were still unpaid. The idea of pay was unthinkable. The few agents who were beginning to mention the notion were thought of as trouble-makers. Even at WEAF there was no thought of paying artists who filled the stretches of unsold time. The policy was clear: "In the case of a lady, a nice bouquet of flowers together with a nice automobile to pick her up at her residence and bring her to 195 Broadway." [21]

Yet the feeling that some *quid pro quo* was needed was strong. The newspaper-owned stations were in a favored position in this respect because they could pay with items in print, and did. At WWJ Elton Plant, the Detroit *News* office boy turned producer, who still wanted to be a

20. Evans, *Reminiscences*, p. 36.
21. Woods, *Reminiscences*, p. 13.

newspaper writer, was in a sense achieving his ambition. At the end of
each broadcast day, having put on—and often participated in—a steady
stream of programs, he would sit down and write reviews of them for the
next day's Detroit *News*. Rex White, who lined up talent for the WWJ
programs, also wrote reviews, always favorable, "or we would have
no show the next night." At WMAQ, the Chicago *Daily News* station, William S. Hedges recalls that "I always saw to it that our talent got a good
plug in the Chicago *Daily News*." At WDAF, the Kansas City *Star* station,
the same policy prevailed. "We used to say that we paid off in publicity.
Every day, following a program, Fitz or I would sit down and write a
story about that particular program." [22]

The payoffs were often lavishly worded. "Scarcely had the strains of
'Souvenir' died away before requests for its repetition began to pour into
WFAA station," its owner the Dallas *News* tells us.[23]

For good measure various papers made a practice of publishing names
and addresses of people who phoned or wrote—apparently as reward and
to keep such applause coming. "A flood of telephone calls was loosed,"
wrote the Detroit *News* after a recital by a Hungarian singer, adding: "A
few of those who called to congratulate Miss Szanto were . . ." Here followed names and addresses.[24]

By quoting the phone calls or letters at length, a newspaper often managed to bestow laurels not only on the artist but also on itself and its
station. The Chicago *Daily News* carried many such items as:

> "If I were to write four thousand words I could only be beginning to
> hint at the worth of the *Daily News* in giving its readers and admirers
> the opportunity of hearing the best," wrote Miss Louise License,
> 1320 South Lawndale Avenue . . .[25]

All this must have reflected audience enthusiasm, but also a determined
policy of encouraging praise through payoffs in print.

It has often been said that radio criticism seldom reached high levels.
One reason may be that it was born in corruption, or perhaps we should

22.*Reminiscences* by Plant, pp. 19-20; Rex White, p. 2; Hedges, p. 23; Patt, p. 12.
"Fitz" was Leo Fitzpatrick, radio editor of the *Star* and known for his late-night
broadcasts of the "Kansas City Nighthawks."
23. Quoted by Stokes, *A Public Service Program History of Radio Station WFAA-
820*, p. 31.
24. Detroit *News*, December 31, 1921.
25. Chicago *Daily News*, July 10, 1923.

say in that state of utter innocence of Adam and Eve who—at first—did not know they were naked.

As artists became difficult or at least needed persuasion, stations began to rely heavily on a special device for obtaining talent. Businesses were encouraged, for the publicity value, to provide programs. No charge was made for time. WLW, Cincinnati, which did not sell time until 1926, had its schedule studded with such programming by 1923. In addition to dance music provided by the Hotel Sinton, it provided stock quotations by Westheimer & Co., market reports by Henry Brow & Co., financial news by the Fifth-Third National Bank, drama readings by the Shuster-Martin School, piano by Baldwin.[26] WJZ, New York, which likewise sold no time until 1926, had its 1923 schedule crammed with such items as the Rheingold Quartet, Schrafft's Tea Room Orchestra, Wanamaker Organ Concert, fashion talks provided by *Harper's Bazaar*, book reviews by *Harper's Magazine*, sports talks by *Field and Stream*.[27] Similarly WFAA, Dallas, offered the Magnolia Petroleum Company Band, and later programs supplied by various department stores, who were sometimes called "chaperones"[28] of their programs, presumably to avoid the term "sponsor."

Among the most faithful program suppliers were music publishers. They had long employed people with passable—and durable—voices to demonstrate the company's songs at music stores, department stores, and other locations. Many stations put these "song pluggers" on the air and let them fill hours, with occasional mention of their companies. A few song pluggers—among them Little Jack Little and Carson Robinson—became radio stars.[29]

Although such devices provided programming, hazards were involved. Stations proclaiming themselves as noncommercial began to sound commercial. As early as November 1922, *Radio Broadcast* was complaining:

> . . . driblets of advertising, indirect but unmistakable, are floating through the ether every day. You can't miss it; every little classic number has a slogan all its own, if it's only the mere mention of the name —and the street address, and the phone number—of the music house which arranged the programme. . . . The woods are full of opportunists who are restrained by no scruples when the scent of profit comes down the wind.[30]

26. Lichty, *The Nation's Station*, pp. 99-100.
27. WJZ Log, May 25, 1923.
28. Stokes, *A Public Service Program History of Radio Station WFAA-820*, p. 34.
29. Patt, *Reminiscences*, p. 15.
30. *Radio Broadcast*, November 1922.

There were other hazards. Some companies sent horrifyingly amateur delegations. Sometimes—with increasing frequency—expected artists
didn't arrive. Every station had to have emergency resources. Phillips Carlin, who joined WEAF in 1923 as announcer, kept a book of Robert W.
Service poems handy to read in emergencies.[31] At WOR, station manager
Joseph Barnett was the emergency baritone. At WJZ, Milton J. Cross was
hired as announcer partly for his value as a crisis tenor. At WWJ, Elton
Plant sang, when needed, with player-piano accompaniment, reading
from the paper rolls.

Most station logs are astringently factual—and uninformative. Yet here
and there they speak volumes with understatement.

The WMAQ log provides a chronicle of non-appearing artists—result-
ing sometimes in premature sign-offs.

May 19, 1925:
Off 4:52. Gunn School did not come.

May 29, 1925:
4:00 p.m., off. Mrs. Carter of Hollywood did not come.

July 14, 1925:
No orchestra. Stood by from 9:47 to 9:53. Signed off.

January 22, 1926:
Mrs. Hiller ill. Major Barclay reading from the *Saturday Evening
Post*. 4:23, speaker failed to arrive. Major Barclay reading from the
Saturday Evening Post.[32]

Worse yet, the reliance on free performances began to generate resentment among musicians, singers and speakers. Heywood Broun gave expression to the changing mood. When radio came along, he said, "gall returned in a most noxious form. The broadcasters do not pay. Instead they
offer the performer publicity. It is a highly depreciated currency."[33]

Rex White speaks of Detroit theaters posting notices in dressing rooms
warning actors not to appear on broadcasting stations.[34]

In 1924 the Kansas City local of the American Federation of Musicians
notified local stations that a musician would have to get $4 per program. At
WDAF, the station of the Kansas City *Star,* the announcement brought

31. Carlin, *Reminiscences*, p. 4.
32. Quoted by Caton, *Radio Station WMAQ*, pp. 124-5.
33. Quoted in *Radio Broadcast*, August 1924.
34. Rex White, *Reminiscences*, p. 3.

consternation. "It was hard to explain to the owners of the paper that we needed some money in order to pay off talent, because we'd never paid a singer a cent." A *Star* board meeting, after long explanations and discussion, produced an appropriation of $120 a week for musicians. To stretch it over the schedule, no groups larger than a string trio could be hired. Singers would remain unpaid.[35]

For three years a seemingly endless parade of willing artists, by thousands, had marched in and out of America's studios and played, sung, or talked—flanked by a fern and a Mason & Hamlin grand piano. The end of the line had not yet come, but it was thinning. Naturally America's stations were looking feverishly for other solutions.

EXPLORATIONS: 1923-24

Among the meaningful explorations of 1923-24 was that of radio drama. This happened not in a theatrical center but in smaller communities—for good reason.

In February 1922 the General Electric Company, spurred by the Westinghouse successes, founded WGY, Schenectady. Martin P. Rice, manager of the company's publications bureau, had been especially insistent on the venture as a competitive necessity. Some executives remained reluctant; however, a sum of $10,000 had been appropriated for an interplant wireless system to link the Schenectady and Erie plants of General Electric. Rice persuaded the company that a broadcasting station could take care of this need, and so managed to divert the $10,000 toward his purposes. As WGY took shape, the interplant communication was forgotten.[1]

The station was built in a structure atop Building No. 40 of the Schenectady works; the transmitter was above the elevator shaft in the room with the elevator motors. Since GE had pioneered in developing tubes for use with high power, WGY started with 1000 watts, soon changed to 5000 watts.[2] From the beginning it had wide, effective coverage. As a start toward programming, president E. W. Rice donated his home reed organ. Kolin Hager of the publicity department was made "studio and program manager."

Raised in nearby Albany, Kolin Hager had won a high school oratory

35. Patt, *Reminiscences*, pp. 13-14.
1. Lang, *Reminiscences*, p. 10; Baker, *Reminiscences*, p. 12.
2. Weir, *Reminiscences*, p. 14.

medal in 1912 with a speech on "The Sinking of the *Titanic.*" In 1917 he left New York State Teachers' College at Albany for the army and reached France in time to act and sing the male lead in the army musical *The Isle of Az-U-Were,* which toured overseas camps. When he joined General Electric in 1921, this histrionic past was enough to win him his WGY assignment.[3]

Broadcasting from a city not bursting with singers, instrumentalists, lecturers, readers, Hager soon gravitated toward drama. The dearth, not the wealth, of talent influenced the decision. He found in the area a nucleus of enthusiasts and other willing volunteers. They included H. Edward Smith, an old-time stock company actor with resonant voice, long black hair. and "Byronic manner," [4] who took a leading role in forming the troupe. Included also was a girl student from New York State Teachers' College at Albany, Rosaline Greene, who had never been on a stage and could not "project." This may explain why she was soon the center of audience attention and was called by newspapers "the first leading lady of radio."

The WGY Players began August 3, 1922, with a full-length production of *The Wolf,* by Eugene Walter. In September the Players became a weekly Friday night offering, broadcasting *The Garden of Allah, Get Rich Quick Wallingford, A Fool There Was, Seven Keys to Baldpate,* and going on to more ambitious attempts such as Ibsen's *The Wild Duck.* Broadcasts averaged two and a half hours in length. An orchestra played bridges or "interludes." For three years not a single playwright asked for a fee.[5]

For some time, to avert anxieties, the company used a microphone disguised as a floor lamp. This absurdity also turned up at other stations but seems to have disappeared by 1924. Perhaps talking to a lampshade seemed no more natural than talking to a microphone.[6]

For some time engineers insisted, for mysterious technical reasons, on placing women at one microphone, men at another some distance away. Actors and actresses found it disconcerting to play love scenes in this way. But "each had his own lampshade." [7]

At first each actor made his own sound effects, but specialization devel-

3. *Ibid.*
4. Greene, *Reminiscences,* p. 3.
5. Hager, *Reminiscences,* p. 6.
6. A related item for the home was the radio loudspeaker disguised as a fringed lampshade, advertised during 1925 by J. B. Ferguson, Inc. as "an acknowledged contribution to both the radio and decorative arts."
7. Greene, *Reminiscences,* p. 8.

oped. One became good at thumping his chest for horses' hoofs and began doing it for everyone. Various principles emerged. The microphones distorted what was very close, favoring low tones. A key-chain close to the microphone could therefore serve as a prison chain. Such sound-effect gadgetry beguiled the press, which soon gave the impression that sound effects were the heart of radio drama. The Players also won publicity by using, for their scripts, "paper especially selected for its freedom from crackling sound." [8] In 1923 the WGY Players launched a $500 Radio Drama Prize Competition, and its rules suggest emerging conceptions of radio drama. An hour and a half was now the preferred length. "Small-cast plays, employing five or six characters, are best adapted to radio." The editorial timorousness of the day was revealed: "PLOTS MUST BE CLEAN with no attempt at questionable situations . . . No 'sex dramas' will be considered." [9] A hundred plays are said to have been submitted and one produced, with disappointing results.[10]

In April 1924 the WGY Players began to be carried via Western Union lines by WJZ, New York, and WRC, Washington—both RCA stations. The first network drama was *Billeted*. Leading lady Rosaline Greene was by now getting $5 per week; two years later she won a raise to $7.50, but lesser actors still received no pay, although a limousine and chauffeur might call for them.[11]

WGY was not the only station attempting drama. On November 9, 1922, three months after WGY's first drama, WLW, Cincinnati, broadcast the one-act play *A Fan and Two Candlesticks*, by Mary MacMillan, followed the next week by the balcony scene from *Romeo and Juliet* and a week later by *Matinata* by Lawrence Langner, with Powel Crosley, Jr. owner of WLW, in the cast. Drama became a weekly feature. On April 3, 1923, the station broadcast an original play for radio by WLW program manager Fred Smith. Entitled *When Love Wakens*—the initials spelled WLW —this may have been the first play written for radio. In this production the narrator was called a "descriptionist." [12]

During these early years plays were occasionally broadcast direct from theaters, but by the mid-1920's this idea was meeting resistance. Mean-

8. *Radio Broadcast,* November 1923.
9. *Radio Drama Prize Competition,* p. 4.
10. Hager, *Reminiscences,* p. 9.
11. Greene, *Reminiscences,* p. 20.
12. Lichty, *The Nation's Station,* pp. 120-23.

while broadcast drama from the studio had at least made a tentative debut.

Stirrings were also appearing in the field of news. Early newspaper-owned stations were not conceived as news media but as devices to publicize the papers. The "bulletins" were largely teasers to stimulate readership. At the Detroit *News* station WWJ, *The Town Crier*, which opened with horses' hoofs, seems to have had this function. At some stations the bulletins were little more than fillers. At the Detroit *Free Press*, which launched WCX to counter WWJ, reporter Herschell Hart was called on in any talent crisis. "Hart, haven't you some news you could come in and read?" the harried WCX manager would ask. Hart would "grab up" some United Press or Associated Press copy and go in to read until he got the signal the emergency was over.[13]

Most stations used items from newspapers, wire services, magazines as freely as they had used songs. Because credit was usually given, the practice was condoned, even encouraged, until the sale of time became general. Personnel without news background, however, caused occasional crises. The text of a speech by President Harding, marked HOLD FOR RELEASE and distributed in advance by International News Service, was broadcast by KYW a full day before the President spoke the words. The act of innocence caused a Washington furor.[14]

One kind of news programming stemmed not from bulletins but from the "talks" that punctuated the musical parade. As we have seen, these occasionally included reviews of current events; it was as a "lecturer" on current events that H. V. Kaltenborn came to appear on WEAF, New York. The lecturer evolved into the radio commentator. Kaltenborn's early experience in this role, and the crises it produced in Washington and New York, are worth examining.

Hans von Kaltenborn was raised in and near Milwaukee.[15] His father, a Hessian soldier-aristocrat, had emigrated from Germany in the 1860's because of the growing dominance of Prussia. For a time Hans attended a bilingual school where severe discipline was practiced; raps on the knuckle with a ruler were used to suppress his natural left-handedness. Hans cultivated physical endurance and as a bicyclist did several "centuries"—a hundred miles in ten hours. He volunteered during the Spanish-

13. Hart, *Reminiscences*, p. 6. WCX later became WJR.
14. Evans, *Reminiscences*, p. 14.
15. The following draws on Chester, *The Radio Commentaries of H. V. Kaltenborn*, and other sources as noted.

American War and became a first sergeant in Company F of the 4th Regiment of Wisconsin Infantry. The war ended two months after he enlisted, and he got only as far as an Alabama training camp, but in later years he liked to refer to his military background and parlayed it into a considerable asset.[16] From the Alabama training camp he wrote dispatches for several newspapers, which earned him a postwar job as city editor of a Wisconsin small-town weekly, the Merrill *Advocate*. He left this for travel in France and Corsica as a salesman of stereoscopes, and on his return in 1902 was hired by the Brooklyn *Daily Eagle* as reporter at $8 a week. He stayed here almost three decades, except for an interruption for study at Harvard, during which he traveled as a tutor. During World War I the much-traveled reporter with the Spanish-American war background was named war editor, dropped the "von" and became H. V. Kaltenborn. He also began giving Tuesday morning current-events talks in the *Eagle* auditorium; and, starting in 1917, to run annual *Eagle* travel tours—sometimes in the United States, sometimes abroad. Kaltenborn would select the place, and go as guide and lecturer. The *Eagle* tours were received by mayors, governors, prime ministers, and presidents, so that Kaltenborn acquired a face-to-face acquaintance with countless dignitaries. He also achieved confidence in discussing extemporaneously a vast range of problems.

In 1921 Kaltenborn bought a crystal set, became a radio enthusiast, and made an appearance on WJZ. When the *Eagle* was invited to contribute a series of talks to the WEAF schedule, H. V. Kaltenborn, now the *Eagle's* associate editor, was the inevitable choice. The *Eagle* got the time free. Kaltenborn's clipped, energetic half-hour reviews of the world situation— later a shorter period was used—began at once to have an impact. He always gave listeners a sense that they had glimpsed, through his analysis, the true complexity of an issue; but in the end he also provided a clarifying feeling. This was often no more than an attitude. He saw hope; or, things looked ominous; or, the situation would have to be watched very closely.

Early in 1924 Kaltenborn discussed United States relations to the Soviet

16. On November 15, 1936, discussing Western hemisphere issues over CBS: "My first contact with the Latin-American problem was as a soldier in the Spanish War." On January 1, 1940, over CBS: "No one who, like myself, shared the tragic responsibility of looking after a company of untrained American soldiers in the Spanish War wants to minimize the criminal mistakes of that unnecessary war." Quoted in Chester, *The Radio Commentaries of H. V. Kaltenborn*, pp. 60-61.

THIS FORM FURNISHED BY
"BENJAMINS"
DE FOREST RADIOPHONES
DANVILLE, ILLINOIS

Danville, Ill. *Jan. 2* 1924

RECEIVED
DATE NO. JAN 4 1924
BY ANSWERED

An appreciation for the *talk* Received by the under-
signed on *Jan 1,* 1924 , *7-8-9* A. M. TO
P. M.
Received on a *De Forest Radiophone*
. Remarks: *Every word clearly heard.*
Think Mr. Kaltenborn most inter-
esting — some one said " He knows
everything."

Reception: Excellent ✓ / Good / Fair / Poor

Name *Mr. and Mrs. Chas. Payne,*
1628 N. Vermilion,
Danville, Ill.

Weather *Very cold.*

Mass Communications History Center

Kaltenborn fan note, written on one of the "applause
cards" distributed by many early radio dealers.

Union. Foreign commissar Maxim Litvinov had written to Washington indicating a desire for diplomatic relations. Kaltenborn considered Litvinov's message "tactful and carefully phrased." However, Secretary of State Charles Evans Hughes had rejected the Soviet Union's bid for recognition, and done so with a curtness Kaltenborn considered unfortunate. "So I criticized Secretary of State Hughes for the abrupt way in which he had responded to the overture from the Russians." According to Kaltenborn's understanding, subsequent events followed these lines. The Secretary of State was tuned to the broadcast in the company of "a number of prominent guests." He was embarrassed and angry. A Washingon representative of the telephone company was called to the phone, and "Secretary of State Hughes laid down the law to him." The word was relayed to New York that "this fellow Kaltenborn should not be allowed to criticize a cabinet member over the facilities of the New York Telephone Company." [17]

William E. Harkness, who was WEAF manager at the time, has essentially confirmed this account, telling us that a Kaltenborn commentary

17. Kaltenborn, *Reminiscences*, p. 104.

"was the cause of a complaint from Washington which resulted in my being instructed to take him off the air." [18]

William P. Banning, who was a public relations executive at AT&T, has written that the company had a "fundamental policy of constant and complete cooperation with every government institution that was concerned with communications." The company's readiness to remove a speaker was presumably an expression of this policy. In its zeal, the company not only responded to objections but anticipated them. According to Harkness, "We used the blue pencil quite freely in the early days." [19]

According to Edgar H. Felix, who joined WEAF to handle publicity, the Kaltenborn episode and other disputes gave the telephone executives "nightmares." They had originally embraced the "toll" conception with the beguiling thought that they could lease facilities without responsibility; this seemed a sound telephone approach. Now they were enmeshed in agonizing policy problems. Should they try to escape them by returning to the wire-broadcasting idea? At AT&T the "wire people" began to be heard again.[20]

In this fashion news analysis made a shaky entry into broadcasting. It is hard to conceive of a policy more inimical to journalism—news or news analysis—than one of "constant and complete cooperation" with government agencies.

While removing Kaltenborn, WEAF also appears to have decided that henceforth the *Eagle* would have to pay for time. The *Eagle* told its readers it was withdrawing from broadcasting because WEAF was asking ten dollars a minute. Letters from listeners fumed over the "rapacity" of the WEAF management. One letter printed by the *Eagle* said: "We will raise that ten dollars a minute for WEAF, even if we have to cut out sirloin steak." [21]

The crisis passed and radio news and comment survived. That summer Kaltenborn led an *Eagle* travel tour of national parks, and en route managed to broadcast current-events talks from cities large and small. Many a long-distance fan had already heard him, and everywhere he was welcomed. The tour gave him a vivid glimpse of broadcasting stations of mid-1924. "I spoke from stations in all sorts of out-of-the-way places—barns,

18. Harkness, *Reminiscences*, p. 35.
19. *Ibid.* p. 34; Banning, *Commercial Broadcasting Pioneer*, p. 172.
20. Felix, *Reminiscences*, p. 50.
21. Brooklyn *Eagle*, June 12, 1924. Quoted, Chester, *The Radio Commentaries of H. V. Kaltenborn*, p. 88.

garages, fraternity headquarters, shops, office buildings, and stores." A Denver station was in a home, with the control room in the kitchen. He also broadcast from WDAF, Kansas City; KHJ, Los Angeles; KPO, San Francisco; KDYL, Salt Lake City; WOAW, Omaha; WLS, Chicago. On his return to Brooklyn he resumed his *Eagle* broadcasts over WAHG, Brooklyn—the station of Alfred H. Grebe, the set manufacturer locked in legal dispute with RCA—and later over WOR, Newark. On WOR he criticized the corrupt New York City administration of James J. Walker. A Walker representative advised the station owners, the Bamberger department store, to restrain Kaltenborn. Municipal functions would otherwise be barred to WOR personnel. The department store, across the river in Newark, decided to ignore the advice. WOR, said Kaltenborn gratefully, "gave me freedom of speech." [22]

While radio was exploring, in halting fashion, news reporting and analysis, it was already on occasion a maker of news. On April 30, 1923, the six-year-old son of Ernst F. W. Alexanderson, developer of the alternator, was lured from home by the promise of a gift of rabbits. He was kidnapped. Bert Jarvis of Theresa (pop. 1000), Jefferson County, New York, heard the news on WGY in the form of an appeal by Alexanderson himself. Jarvis was caretaker of a group of summer cottages. The broadcast description seemed to fit that of a child brought to one of the cottages by a man and woman. Jarvis alerted police. As a result the boy, Verner Alexanderson, was restored to his parents. "RADIO REPAYS ITS GENIUS," *Radio Broadcast* headlined the story.[23]

On a stormy night in January 1924, at about eight o'clock, operators at all New York City stations heard a broadcast SOS and, according to law, promptly left the air. For hundreds of thousands of listeners, a sudden silence.

At WOR the artists for several scheduled programs, about thirty or forty in number, stood waiting—baritones, tenors, sopranos, contraltos, instrumentalists, announcers. Station manager Joseph Barnett was informed by his engineer Jack Poppele that the dirigible *Shenandoah*, while being moored at Lakehurst, had broken loose and was adrift. Barnett called Lakehurst for confirmation. He learned that the Lakehurst wireless transmitter had at the same time been blown down; the ground crew was out

22. Kaltenborn, *Reminiscences*, pp. 111, 129, 158.
23. *Radio Broadcast*, August 1923.

of touch with the dirigible. "Can we communicate with them for you?" Barnett asked. A Commander Klein welcomed the idea. "Do you order us back on the air?" asked Barnett. The Commander then designated WOR the official voice of the Lakehurst installation. On the basis of this authorization, WOR returned to the air, and had a local monopoly. It began asking listeners to phone the broadcasting station if they heard the *Shenandoah*'s motors. The waiting performers were posted at telephones in various parts of the Bamberger store. As calls came in, others rushed the information to the studio. With pins on a map the course of the *Shenandoah* was plotted in the studio. With a vast and growing audience listening, WOR now began addressing the crew of the *Shenandoah*. Careening through black clouds, it did not know its position or course until informed by WOR. Guided by WOR—which kept getting calls from listeners—the *Shenandoah* began struggling back toward Lakehurst. Listeners did not see the ship; it was the roar of the motors that made possible the charting of the path. During much of the night the ship's crew could not see the ground; minute by minute it was told its position. The crew replied in code, received by operator Poppele on the roof of the store. At about midnight the *Shenandoah* neared home. On the roof of Bamberger's, Poppele heard the roar of the motors above. "And all of a sudden there was a rift in the clouds and there she was!" The *Shenandoah,* at the same time, began to glimpse land. At about four o'clock in the morning she was brought down at Lakehurst. Later that day WOR resumed the potted-palm ritual, perhaps with some feeling that more meaningful roles awaited broadcasters.[24]

That feeling gave importance to other concurrent explorations—of a technical sort. Especially important were those that followed the path of the AT&T long lines. Though technical, they eventually revolutionized programming and raised social problems of wide ramifications. The explorations began in a way that was modest, even quaint.

Remote pickups using telephone, telegraph, or special wires—from stadiums, theaters, churches, banquet halls, lecture halls, hotels—had been familiar since 1921, but the linking of two stations for the same broadcast presented more difficulty. In October 1922, WJZ, Newark, and WGY, Schenectady, were linked by telegraph wire for broadcasts of the World Series. In January 1923, WEAF, New York, and WNAC, Boston, were linked by

24. Barnett, *Reminiscences,* p. 28.

telephone line for a musical program. Neither broadcast was technically satisfactory. The WEAF-WNAC hookup convinced AT&T engineers that they would have to set aside and maintain special circuits for broadcasting, and that a specially developed cable would be needed, on which work progressed during the following months. They would also need more experience. That summer they were offered the experience by a bizarre development.

Colonel Edward H. R. Green, an eccentric millionaire, had built a broadcasting station on his estate at South Dartmouth, Mass., with call letters WMAF. He was proud of his hobby and, to share its blessings with the town people, he had loudspeakers mounted on telephone poles in the area.[25] He sat at home and played favorite records for the neighborhood via a Western Electric transmitter. Everything was of the best quality. To his chagrin he found the town people not especially grateful; some were even resentful because WMAF prevented them from getting WEAF and other New York stations.

Colonel Green knew AT&T President Thayer and knew of the special line run to the executive's home in New Canaan, Conn. Why not to Massachusetts? The colonel notified WEAF that he would like its entire program schedule sent by telephone lines to his estate for broadcast over WMAF; he requested an estimate of costs. Journeying to New York to get the details, he was visited at his Waldorf-Astoria suite by William E. Harkness of WEAF, who told him it would cost about $60,000 a year. "After some discussion and joking on his part, he accepted our proposition." By July 1, 1923, the required cable was installed—the first permanent hookup between two stations—and provided WEAF engineers with just the experience they needed in line amplification and equalization. Each month Colonel Green received a bill. In addition to line rental, he paid for unsponsored programs at a fixed rate; he carried sponsored programs free of charge.[26]

Having lost a leg early in life and also suffering from rheumatism, Colonel Green was confined to a wheel chair. His whims and demands often seemed to spring from an urge for human contact. Each month he found something in his bill to protest and would journey from South Dartmouth to New York to confer about it. Having made his point and having re-

25. Felix, *Reminiscences*, p. 37.
26. Harkness, *Reminiscences*, p. 54. Archer, *History of Radio*, p. 314.

ceived a concession, however small, he would return home. There he delighted in the service he was providing his neighbors. For fight broadcasts he erected a loudspeaker on the water tower of his estate and allowed people from miles around to drive in and cut up his lawns.[27]

Because the cable from New York to South Dartmouth ran via Providence, R.I., AT&T decided at the end of the summer of 1923 to offer an arrangement to WJAR, Providence—an AT&T-licensed station. It was operated by the Samuels brothers at their store, the Outlet. Under the arrangement, WEAF was to have the right to sell time over WJAR; for each sponsored hour WEAF would recompense the Samuels brothers with two hours of unsponsored programming without charge. A plan for network operation thus began to take shape; other stations were soon added.

AT&T had originally mapped a chain of thirty-eight stations of its own for nation-wide coverage. In view of the already congested state of the spectrum, the plan as envisioned would not be easy to put into effect. A new plan gradually superseded it: stations equipped or licensed by AT&T would in one way or another be incorporated into the toll plan. AT&T would thus without delay be able to offer sponsors a group of stations as a package.

The AT&T web of wires and the spectacular events they could bring to the broadcasting station and its listeners were powerful elements in furthering the AT&T plan.

From the summer of 1923, when three stations were first linked, the technology of chain operation was rapidly developed and its possibilities dramatized. By the end of the year a six-station hookup was used; by the end of 1924, a coast-to-coast hookup of twenty-six stations.

Public events were usually the occasion for unveiling progress. The growth of the chain thus became a chronicle of moments holding national attention. Some provided little more than platform platitudes; others, moments of astonishment in which the world made a jarring intrusion into the ritual of the ferns. A few events are worth mentioning.

On June 21, 1923, President Warren G. Harding, starting on a westward trip, spoke on "The World Court" in St. Louis. Adherence to the World Court was recommended within an isolationist framework that still rejected the League of Nations. The speech was heard in St. Louis over KSD and in New York and Washington over AT&T stations WEAF

27. Harkness, *Reminiscences*, p. 91.

and WCAP. It seemed possible, said *Radio Broadcast*, that a million people had heard him.[28] No President had even spoken to such numbers.

The President's destination was Alaska, and the schedule called for a homecoming speech in San Francisco on July 31. AT&T planned its first coast-to-coast chain broadcast for the occasion—linking KPO, San Francisco, with WEAF, New York and several other stations. Secretary of Commerce Hoover joined the auspicious presidential tour. During the trip he found Harding "exceedingly nervous and distraught"; in one conversation the President hinted at "a great scandal in our administration." Late in July he fell ill; the speech and broadcast were canceled. On August 2 he was dead.[29]

In the transition that followed, broadcasting played virtually no role. As Calvin Coolidge was sworn in by his father—a notary public—in a Vermont kitchen by kerosene light, no broadcasters were on hand. At news of Harding's death, some stations had even left the air "as a mark of respect." Some played religious music—especially "I Know That My Redeemer Liveth," which was said to be Harding's favorite religious song.

Within a few months, chain broadcasting found occasion to renew its progress. On December 4, 1923, the opening of Congress was broadcast for the first time. President Coolidge's message to Congress was broadcast by a chain of seven stations linked by AT&T cables and extending westward to WFAA, Dallas.

The broadcast produced a surprise. To those who had met Coolidge, his voice seemed flat, uninteresting. But on the air an unexpected resonance appeared. The close pickup made necessary by his uninflated delivery emphasized lower tones. Whereas Harding's more traditional oratory had sounded hollow on the air, the Coolidge face-to-face manner proved a revelation, striking in its absence of artifice. Even the nasal quality of his voice seemed to contribute to this. At the same time the wide-open microphone allowed millions to hear clearly the turning of pages, which seemed to provide a gratifying touch of intimacy.[30] During the following weeks President Coolidge made other radio appearances and firmly established himself as a radio personality.

He also began to be interviewed by journalists—among them, *Eagle* editor and broadcaster H. V. Kaltenborn. This interview took place in the

28. *Radio Broadcast*, September 1923.
29. Hoover, *Memoirs: The Cabinet and the Presidency*, p. 49.
30. Archer, *History of Radio*, p. 324.

Oval Room. The President stood up to receive him. "Sit down (pause) for a minute." Kaltenborn asked whether the President favored some form of co-operation with the League of Nations. Would he make a statement on the subject? He would. "I think we are very snug as we are." [31]

While the Coolidge personality was impressing itself on the nation, especially through radio, another presidential voice had been heard on the air. This broadcast and its aftermath were among the strangest episodes in radio annals.

In the fall of 1923 it occurred to Bernard Baruch's daughter Belle, who was working for United States entry into the League, to ask Woodrow Wilson to broadcast a few words the day before Armistice Day. He was living in seclusion in a house on S Street in Washington, a sick man with ashen skin, one arm helpless, a face twisted to one side. He was almost forgotten. For a time a guard had been posted, but this seemed unnecessary and he was removed. Mr. Wilson sometimes tried to write but found it hard to keep his mind focused; he was failing fast. He had heard a few broadcasts and disliked them intensely. But the request for an Armistice Day message was something he did not want to refuse.[32]

On November 10 he stood—he insisted on standing—in front of a microphone in the library of his house on S Street. The announcer said: "Mr. Woodrow Wilson will now say a few words." AT&T had arranged a hookup of WCAP, Washington; WEAF, New York; and WJAR, Providence; but the broadcast was going farther. Without telephone company authorization, the chief engineer at WGY, Schenectady, decided to pick it up on an ordinary receiver and rebroadcast it simultaneously over the General Electric station.[33]

Ex-President Wilson, struggling to recall the words he had written with the help of his wife, could not remember them. A typed script was before him but he had trouble seeing it. His voice began so feebly—with intermittent gasps—that many listeners could hardly hear him. But from some resource he gathered strength and continued. A few times he stopped completely and Mrs. Wilson was heard whispering the next words in the background. Finally he finished. The last words heard by the radio audience, after a pause, were Wilson's question: "That is all, isn't it?" [34]

It wasn't quite all. On the next day, Armistice Day, coming on foot, by

31. Kaltenborn, *Reminiscences*, p. 154.
32. Smith, *When the Cheering Stopped*, p. 223.
33. Wagoner, *Reminiscences*, p. 25.
34. Smith, *When the Cheering Stopped*, p. 224.

trolley and by car, an estimated twenty thousand people came to stand in front of the S Street house. They gathered in the early afternoon and stood there. At one time they covered an area five blocks in every direction. It was as though the broadcast had helped to remind them of a ghost who still walked among them. Or perhaps, as some suggested, he was a link with something within themselves, almost suppressed and forgotten, that would not quite die. The ex-President came out to say a few words and managed to exclaim, with surprising spirit and volume: "That we shall prevail is as sure as that God reigns!" [35]

A few weeks later he was dead. The funeral services on February 6, 1924, were carried by WCAP, Washington; WEAF, New York; WJAR, Providence; and perhaps others.

Meanwhile President Coolidge had been heard again on the air, speaking from the White House, and during the following months was heard often. The 1924 campaign had begun.

That campaign was momentous in the development of chain operation. The conventions of 1924 provided sensational stimulus at precisely the time the broadcasters were technically ready for the challenge. The year saw an economic recession, but broadcasting hardly felt it. Under the impact of the conventions, set sales skyrocketed.

The Republican convention in Cleveland, June 10-12, provided little hint of the drama to come. The Coolidge-Dawes ticket was quickly chosen; Will Rogers said it could have been done by postcard.[36] But for broadcasters it was a useful dress rehearsal.

On June 24 the scene shifted to New York City, to the Democratic convention in the old Madison Square Garden. Here the drama began. By the end of the Democratic convention, which lasted fifteen days and saw 103 ballots for the presidency, eighteen stations were linked by AT&T cables, receiving broadcast descriptions from WEAF. These stations included some with Western Electric transmitters and some that had, by this time, paid the AT&T license fee. To receive the convention broadcast they also paid cable charges.

General Electric and RCA, locked in a behind-the-scenes feud with AT&T, put together a few stations linked by telegraph lines and fed by WJZ. The public felt it was witnessing a zealous, friendly rivalry, but far more was involved.

35. *Ibid.* pp. 225-8.
36. New York *Times,* June 19, 1924.

In equipment and coverage, the AT&T group easily had the better of it.

The WEAF chain heard a broadcast description by Graham McNamee, who had begun to make an impression describing sports events; he was assisted by a newcomer, Phillips Carlin. The WJZ chain had Major J. Andrew White, editor of *Wireless Age*, who had begun his broadcasting career with the Dempsey-Carpentier fight; he was also assisted by a newcomer, Norman Brokenshire. Each of the main announcers worked in a small glass box on the platform. For added perspective Carlin was in a "birdcage-like contraption hanging high above the floor among the steel girders of the arena." [37] There were microphones to pick up speeches, band music, pipe organ, and crowd sounds. For emergencies, participating stations had musical artists standing by, ready with studio programs.

The Democratic convention provided listeners with something they had never heard before. In contrast to the smooth, well-managed Republican meeting, it thrust on the listening audience a no-holds-barred struggle in which raw emotion came to the surface. Again and again listeners heard it in the hoarse roar of the crowd and in disputes that erupted into violence within earshot of microphones. One element in the tension was the issue of the Ku Klux Klan, rumored to control a large block of votes. Roman Catholic Alfred E. Smith, one of the two leading candidates, pressed for condemnation of the Klan. William G. McAdoo, the other leading candidate—a beneficiary of the Klan's anti-Catholicism—quietly opposed the move as divisive. William Jennings Bryan, aging standard bearer of the party and by now a kind of curio, still revered by many, essayed the role of peacemaker. In a resolutions committee meeting, when two delegates came to blows on the Klan issue, Bryan thrust himself between them and fell on his knees and prayed, apparently averting bloodshed. McNamee described the incident on the air. Later Bryan, from the platform, begged the convention not to mention the Klan by name in any resolution. Many cheered him but in reply an angry, throaty roar rose from the galleries and floor, engulfing speaker, chairman and gavel. Ben Gross, a reporter who would soon turn radio columnist, was astonished and frightened by its anger.[38]

Democratic party officials, alarmed at the tension within the party, had stationed an official censor on the platform to interrupt the radio coverage

37. Gross, *I Looked and Listened*, p. 205.
38. *Ibid.* p. 206.

of any speech that might sound divisive. But the roar, not the speeches, told the story to the millions.

Newcomer Norman Brokenshire had the job of leg man for Major White. Racing around Madison Square Garden, young Brokenshire gathered bits of information, anecdotes, and rumors of switches in votes. When the major went out to lunch, Brokenshire also had brief periods on the air. During one of these a fight developed nearby.

> Spotting it, wanting to do well for the glory of WJZ, I concentrated on the fight and let everything else go by. I explained that one whole delegation had blustered across the aisle to register a complaint, following with a blow-by-blow eyewitness account of one of the finest donnybrooks I'd ever seen. Delegation signs were banged on opponents' heads, chairs and decorations destroyed: I had a ringside seat. I was letting the listening audience in on the fracas when Major White walked in. When he grasped what I was doing, his face turned pale, he grabbed the microphone from me, signaled the operator to take us off the air, picked up a telephone, and called the studio. We were off the air only a few seconds. Keith McLeod came on, playing "Träumerei."

A short while later Major White, "with elegant composure," began broadcasting again. "And now, ladies and gentlemen, we resume from Madison Square Garden and the Democratic National Convention." In a spare moment he explained to the raw recruit that the Democratic party had granted WJZ the right to broadcast the convention with the distinct understanding that no disorders of any kind would be reported.[39]

This convention, in the course of the 103 roll-call votes in stifling summer heat that finally produced the nomination of John W. Davis, also generated humor. Each roll-call began with the words of Alabama's Governor Brandon, sung to the rafters: "A-la-ba-ma casts twenty-four votes for Oscar W. Underwood!" After a few ballots the galleries began to join in the refrain. In communities far and wide groups before loudspeakers—in restaurants, clubs, radio stores, homes—took up the game. For years it was a vaudeville joke.

The conventions of 1924 had a fateful impact on broadcasting. The stations that had become associated with AT&T via transmitter purchases or licenses and were prepared to pay the substantial line charges won the radio spotlight. They became prestige stations. To be sure, they paid for this with increasing costs which would soon produce policy crises, at one

39. Brokenshire, *This Is Norman Brokenshire*, pp. 41-9.

station after another. On the other hand, stations not participating in these chain developments were slipping into a lesser role.

The power thus exerted by AT&T through its web of cables was deeply disturbing to General Electric and Westinghouse and their sales agent, RCA. The cables seemed to them a weapon used by AT&T to achieve dominance of radio. Not surprisingly, they pressed the search for alternative means of chain operation. They were using telegraph lines and seeking desperately to "doctor the hum." [40] But they were also looking in another direction.

In 1923 Conrad and others at Westinghouse began relentlessly to explore a new realm—the short waves. A corresponding exploration went on at General Electric.

When KDKA began broadcasting church services from the Point Breeze Presbyterian Church, there was more involved than a contribution to religion. Westinghouse arranged a wire connection with the church but also placed in the church steeple a 200-watt short-wave transmitter. Two ways of relaying the services to KDKA were thus available. During broadcasts the engineers sometimes switched from one to the other to compare results. When the short-wave link was in use, the engineers at each end conversed via the wire link, and vice versa. Once they talked via the wrong link so that a prayer was broadcast with an obbligato by Donald Little: "One, two. three, four, testing . . ." To extend this exploration, Westinghouse began sending out KDKA programs via an experimental short-wave transmitter. It also established a broadcasting station in Cleveland—KDPM, a "satellite" station—which merely rebroadcast KDKA programs picked up by short-wave. Results were often brilliant; sometimes "hash." To pursue the experiment further Westinghouse built KFKX, Hastings Nebraska, feeding it programs via short-wave. The tests made it increasingly clear that short waves, while erratic, could achieve fantastic distances.[41]

Others were discovering the same thing, and there was irony in this. With the advent of broadcasting, amateurs had been banished to the short-wave region, which was thought of as a kind of Siberia, commercially and militarily useless. After initial indignation they had begun to explore this wilderness and found it fruitful beyond their imagining. During 1923 American and French amateurs began chatting with each other across the

40. Hager, *Reminiscences*, pp. 16-17.
41. Little, *Reminiscences*, pp. 35-6.

Atlantic Ocean.[42] By now Guglielmo Marconi was also saying that the
short waves had been mistakenly neglected.

In 1924 Conrad went to an international conference in London, also
attended by David Sarnoff. According to Donald Little, Conrad was a
baseball enthusiast and had arranged for the Westinghouse short-wave
transmitter in Pittsburgh to report the baseball scores at particular times
each day. He took with him a single-tube set designed for short-wave
reception and thus got his scores. He invited Sarnoff in for a demonstration, and using his hotel-room curtain rod as antenna, he let Sarnoff hear
Pittsburgh on the one-tube set.[43] Such moments spelled the doom of the
Alexanderson alternators; those huge machines, which had hurled their
signals across the Atlantic with overwhelming power, were now an anach-
ronism. The future was not in great power but in short waves.

While such findings brought a reorientation in the RCA transoceanic
message business, they also held revolutionary implications for broadcasting. In March 1924 the speeches at a Massachusetts Institute of Technology alumni dinner were short-waved to England and rebroadcast there. In
October, a station in Cape Town, South Africa, rebroadcast a KDKA program relayed by short-wave.[44] The whole world loomed as a program
source.

In the final months of the 1924 election campaign these developments
injected themselves in odd fashion into the contest.

On October 11 the H. J. Heinz Company, celebrating its fifty-fifth anniversary, was holding simultaneous banquets in a number of cities. President Coolidge agreed to address the banqueters, and Westinghouse arranged to send his and other speeches by short-wave from the Pittsburgh
transmitter and rebroadcast them from various broadcasting stations.
Thus ten thousand banqueters in a number of cities—and of course many
other people—heard the Coolidge address from KDKA, Pittsburgh; KYW,
Chicago; WBZ, Springfield; KFKX, Hastings; and other stations. A network reaching millions had been linked by short-wave. Would it prove a
weapon in the struggle for dominance?

Three weeks later President Coolidge, on election eve, again spoke to
the nation. This time it was on an AT&T network of twenty-six stations,

42. Dunlap, *Radio and Television Almanac*, p. 73.
43. Little, *Reminiscences*, p. 34.
44. Dunlap, *Radio and Television Almanac*, pp. 72-9.

coast to coast. He was thought to have reached "twenty to thirty million people." Again, no President had ever addressed so many.[45]

Each of these Coolidge broadcasts was an historic step in the growth of a medium; also, a move in an industry struggle.

We have noted that after World War I, Lee de Forest devoted his main attention to the sound film. By April 1923 his experiments had reached the demonstration stage. At New York's Rivoli Theater a monologue and song by Eddie Cantor and several other vaudeville acts were used to unveil the De Forest Phonofilm process.[46] Again various researchers were moving along parallel lines. Western Electric was at the same time demonstrating a system for synchronizing disc and film. General Electric had a development of its own, the Pallophotophone. This had emerged from wartime experiments in recording radio signals for reference and decoding. The Pallophotophone recorded signals photographically on a moving tape. GE, with no thought of nursing this into a talking-film device, saw it as an adjunct to radio. On December 24, 1922, Calvin Coolidge as Vice President recorded a holiday message by Pallophotophone for broadcast over WGY. When the recording was played for him, Coolidge heard his own nasal voice for the first time and was shocked, but Mrs. Coolidge said the recording sounded "quite natural" and it was used.[47] A few months later GE researchers, apparently goaded by the work of De Forest and Western Electric, demonstrated that the Pallophotophone could be synchronized with film. It later became the RCA Photophone process.

Meanwhile research was jabbing in other directions. At a 1923 luncheon of GE engineers, Owen D. Young said, according to the recollection of Ernst F. W. Alexanderson: "I'm getting tired of dots and dashes. Why don't you make a system so that you can put in a written letter and *zip*—it will come out just as it is written at the other end?"[48] The engineers smiled; Young liked to make suggestions, without any notion of what was involved. But the transmission of documents and pictures in "facsimile" by the scanning method became a reality within months. In July 1924 RCA was sending a "radio photo" of Charles Evans Hughes across the Atlantic; the idea of a radio newspaper, a "facsimile newspaper," began to be discussed. Facsimile was basically television in slow-motion form. The same

45. Weeks, "The Radio Election of 1924," *Journal of Broadcasting,* Summer 1964.
46. De Forest, *Father of Radio,* p. 370. *Variety,* April 15, 1923.
47. Hager, *Reminiscences,* p. 5.
48. Alexanderson, *Reminiscences,* pp. 37-8.

procedure, speeded for the televising of motion, was already being developed at Westinghouse. Late in December 1923, Vladimir Zworykin demonstrated for Westinghouse executives in crude yet practical form a partly electronic television system.[49] On December 29 a patent application was filed. Throughout 1924 the research was pursued—and paralleled by research elsewhere. Meanwhile Edwin H. Armstrong, having sold to RCA his patent in a new idea—the super-regenerative circuit—was turning his attention to still another and more radical notion: the elimination of static through frequency modulation.

The years 1923 and 1924 can be seen as a period of constant technical probing in the broadcasting field. During this time a community antenna system even made its appearance: in Dundee, Michigan, a company was offering subscribers a wire service to the home at $1.50 per month, with a choice of programs from several stations.[50]

In 1924 Americans invested a fantastic $358,000,000 in radio sets and parts—up from $136,000,000 spent in the previous year.[51] Radio listening was becoming a major occupation. The silent film was likewise holding audiences spellbound. In both media the *status quo* appeared to have solid support. Yet laboratory explorations were diagramming upheavals that would shake both—and bring them together in the arena of television.

If explorations in programming and technology were preparing for change, still other explorations were making change inevitable. These were in the realm of economics.

The economic explorations were spurred by a number of factors. Broadcasts of public events via telephone lines involved seemingly fantastic costs, which had not been foreseen. Demands for payment of artists increased the pressure. The question, "How will broadcasting be financed?" had hardly been asked in 1921. During 1922 it became a conversational topic. In 1923 and 1924 it was asked with increasing urgency. In 1925 it reached a crisis stage.

The industry discourse on the topic had begun almost academically. The magazine *Radio Broadcast* had raised the question in its first issue in May 1922. The magazine considered it likely that equipment manufacturers—the first to create a demand for radios by regular broadcasting—

49. Dunlap, *Radio and Television Almanac*, p. 75.
50. *Radio Broadcast*, May 1923.
51. *Broadcasting*, 1939 Yearbook, p. 11.

WJZ: Thomas H. Cowan in "cloak-room" studio, 1921.

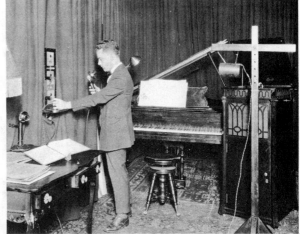

Cowan collection

KYW: Walter C. Evans at Chicago Civic Opera, 1921.

NBC

KDKA: Tent on roof for orchestral performance, 1921.

NBC

Olga Petrova: just a nursery rhyme
—her own version.

Cowan collection

Eddie Cantor: joins the parade.

Smithsonian Institution

Billy Jones and Ernie Hare: with Helen Hann,
WEAF hostess-accompanist.

NBC

would have less interest in bearing the cost after the radio-buying boom subsided. For this reason "some different scheme of financing" would have to emerge, and the magazine mentioned several possibilities.[52]

One was "endowment of a station by a public-spirited citizen." Only a decade or so earlier Andrew Carnegie had spent his final years founding libraries, sometimes at the rate of several a day. He would come to his office and find a small pile of the necessary documents on his desk, ready to be signed. He would ask his secretary a few questions about each, and add his signature—$60,000 here, $78,000 there. There was no sin in getting rich, he liked to say, but there was in dying rich. Signing diligently, he converted imminent sin into more than 2500 libraries. The memory of this orgy of giving lent plausibility to the suggestion made by *Radio Broadcast*. But although a few Colonel Greens had started hobby stations, and some college stations had been helped by gifts, no one resembling a Carnegie had yet appeared on the radio scene.

A second suggestion was "municipal financing." The magazine recognized that some would consider this socialistic, but expressed the opinion that the idea was "not so strange," considering that cities financed schools, museums, and other institutions of learning and culture. This view, as we have seen, coincided with that of Grover Whalen and Rodman Wanamaker, who in that same year began determined efforts to establish a New York City station. But their success in founding WNYC in 1924 was achieved against strong and highly placed opposition. Whalen found the Department of Commerce suspicious. Secretary Hoover, with whom he discussed the project, "had to be convinced."[53] AT&T informed Whalen that lines for remote broadcasts would not be provided. The telephone executives continued efforts to head off the plan, urging the city to use WEAF. Time would always be available, they told Whalen. He replied that this would last "for a honeymoon period."[54] His stubbornness made "municipal financing" a reality in New York; the idea also materialized in a few other cities, but on a small scale.

Financing by states, not mentioned by *Radio Broadcast*, appeared more widely. From the start, some of the most stable educational stations were those founded by states, in many cases on state university campuses.

52. *Radio Broadcast*, May 1922.
53. Whalen, *Reminiscences*, p. 11.
54. Cowan, *Reminiscences*, p. 40. During this period, according to Edward L. Bernays, Whalen was seeking his advice on how to become President. Bernays, *Biography of an Idea*, p. 362.

Another possibility suggested by *Radio Broadcast* was "a common fund . . . controlled by an elected board." Contributions to the fund might come from many sources. The idea of inviting donations from the public was discussed from time to time and even tried—curiously enough—by AT&T. We have noted that WEAF, the original toll station, did not pay talent performing in unsponsored periods. The telephone company was occasionally told that this was an outrage. Early in 1924, expressing its agreement that performers should be paid, the telephone company announced that it was establishing a fund, to which anyone might contribute and thus help support talented and deserving artists appearing on WEAF. A goal of $20,000 was announced and the fund promoted on WEAF. After about $1000 had been collected, the idea was abandoned.[55] Its quasi-philanthropic nature had aroused some skepticism; contributions are said to have been returned.[56]

Another fund scheme was developed by WHB, Kansas City. Listeners were invited to send money for imaginary seats in an "invisible theater" of radio. Ten dollars entitled the contributor to a box seat, five dollars to a loge seat, three dollars to a parquet seat, two dollars to a balcony seat, one dollar to a gallery seat—all equally mythical but bringing in some three thousand genuine dollars.[57]

It is worth noting that in its first discussion of economic alternatives, *Radio Broadcast* did not mention advertising as a possible means of support. The WEAF experiment was still to come.

It should also be noted that the plan soon to be adopted by Britain and others—a tax on receivers to support a broadcasting service—likewise went unmentioned by *Radio Broadcast* at this time. However, when the magazine later offered a $500 prize for the best essay on the topic, "Who is to pay for broadcasting—and how," the award went to an essay that recommended a version of the British plan. The writer proposed that each set be taxed at the rate of $2 per tube, or 50¢ for a crystal set—a graduated tax, instead of a flat fee such as the ten-shilling fee adopted in Britain. The writer estimated that his plan would provide an annual fund of $18,000,-000 to be turned over to a central broadcasting organization.[58]

A variation of this plan was long championed by David Sarnoff. Since 1922 he had urged that a separate organization be set up to carry on

55. Carlin, *Reminiscences*, p. 13.
56. Archer, *History of Radio*, p. 329.
57. Landry, *This Fascinating Radio Business*, p. 46.
58. *Radio Broadcast*, March 1925.

broadcasting as a national service, and that this be financed by a levy on the sale of equipment. Under the Sarnoff plan the collection would be handled by the industry itself, not by government. The service would be controlled by a board on which the industry and the public would be represented. "A fair method of determining the amount to be paid by each member, or portion of the industry, will be worked out and this will be based on a percentage of the sale price of the radio devices." [59]

This variation of the license-fee plan, like other Sarnoff blueprints, was impressive and convincing in its reasoning. If it did not materialize in the form in which Sarnoff proposed it, one reason may have been that RCA and its manufacturing partners, GE and Westinghouse, were divided from the rest of the industry by a chasm of hostility. Virtually all other set manufacturers had been pilloried by the allies as patent-infringers, and were in turn assailing the allies as "the trust." Under the circumstances the co-operative plan outlined by Sarnoff seemed only a remote possibility.

But all such plans tended in any case to remain doctrinaire notions because toll broadcasting was surviving and gaining. Every development at WEAF was watched and studied by the industry. All broadcasters seemed to be feeling WEAF's pulse. Their own decisions depended on WEAF developments. All felt the pressure of its successes, which came slowly, then quickened.

For a time advertisers were baffled as to how to use this new access to public attention. Several early toll users emulated the Jackson Heights promoters and looked to history—or quasi-history. An association of greeting card manufacturers presented a talk on the history of Christmas cards. The Haynes company presented the story of the Haynes automobile as told by Mr. Haynes.[60] Gillette offered a talk on fashions in beards since medieval times, culminating in the delights of the safety razor. The resemblance to a carnival pitch was close enough to be uncomfortable, and the telephone executives sought to minimize this. A talk on cigarettes was "heavily censored." [61] A "discreet" talk on the teeth and their care, offered by a toothpaste company, was delayed while executives argued whether anything so personal as tooth-brushing should be mentioned on the air. It

---

59. *Ibid.* July 1924. A 10 per cent tax such as that proposed by Sarnoff was used in Britain from 1922 to 1924 to provide additional revenue for the BBC; it was abandoned because it gave advantage to imported equipment. Briggs, *The Birth of Broadcasting*, pp. 10-11.
60. Archer, *History of Radio*, pp. 288-9.
61. Felix, *Reminiscences*, p. 29. Harkness, *Reminiscences*, p. 64.

finally was. The executives yearned for profits but also for total respectability, and therefore kept devising rules. Prices were not to be mentioned. The color of a can or package was not to be mentioned. Store locations were a taboo subject. Samples were not to be offered. A vacuum cleaner company was not to use the line "sweep no more, my lady" because lovers of the song "My Old Kentucky Home" might be offended.[62]

Most of the early talks were individually booked. Economically they seemed a blind alley, and each involved prolonged sales effort and editorial anxiety. For this reason the creation of the "Browning King Orchestra" —achieved by salesman Harry C. Smith, who had also negotiated the Jackson Heights coup—seemed to WEAF staff members a "milestone." [63] Browning, King agreed *not* to offer a talk but simply to attach its name to an orchestra—Anna Byrne's orchestra. The germ of this notion already existed in such institutions as Wanamaker organ concerts and other musicales held at stores. The revolutionary ingredient was the idea that such a concert need not take place in a store, required no store studio, nor an orchestra having any real connection with the store. The link would be solely in the name "Browning King Orchestra" and the financial arrangements behind it. From this linkage good-will would flow. Seeking goodwill, Browning, King did not even mention that it sold clothing. The venture led to a rash of similar creations: the "Cliquot Club Eskimos," the "Gold Dust Twins (Goldy and Dusty)," the "Lucky Strike Orchestra," the "Ipana Troubadours," the "A&P Gypsies," the "Goodrich Silvertown Orchestra" and its "Silver Masked Tenor." To the delight of WEAF management, artists could appear under various guises. Billy Jones and Ernie Hare could be the "Happiness Boys" for Happiness candy stores, the "Interwoven Pair" for Interwoven socks, the "Best Foods Boys" for Best Foods, and the "Taystee Loafers" for Taystee bread. On the wings of such inspiration, WEAF revenue picked up in 1923 and "turned the corner" in 1924.[64]

The new formula had magic results. It quickly led to series contracts in place of single-program sales. It also reduced policy headaches. Sponsors seemed to enjoy the new approach. They were willing—for a time, at least—to settle for good-will and forgo selling effort. The 1924 trend even led H. V. Kaltenborn to write in the Brooklyn *Eagle:* "Direct advertising

62. Banning, *Commercial Broadcasting Pioneer*, pp. 108, 147-50.
63. Felix, *Reminiscences*, p. 33.
64. Chase, *Sound and Fury*, p. 29. Woods, *Reminiscences*, p. 19.

has already been abandoned by most advertisers who have tried radio as a medium." [65]

Many early WEAF sales—they included time and talent—were negotiated directly with sponsors, but WEAF began to insist that the advertising agencies sign the contracts. It also insisted on paying the agencies a 15 per cent commission, matching the commissions paid by magazines and newspapers on space sales. Thus advertising agencies were given a financial stake in growing business and in rising budgets.

With success, budgets rose rapidly. A series launched in December 1923 to sell Eveready batteries became the most ambitious effort to date. As the *Eveready Hour,* it may have been the first program to become known by its series title rather than by the name or pseudonym of a performer or group. Under supervision of the N. W. Ayer advertising agency it received lavish attention and financial backing. It sometimes offered concert music, sometimes dance music, sometimes drama. For a single program it is said to have paid Will Rogers an unheard-of $1000. The Eveready broadcasts over WEAF promptly won such favorable attention that the sponsor began to finance travel junkets for appearances of the artists over other stations under Eveready sponsorship. The proliferation of Eveready programs was obviously absurd; early in 1924 Eveready ordered a WEAF-WJAR hookup and expanded this as quickly as WEAF could add stations. The advertising agency meanwhile introduced a degree of professionalism into the production. Everything was rehearsed—an unprecedented development. All announcements were written. Bookings involved a search for spectacular novelty. In June 1924 the singer and ukulele player Wendell Hall was married on the *Eveready Hour* to a newspaper girl.[66] Such ventures won wide attention and lured other sponsors.

While the salesmanship of early entertainment sponsors on WEAF was extraordinarily restrained, there was constant effort to win audience expressions of gratitude. A sack of grateful letters was a novel experience for many advertisers and seemed at first ample proof of the good-will being purchased via the phone booth. The effort to get letters sometimes ran to aggressive coyness. In a closing announcement for the "Gold Dust Twins" the announcer said:

65. Brooklyn *Daily Eagle,* February 3, 1925.
66. Chase, *Sound and Fury,* p. 25. There had already been several local radio weddings, but the Wendell Hall broadcast probably deserves the title of "first network nuptials" and first to be solemnized under advertising agency auspices.

Perhaps you open your hearts and homes to them each week—Goldy and Dusty, the Gold Dust Twins, who come to "brighten the corner where you are," and perhaps you have written them of your pleasure, or perhaps you have delayed. Won't you then do it tonight? Notes of encouragement from the audiences of WEAF, New York; WGR, Buffalo; WEEI, Boston; WFI, Philadelphia; and WEAR, Cleveland, serve to brighten these dusky entertainers. Address the Gold Dust Twins, care of station WEAF, 195 Broadway, New York City, or the station through which this program has reached you.[67]

The letters came in a flood.

WEAF with its growing hookups and budgets became a mecca for artists. They were now less available for free performances. If stations everywhere felt the pressure of these developments, it was sensed especially by RCA's New York outlets, WJZ and WJY. RCA, still trying to program its stations on modest budgets and still fighting off ASCAP, resented WEAF's escalation of radio finances. WJZ too began to pay artists, and at the same time stepped up its campaign to persuade other companies to share the cost. Offering free time—and publicity—to companies willing to finance programs, WJZ was in essence giving away what WEAF was trying to sell. This was in turn resented by WEAF and its parent AT&T. They felt RCA was jeopardizing the toll venture. AT&T also claimed that RCA had no right, under the terms of the cross-licensing alliance, to use its station for such business purposes.

This was one element—the one clearly visible element—in the growing feud between AT&T on the one hand and RCA and its manufacturing partners on the other. Another issue between them was that of pickup and network lines, still withheld from RCA by AT&T. But a far more crucial issue was now appearing.

WASHINGTON GIFTS

During 1923 RCA had found increasing evidence that the AT&T subsidiary, Western Electric, was preparing to put a receiving set on the market. At RCA, GE, and Westinghouse this brought consternation. The alliance agreements were reread and protests conveyed to AT&T. This field, they

67. Banning, *Commercial Broadcasting Pioneer*, p. 262. On early chain broadcasts all interconnected stations were mentioned. According to Phillips Carlin, "McNamee and I used to vie with each other to see who could give the list of cities in one breath." The list finally grew too long. Carlin, *Reminiscences*, pp. 23-4.

warned, was out of bounds for the telephone company. Not so, said AT&T; its allies must have misunderstood the agreements.

At the start of 1924, RCA sets and parts, made by GE and Westinghouse, were selling at the rate of $50,000,000 a year—double the rate of the previous year. Was AT&T, while claiming sole right to broadcast for toll and to sell transmitters, also eying a slice of this $50,000,000 pie? What would such competition mean to RCA? Could its cumbersome arrangements, under which it had to co-ordinate GE and Westinghouse assembly lines, compete with the telephone colossus? Major General Harbord wrote to Owen D. Young: "It would possibly put us out of business." [1] They had ample respect for the prowess of AT&T.

RCA was in a state of alarm. A Washington episode added a note of fury. Early in 1924 RCA arranged to present a new radio to the White House for presidential use. While awaiting the setting of a presentation date, RCA learned that another set had been delivered to the White House —a superheterodyne donated by AT&T. Spies reported that it was large, magnificent, and much admired by the recipient.

The alliance agreements provided an arbitration machinery. Even before the White House incident the allies—AT&T, RCA, GE, Westinghouse, United Fruit, and subsidiaries—had agreed to arbitrate their conflicting interpretations of the alliance agreements, rather than air them in public. The machinery had been set in motion. In highest secrecy, with billions of dollars in expected revenue at stake, the case was to be argued in New York City before a single referee. His sole decision, said the arbitration agreement,

> shall constitute an adjudication binding upon each party hereto as finally and conclusively as an adjudication of a court having jurisdiction. . . . Each party hereto agrees that it will accept and conform to such determination, and after such determination has been made will not take any proceedings intended either to modify it or set it aside. . . .[2]

In January 1924, as the parties were submitting preliminary statements to referee Roland W. Boyden, they were startled by a bombshell from Washington. The Federal Trade Commission, which had recently completed its study of radio—*Report of the Federal Trade Commission on the Radio Industry*—and submitted it to Congress, now followed this with a formal

1. Archer, *Big Business and Radio*, p. 112.
2. *Ibid.* pp. 128-9.

complaint. It charged that the allies—AT&T, RCA, GE, Westinghouse, United Fruit, and subsidiaries—had "combined and conspired for the purpose of, and with the effect of, restraining competition and creating a monopoly in the manufacture, purchase and sale in interstate commerce of radio devices . . . and in domestic and transoceanic communication and broadcasting." [3] FTC hearings would look further into their agreements and competitive practices.

The FTC, like the public, seems to have been totally unaware of the behind-closed-doors arbitration launched in New York, in which the division of empire was being reviewed. The irony of the timing could therefore be appreciated by very few people.

The FTC action produced anxiety, especially in RCA. Its program of litigation was now held in abeyance as FTC developments were awaited and watched. But the highly secret arbitration was even more feared. Here the status quo faced an imminent, decisive threat.

In the arbitration the presentation of testimony began in May 1924. The FTC hearings did not begin until October of the following year. Both moved with agonizing deliberateness, and in time would converge with still other struggles. As the 1920's approached their midpoint, radio would be gripped by converging crises—in courts, Congress, Federal Trade Commission, secret arbitration. From these crises would come a new structure in American broadcasting.

Meanwhile the boom went on—in broadcasting, manufacture, setbuying. Business failures increased in number, but new entrepreneurs plunged in. The deluge of programs continued.

DEAR, DEAR FRIENDS

Christmas in 1924 was widely advertised as a "radio Christmas." In the December issue of *Radio Broadcast* more than two hundred companies advertised their equipment. They vied for attention with scores of brand names, a number of which would not face another Christmas. Among pages of slogans and promises the reader could learn about RCA's Radiola radios and Radiotron tubes and also about the De Forest Radiophone ("how many radio miles did you go last night?"), the Golden-Leutz Pliodyne-6 ("the 'perfect' receiver"), the Newport radio ("makes every day a

3. New York *Times,* January 28, 1965.

Christmas"), the Dynergy ("authorities agree on the Dynergy"), the
Splitdorf 5-tube radio ("coast-to-coast with Splitdorf"), the Crosley ("of
course it's a Crosley"), the Freed-Eisemann ("the difference is—finesse"),
the Timmons ("housed in cabinets of rare beauty"), the Brandola ("one
dial"), the Mercury ("the Stradivarius of radio"), the Sherma-Flex
("shipped on approval—send no money"), the Melco Supreme ("Aladdin
had his lamp, you have the Melco Supreme"), the Marshall ("embodying
a marvelous new, non-oscillating principle"), Magnavox ("the utmost in
quality and value"), the Kennedy ("ask Santa to bring you a Kennedy"),
not to mention such items as Na-Ald sockets and dials, the Bel-Canto
loudspeaker, and the Danziger-Jones Kit of a Thousand Possibilities.[1]

What was America hearing, as 1925 began, on this profusion of equipment? Much was as it had been a year or two earlier, but there was a
crucial new factor.

In its first years broadcasting had been dominated by anonymous personalities. The only people on the air regularly, the announcers, were
largely nameless. In this respect as in others, early radio resembled early
film, with its "Biograph girl" and other stirring mysteries. Aside from the
announcers, most performers made such fleeting appearances that few became fixed in public consciousness. The announcers, anonymous or not,
became recognizable.

In the first months at WJZ, Tommy Cowan adopted the practice of
identifying himself with a set of initials—ACN. A stood for announcer, C
for Cowan, N for Newark (later New York). The practice was considered
an echo of wireless, and continued at WJZ until 1925. Each new announcer and each "operator"—another wireless echo—received a set of
initials, starting either with A for announcer or O for operator. Because
Cowan had preempted C, Milton J. Cross became AJN.[2] Because Bertha
Brainard was ABN, Norman Brokenshire became AON. The policy apparently appealed to management for a reason that had also operated in the
early film field: the fear that performers, if identified, might become un-
manageable celebrities. There was basis for the fear. As voices became
familiar, listeners developed a compulsive curiosity about the people behind them. Everywhere stations received innumerable queries about
them. At WHAS, Louisville, these were answered with a form letter:

1. *Radio Broadcast*, December 1924.
2. Popenoe, *WJZ*, p. 16.

Dear Madam:

It is against the rules of this radio station to divulge the name of our announcer.

With deep regret, I am——[3]

This executive resistance was futile. Whether known by initials or merely by a voice, the elusive personality aroused ungovernable interest, admiration, affection, and passion.

As program patterns changed and the parade of momentary appearances gave way to weekly features, similar feelings were lavished on singers, poetry readers, and actors. As the anonymity policy broke down, unabashed idolatry followed.

The idolatry must have been furthered by changing styles of performance. In 1922 performers still imagined themselves in a vast auditorium "where rear seats are hundreds of miles from the stage," but by 1925 a cozier image was established. Many artists liked to imagine the audience as "a single person." Letters encouraged this; no other medium had ever afforded an audience this illusion of intimacy shielded by privacy.

Many a performer began getting letters by hundreds and thousands. Listeners often wrote as though he had spoken directly to them. Accepted without question was the premise that they were friends and that it was possible to speak frankly of one's problems. Many poured out their hearts. A few wrote love letters. This could be disconcerting to a beginning announcer. "The first such epistle," wrote Credo Harris of WHAS, Louisville, "nearly jumped me out of my skin. In all my young and sheltered life no woman had ever come at me like that! Its fire and fervor were terrifying." [4] Some writers, with few preliminaries, made proposals or other suggestions. To Ted Husing, who joined WJZ in 1925, a woman wrote: "Would you like to thrill a lady in person?" She explained that her husband teased her about her complete infatuation for Husing, but nothing could be done about it. Now she was to go on a trip and could arrange her itinerary to include a rendezvous.[5]

During 1924 and 1925 the spotlight of broadcasting began to center itself on idols and the business of developing them. Candidates for idolatry were numerous and flocked to the microphone. "Each announcer knew in

3. Harris, *Microphone Memoirs*, p. 86.
4. *Ibid.* p. 115.
5. Husing, *Ten Years Before the Mike*, p. 196.

his heart," wrote Norman Brokenshire, "that he was God's gift to radio." Brokenshire described the apparent camaraderie among WJZ announcers as pretense. "Actually each man was strictly out for himself." [6] Brokenshire exuded charm at all times and seemed to have no doubts about his destiny. His elaborate jauntiness may have masked severe doubts; between periods of success he struggled with alcoholism.

Like many a radio personality, Brokenshire was the child of a minister and was raised for religious service. Both his father and mother—daughter of a missionary—played the cornet, which almost inevitably led them to the Salvation Army and endless mission journeys. Eventually the father became a preacher in remote sections of Canada, where young Brokenshire was born near Hudson's Bay with the aid of an Indian midwife. During his childhood the family was constantly pulling up stakes. The father was strict and the boy feared him. "He was a restless, I now think unhappy, soul, irritably communicating to his children reflections of an inner turmoil." [7] When the boy eventually sought Broadway and then the microphone, he may have felt he was repudiating his father, while even then following in his footsteps.

As AON, making his appearance in 1924 over WJZ, Norman Brokenshire at once attracted attention. He quotes Stuart Hawkins, radio editor of the New York *Herald Tribune,* as asking, "Who is this new AON? He speaks with perfect enunciation and exceptional modulation." [8] The following year WJZ, pressed by competition, abandoned the cryptic initials. At WEAF Graham McNamee, announcing under his own name, was becoming a legendary figure. During the 1925 World Series he received 50,000 letters. [9] The WJZ staff fretted under anonymity. The RCA management relented, and AON became Norman Brokenshire. For a day or two he felt exposed and vulnerable, then he began to relish the role.

Assigned to introduce a Mrs. Heath, who was conducting one of the first series of homemaking advice, Brokenshire devised introductions that, in one way or another, injected himself into the spotlight. He might begin: "You know, Mrs. Heath, I have a confession to make; this morning I wiped my razor on one of my landlady's best towels." Mrs. Heath, playing along with this, was shocked. "But you must never, never do that. You, ladies, do remind your husbands to use a bit of tissue paper; otherwise

6. Brokenshire, *This Is Norman Brokenshire,* p. 55.
7. *Ibid.* p. 4.
8. *Ibid.* p. 43.
9. Banning, *Commercial Broadcasting Pioneer,* p. 144.

they'll cut the fibers in your cloth towels . . ." According to Brokenshire, more and more of the mail began to be addressed to him instead of to Mrs. Heath. Through this and other assignments he was getting at least a hundred letters per day. "I would cram my pockets with them and read them between announcements and on the outside jobs." [10]

In March 1925 Brokenshire was sent by WJZ to Washington to cover the inauguration of President Coolidge. Except for the engineers, he was alone on the assignment. Without precedents, he was given no instructions except to "do the job." For WEAF, Graham McNamee went with leg men, researchers, and publicity representatives. Early on inauguration day, as Brokenshire surveyed the podium, he was asked by a press photographer: "Are you going to be the announcer?" Yes indeed, Norman Brokenshire told him, and he had his picture taken standing by the podium microphones, wearing his new hat. Next day this United Press photo was in countless newspapers. Meanwhile Brokenshire had ad libbed for over two hours for the WJZ-WRC audience and displayed an inexhaustible gift for banter and bonhomie. "I used my name at every decent opportunity. For the nice listeners I think I even spelled it several times." [11]

As his mail snowballed, station manager Charles Popenoe felt it might go to Brokenshire's head. He also considered the mail to be station property, and so ordered the mail department to withhold it. Brokenshire countered this with a visit to the main New York City post office, where he rented a large mail box and filled out a change-of-address card. At WJZ Popenoe was puzzled at the sudden drop in Brokenshire mail, especially when he saw the young man walking about with huge bundles of letters.[12]

Idols and management struggled not only over mail and the use of names, but over personal appearances as well. The rising stars were deluged with invitations. Some stations permitted them to appear as station representatives but not to accept remuneration. Instead they were plied with gifts. To Brokenshire came monogrammed cigarette cases, belt buckles, pigskin wallets with gold corners. He received a plaque that held a twenty-dollar gold piece—removable. Everywhere radio personalities were treated like war heroes. Said Phillips Carlin of WEAF: "We received keys to the cities on many occasions and were met with bands and driven through the streets in automobiles . . . We were quite something." [13]

10. Brokenshire, *This Is Norman Brokenshire*, pp. 46-56.
11. *Ibid*. pp. 60-61.
12. *Ibid*. p. 93.
13. Carlin, *Reminiscences*, pp. 17-18.

The no-fee policy could not survive. Announcing salaries were still modest. Husing began at $45 per week. Brokenshire, announcing the presidential inauguration, was getting $65 a week. The effort to keep salaries at such levels made the outside fees a bargaining point. On many stations artists worked regularly for minimal fees—and even without fees—for the sake of money earned outside via a radio buildup. In Detroit, Elton Plant of the Detroit *News* station WWJ began to appear in theaters as the Boy Baritone of the Air, dressed in patched knickers with a bundle of papers under his arm.[14] In Chicago, Patrick Barnes joined WHT in 1925 as chief announcer and was soon earning huge sums through appearances. "Very often we would get a thousand dollars in a night. Oh, it was very profitable." [15]

Among the most widely celebrated of the new idols were those featured on late-night programs, when stations were heard over great distances and Silent Night helped them win vast audiences. Many a station became known by its late-night personality. Much of the nation knew Lambdin Kay, the Little Colonel of WSB, Atlanta; George Hay, the Solemn Old Judge of WLS, Chicago; Harold Hough, the Hired Hand of WBAP, Fort Worth; and Leo Fitzpatrick, the Merry Old Chief of the Kansas City Nighthawks of WDAF. Fitzpatrick went on a personal-appearance tour that covered 101 towns in 100 days. He was famed for his sign-off, borrowing from Longfellow: "And the night shall be filled with music, and the cares that infest the day shall fold their tents like the Arabs and as silently steal away . . . Goodnight to all on the Atlantic Coast, goodnight to those on the Pacific Coast, and goodnight to everyone until tomorrow night." Fitzpatrick offered listeners membership cards in a mythical society of "Nighthawks." Two million people are said to have enrolled.[16]

That this door to greatness should have attracted to radio some strange characters is not surprising. To some extent the rise of the personality coincided with the rise of commercialism. The influx of 1924-25 included many men with something to sell.

The first program for which time was sold over WOR, Newark, brought to the air the colorful Bernarr Macfadden. Short of stature, he had become obsessed with physical culture and, through the magazine *Physical Culture*, parlayed his obsession into a magazine empire. In 1919 he had

14. Plant, *Reminiscences*, p. 18.
15. Barnes, *Reminiscences*, p. 10.
16. Patt, *Reminiscences*, pp. 21-2.

launched its fitting companion piece, *True Story*, which specialized in confessions of sex and repentance; by 1925 it had a circulation of over a million and a half copies and a year later was close to two million. Meanwhile he was adding other magazines and challenging the New York tabloid field with his daily *Graphic* and its bizarre "composographs," in which bedroom scandals of the day were restaged for the camera by models—with the proper celebrity faces inserted. These new interests had by no means reduced his concern for physical culture, for in 1925 Bernarr Macfadden took over the newly launched morning calisthenics broadcasts over WOR. Started as an experiment, this series had soon won the largest following among all WOR programs.[17] During the Bernarr Macfadden regime it began at 6:45 each morning and lasted for an hour and a quarter, with alternating segments of music and exercise. Music was provided by piano, saxophone, and violin. Listeners could send for charts showing the movements; exercises were identified by number. Letters indicated that many listeners exercised with earphones on. The studio engineer, a former ship wireless operator in the British merchant marine, was John Gambling.[18] He eventually took over the program when Macfadden, with ever-larger involvements and thoughts of the Presidency, withdrew.

Macfadden paid WOR for the privilege of conducting the exercises and in return was allowed to promote the *Graphic* as well as *Physical Culture*. Sometimes he brought a chorus girl to exercise with him; she would get her picture in the *Graphic*. Sometimes the chorus girl spoke a testimonial for physical fitness. One such visitor, in refined tones, read a statement penciled for her by Gambling.

> I am so happy to be here with Mr. Macfadden. I do these exercises *every* morning, and I am sure I keep my figure and keep in condition just through these exercises. Thank you. (GASP OF RELIEF) My gawd, I'm glad that's over.[19]

There were other faddists, medicine men and messiahs who attracted audiences in the mid-1920's and played their part in the changing atmosphere of broadcasting. By far the most remarkable, and a pivotal figure in the story of radio, was John Romulus Brinkley—Dr. Brinkley.

His beginnings are lost in mist; Brinkley himself told various versions of his life. Most began in a log cabin in the Smoky Mountains with holly-

17. Barnett, *Reminiscences*, pp. 18-19.
18. Gambling, *Reminiscences*, pp. 1-7.
19. *Ibid.* pp. 21-6.

hocks at the door and a spinning wheel inside. Brinkley had a feeling for symbols of America's rural past. His mother died early, and he spent part of his childhood with an uncle, a general practitioner, picking up a smattering of medical lore. Like many later broadcasters, the boy took his first step toward radio in a telegraph office. Without pay he assisted the railroad agent at Sylva, N.C., and was taught telegraphy. "I was first attracted to him by his curiosity," the agent later recounted. "He just wanted to tear my instruments off the table, he was so interested in them." Brinkley subsequently worked for Western Union in Chicago, studied medicine, quit his studies, and instead bought medical diplomas from diploma mills in Kansas City and St. Louis. The Kansas City $100 parchment won him a license to practice in Kansas. Thanks to reciprocal courtesies between states, other licenses followed. He and a partner opened a medical office in Greenville, N.C., with the sign "Greenville Electro Medic Doctors." Their advertisements in the Greenville Daily News asked, "Are you a manly man full of vigor?"—a question Brinkley was to ask most of his life, and before long, on the air. The Greenville partners gave $25 injections of distilled colored water and after two months left town. At a later time Brinkley worked for less than a month in the medical office at Swift & Company in Kansas City, which he later said gave him an unparalleled opportunity to study animal glands.[20]

Further wandering—and brushes with the law—brought Brinkley and his wife in 1917 to Milford, Kansas, population 200. The village drugstore was empty, and Brinkley took it over for $8 a month. In back were two rooms, one of which became the Brinkley home, the other his consultation room, while Mrs. Brinkley sold patent medicines in the store. One day an elder citizen of Milford insisted that the doctor do something about his problem of failing manhood. The conversation turned to the goats Brinkley had seen at Swift & Company. "You wouldn't have any trouble if you had a pair of those buck glands in you," Brinkley said. The man asked, "Well, will you put 'em in?" Eventually it was done in the back room, and a career was launched. Other men came to say they had the same trouble as Jake had had. The Brinkley operation fee went up to $750, $1000, $1500. When Mrs. Brinkley received a legacy, they used it to build, in 1918, a small Brinkley Hospital. It was expanded rapidly.[21]

About 1922 the Brinkley legend reached the ears of Harry Chandler,

20. Carson, The Roguish World of Dr. Brinkley, pp. 12-26.
21. Ibid. pp. 30-40.

who owned the Los Angeles *Times* and was also starting KHJ, Los Angeles. He persuaded Brinkley to come to California and vowed to make him famous if his treatment was good. We are told that "several staff members" of the *Times* had the treatment and that several screen stars also became "Brinkley alumni." Besides spreading the word, the trip brought a new element into Brinkley's life. Impressed by KHJ and $40,000 richer from the California trip, Brinkley applied for a broadcasting license from the Department of Commerce and in 1923 founded KFKB, Milford. Starting with a 1000-watt transmitter, it was immediately one of the most powerful stations and its power was subsequently increased several times. Under Department of Commerce rules this entitled the station to a preferred dial position; KFKB was soon heard far and wide. On every night except Sunday a Brinkley lecture was heard; the rest of the schedule presented fundamentalist religion, guitar and banjo ensembles, accordionists, cowboy singers, yodelers, crooners, hymn-singers, story-tellers. The doctor's lectures held a vast audience spellbound. "Don't let your doctor two-dollar you to death . . . come to Dr. Brinkley." He delighted in images of rural life.

> Note the difference between the stallion and the gelding. The stallion stands erect, neck arched, mane flowing, champing the bit, stamping the ground, seeking the female, while the gelding stands around half asleep, going into action only when goaded, cowardly, listless, with no interest in anything.

Was the listener listless? The doctor recommended his "compound operation." In response to inquiries a steady stream of literature backed up the radio message. "Are you a man of your own mind? Men like Edison, Marconi, Burbank, and Brinkley have always *thought for themselves.*" A daily KFKB feature, *Medical Question Box,* quoted letters from listeners describing their symptoms. If they were not candidates for the compound operation, Dr. Brinkley would tell them on the air what medicines to use. A huge mail-order drug business was developed, which was to continue for thirteen years and probably exceed the hospital business in income and profit. Shipments of goats came in from Arkansas. Shipments of drugs went out to all points of the compass. Whereas the operations catered to men, 95 per cent of the mail-order business involved women. "Now here is a letter," said the doctor on KFKB, "from a dear mother—a dear little mother who holds to her breast a babe of nine months. She should take

Number 2 and Number 16 and—yes—Number 17 and she will be helped. Brinkley's 2, 16, and 17. If her druggist hasn't got them, she should write and order them from the Milford Drug Company, Milford, Kansas, and they will be sent to you, Mother, collect. May the Lord guard and protect you, Mother. The postage will be prepaid." [22]

Dr. Brinkley was a genius in what came to be known as public service. Through his bequests a local Sunday school became the Brinkley Methodist Sunday School. Similarly a local baseball team became the Brinkley Goats. He served the children of America with a "Tell Me a Story Lady" over KFKB; she also happened to be the wife of the local banker. But his most impressive achievement was a relationship established with Kansas State College of Manhattan. A student, a go-getter named Sam Pickard, is said to have been the intermediary in making arrangements. Over KFKB the college launched a College of the Air which by 1924 had for-credit enrollments from 39 states and from Canada, thanks to the vast range of the Brinkley station. Among the radio students, 311 that year received certificates from Kansas State.[23] In dealings with government agencies Dr. Brinkley could always cite beneficences such as these and present letters of praise and gratitude and plaques in his honor. "We are prospering," said Brinkley, "because our keynote is service." [24] Sam Pickard became radio director for the Department of Agriculture and then a member of the Federal Radio Commission, which may have proved helpful to Brinkley.

Meanwhile the American Medical Association was stirring itself. The diploma mills from which Brinkley had purchased his degrees were being exposed. Brinkley himself, in his applications for state licenses, was found to have made numerous false claims. The American Medical Association declared his operation a fraud. By 1925 several states took steps to revoke his licenses. Over KFKB Brinkley counterattacked; he referred to the American Medical Association as a "meat cutters' union." He also began to give his "dear, dear friends" of the radio audience a continuing autobiography, constantly elaborating the Brinkley legend and heaping scorn on his enemies—who were at the same time piecing together the details of the Brinkley career. Meanwhile he prospered, drove a 16-cylinder Cadillac,

22. *Ibid.* pp. 89-103. Chase, *Sound and Fury*, 61-5.
23. Frost, *Education's Own Stations*, p. 144.
24. Carson, *The Roguish World of Dr. Brinkley*, p. 82.

wore large diamonds, built a mansion, bought airplanes, and spent $65,-
000 on new and more powerful station equipment.[25] The famous goat-
gland doctor—goateed himself—became a folk hero.

Milford became Brinkley and Brinkley Milford. He was its patron saint,
and the town's life was inextricably meshed with his. The daughter of the
county sheriff was his secretary. The local banker was a stockholder in the
radio station. The local newspaper editor did the Brinkley printing. When
exposures began to be printed in newspapers like the Kansas City *Journal-
Post*, they were simply not distributed around Milford.[26]

By 1925 strong forces were arrayed against him, but Brinkley rode high
and had years of success ahead of him. In a few years a station popularity
contest run by *Radio Digest* of Chicago would give first place—among all
the stations of the nation—to KFKB, Milford.[27] By then he would even
loom as a political power.

Brinkley had already made an indelible mark on radio. He had swept
aside the potted palms and spoken to a rural audience in its idiom. The
radio careers of many a later figure, including that of Huey Long, were to
follow a trail blazed by Dr. Brinkley.

He had done more. With his drug business—built entirely by radio—he
had made clear there was gold in the kilocycles. Many had caught the
message and were descending on radio. They knew what was needed—a
wave length and personality.

They made their contribution to a period of crisis.

CRISIS IN THE AIR

The crisis atmosphere that engulfed broadcasting in the mid-1920's
stemmed from various tensions we have seen developing: small versus
powerful stations; patent allies *v.* competitors; patent allies *v.* antimonopolists; telephone *v.* manufacturing groups; copyright owners *v.* users; educational *v.* commercial interests; politicals ins *v.* outs. In 1925 these
erupted in scattered disturbances, which by 1926 merged in a common
convulsion, from which new patterns of control would issue.

While Kansas State College was winning radio triumphs through cour-
tesy of Dr. Brinkley's KFKB, another Kansas educational institution was

25. Chase, *Sound and Fury*, pp. 66-70.
26. Carson, *The Roguish World of Dr. Brinkley,* pp. 122-3.
27. *Ibid.* p. 143.

in trouble. The University of Kansas at Lawrence had been an early licensee, with call letters KFKU. It was originally licensed without time restriction, and like various other universities had organized home study courses for credit. Soon almost all departments of the university were involved, and there was an enthusiastic "rush by the faculty to broadcast." However, by 1925 the wave length was being used by twenty-seven stations. Time sharing was required, and even during its own hours KFKU ran into a barrage of interference. Enrolled home-study students said they could not hear the broadcasts. Faculty members became disillusioned and withdrew. The home study courses were abandoned.[1]

This reversal epitomized the dilemma of educational institutions. Their own stations were squeezed into shared channels, bristling with voices; but by hanging onto the coattails of a Dr. Brinkley, it was possible to be heard in thirty-nine states. The University of Kansas continued with its own station nonetheless. Kansas State decided after a time to let go of the Brinkley coattails and also to start its own station, against large odds. But the pressures at work in Kansas were active everywhere. To many educational stations they now brought surcease.

By the end of 1924, some 151 colleges and universities had been licensed by the Department of Commerce, and forty-nine of these had in the same period expired. The death rate among these stations was thus 31 per cent —somewhat lower than the average among all stations, which was over 50 per cent.[2]

But in 1925 the fortunes of the college and university stations took a plunge. That year, while twenty-five new stations joined this group, thirty-seven expired. It was the year of highest mortality.

In some cases stations simply gave up, discouraged by chaos and rising costs. This was the case with KFAJ of the University of Colorado, which could not be heard—even locally—when General Electric's powerful KOA, Denver, was on the air. In 1922 the university had been authorized to operate at 1000 watts but the following year was reduced to 100 watts by the Department of Commerce. The situation seemed to offer no prospect of a useful educational service, so the university allowed its license to lapse in 1925. Such actions have been referred to as "apathy," but disgust and weariness were active ingredients.

1. Frost, *Education's Own Stations*, pp. 170-72.
2. Jome, *Economics of the Radio Industry*, p. 174. By August 1924, 1105 licenses had been issued; 533 stations survived.

In that year another factor entered the radio situation and began to affect the educational broadcaster and his license. Until 1925 the Department of Commerce had given licenses to all who asked. The 1912 radio law seemed to require it. Nevertheless, at the third and fourth Washington radio conferences—held in 1924 and 1925 respectively—industry leaders urged Secretary of Commerce Hoover to discontinue giving licenses and even to attempt to reduce the number of existing stations. At the 1925 conference—the Fourth National Radio Conference—he agreed and began telling applicants that "all wave lengths are in use," and that no further licenses could be issued.

This situation produced a new phenomenon. Though a channel could not now be obtained by applying, it apparently could by purchase. A traffic in licenses quickly developed. The Department of Commerce, far from discouraging it, furthered it by a policy it adopted. "We take the position," a Commerce Department spokesman told a Senate committee, "that the license ran to the apparatus, and if there is no good reason to the contrary we will recognize that sale and license the new owner of the apparatus."[3] Thus via the market place, channels were still available.

It was natural that prospective purchasers should begin to eye some of the channels occupied by nonprofit institutions, most of which were feeling financial pressure. It was for commercial use that Stephens College in Columbia, Mo., sold its station KFRU.[4]

Church-owned stations were also getting offers. In some cases a promise of free time clinched a transfer without cash. We have noted that the station started by "Doc" Herrold in 1909 was purchased after the war by the First Baptist Church of San Jose, Cal. In 1925 Fred J. Hart, a local businessman, "took it over." No money seems to have been involved. The church was assured of free broadcasting time for twenty years. Sundays were allotted to the church, which was undoubtedly relieved to rid itself of repair and maintenance costs. Thus KQW, the station that was to become KCBS, San Francisco, changed hands and became commercial.[5] Similarly the first station in Nashville, Tenn., WCBQ of the First Baptist Church of Nashville, was transferred to a local druggist for commercial use on condition that church services would be broadcast.[6]

It did not take long for the license traffic to raise political heat. Chicago

3. *Radio Control*, p. 39.
4. Frost, *Education's Own Stations*, p. 419.
5. Hart, *Interview*, pp. 41-2.
6. Ward, *Reminiscences*, p. 3.

already had some forty stations, and twenty groups still wanted licenses. In this situation *Liberty* magazine, intent on a Chicago station, bought one for a reported $50,000; the license was automatically transferred.[7]

The Chicago Federation of Labor was meanwhile making plans for a station, but before it had even applied for a license it was surprised by a letter from the Department of Commerce.

January 13, 1926

Sir:

The department has been informed that your organization is contemplating erecting and operating a radio broadcasting station.

At the present time all wave lengths available are in use and I see no possibility of providing an operating channel for the station if erected. If the station is erected a license cannot be issued for its operation.

Because of the present congested conditions, the Fourth National Radio Conference recommended that until there has been a substantial reduction in the number of broadcasting stations no further licenses be issued.

Respectfully,
Stephen Davis
Acting Secretary of Commerce[8]

The Chicago Federation of Labor, in reply, expressed surprise over the role of a "so-called" national radio conference, and submitted its license application. It pointed out that WEAF, in New York City, had a clear channel—shared only with a west coast station—and expressed the hope the department was not helping to establish a radio monopoly. In a prompt response, Secretary Davis assured the Federation that the department had no desire to discriminate. He presented an ingenious defense of its policy: "The Secretary of Commerce has no right under existing law to select the individuals who should exercise the broadcasting privilege." [9]

Senator James Couzens of Michigan expressed shock over the situation. *Liberty* was financially related to the Chicago *Tribune*, which had previously bought a station. The Commerce Department policy seemed to Senator Couzens to invite a private auctioning of channels to the highest bidders. "Anyone that buys the apparatus controls the situation." [10] The

7. *Radio Control*, pp. 37-9.
8. *Ibid.* p. 218.
9. *Ibid.* p. 219.
10. *Ibid.* p. 39.

department defended its policy. The Chicago Federation of Labor continued to protest.

During 1925 the quest for licenses, in many cases for commercial use, added an aggressive note to the broadcasting environment. It was encouraged by continuing AT&T successes.

The AT&T suit against WHN, New York, launched in 1924, had ended out of court. After a show of defiance, which won applause in the press, WHN quietly settled for a $1500 license fee. Both sides appear to have been much relieved—AT&T, because it had been pictured in monstrous terms in editorial and cartoon; WHN, because it could not possibly afford a court fight. Now it was authorized by AT&T to sell time and could hope for telephone pickup lines. This settlement was followed by a wave of others. Within a year 250 stations paid AT&T license fees of $500 to $3000.[11] Some did so largely for the sake of pickup lines, but many "went commercial."

One of the stations that began to sell time in 1925 was WWJ, Detroit. Another was WJR, Detroit, which by 1926 had several religious programs on a commercial basis and found Sunday especially profitable. That year Leo Fitzpatrick, former Kansas City Nighthawk, became WJR manager and persuaded Father Charles Coughlin of the Shrine of the Little Flower in Royal Oak to experiment in using radio for fund-raising.[12]

In 1925 AT&T offered the following stations as a group that could be linked by its long lines:[13]

		COST PER HOUR
WEAF	New York	$500
WEEI	Boston	250
WJAR	Providence	250
WCCO	Minneapolis-St. Paul	250
WOO	Philadelphia	200
WFI	Philadelphia	200
WCAE	Pittsburgh	200
WGR	Buffalo	200
WSAI	Cincinnati	200
WWJ	Detroit	200
WCAP	Washington	150
WEAR	Cleveland	150
WOC	Davenport	150

11. Banning, *Commercial Broadcasting Pioneer*, p. 213.
12. Tull, *Father Coughlin and the New Deal*, p. 3. Patt, *Reminiscences*, pp. 42-3.
13. Archer, *History of Radio*, pp. 360-61.

A sponsor could purchase the group or part of it. Receipts from the earliest sponsored hookups had been kept by AT&T—the station got free programming—but various "station compensation" plans were later evolved which allowed the stations to share in expanding revenues. In 1925 these were creating promising vistas: one sponsor committed himself to a year's expenditure, in time and talent, of $120,000; another to a budget of $108,000; another, to $73,000.[14]

Throughout the spread of the AT&T toll venture, there were protests. In *Century* magazine Bruce Bliven wrote: "The use of the radio for advertising is wholly undesirable and should be prohibited by legislation if necessary." He saw a medium of magnificent promise being given over to "outrageous rubbish." [15] In 1925 Representative Sol Bloom of New York (D.) announced that he would sponsor legislation to ban radio advertising.[16] The subject was feverishly discussed. H. V. Kaltenborn offered a lecture titled "Radio—Prophet or Profiteer?" [17] The Newspaper Publishers Association urged newspapers not to give free publicity to sponsored programs.[18] Important stations, including WJZ, WRC, WGY, WLW, WMAQ, WFAA, and many others, were still not selling time and many were vocal in opposition. The publishers of the Kansas City *Star*, owners of WDAF, were insisting as late as 1926—"vehemently"—that the station would advertise only the *Star*.[19]

Attacks on advertising, however, were often ambiguously worded. They attacked, as Hoover had done, "direct advertising." Just what this permitted, and what it barred, was not defined. The phrase seemed to take a righteous stand while leaving the door open.

The attitude of Secretary of Commerce Hoover on this—as on other issues—was not clear. He seemed to many a bulwark against commercialization, sometimes making quotable, sardonic statements on the subject. At the third Washington conference, in October 1924, he said: "If a speech by the President is to be used as the meat in a sandwich of two patent medicine advertisements, there will be no radio left." [20] Yet he had given toll broadcasting its most important boost in providing it with a clear channel. And when the 1925 Washington conference went on record as

14. Banning, *Commercial Broadcasting Pioneer*, p. 261.
15. Bliven, "How Radio Is Remaking Our World," *Century*, June 1924.
16. *Radio Broadcast*, October 1925.
17. Kaltenborn, *Reminiscences*, p. 128.
18. Archer, *History of Radio*, p. 360.
19. Patt, *Reminiscences*, p. 20.
20. *Radio Broadcast*, December 1924.

deprecating "the use of radio broadcasting for direct sales effort," it also adopted, at the urging of Secretary Hoover himself, another resolution: "The problem of radio publicity should be solved by the industry itself, and not by Government compulsion and legislation." [21] A key issue in the use of the air was thus set aside by Hoover as something to be settled not by elected representatives but by private interests.

Some other attitudes of Hoover's seemed to involve similar contradictions. In 1924, when the Federal Trade Commission action had brought attention to the monopoly issue, he said it would be most unfortunate if broadcasting should be controlled by any "corporation, individual or combination." [22] But the patent allies continued to be among his chief advisers and to receive favored treatment. That fall David Sarnoff again urged a limited group of "superpower" stations strategically located to serve the entire country—a favorite theme with RCA, GE, and Westinghouse. Over the protests of small stations and in spite of air congestion, Hoover promptly authorized WJZ and WGY to experiment with 50,000 watts.

There were other contradictions. In his *Memoirs* Hoover wrote that as Secretary of Commerce he was under constant pressure to support the preemption of channels as private property. This, he was urged, would encourage investment in broadcasting.[23] The existence of such backstairs pressure is understandable enough. These years saw a plunder of government oil resources through private deals; the Secretary of the Interior looked after his friends and they after him. The Secretary of Commerce, in proclaiming the air as a national resource to be guarded, may well have resisted strong undercurrents. Yet the policy adopted on the selling of stations did in fact treat channels as private property.

Perhaps the contradictions were apparent rather than real. That Hoover should turn for counsel to the most successful elements in the industry was taken for granted. This was co-operation—an administration policy. That their initiative would, in the nature of things, produce public benefit was an accepted article of faith. Another was that excesses would create their own antidotes through public reaction. Where enlightened business leaders were involved, all that would be needed would be an executive word of caution. Secretary Hoover provided such admonitions—against monop-

21. *Radio Control*, p. 67.
22. *Radio Broadcast*, June 1924.
23. Hoover, *Memoirs: The Cabinet and the Presidency*, pp. 140-41.

oly, vested interests, excessive advertising—but continued to give dominant groups virtually what they asked for.

In the absence of legislation he proceeded more and more as though the advice of industry leaders, as embodied in resolutions of the Washington conferences, were legislation, and as though he had the powers he had urged Congress to give him. The 1924 conference urged abolition of the cluster of 86 stations still operating at 360 meters. Secretary Hoover promptly began their dispersal. Stations of 500 watts were given assignments among the regional medium-power stations. Lower-power stations were tucked away in available—often miserable—time-sharing pockets.

Protests came. From WBT, Charlotte, N.C., manager Fred M. Laxton wrote: "Why should 500 watts output make one station a broadcast and 250 make another station an outcast?" WBT's own history underlined the question. It had once operated at 500 watts with a locally made transmitter. It later decided to become AT&T-licensed in order to obtain telephone pickup lines, which had been refused by the local telephone company. Because the AT&T license fee was $4 per watt, the station decided to use only 250 watts so that the license fee would be $1000 rather than $2000; the 250 watts adequately covered Charlotte. This action now threatened the station with an unfavorable shift by the Department of Commerce. Laxton suggested that the Secretary was paying too much attention to his advisory committees, dominated by "the manufacturers" and their powerful stations, who wanted "the stage" to themselves.[24]

Throughout 1925 Secretary Hoover was busy with innumerable station shifts and power and time changes. Abandoning earlier policy, he even intervened in local time-sharing disputes. In Cincinnati WLW and WMH (later WKRC) were unable to agree and for weeks broadcast simultaneously on their shared wave length. Hoover stepped in and imposed a settlement schedule.[25]

He began to deal with increasing assurance with those who did not hold to assigned wave lengths. Many small stations tended to wander, either because of equipment defects or deliberately, in search of clear air. In earlier days such deviations had often been ignored by the Department, but no longer. In Los Angeles a chronic wanderer was a station operated by evangelist Aimee Semple McPherson. Hoover, after warnings, ordered

24. Wallace, *The Development of Broadcasting in North Carolina*, pp. 90-91.
25. New York *Times*, February 15, 1925.

a Department of Commerce inspector to seal the station. She wired Hoover:

PLEASE ORDER YOUR MINIONS OF SATAN TO LEAVE MY STATION ALONE
STOP YOU CANNOT EXPECT THE ALMIGHTY TO ABIDE BY YOUR WAVE
LENGTH NONSENSE STOP WHEN I OFFER MY PRAYERS TO HIM I MUST
FIT INTO HIS WAVE RECEPTION STOP OPEN THIS STATION AT ONCE[26]

Hoover's increasing firmness was encouraged by industry leaders. And without it, chaos would have developed far earlier than it did. Yet with disgruntled broadcasters increasing in number, it was inevitable that the Secretary's authority would be challenged in court. A challenge began in 1925.

It started unspectacularly. Among the dissatisfied of Chicago was Eugene F. McDonald of Zenith—one of the first to sell a tubeless tube radio. McDonald also had a Chicago radio station, WJAZ, but was allotted only two hours a week on a wave length shared with the General Electric station, KOA, Denver. According to a Zenith company history, McDonald objected to what he considered "one-man control of radio with the Secretary of Commerce as supreme czar." [27] Since Hoover had said he would welcome a test case, McDonald decided to provide one. He moved WJAZ to a more attractive channel, challenging the authority of the Department of Commerce. It promptly brought suit. It hardly had a choice, particularly since the occupied channel had been ceded to Canada. A test case now moved toward a decision.

The numerous disputes between Hoover and licensees, including the WJAZ case, received only minor attention in the trade press. They hardly seemed crucial. The authority of the Secretary of Commerce was generally unquestioned. At his weekly press conferences—well attended, since Hoover already seemed destined for higher things—he seemed in firm control. Besides, the broadcasting press—magazines, supplements, columns—increasingly concentrated on other matters, such as the rise of "Roxy," or the life of J. Andrew White, or pictures of Graham McNamee at the microphone, or of the Gold Dust Twins in burnt-cork make-up, or the Cliquot Club Eskimos in their broadcasting parkas. Even *Radio Broadcast* was tending to become a fan magazine, and personality items displaced industry problems and set diagrams.

26. Hoover, *Reminiscences*, p. 11.
27. *The Zenith Story*, p. 8.

Amid the star obsession, the most crucial struggle of the day went entirely unchronicled; even top station executives were unaware of it. In a New York office the forces of AT&T were arrayed against RCA, GE, Westinghouse—the "radio group"—in a bizarre industrial drama.

At first there was no hint of surprise—only of insoluble deadlock.

The odd quality of the arbitration derived from its irrationality. The disputants were arguing about agreements written early in 1920, just before the broadcasting era. Broadcasting had existed in rudimentary form, and the word crept into the documents, but in the main they had nothing to do with broadcasting, but concerned telephony (wired and wireless) and telegraphy (wired and wireless).

Now each side claimed segments of the broadcasting world—of today and tomorrow—on the basis of the 1920 language.

To add to the confusion, the 1920 contract language was so turbid that the lawyers who wrote it could not now agree on what it had been meant to convey.

The turbidity encouraged the dispute: the more each disputant read and reread the spiraling phrases, the more he found. The vastness of the stakes also encouraged the dispute.

There was—for instance—television. Television, they all felt, would soon be upon them. The agreements had not mentioned television. But was it perhaps—basically—a form of telegraphy? Of course! argued GE's Albert G. Davis in a backstage caucus. With television, telegrams would be sent in fascimile, so of course it was a form of telegraphy. Frederick P. Fish, harried attorney representing the radio forces, had difficulty absorbing this argument. At one point in the arbitration he dispatched a pleading note to Davis on the television matter: "Can you get someone to write an argument in favor of your view that this is telegraphy?" [28]

A number of issues hinged on similar debating niceties.

> . . . it is agreed that the Telephone Company has no license under this agreement to make, lease or sell wireless telephone receiving apparatus except as part of or for direct use in connection with transmitting apparatus made by it.[29]

According to the radio group, this meant that AT&T could make receivers for two-way telephones, but not radio receivers. According to AT&T, it

28. Archer, *Big Business and Radio*, p. 163.
29. *Agreement*, July 1, 1920, between General Electric Company and American Telephone and Telegraph Company, Article V, 4(d)(2). See *Report of the Federal Trade Commission on the Radio Industry*, Exhibit D.

allowed AT&T to make radio receivers so that listeners would be able to listen to its toll broadcasting stations.

> . . . to the Telephone Company. . . . exclusive licenses. . . . to make, use, lease and sell all wireless telephone apparatus connected to or operated as a part of a public service telephone communication system.[30]

According to members of the radio group, this merely prohibited them from competing with an operation like the radio link to Catalina Island. According to AT&T, it also prohibited the radio group members from connecting their broadcasting stations with any public-service system of wires including Western Union and Postal Telegraph.

> . . . to the General Company nonexclusive licenses in the field of wireless telephony for its own communication or for purposes of convenience, or to save expense in connection with its commercial operation of wireless telegraph systems, but not for profit or for transmission of messages to the public.[31]

According to AT&T, this enjoined the radio group from conveying any sponsored messages to the public. According to the radio group, it permitted others to help defray broadcasting costs.

Similar disputes ranged over a score of passages and dealt with loudspeakers, head sets, public address systems, hotel and apartment house systems. There was even argument over whether AT&T had the right to broadcast.[32]

For weeks referee Boyden listened to witnesses and lawyers. Neither by question nor expression did he give a hint of his thoughts. Then, for months, he was in seclusion with piles of documents. Late in 1924 he sent a draft of his opinion to each of the disputants. If there were objections he would consider them, then put his ruling in final form.

As the members of the radio group read the draft, they could hardly believe their eyes. Point after point, their contentions had been upheld. AT&T had been routed. To Owen D. Young, en route to the United States after work on the Dawes Plan—designed to save Germany from economic collapse—Major General Harbord sent a jubilant radiogram:

30. Ibid. V, 4(e).
31. Ibid. V, 4(a). The same paragraph applied to Westinghouse and RCA.
32. Archer, Big Business and Radio, pp. 109-65.

DRAFT DECISION BOYDEN JUST RECEIVED STOP APPEARS SO FAR AS
STUDIED TO GIVE US EXCLUSIVE RIGHT SALE RECEIVING SETS RIGHT TO
PICKUP WIRES RIGHT TO INSTALL SYSTEMS IN HOTELS AND APARTMENT
HOUSES PROBABLE RIGHTS TO SELL LOUDSPEAKERS AND HEAD SETS IN
CONNECTION WITH RECEIVING SETS ALTHOUGH STATED TO BE IN WIRE
FIELD AND GIVES RIGHT TO COLLECT TOLLS FOR BROADCASTING STOP

He followed with another:

FURTHER STUDY BOYDEN DECISION SHOWS TELEPHONE GROUP HAS NO
RIGHTS BROADCAST TRANSMISSION UNDER PATENTS RADIO GROUP STOP[33]

The victory had been sweeping—so sweeping as to create a peril for the
victors. AT&T, backed against a wall, was likely to use whatever weapon
it might have. And it had one.

Meanwhile Owen D. Young, arriving on American shores, had plans of
his own. His brilliance as negotiator, A. G. Davis of General Electric once
said, was an "uncanny way of sensing what was essential to each
interest." [34] Young saw the moment as fruitful for diplomacy. With a
sweeping victory behind it, the radio group could be generous, yield a
point or two, and in yielding obtain clarifications that would be of advantage to all. A new, realistic division of spheres could be made. Young and
associates became busy with lists—of possible trading points.

Both AT&T and the radio group filed comments on the referee's draft,
without bringing about substantive changes. In March 1925, Referee Boyden got his ruling into final form. After a few weeks it was to go into
effect.

Now AT&T made its move. It presented to the radio group an advisory
memorandum by no less a person than John W. Davis, recent Democratic
party candidate for President. It said simply that if the cross-licensing
agreements of 1920-21 meant what Referee Boyden said they meant, they
were illegal in the first place—a conspiracy in restraint of trade—a violation of the United States anti-trust laws. AT&T could of course not contem-
plate an illegal course.

Nothing could have altered more stunningly the situation confronting
the radio group. Since John W. Davis had helped to draft the Clayton Act
and was a former United States Solicitor-General, his words could not be
lightly dismissed.

Each side in the arbitration had bound itself to accept the referee's deci-

33. *Ibid.* 170.
34. Tarbell, *Owen D. Young*, pp. 111-12.

sion and not to take "any proceedings intended either to modify it or set it aside." [35] But how could AT&T be held to this?

AT&T had presented its opponents with a torturing dilemma. If the quarrel were brought into open court, it would add fuel to monopoly charges of the Federal Trade Commission—enough to make a brilliant public bonfire. Moreover, AT&T would be aligned with government against RCA, GE, Westinghouse. To a large extent AT&T had put itself in position for such a move by selling its RCA stock and withdrawing from the RCA board. It could say—this was implicit in the John W. Davis memorandum—that it had not been aware of such illegality as the agreements proved "upon subsequent construction" to have.[36]

There was an additional fascinating aspect to the memorandum. The cross-licensing agreements were still in effect, he advised—except for their illegal aspects. AT&T should continue to use the patents of the group. Only the illegal portions were not binding—those which allegedly bound AT&T to stay out of available fields, such as the radio set field, in spite of the fact that its experience could "vastly benefit the industry and, in consequence, the general public." [37]

In accordance with the plans of Owen D. Young, talks began—but under greatly changed circumstances. There was now a quiet, dogged drive for solutions, amid utmost secrecy. Details of these negotiations would not be revealed for years,[38] although the final outcome would be clear.

Now came long, grueling explorations, digressions, deadlocks, confrontations, retreats, new beginnings. David Sarnoff, with his detailed knowledge of every phase of radio, moved gradually into a pivotal position. His idea of a "central broadcasting organization" began to occupy attention.

AT&T's wish to market radio sets and tubes had been a principal source of bitterness. Once its right to do so was fully conceded—with a royalty feature intended to limit its production[39]—the talks began moving ahead. Curiously, the hard-fought right was to go almost unused by AT&T. Other prospects would take precedence.

35. Archer, *Big Business and Radio*, pp. 128-9.
36. *Ibid.* p. 196.
37. *Ibid.*
38. In 1938 David Sarnoff made his records of these negotiations available to Gleason L. Archer, president of Suffolk University, for use in *Big Business and Radio*.
39. Sales over $5,000,000 in any one year would be subject to a 50 per cent royalty to the others of the patent group. *Ibid.* p. 265.

Among crucial elements in the situation was the AT&T web of cables. Alternative means for a national service—short-wave links, telegraph wires, superpower—existed but were inadequate or not ready.

On the other hand, AT&T had painful scars. It still smarted from the vituperation heaped on it in its licensing campaign. Such matters as the Kaltenborn crisis were also unpleasant memories. AT&T, government-regulated, had little appetite for such disputes.

Then there was toll broadcasting, which in 1925 was bringing AT&T a net profit of $150,000 and was surging forward.

The pieces began to fit together.

In February Sarnoff, jotting down possible trading points, had written:

> Put all stations of all parties into a broadcasting company which can be made self-supporting and probably revenue-producing, the telephone company to furnish wires as needed.[40]

It was the first hint that Sarnoff was ready to take up toll broadcasting. By mid-summer it played a part in all discussions. Should the company claim *exclusive* right to broadcast for tolls? Yes, thought Sarnoff at first. By all means, wrote A. G. Davis of General Electric in December, "in so far as the parties can give it that right." [41]

In January 1926 the RCA board of directors approved the idea of the new company. It would be owned by RCA (50%), GE (30%), and Westinghouse (20%).

It would lease, under long-term contract, the AT&T web of wires. How much would their use be worth? It became clear that a chain spanning fifteen cities should plan to pay a telephone bill of at least $800,000 the first year, and that it would rise into millions as the chain grew. A ten-year contract was discussed.[42]

The new company would buy WEAF. For how much? AT&T suggested $2,500,000.[43] The physical facilities, it was agreed, were worth $200,000. What would the remainder be for—a clear channel? A final price of $1,-000,000 was set—$200,000 for "physical facilities," $800,000 for "goodwill." The $800,000 would be returned if AT&T should resume broadcasting.

AT&T would discontinue WCAP, Washington; WRC would acquire its

40. *Ibid.* p. 184.
41. *Ibid.* pp. 186-7, 251.
42. *Ibid.* p. 248.
43. *Ibid.* p. 253.

air time. Commerce Department policies presented no obstacle to this arrangement.

In May AT&T organized its broadcasting activities into a separate corporation, Broadcasting Company of America, as a move toward transfer.

On July 7, 1926, twelve documents were signed. One was a service contract for the web of wires. The others readjusted the innumerable interrelationships between the allies. A new division of empire had been made.

AT&T was stepping out of active broadcasting, but on terms that would secure it a lucrative and steadily mounting revenue, with freedom from editorial troubles. It had its toll as it wanted it.

The outlines of the proposed organization—still unnamed, still unformed—were now clear. Owen D. Young began to survey the nation for a suitable president for the new company.

Until this time not a hint of the negotiations had appeared in the press. In mid-July, as the story began to leak, various announcements were made. On July 21 the WEAF staff was informed that the station would be sold to RCA. The staff appears to have felt it had been sold down the river, but press releases soon began to paint a vision of a glorious future.

In August the proposed new company acquired its name—National Broadcasting Company. On September 9 it was incorporated under the laws of Delaware. A few days later RCA in full-page advertisements proclaimed the formation of the new company. A few weeks later NBC sent the telephone company a check for $1,000,000 and became the owner of WEAF—as well as good-will and a 491.5-meter clear channel.

A divide had been crossed. The toll venture had been formally transferred to the national scene. The mantle of toll had fallen on NBC.

RCA's full-page announcements did not say this. Perhaps Owen D. Young and Major General James G. Harbord, who jointly signed it, were unsure how the toll aspect would be received. The term "toll" would now be quietly dropped from the vocabulary of broadcasting.[44]

The emphasis of the announcement was on other matters. Through NBC, events of national importance would be broadcast throughout the United States. The public was assured of the very best programming.

It was estimated that five million homes already had radios; twenty-one million homes remained to be supplied. If assured of highest quality programming, all would buy. Therefore RCA, as the world's largest distribu-

---

44. "Toll" would return in the television era with a directly opposite meaning, that of audience-supported broadcasting.

A tower for Cedar Rapids: WJAM, 1922.

Fall catalogue, 1922: Montgomery Ward's first receiver.

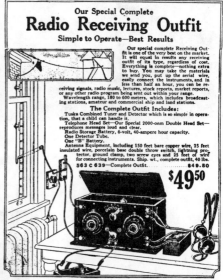

Our Special Complete

Radio Receiving Outfit

Simple to Operate—Best Results

Our special complete Receiving Outfit is one of the very best on the market. It will equal in results any receiving outfit of its type, regardless of cost. Everything is complete—nothing extra to buy. You may take the materials we send you, put up the aerial wire, easily connect the instruments, and in less than half an hour, you can be receiving signals, radio music, lectures, stock reports, market reports, or any other radio program being sent out within your range.

Wavelength range, 180 to 600 meters, which includes broadcasting stations, amateur and commercial ship and land stations.

The Complete Outfit Includes:

Tuska Combined Tuner and Detector which is so simple in operation, that a child can handle it.
Telephone Head Set—Our Special 2000-onm Double Head Set—reproduces messages loud and clear.
Radio Storage Battery, 6-volt, 40-ampere hour capacity.
One Detector Tube.
One "B" Battery.
Antenna Equipment, including 150 feet bare copper wire, 25 feet insulated wire, porcelain base double throw switch, lightning protector, ground clamp, two screw eyes and 25 feet of wire for connecting instruments. Ship. wt., complete outfit, 40 lbs.

563 C 639—Complete Outfit. $49.50

$49⁵⁰

WMT

Smithsonian Institution

Tent-like studio: WHK, Cleveland, c. 1923.

EXPLORATIONS

General Electric

Loudspeaker radio: Sears, Roebuck 1924 catalogue item.

Christmas message: Coolidge at the Pallophotophone—beginning of the Photophone sound-on-film process.

The big news: 1922 crowd gatherer.

Detroit Historical Museum

Good-will: the Browning, King Orchestra, with Anna Byrne, WEAF, 1923.

NBC

Announcing the

National Broadcasting Company, Inc.

National radio broadcasting with better programs permanently assured by this important action of the *Radio Corporation of America* in the interest of the listening public

THE RADIO CORPORATION OF AMERICA is the largest distributor of radio receiving sets in the world. It handles the entire output in this field of the Westinghouse and General Electric factories.

It does not say this boastfully. It does not say it with apology. It says it for the purpose of making clear the fact that it is more largely interested, more selfishly interested, if you please, in the best possible broadcasting in the United States than anyone else.

Radio for 26,000,000 Homes

The market for receiving sets in the future will be determined largely by the quantity and quality of the programs broadcast.

We say quantity because they must be diversified enough so that some of them will appeal to all possible listeners.

We say quality because each program must be the best of its kind. If that ideal were to be reached, no home in the United States could afford to be without a radio receiving set.

Today the best available statistics indicate that 5,000,000 homes are equipped, and 21,000,000 homes remain to be supplied.

Radio receiving sets of the best reproductive quality should be made available for all, and we hope to make them cheap enough so that all may buy.

The day has gone by when the radio receiving set is a plaything. It must now be an instrument of service.

WEAF Purchased for $1,000,000

The Radio Corporation of America, therefore, is interested, just as the public is, in having the most adequate programs broadcast. It is interested, as the public is, in having them comprehensive and free from discrimination.

Any use of radio transmission which causes the public to feel that the quality of the programs is not the highest, that the use of radio is not the broadest and best use in the public interest, that it is used for political advantage or selfish power, will be detrimental to the public interest in radio, and therefore to the Radio Corporation of America.

To insure, therefore, the development of this great service, the Radio Corporation of

America has purchased for one million dollars station WEAF from the American Telephone and Telegraph Company, that company having decided to retire from the broadcasting business.

The Radio Corporation of America will assume active control of that station on November 15.

National Broadcasting Company Organized

The Radio Corporation of America has decided to incorporate that station, which has achieved such a deservedly high reputation for the quality and character of its programs, under the name of the National Broadcasting Company, Inc.

The Purpose of the New Company

The purpose of that company will be to provide the best program available for broadcasting in the United States.

The National Broadcasting Company will not only broadcast these programs through station WEAF, but it will make them available to other broadcasting stations throughout the country so far as it may be practicable to do so, and they may desire to take them.

It is hoped that arrangements may be made so that every event of national importance may be broadcast widely throughout the United States.

No Monopoly of the Air

The Radio Corporation of America is not in any sense seeking a monopoly of the air. That would be a liability rather than an asset. It is seeking, however, to provide machinery which will insure a national distribution of national programs, and a wider distribution of programs of the highest quality.

If others will engage in this business the Radio Corporation of America will welcome their action, whether it be cooperative or competitive.

If other radio manufacturing companies, competitors of the Radio Corporation of America, wish to use the facilities of the National Broadcasting Company for the purpose of making known to the public their receiving sets, they may do so on the same terms as accorded to other clients.

The necessity of providing adequate broad-

casting is apparent. The problem of finding the best means of doing it is yet experimental. The Radio Corporation of America is making this experiment in the interest of the art and the furtherance of the industry.

A Public Advisory Council

In order that the National Broadcasting Company may be advised as to the best type of program, that discrimination may be avoided, that the public may be assured that the broadcasting is being done in the fairest and best way, always allowing for human frailties and human performance, it has created an Advisory Council, composed of twelve members, to be chosen as representative of various shades of public opinion, which will from time to time give it the benefit of their judgment and suggestion. The members of this Council will be announced as soon as their acceptance shall have been obtained.

M. H. Aylesworth to be President

The President of the new National Broadcasting Company will be M. H. Aylesworth, for many years Managing Director of the National Electric Light Association. He will perform the executive and administrative duties of the corporation.

Mr. Aylesworth, while not hitherto identified with the radio industry or broadcasting, has had public experience as Chairman of the Colorado Public Utilities Commission, and, through his work with the association which represents the electrical industry, has a broad understanding of the technical problems which measure the pace of broadcasting.

One of his major responsibilities will be to see that the operations of the National Broadcasting Company reflect enlightened public opinion, which expresses itself so promptly the morning after any error of taste or judgment or departure from fair play.

We have no hesitation in recommending the National Broadcasting Company to the people of the United States.

It will need the help of all listeners. It will make mistakes. If the public will make known its views to the officials of the company from time to time, we are confident that the new broadcasting company will be an instrument of great public service.

RADIO CORPORATION OF AMERICA

OWEN D. YOUNG, *Chairman of the Board*   JAMES G. HARBORD, *President*

tor of radios, handling all those made by General Electric and West-inghouse, had the greatest stake in program quality. To that end this "instrument of great public service" had been created. Thus the birth of NBC was explained in somewhat the same terms as the birth of KDKA.

From his position as managing director of the National Electric Light Association, Merlin H. Aylesworth—a stranger to broadcasting who did not own a radio[45]—was transplanted by Owen D. Young to the $50,000-a-year presidency of NBC.

WEAF's supersalesman George McClelland became general manager of NBC. Bertha Brainard of WJZ became program manager. It was announced that NBC would make its debut on November 15 with "the most pretentious broadcasting program ever presented." [46] On this note, amid nation-wide attention, NBC prepared to usher in the network era.

45. Gross, *I Looked and Listened,* p. 100.
46. NBC release, November 1, 1926.

"The chief business of the American people is business."   CALVIN COOLIDGE

NBC, like RCA, was born with a silver spoon. It had behind it the wealth
of huge corporations. It entered the world at a moment of business affluence. Godfather-sponsors stood ready with rich gifts.

It had a promising commercial purpose—played down in public announcements—but along with this it had a service to perform, for which it
was uniquely equipped. It could speak at once to east and west, city and
country, rich and poor. Awareness of this touched off expressions of idealism that matched the euphoria of the first year of broadcasting. NBC
seemed a child of destiny. That there was, or ever might be, conflict between the commercial purpose and the destiny of service did not apparently occur to those who brought NBC into the world. If it did, the record
does not show it.

As NBC prepared for its career, ready to lead the world of broadcasting, there was one dark cloud—that world itself was verging on chaos.

The U. S. District Court for the Northern District of Illinois, in the case
of *United States* v. *Zenith,* had decided in April 1926 that Eugene McDonald was right: the Secretary of Commerce did not have the authority he
had been exercising. The court observed that our system of government
does not permit "the play and action of purely personal and arbitrary
power." [1] The broadcast industry expected a vigorous appeal—to the U. S.
Supreme Court, if necessary. But on July 8 a memorandum was released
by the Acting Attorney General. He expressed the opinion that the Secre-

1. *United States* v. *Zenith,* 12 Fed. (2nd) 614 (1926).

189

tary of Commerce, under the radio law of 1912, did not have the right to refuse a license, assign hours, or limit power. Even his right to specify wave lengths was limited.[2] The memorandum quietly anaesthetized the law. A new law was clearly needed, but Congress had just gone home.

That summer and fall, various stations began to increase their power, move to more attractive dial positions, and use the hours they liked best. Scores of new stations erupted. Bedlam mounted. By November, as NBC approached its debut and congressmen headed back to Washington—they were to reconvene December 8—the demand for a new law was shrill.

The place that broadcasting had won in the life of the nation was clearly revealed in events that followed. As Congress prepared to frame a new law, a vast array of financial interests and sharply clashing ideological drives was brought into play. For broadcasting it was an hour of decision.

Already many of the interests and drives were embodied in legislative proposals. Thirteen laws and resolutions had been submitted to the 68th Congress (1923-25); in the 69th Congress (1925-27) the total would be eighteen. The White bill, in various forms, had been before the lawmakers since 1923. If nothing had come of all this, it was partly because of Hoover's substantial success in winning adherence to his edicts. When he had pleaded for new legislation, congressmen told him, "Why bother us? You're doing fine." [3] Now the threat of anarchy would bring action.

As the legislative machinery gathered steam, NBC made its spectacular debut. On November 15, 1926, a thousand people—captains of industry and finance, stars of the music and theater worlds—assembled in the Grand Ballroom of the Waldorf-Astoria. Around the building, at 34th Street and Fifth Avenue, crowds surged for a look at celebrities. "A new epoch in American life" was being inaugurated. At 8:05 the program began. The newly appointed president, Merlin Aylesworth—tall, suave, entirely charming—spoke briefly. Twelve million people, he said, "may be hearing what takes place in this ballroom tonight." There was the New York Symphony, with Walter Damrosch conducting; also, the New York Oratorio Society. There were "remote" features. Mary Garden sang "Annie Laurie" from Chicago—marred by a "feedback" whistle in the Grand Ballroom. Will Rogers did a monologue from Kansas City, Mo., mimicking President Coolidge. From various locations came the dance bands of Vincent Lopez, Ben Bernie, George Olsen, and B. A. Rolfe. Also presented

2. New York *Times,* July 9, 1926.
3. Hoover, *Reminiscences,* p. 10; retold in *Memoirs: The Cabinet and the Presidency.*

were Edwin Franko Goldman's band; Titta Ruffo, Metropolitan Opera star; the comedy team of Weber and Fields. When the show ended after midnight, radio columnist Ben Gross heard a dowager say, "My dear, I had no idea! We simply must get one of these radios." Newspapers reported that the premiere had cost NBC $50,000. Aylesworth confided to Gross, "Hardly a cent." The stars had given their services. But from now on, said Aylesworth, sponsors would pay for the big shows.[4] He knew precisely what he was saying.

By January NBC had two networks in operation—a "red" network fed by WEAF and a "blue" network fed by WJZ.[5] Available stations on each grew rapidly in number. As 1927 began, a number of lavish sponsored series were already in operation. Concerts, classical or semi-classical, were presented by the *Maxwell House Hour*, the *Ampico Hour*, the *Palmolive Hour*, the *General Motors Family Party*, the *Cities Service Orchestra*. Brunswick was sponsoring the Chicago Civic Opera. In somewhat lighter vein were the *Seiberling Singers*, the *Stetson Parade*, the *Wrigley Review*. Continuing were the *Cliquot Club Eskimos*, the *Ipana Troubadours*, and the always varied *Eveready Hour*.[6] The potted-palm atmosphere was still dominant.

Advertising was brief, circumspect, and extremely well-mannered. In production, professionalism continued to develop. Everything was written and rehearsed. Except in the description of public events, *ad lib* talk was virtually banished from NBC. The ambitious dramas produced once a month for the *Eveready Hour* were auditioned for the sponsor three weeks before air time; if not satisfactory, they were revised or abandoned. Among its actors was Rosaline Greene. Having left WGY in 1926 to become a schoolteacher, she changed her mind because of the *Eveready Hour*. Instead of $7.50, the pay was now $75 to $125 per performance.[7] Her portrayal of Joan of Arc—often repeated—was widely praised.

At first there was little innovation, but the stage was set for change. In

4. Gross, *I Looked and Listened*, pp. 99-101.
5. The terms "red" and "blue" originated, according to RCA chief engineer Alfred N. Goldsmith, on the *Congressional Limited* en route to Washington, shortly before the formation of NBC. He was riding with Elam Miller, AT&T operations engineer. "We had some blank maps of the United States . . . We drew on these maps the networks that we hoped would come into existence in their entirety, based on WJZ and WEAF. WEAF stations and connections were drawn with a red pencil, those of WJZ with a blue pencil." Goldsmith, *Interview*, pp. 21-2.
6. Summers (ed.), *A Thirty-Year History of Programs*, pp. 7-9.
7. Greene, *Reminiscences*, p. 19.

January 1927, NBC appropriated $400,000 for new studios to be built at 711 Fifth Avenue, with an air-conditioning system said to be the largest except in South African mines. The studios would float on springs, for sound-proofing.[8] Each studio would have its own control room. Gustave Bosler, an alumnus of the American Marconi experimental laboratory of the World War I period, was given the task of organizing a model shop to develop studio and control room equipment. A director wanted a machine for marching feet; Bosler devised a frame holding many rows of wooden pegs. Roxy wanted a mixer for eight microphones; the shop built one, as well as a system of tally lights to show which microphone was in operation.[9] The equipment and facilities in the new quarters would for the first time encourage the director to make free use of fades, cross-fades, and background effects; their uses in drama were just beginning to be understood.

The first months of NBC were among the most frenetic in radio history. Two broadcasting organizations were being merged, and both were moving amid a dusty turmoil of studio construction. Because both WEAF and WJZ had previously examined 711 Fifth Avenue as a possible studio site— via different brokers—NBC found itself having to pay two brokerage fees.[10] But that was a mere detail.

On June 11, 1927, came a high spot of the broadcasting year. Charles Lindbergh's return from his solo flight across the Atlantic became the occasion for the first grand multiple-announcer broadcast. Spaced along the ticker-tape route, with a background of screaming throngs, famous announcers passed the air spotlight to each other like a flaming torch. Fifty stations carried the broadcast.

In rapid order, crucial programming decisions were made: Walter Damrosch was engaged as musical counselor; Frank Mullen of KDKA was deputized to develop an NBC farm service; Frank A. Arnold, advertising executive, became "director of development"—time salesman on an ambassadorial level, providing liaison with the world of big business.

The outburst of activity within NBC was matched by similar bursts at higher corporate levels. It was as though the patent allies, at last released from stalemate, were ready to venture in numerous directions. Their moves brought them suddenly into a tangle of relationships with other

8. Woods, *Reminiscences*, p. 33.
9. Bosler, *Reminiscences*, pp. 12-17.
10. Woods, *Reminiscences*, p. 33.

fields; phonograph, film, vaudeville, theater, automobiles. Deals and mergers followed in breathless succession. Broadcasting was having a cumulative impact on other fields, paving the way for new alignments. The moves that filled the years 1927-29 were as dazzling as the moves made by Owen D. Young in 1919-21. They also stirred such dreams of wealth and glory that rumor mounted on rumor, all adding momentum to an accelerating stock market spiral. In that delirium, radio stocks were among the leaders.

We shall presently pursue some of the details of that explosion of merger and boom. But first we must take note of a shoestring enterprise that began in its shadow and seemed for a time ludicrous and futile. It had its start, strangely enough, in the office of David Sarnoff.

UPSTART

Arthur Judson had begun as a violinist but, finding he was not a Kreisler or Heifetz, turned to artist management. He managed, at various times, the Cincinnati Orchestra, the Philadelphia Orchestra, the New York Philharmonic, and hosts of individual artists. "Concert Management Arthur Judson" conveyed distinction and success.

He knew little about the broadcasting world but, viewing it from some distance, was naturally concerned about its impact on the concert field and its policies toward the performing artist. In mid-1926 the rise of well-financed sponsorship stirred him to action. Among rumors of impending developments at RCA he visited David Sarnoff. He proposed organizing a bureau that would provide leading artists for chain broadcasting at fees "sufficient to make it worth while and yet not ruin the business." According to Judson, Sarnoff asked him to submit a plan, which Judson presently did. "Sarnoff read the plan with great interest and said that if it was within his power when he got his chain organized—which he was then doing—he would certainly put me in charge of the programs and of supplying the artists." [1]

When the creation of NBC was announced, Judson was sure he would hear from Sarnoff. He had organized, in September 1926, the Judson Radio Program Corporation. When he learned that there would be two chains—a red and a blue—both controlled by NBC, and he had still not heard from Sarnoff, he became uneasy. Would there be a monopoly situa-

1. Judson, *Reminiscences*, p. 5.

tion from which he would be shut out? With his associate George A. Coats he visited Sarnoff again, and asked what was planned concerning the Judson proposals. "Nothing," Sarnoff told him. Judson was taken aback. "Then we will organize our own chain," he announced. Sarnoff, having just completed a full year of hand-to-hand combat with AT&T negotiators, looked at Judson and, according to the latter's account, leaned back in his chair and roared with laughter. "You can't do it!" he said. Sarnoff offered the information that he had just signed a contract with AT&T for a million dollars' worth of long lines. Even if Judson had a station, he would not be able to get lines, Sarnoff told him.[2]

Stung by the challenge, Judson and Coats and two other associates formed, in January 1927, United Independent Broadcasters. The word "independent" was meant to sound a note of protest against "monopoly."

George A. Coats was a promoter who operated in various fields including manufacture of road equipment. Promotion was his specialty, choice of field secondary. He had recently become indignant about ASCAP and seems at first to have visualized the Judson venture as an anti-ASCAP move. If performers could be united as a power bloc, composers and music publishers could be brought to terms, he argued. Judson seems to have been driven by a different motivation: to win for concert artists— and their management—a deserved place in the broadcasting sun.

They were soon joined by J. Andrew White. Veteran editor of *Wireless Age* and a pioneer sportscaster, he was rapidly being eclipsed by younger idols such as McNamee, Brokenshire, and Husing. But his name held renown and was of value to the promoters. They resolved on a September debut.

Coats went on the road and soon had contracts with a number of stations. He began with WCAU, Philadelphia, owned by Leon and Isaac Levy—the first a dentist, the second a lawyer. Leon Levy put Coats in touch with other broadcasters and helped him work out the terms that were extended to all the stations. Twelve stations quickly accepted them, including WOR, which would be their New York origination point.

The speed of these developments resulted from the nature of the terms. Coats was generous with the revenue expected from network sponsors. Each station was guaranteed $500 a week for ten hours of its broadcast time. The venture was thus committed to an outlay of $6000 per week

2. *Ibid.* p. 7.

before it had a hint of a sponsor. There would also be line costs. However —a more perilous circumstance—they had no lines.

Early in 1927 the promoters approached AT&T. Its attitude was unpromising. It would be at least three years, said AT&T, before lines could be furnished. Argument and protest brought no result. But Coats would not accept this answer and headed for Washington, intent on stirring up pressure at the Interstate Commerce Commission,[3] which had jurisdiction over telephone matters.

He also went armed—according to Judson—with a $1000 check and a $10,000 check.[4] Coats said he knew a man who fixed things.

Judson stayed in New York.

A LAW IS MADE

The new broadcasting law that reached its final form with remarkable speed late in January 1927 was in many ways an historic document. Burning issues of the day made their mark on it.

One such issue was *conservation.* During the Coolidge regime the scandals of Elk Hills and Teapot Dome came to light. Oil reserves held for future national needs had been quietly—without competitive bidding—made available by the Secretary of the Interior to friends, after which he had gone home with a satchel full of $100 bills, amounting to $100,000. The rationale for the oil leases had been that the private exploiters paid a royalty in the form of oil to be stored at Pearl Harbor for defensive needs. But meanwhile private fortunes as well as oil had been extracted from government property, and some of the oil appeared to have been sold to Japan.[1] For his role in the affair, Secretary of the Interior Albert B. Fall eventually went to jail.

Conservationists of both parties, indignant over the oil plunder, were also getting agitated over private exploitation of other national resources. A leader in the agitation was Senator George W. Norris of Nebraska. He saw the innumerable rivers and streams of America, tumbling from thousands of mountains, as a resource belonging "to all of us, a source of

3. Archer, *Big Business and Radio,* p. 308.
4. Judson, *Reminiscences,* p. 9. Judson does not say for whom the checks were intended.
1. Allen, *Only Yesterday,* p. 149.

human happiness." [2] He felt its development should be a public responsibility. In his battle his most formidable opponent was the National Electric Light Association, propaganda arm of electric utilities and holding companies, and until recently managed by Merlin H. Aylesworth. It campaigned vigorously against public power as a communist threat. It also put professors and teachers secretly on its payroll, attacked textbooks unfavorable to its views, dispatched speakers to schools and churches, and courted legislators.[3] Little was yet known of the role of Merlin H. Aylesworth in all this before his transplantation to the NBC presidency. But broadcasting, like hydroelectric power, was ultimately based on a national resource; the parallel made the use of the air another crucial conservation issue.

The issue left its mark on the new law. Its stated purpose was *"to maintain the control of the United States over all channels"* and to provide for the use of channels, *"but not the ownership thereof,"* by licensees for limited periods; *"and no such license shall be construed to create any right, beyond the terms, conditions, and periods of the license."* [4] In the granting of a license or transfer of a station, the guiding standard was to be the *"public interest, convenience or necessity."* [5] And every applicant for a license was to sign *"a waiver of any claim to the use of any particular frequency or wave length or of the ether as against the regulatory power of the United States."* [6]

Another issue was *censorship*. The suppression mania of the early 1920's had to some extent subsided. The year 1925 had brought it to great heights but also to a turning point. In Dayton, Tenn., John Thomas Scopes had that year been brought to trial under a state law forbidding the teaching of evolution. In an enterprising move, Chicago station WGN, expending $1000 per day in wire charges,[7] had broadcast the final portions of the trial, bringing to large audiences bizarre confrontations between Clarence Darrow as defense attorney and the aging William Jennings Bryan, volunteer prosecutor:

DARROW: Mr. Bryan, do you believe that the first woman was Eve?
BRYAN: Yes.

2. Quoted, Schlesinger, *The Crisis of the Old Order*, p. 123.
3. *Ibid.* p. 121.
4. Public Law No. 632, 69th Congress, Sec. 1. (See Appendix B.)
5. *Ibid.* Sec. 11.
6. *Ibid.* Sec. 5 (H).
7. *WGN*, p. 22.

DARROW: Do you believe she was literally made out of Adam's rib?
BRYAN: I do.
DARROW: Did you ever discover where Cain got his wife?
BRYAN: No, sir; I leave the agnostics to hunt for her.
DARROW: You have not found out?
BRYAN: I have never tried to find out. . . .
DARROW: Were there other people on the earth at that time?
BRYAN: I cannot say.[8]

Scopes and Darrow had lost the case. Bryan, who died five days later, had won. What residue had the trial, via newspaper accounts and broadcasts, left in public thinking? In the 69th Congress the issue stirred again in a proposed amendment to ban from radio all "discourses" on evolution. Senator Coleman L. Blease of South Carolina spoke forthrightly on behalf of the ban: "I am willing for the world to know that on this proposition I am on the side of Jesus Christ." [9] But the amendment had no chance; there was change in the air.

Another 1925 event had contributed to this. In that year the U. S. Supreme Court had taken up the case of *Gitlow* v. *State of New York*. Benjamin Gitlow, a socialist, had written a pamphlet and been jailed for it under the New York State Criminal Anarchy Act of 1902. The Supreme Court did not reverse the conviction but in its decision made an historic pronouncement. Until that time established doctrine had considered the Constitution a barrier against federal censorship but not against state censorship. Under laws like the New York Criminal Anarchy Act, states had for decades freely imprisoned those who expressed unpopular or "dangerous" opinions. In the Gitlow case the U. S. Supreme Court, climaxing long agitation, officially took the view that freedom of speech and press were among those unspecified "privileges" and "immunities" which the Fourteenth Amendment guarantees against state abridgement.[10] This decision seemed to Professor Zechariah Chafee of Harvard "the greatest victory for freedom of speech in my lifetime," [11] and it became a stepping stone for countless later advances in civil-rights and censorship struggles. To all communication media it brought a change of environment. A thaw had set in.

The new climate was reflected in the 1927 radio law. *"Nothing in this*

8. *American Heritage*, August 1965.
9. *Congressional Record*, 69th Congress, Vol. 67, Part II, p. 12615.
10. *Gitlow* v. *State of New York*, 268 U.S. 652 (1925).
11. Chafee, *Freedom of Speech and Press*, p. 54.

act shall be understood or construed to give the licensing authority the power of censorship over the radio communications or signals transmitted by any radio station, and no regulation or condition shall be promulgated or fixed by the licensing authority which shall interfere with the right of free speech by means of radio communications." This right did not, however, extend to *"obscene, indecent, or profane language."* [12] The licensee, while not required to give time to candidates for office, was obliged to treat rival candidates equally and had *"no power of censorship over the material broadcast under the provisions of this paragraph."* [13]

Still another issue was the struggle against *monopoly.* Antimonopolists too left their mark on the law. The licensing authority was forbidden to license *"any person, firm, company, or corporation, or any subsidiary thereof, which has been finally adjudged guilty by a Federal court of unlawfully monopolizing or attempting unlawfully to monopolize, after this Act takes effect, radio communication, directly or indirectly, through the control of the manufacture or sale of radio apparatus, through exclusive traffic arrangements, or by any other means or to have been using unfair methods of competition."* [14] Federal Trade Commission findings of monopolistic practices were mentioned as a possible basis for license revocation.[15] There were also clauses intended to prevent telephone interests from controlling radio, or vice versa.[16] There was also a check on the power of the licensing authority itself; certain of its decisions could be appealed to the Court of Appeals of the District of Columbia and others to United States district courts.[17]

That such passages found their way into the new law was a remarkable achievement for their proponents. The desperate need for radio legislation probably helped them establish these beachheads.

Yet in the long run these written guarantees would find their meaning in administrative decisions. Such phrases as "public interest, convenience or necessity"—like "due process" in the Constitution—would acquire flesh and blood gradually, case by case. Words would ultimately mean what men had decided they meant. A crucial issue overhanging all other issues therefore was: "Which men?"

12. Public Law No. 632, 69th Congress, Sec. 29. (See Appendix B.)
13. *Ibid.* Sec. 18.
14. *Ibid.* Sec. 13.
15. *Ibid.* Sec. 15.
16. *Ibid.* Sec. 17.
17. *Ibid.* Sec. 16.

Here a long conflict gradually moved toward compromise. In the bills offered by Representative Wallace White of Maine in 1923 and subsequent years, the licensing authority was the Secretary of Commerce. An opposing view demanded an independent commission, and this was embodied in a proposal submitted by Senator Clarence C. Dill of Montana. President Coolidge was said to frown on this, and Secretary Hoover was likewise quoted as saying: "The tendency to create in the government independent agencies whose administrative functions are outside the control of the President is, I believe, thoroughly bad." [18] In January 1927, crisis brought compromise. The Dill-White bill, which became the radio law, gave the licensing authority to an independent bipartisan commission of five members for a period of one year. These men were to bring order out of chaos. After the one-year period the licensing authority was to revert to the Secretary of Commerce. At least, so the law contemplated. "But I knew," Senator Dill said later, "if we ever got a commission, we would never get rid of it." [19] Later amendments prolonged the life of the commission; its work never seemed finished.

The enactment of the Radio Act of 1927 deserves several postscripts. Although it represented important advances over the 1912 law and embodied significant principles, it was already obsolete when passed. Its general pattern was descended from the White bill of 1923, its direct ancestor. This was written when stations were separate entities. The law assumed that each station controlled its own programming. The lawmakers could not know the extent to which negotiations just concluded in New York City would make their picture of the radio world a thing of the past. To be sure, talk about "chain broadcasting" was everywhere, and at the final moment the subject squeezed into the law: The commission was authorized to make *special regulations applicable to radio stations engaged in chain broadcasting.* [20] Only in this one sentence, added in the final Senate-House conference committee,[21] did the law take note of a development that was to dominate broadcasting for decades to come.

Another crucial development similarly escaped full attention. The sale of time, like chain broadcasting, crept into the document briefly, even obliquely. Matter broadcast for a consideration, said the law, must be *announced as paid for or furnished, as the case may be, by such person, firm,*

18. *Radio Broadcast,* July 1926.
19. Dill, *Interview,* p. 9.
20. Public Law No. 632, 69th Congress, Sec. 4(n). (See Appendix B.)
21. *Jurisdiction of Radio Commission,* p. 134.

company, or corporation." [22] Radio advertising was thus mentioned as an almost peripheral topic. At this juncture the time-selling stations were still a minority; the climax of a struggle between commercial and noncommercial interests lay ahead. But the balance was rapidly shifting. All this the lawmakers failed to note, or else sidestepped.

Thus the Radio Act of 1927, in spite of impressive achievements, perpetuated a state of affairs that had existed from the start of broadcasting. The field would still be governed by a law written for a world that no longer existed.

If the word "advertising" did not enter the law, neither did "education." One senator is said to have urged that channels for education receive a specific guarantee in the law. He was persuaded that the standard of "public interest" inevitably protected education.[23] This too would be left to another arena.

Senator Dill of Montana, one of the chief authors of the new law, would remain a leading figure in radio legislation. He later told the curious circumstances that had thrust him into this role and made him a radio specialist. About 1925 he had been "called out of the Senate" one day by an old acquaintance who represented two western newspapers, one of which —the *Oregonian*—had a broadcasting station. The man asked, "Dill, how would you like to have a story in the morning paper?" "What is it about?" asked Dill. The *Oregonian* station was having ASCAP trouble. The man had a bill he wanted Dill to present to the Senate—an amendment to the Copyright Act, exempting musical broadcasts from any obligations under copyright law. The Senator, after consideration, offered the bill—S. 2328, 69th Congress—and suddenly found himself a celebrity among broadcasters. "Next day my office was filled with a number of men I had never seen." They represented stations in various parts of the country and were very enthusiastic. "We've been in trouble with the ASCAP people . . . and you, a Senator from the far northwest . . . have proposed a solution!" They all wanted to take part in hearings. ASCAP also knew how to put on pressure—"What are you trying to do to us, do you want to destroy our means of livelihood?" Victor Herbert and John Philip Sousa were presently asking in Senate visits—and the bill eventually died in committee. But Senator Dill had meanwhile become a focal figure, and thus it was

22. Public Law No. 632, 69th Congress, Sec. 19. (See Appendix B.)
23. *Education on the Air* (1931), p. 33.

around him that the movement against Hoover suzerainty coalesced. Before that "I didn't know what a wave length was." [24]

The new law, through its belligerent stance on monopoly, seems to have put pressure on the patent allies. The month in which the bill reached final form saw a decisive shift in RCA policy. RCA offered to license a limited number of competitors—including recent "infringers"—to make radios under patents of the allies. The peace achieved with AT&T had paved the way for this. Each licensee would pay 7.5 per cent of gross sales, with a minimum of $100,000 per year. Zenith, Crosley, Atwater Kent, Philco, and others quickly became licensees. Some became early sponsors of NBC network programs. In 1927 RCA would receive from 20-odd licensees approximately $3,000,000 in royalties—one-fourth of its net revenue. All this would not end the hostility toward RCA; before long they would be detailing bitter complaints against it. But for the moment it brought a detente, and also a slackening in the Federal Trade Commission action. In 1928 the FTC dropped its complaint.

Perhaps the new law with its warlike words also aided Arthur Judson. While he continued to plead with AT&T officials in New York and to get discouraging answers, a telephone call came from Coats in Washington. The availability of telephone lines was assured, Coats cheerfully announced. Miraculously, the lines would be ready in the fall. The odds against the new network were still staggering. It still had no sponsors. Its cash was exhausted. But the desperate gamble went on.

The Radio Act of 1927 was signed by President Coolidge on February 3. Sixty days after passage of the act all existing licenses were to become void. New applications would form the basis for a new start. More than seven hundred stations watched and waited.

President Coolidge was to appoint, with the advice and consent of the Senate, a five-man commission to administer the new era. Not more than three were to belong to one party.

The crucial question still was, "Which men?"

Hoover tells us: "President Coolidge asked me to select its members, which I did." [25] On March 1 the President sent their names to the Senate.

24. Dill, *Interview*, pp. 3-5.
25. Hoover, *Memoirs: The Cabinet and the Presidency*, p. 145.

THE COOLIDGE HOUR

In 1927 the Coolidge era began its most exhilarating moments. There was affluence, at least for business. To be sure, there was awareness that farmers were in a depression but, as Coolidge pointed out, farmers had never made money. "I don't believe we can do much about it." [1] At least business boomed, and some of the wealth was expected to trickle into other segments of society. Never had confidence in the world of business been so high, or had business been so surely in control. "Never before, here or anywhere else," said the *Wall Street Journal*, "has a government been so completely fused with business." [2]

Sitting as chairman of this fusion was President Calvin Coolidge. In the words of Arthur Schlesinger, Jr., "His frugality sanctified an age of waste . . . his taciturnity an age of ballyhoo." [3]

The ballyhoo had been mounting steadily. The stage had been set for it by mergers of earlier decades. At the start of the century advertising was still a marginal, grubby business. Albert Lasker, due to become one of the titans of radio advertising, was working at Lord & Thomas at the turn of the century; it was already one of the three largest advertising agencies. But it needed only one copy writer; in the morning he worked for Lord & Thomas, in the afternoon for Montgomery Ward. [4]

Various kinds of business combinations turned the tide for advertising. The first million-dollar advertising account was created when several hundred local cracker factories were combined into the National Biscuit Company—each getting stock in the new corporation—for the sake of a common trademark in national advertising. [5] Similar unity operations swept through the business world. As the big national advertising campaigns proved successful, they brought other changes. The American Tobacco Company, instead of splitting its advertising into budgets for fifty different brands, began in the 1910's to join them into massive splurges for Lucky Strike cigarettes. [6] The gamble won fortunes for the American Tobacco Company and its advertising agency, Lord & Thomas, which was by now owned by Albert Lasker. Throughout the 1920's the trend toward

1. Schlesinger, *The Crisis of the Old Order,* p. 67.
2. *Ibid.* p. 61.
3. *Ibid.* p. 58.
4. Lasker, *Reminiscences,* p. 16.
5. *Ibid.* p. 19.
6. *Ibid.*

concentration continued. By the end of the decade the two hundred largest American corporations—other than banks—controlled almost half the
corporate wealth,[7] and leading advertising agencies grew rich in the process. Their executives were now men of the world with a statesmanlike look
who talked about advertising as a profession. Advertising proclaimed
codes of ethics and a theology. Bruce Barton, one of its prophets, in 1924
depicted Jesus as a great businessman and advertiser. The flabby Sunday
school picture of Jesus was wrong, said Barton, partner in Batten, Barton,
Durstine & Osborn, which was to represent DuPont, United States Steel,
and other industrial giants. The real Jesus "picked up twelve men from the
bottom ranks of business and forged them into an organization that con-
quered the world." Barton decided to write a book about "the real Jesus"
because he was sure every businessman would want to read it and send it
to his partners and salesmen. "For it will tell the story of the founder of
modern business." [8]

During the 1920's advertising carried all before it. It seemed to dispose
of opposition without difficulty by forming associations, which in turn
framed codes. Protests against billboards mounted, but in 1925 the Out-
door Advertising Association announced a code which said there should
be no structures which destroyed scenic beauty, and that seemed to take
care of the matter. In 1928 the National Association of Broadcasters also
formed a committee to frame a code of ethics, proclaimed the following
year. Its first edition said: "Commercial announcements, as the term is
generally understood, should not be broadcast between seven and eleven
P.M." [9] Daytime hours belonged to the business day, it was explained, but
the evening did not.

Such agencies as the Federal Trade Commission occasionally slowed the
consolidation process, as in the 1924 action against the radio patent group.
But in 1925 President Coolidge made a personnel change which brought a
policy shift. The new chairman, William E. Humphrey, promised that the
FTC would no longer be "an instrument of oppression and disturbance"
but would help business.[10]

The formation of NBC as a coast-to-coast web of independent units,
linked by agreements and common interests, put it in the mainstream of
the consolidation movement. Coming when it did, it also provided an

7. Berle and Means, *The Modern Corporation*, p. 32.
8. Barton, *The Man Nobody Knows*, pp. i-v.
9. White, *The American Radio*, pp. 240-41.
10. Schlesinger, *The Crisis of the Old Order*, p. 65.

ideal instrument of expression for other consolidations, and thus furthered
the trend. It also fostered the developing self-image of the business magnate. He was ready to become a patron of the arts; NBC gave him this
chance.

The air of distinction and vision which NBC managed to impart to its
operation in its formative months was an extraordinary phenomenon. It
left little room for doubt that broadcasting was in the best possible hands.
The range of symphonic combinations that filled the evening hours contributed to this aura. Another factor was a creation of Owen D. Young:
the Advisory Council of the National Broadcasting Company. This unique
body, outshining any presidential cabinet of modern times, held its first
meeting in February 1927.

In telling a congressional committee about the Advisory Council, Merlin
Aylesworth spoke of "the enormous power concentrated in the hands of a
few men controlling a vast network of radio stations." This power, he said
—conveying a sense of awe—was "a matter for the consideration of statesmen." It involved such far-reaching responsibilities that the NBC board of
directors had created a council of outstanding citizens, "to which appeals
can be carried over the heads of the operating executives." [11] The Advisory
Council included:

> Edward A. Alderman, president, University of Virginia
> Walter Damrosch, conductor, New York Symphony Orchestra
> John W. Davis, lawyer
> Francis D. Farrell, president, Kansas State Agricultural College
> William Green, president, American Federation of Labor
> James G. Harbord, president, RCA
> Charles E. Hughes, lawyer
> Rev. Charles F. MacFarland, general secretary, Federal Council of
>   Churches of Christ in America
> Dwight W. Morrow, banker
> Morgan J. O'Brien, lawyer
> Henry S. Pritchett, president, Carnegie Foundation
> Henry M. Robinson, president, First National Bank, Los Angeles
> Elihu Root, lawyer
> Julius Rosenwald, president, Sears, Roebuck & Co.
> Mrs. Mary Sherman, president, General Federation of Women's Clubs
>   in America
> Guy E. Tripp, chairman of the board, Westinghouse Company
> Owen D. Young, chairman of the board, General Electric Company

11. *Commission on Communications*, p. 1702.

That such a body could strengthen NBC's position and help ward off any possible governmental obstruction can hardly be doubted. Yet the council, under the chairmanship of Owen D. Young himself, does not seem to have thought of itself in that light, but rather as guardians of the network's higher aims. In that respect, it could view the situation with some assurance. At its second meeting it reviewed the achievements of the year 1927. The six hundred commercial sponsors who had brought NBC a flow of funds had at the same time contributed notable programs. While filling a quarter of the network hours, they had provided the revenue that had also paid for hours of farm programs, religious programs, talks, concerts—including music-appreciation broadcasts by Dr. Damrosch, which many schools were utilizing.

The meeting was a festival of congratulations. William Green praised NBC's "liberal policy of giving both sides a hearing." Dr. Alderman described the world of education as "dazed over the vast possibilities of radio as an instrument of education." Mrs. Sherman reported that the General Federation of Women's Clubs had urged that "no home is complete without a radio." Dr. MacFarland said that religious leaders had found the company invariably "fair, just, and wise." Dr. Damrosch was ecstatic. No doubt some people still dwelt, he thought, "in the lower depths and darkness of accepting mere rhythmic noise as a substitute for music." But for millions, things were changing. If he could just bring the little red schoolhouses all over the land within the sphere of NBC's musical activity, it would be "the crowning arch of our building." [12]

The great men fell to chatting. Elihu Root, distinguished Secretary of State under President Theodore Roosevelt, wondered if one might pursue scientific research to learn the relative numbers of those who are primarily ear-minded as opposed to those who are primarily eye-minded. Owen D. Young offered the information that Bruce Barton, before advising General Motors to go on the air, had made an investigation of precisely that question—"necessarily somewhat limited"—and found 20 per cent "markedly ear-minded." Dr. Damrosch said that Socrates' pupils must have been ear-minded. But, he said, Montaigne had found that if he wanted even his dearest friend to know what he thought, he would have to have it published so his friend would read it. Dr. Alderman suggested that radio might make us ear-minded again.[13] The distinguished leaders went home

12. *Memorandum of Minutes,* 2nd meeting (March 1928), pp. 10-14, 43.
13. *Ibid.* p. 16.

and each received a printed copy of the minutes, immortalizing even their intellectual chit-chat. It was bound in cloth. In each copy were printed such words as:

> Only 30 Copies Printed
> This is No. 19
> For the Personal Use of
> Hon. Elihu Root

There is no indication that any citizen ever appealed to this Advisory Council "over the heads of the operating executives." Perhaps few knew where to reach it, or even that it existed. Management apparently did not make a practice of relaying complaints to it. In 1934, when commercial broadcasting was under sharp attack and the Federal Radio Commission was noting a steep increase in protests, the minutes of the NBC Advisory Council noted: "Mr. Aylesworth observed that there were no new complaints to bring before it." [14]

While the Advisory Council dwelt at a rarified level, the network operation was already beginning to affect radio.

NBC was paying each station $50 per hour for the sponsored network programs carried by the station, and charging it $45 an hour for unsponsored—already called "sustaining"—programs.[15] The 1930's were to bring various modifications of these terms.

At many stations the advent of NBC brought a sharp policy shift. WMAQ, Chicago, was asked by NBC to take part of the network schedule. This meant programs of prestige from the entertainment capital; it also meant sponsored programs. William S. Hedges now found himself able to persuade the Chicago *Daily News* to take the plunge. WMAQ began to sell time locally. Within six months it was on a paying basis.[16] In Kansas City, WDAF became an NBC outlet. As the *Eveready Hour* and *Atwater Kent Hour* came over the network lines, the Kansas City *Star*, owner of the station, likewise decided to sell time locally. It had, only a short time before, rejected such a move.[17] Likewise WSB in Atlanta began for the first time to sell time.[18]

14. *Memorandum of Minutes*, 8th meeting (1934), p. 11.
15. *Federal Radio Commissioners*, p. 276.
16. Hedges, *Reminiscences*, p. 17.
17. Patt, *Reminiscences*, p. 20.
18. Arnold, *Broadcast Advertising*, p. 227.

Such decisions, in cities across the country, precipitated still other decisions. As radio began to siphon local advertising funds away from newspapers, uneasiness and hostility developed—especially among newspapers not involved in radio. Radio listings were dropped in many cities.

This development followed an erratic course. In New York City, in 1927, several newspapers began a radio boycott: no schedules would be printed unless paid for. But the papers that ignored the boycott—and carried schedules—gained readers. The boycott therefore quickly collapsed. But tensions continued to increase. Radio columns shrank or vanished. The *Herald Tribune* discontinued program news and criticism in 1928 and maintained the blackout for years. In a few years the tensions would erupt into warfare.

Another effect was the death of long-distance listening. In the mid-1920's newspapers still carried program notes concerning distant stations. During 1925 the Cedar Rapids *Gazette* told its readers about special programs scheduled on WGN, WLS, WMAQ, Chicago; KDKA, WCAE, Pittsburgh; WLW, Cincinnati; WGY, Schenectady; WEAF, WJZ, New York; WHO, Des Moines; KGO, Oakland. In 1927 such information was dropped because the same programs appeared on station after station. Moreover, Silent Night was being swept aside. Affiliates were pressed by networks to carry sponsored programs regardless of traditional silent periods. Local sponsors, too, were bringing this pressure. Night-time hours—the long-distance listening hours—also seemed best to sponsors. In Chicago, WHT decided to defy tradition with sales on Monday night, Chicago's long-established Silent Night. The station persisted in the face of furor and of organized protest. "This is a *business!*" station manager Pat Barnes later explained. "We are not going to be ruled by mobs and committees, this is our *business* and our hours are at *night!*" [19] In San Jose, Fred J. Hart of KQW stirred up similar storms by defying the daily 7-7:30 silent period, which had existed before he entered broadcasting. "I thought, well, I'm not under that ban and anyway, that's when agriculture can listen. So boom! I go on the air and boom! everybody hollers." [20]

Another effect was on local talent. In San Francisco, Wilton Gunzendorfer led a twelve-man orchestra that broadcast every evening—most of the evening—over KPO from the Whitcomb Hotel. The program was dinner and dance music for the area. One day in 1927 the KPO manager

19. Barnes, *Reminiscences*, p. 10.
20. Hart, *Interview*, p. 77.

got word from New York that NBC would take over the time except on Saturdays.[21]

For a number of years, hundreds of stations had given birth to millions of local broadcasts. Quantities of local and transient talent had been brought into action. At many stations the rise of local sponsorship would continue for a time to maintain local production. But at some a decline now began. As network programs expanded, the word came to many—orchestra leaders, lady organists, pianists, singers, monologists, speakers— that they would not be needed. Many dropped from sight.

This transition, which had its tragedies, was poignantly summed up in the humorous column the *Sun Dial*, written by H. I. Phillips for the New York *Sun*. The formation of NBC inspired Phillips to invent a network executive, who was interviewed:

> "What is your plan in regard to Bedtime Stories?" was the next question.
> "Ah," was the reply. "I'm glad you asked. Centralization of the Bedtime Story industry will be brought about at once. Do you realize that at present there are over 1,167 concerns turning out Bedtime Stories east of the Mississippi alone? Do you know that none of them is making money and that the product is far from satisfactory? Our plan is to close all these factories and open one big Bedtime Story plant in Long Island City and produce a complete Bedtime Story by one operation in which the human element is reduced to a minimum." [22]

But it was not twilight for all local talent. In some cases a local performer caught the ear of network or sponsor and suddenly found himself a national commodity. In 1925 Charles Correll and Freeman F. Gosden began broadcasting over WEBH in Chicago's Edgewater Beach Hotel and were paid with free hotel dinners. They passed into the employ of the Chicago *Tribune*'s WGN, which paid $50 a week for both. Later they moved to WMAQ. It was not long afterward that they were able to get $100,000 from a network sponsor—as *Amos 'n' Andy*, of whom more will be heard.

Another effect was on talent agents. Immediately after its formation NBC organized an artist bureau and began representing artists on a percentage basis. The venture was backed by on-the-air promotion. The entry

21. Gunzendorfer, *Reminiscences*, pp. 1-9. He became a broker who bought and sold radio stations.
22. Quoted, Goldsmith and Lescarboura, *This Thing Called Broadcasting*, p. 338.

"Artist Bureau Announcement" first appeared in the WJZ log on November 26, 1926, at 9 P.M. Because NBC would also be a major employer offering a nation-wide platform, artists quickly gravitated to its management service. Talent agencies without a network base would soon feel their livelihood threatened.

In March 1927, as the Federal Radio Commission was being formed, there were 732 broadcasting stations in the United States.[23] Less than a hundred were network-affiliated, but they were making news and getting major attention. More than six hundred stations were still operating independently. The majority of these were not selling time. Many were still publicity vehicles, representing newspapers, stores, manufacturers, hotels. About ninety stations were operated by educational institutions, offering concerts and talks, including full college courses. There were also a number of religious stations. There were, in addition, a number of more or less anomalous stations. In Chicago the Chicago Federation of Labor had persisted in its struggle and in 1926—after the Zenith litigation—obtained a license for its WCFL. In New York City there was WEVD, named after Eugene Victor Debs, several-times Socialist party presidential candidate who had spent much of World War I in prison for contesting the draft. In New York City there was also WNYC, the New York City station, often a subject of controversy; Mayor John F. Hylan had used the station to attack his political enemies and had been stopped in 1926 by court injunction forbidding such use.[24]

This welter of stations had continued to grow until almost the moment the FRC was appointed. Some new stations began as primitively as stations of earlier years. Here and there the whole story of broadcasting seemed to start from its beginning. In Vida (pop. 25), Montana, KGCX was launched on October 5, 1926, by the First State Bank of Vida in a back room of the bank. The broadcasting was done by Ed Krebsbach when he could "slip away from the front counter." [25] In San Diego, Lyman Bryson, a young extension teacher for the University of California, was asked to discuss current events on a radio station in the corner of a hotel. The engineer and control equipment were in the same room as Bryson, but during the broadcast someone warned the engineer that a policeman was going down the street with parking tickets. Leaving the equipment

23. Schmeckebier, The Federal Radio Commission, p. 23.
24. Fletcher v. Hylan, 211 N.Y.S. 727. See Nobel, The Municipal Broadcasting System, p. 10.
25. Richards, "Montana's Pioneer Stations," Montana Journalism Review, Spring 1963.

on, the engineer dashed off. As Bryson finished reading his talk, no engineer was in sight. Bryson ad libbed twelve minutes until the engineer returned.[26]

While new stations still sprouted, others prepared to follow. In North Carolina, Governor Angus Wilton McLean was campaigning vigorously for a high-powered station to be operated by the state as an educational service to rural areas. He argued that such stations should have priority over private stations in channel assignments.[27]

Listeners, too, were still multiplying. Purchases of sets and parts had slackened during the chaos, then shot up again:[28]

1925	$430,000,000
1926	506,000,000
1927	425,600,000
1928	650,550,000

Sets operated on house current were becoming common in 1927—Zenith was a leader in this—but battery sets remained important in rural areas. In a curious way radio and automobile, whose stocks were leaders in the stock market rise, also swept jointly through the countryside. "We would always sell the farmers the battery sets," recalled an Atwater Kent salesman who rode the West Virginia hills, first on horseback and later, as he grew prosperous, in an automobile. "If they had a Ford car, why, we'd put a Ford battery on their radio. If they had a Chevrolet, we put a Chevrolet battery, so that when the battery on the radio ran down, they'd switch it with the one in the car and get it recharged." [29] Also in 1927, car radios began to appear. Philco was a leader in this.

As radio still pushed in all directions, television moved ahead. Early in 1927 Philo Farnsworth patented a "dissector tube" that proved an important link in the development of all-electronic television. Meanwhile experiments using a mechanical scanning system also looked promising. In Schenectady, Ernst F. W. Alexanderson began experimental telecasts. In Pittsburgh, Edgar S. Love, a seasoned amateur, built himself a television set and picked up the Schenectady experiments—mostly silhouettes.[30] Also in Pittsburgh, Vladimir Zworykin pushed forward with his experiments. In

26. Bryson, *Reminiscences,* p. 108. He became Educational Counselor, Columbia Broadcasting System.
27. Wallace, *Development of Broadcasting in North Carolina,* pp. 123-6.
28. *Broadcasting,* 1939 Yearbook, p. 11.
29. Robinson, *Interview,* p. 3.
30. Love, *Reminiscences,* p. 6. Alexanderson, *Reminiscences,* p. 40.

New York AT&T held public television demonstrations. A magazine called *Television* appeared in New York. One of its advertisements said:

> I Thought Radio was a Plaything
> But Now My Eyes Are Opened, And
> I'm Making Over $100 a Week.[31]

There were others on the "get in on the ground floor" theme. Television fever was spreading.

Over this spectrum of nation-wide activity and its hopes and fears, the Federal Radio Commission now assumed supervision.

BIRTH OF THE FRC

In almost every respect the career of the Federal Radio Commission was weird, to the point of straining belief. It belongs in the annals of politics but had a fateful impact on broadcasting.

"Probably no quasi-judicial body was ever subject to so much congressional pressure as the Federal Radio Commission," said a Brookings Institution monograph.[1] The stakes were high.

The list of five FRC appointees drawn up by Secretary of Commerce Hoover and sent by President Coolidge to the Senate for confirmation was made up of Admiral W. H. G. Bullard (chairman), Colonel John F. Dillon, Eugene O. Sykes, Henry A. Bellows, and Orestes H. Caldwell. The first three were confirmed March 4, 1927, just before the 69th Congress adjourned and went home. However, one of them, Admiral Bullard, was in China at the time and died soon after his return. Another, Colonel Dillon, had cancer and also died within a few months. Until the following spring the FRC had only one confirmed member—Eugene O. Sykes, former Mississippi supreme court justice.

Meanwhile Henry Bellows and Orestes Caldwell, both unconfirmed, could not receive government salaries, but stayed on. During much of 1927 they carried the burden of the work and made crucial reallocations.[2] Bellows, still unconfirmed and still not on the government payroll, resigned in October and went back to Minneapolis, where he had been a broadcaster.

31. *Television*, Fall 1927. A magazine of the same title appeared at about the same time in Britain, where parallel television experimentation was in progress.
1. Schmeckebier, *The Federal Radio Commission*, p. 55.
2. Caldwell, *Reminiscences*, p. 10.

The list of five names sent by President Coolidge to the Senate had posed questions. That the FRC chairman should be a naval officer closely connected with the birth of RCA—he had, in fact, been its principal god-father and had sat with its board of directors—raised eyebrows. RCA was still under investigation by the Federal Trade Commission for monopo-listic practices. But the much-decorated retired admiral was confirmed as a matter of course. Not so with others.

The law provided that there should be one commissioner from each of five districts. The arrangement contemplated that each commissioner would become a specialist in the problems of his zone. In fact, each was to become virtually a satrap for his portion of the country.

This centered particular interest on Orestes Caldwell, appointed to rep-resent the First Zone—Maine, New Hampshire, Vermont, Massachusetts, Connecticut, Rhode Island, New York, New Jersey, Delaware, Maryland, the District of Columbia, Puerto Rico, and the Virgin Islands.

It is likely that few senators had previously heard of Orestes Caldwell. He had worked for various trade periodicals in the electrical equipment field: *Western Electrician, Electrical World, Electrical Merchandising,* and finally *Radio Retailing,* which he had started for McGraw-Hill in 1925. Its chief income was from advertising placed by radio manufactur-ers, with whom he was well acquainted. In the course of his editorial work he had also known Hoover since 1926 and had agreed with him that li-censing should be controlled by the Secretary of Commerce.[3]

Editorial statements of *Radio Retailing* became a subject of special in-terest to senators. *Radio Retailing* was quoted as having denounced—as "vicious in the extreme"—the clause in the Radio Act barring licenses to those convicted of anti-trust violations.[4] Another provision, barring from the commission those with financial interests in the radio industry, had also been denounced by *Radio Retailing*.[5] Such statements raised ques-tions of whether Caldwell was out of sympathy with the act he was to administer, and committed to one industry element.

Caldwell was anxious to be confirmed. He regarded himself as unpreju-diced. He felt he knew radio and could help. Cleaning up the chaos of the ether seemed to him important. In any event, *Radio Retailing* would have no future if the chaos were not ended. Caldwell at first expected to spend

3. *Ibid.* pp. 4-5.
4. *Jurisdiction of Radio Commission,* p. 196.
5. *Radio Retailing,* November 1926. Quoted, *Federal Radio Commissioners,* p. 159.

one or two days a week at his commission task and also carry on his editorial work.[6] But this would prove difficult.

When, in the hectic closing days of the 69th Congress, the FRC appointments were referred to the Senate committee on interstate commerce, this committee simply deferred action on Bellows and Caldwell, apparently wanting more information. The committee chairman, Senator James E. Watson of Indiana, was regarded as a presidential hopeful. Caldwell concluded that Senator Watson looked on him as a "Hoover man." Watson was thought to consider most New Yorkers to be "Hoover men." Caldwell decided to have a talk with Senator Watson.

The situation was complicated by the fact that the final days of the 69th Congress were taken up by a filibuster.

> So for three nights, I sat up in the Senate galleries all night long watching Senator Watson at his desk on the floor, and other committee members, so that if at any time they ducked out I could hurry out and get hold of Senator Watson.[7]

On the third night Caldwell had his chance, getting in hurried words in the corridor before the committee door closed on him. Caldwell told the Senator:

> Senator Watson, you feel I am a New Yorker. That is true, I do live in New York. But Senator Watson, I am a graduate of Purdue University in Indiana, and my friends in Purdue and Indiana are counting on you as Senator from Indiana to protect my interests in this committee meeting. Therefore I insist that you recognize me as a Purdue boy.[8]

Although this did not produce confirmation, the committee at least did not reject him. Caldwell decided to start work under his interim appointment, without salary, on the chance that he might be confirmed by the next Congress.

This decision, made with a feeling of devotion to the cause, would not be so interpreted by others. It was facilitated by the fact that Caldwell was continuing to receive $7000 a year from *Radio Retailing*. Caldwell himself said he was "not on the payroll" of the magazine, that this was only a "retainer." Senator Burton K. Wheeler scoffed at this. "That is just

6. Caldwell, *Reminiscences*, pp. 6-7.
7. *Ibid.* p. 8.
8. *Ibid.* pp. 8-9.

another way of saying you are on the payroll." [9] Caldwell served as an unconfirmed, unsalaried commissioner—with support from *Radio Retailing*—for more than a year. On March 30, 1928, his appointment was finally confirmed in the Senate by a one-vote margin, 36-35.[10]

Meanwhile a staggering load of work had been carried. To aggravate matters, the filibuster had prevented the 69th Congress, before it disbanded, from making an appropriation for the new commission. The FRC therefore began life without staff or funds of its own and lived on the charity of the Department of Commerce. Secretary Hoover provided space.

The FRC started with "one desk, two chairs, a table and a packing box." Caldwell insisted that Sykes, as a former state supreme court justice, take the desk. This seemed to make him temporary chairman in Bullard's absence. The Navy sent Captain Hooper to help with allocations.[11] Secretary Hoover provided clerical help.

The situation confronting the small group was "almost hopelessly involved" and "without parallel." The problem was what to do with 732 broadcasting stations. The commission was swamped with telegrams and letters of advice. Leading recommendations included: punishment of wave pirates; abolition of direct advertising; confinement of advertising to daytime hours." [12]

As a basis for decision, the commissioners began sending questionnaires to all stations. Somewhat ominously, they pronounced their belief in "open covenants openly arrived at." [13]

That spring they extended all licenses temporarily. Then they made a reallocation involving almost all stations. All licenses were at this time made for 60-day periods, facilitating early revision. Then the commissioners went home to review. That fall it seemed clear to them that far more drastic action was needed. At least a hundred stations would have to be abolished.

In November two new commissioners joined the group: Harold Lafount, who had been in the hardware field and in radio manufacture in Salt Lake City; and Sam Pickard, who had started the Kansas State Col-

9. *Federal Radio Commissioners,* p. 153.
10. New York *Times,* March 31, 1928. Henry Bellows was also retroactively confirmed, and was reimbursed for past services by a special joint resolution.
11. Caldwell, *Reminiscences,* p. 9.
12. *Annual Report of the Federal Radio Commission* (1927), pp. 1, 8.
13. *Ibid.* p. 6.

lege programs over KFKB, the Brinkley station, and then directed radio activities of the Department of Agriculture. Soon they were also aided by Louis G. Caldwell as FRC counsel.

In all their actions that winter, the commissioners felt the need for speed, "to get the allocation into effect and to prevent any legal injunctions being brought." [14] In spite of widespread feeling against "wave pirates," the commission had to remember that these had not, in the opinion of a district court and of the Acting Attorney General, broken the law; rather, the Department of Commerce had overstepped its authority. Decisions that seemed punitive might not stand up in court. What decisions would? How could one rightly weigh, as Commissioner Bellows asked with appropriate desperation, "the conflicting claims of grand opera and religious services, of market reports and direct advertising, of jazz orchestras and lectures on the diseases of hogs?" [15]

Without investigators, the commissioners had to rely on themselves. They often worked through week ends. The avoiding of litigation "before we would get a system working" became an obsession. "Personally I can tell you," Commissioner Caldwell recounted later, "the commissioners were more scared than the broadcasters were." If a station sent a lawyer, or a Congressman interceded, a compromise usually resulted. "We felt that at that time we did have to make a lot of trades . . . But we were just a handful of men there—three or four men." [16]

Early in 1928 an amendment, the "Davis Amendment," required the FRC to make "equitable" allocations to each region—in number of licenses, wave lengths, time, and power. This added almost insoluble complications.

In March 1928, Ira Robinson of West Virginia, a former judge, was appointed to the commission and became its chairman; the FRC became complete for the first time.

Soon thereafter the FRC made its most drastic move. Its General Order #32 told 164 stations to show cause why they should not be abolished. Hearings would be held.

Louis G. Caldwell, FRC counsel, described the ensuing events.

> On July 9, 110 out of 164 stations appeared in a body in the auditorium in the Interior Department building, where the hearings were

14. Caldwell, *Reminiscences*, p. 11.
15. *Annual Report of the Federal Radio Commission* (1927), pp. 7-8.
16. Caldwell, *Reminiscences*, pp. 12-15.

to be held. We had almost no procedure devised. We had no files. We had affidavits and letters piling in from all stations. Some stations were soliciting letters from their listeners. . . . Stations were able to send in as high as 400,000 and 500,000 letters. They would come in packing cases. That is the sort of record that threatened to swamp the commission. We had to devise rules and regulations. We had to get up a filing system, and do a lot of miscellaneous things in order to permit us to handle those hearings and avoid injustice to the stations. All stations were heard in about two weeks.

Throughout this action the FRC remained painfully aware that its decisions might be tested in court. Louis Caldwell was especially conscious of this aspect. "I considered it my chief duty to try to guard the record with that end in mind." [17] Because programming offered no objective standards, the FRC began to give special attention to technical standards, such as quality of equipment. Every station representative was pressed on technical questions. Most decisions were explained by the FRC on several grounds, always including "the public interest, convenience and necessity," [18] and often citing technical shortcomings.

Among the 164 stations summoned to defend their right to exist, eighty-one made sufficient protests to survive in some form, usually with reduced time and power. Among them was WEVD, New York. It had entered into the record the following statement:

This station exists for the purpose of maintaining at least one channel of the air free and open to the uses of the workers. We admit without apology that this station has no deep concern with reporting polo matches. . . . We are not convinced that the public necessity dictates the broadcasting of descriptions of ladies' fancy dresses at receptions in Fifth Avenue ballrooms. . . . If WEVD is taken off the air and in fact if it is not treated on a parity with others who are richer and more influential with the government, the people of the nation can truly recognize that radio which might be such a splendid force for the honest clash of ideas—creating a free market for thought —is nothing but a tool to be used by the powerful against any form of disagreement, or any species of protest.[19]

The FRC's decision to renew was to become one of its most cherished exhibits. It would long be cited in answer to any accusation of political partiality. It also provided the germ for what became in later years the

17. *Commission on Communications*, p. 68.
18. *Annual Report of the Federal Radio Commission* (1928), p. 9.
19. Quoted, Brindze, *Not To Be Broadcast*, pp. 152-3.

"fairness doctrine." The station would have to be conducted, the FRC said, "with due regard for the opinions of others." [20]

Throughout this period there was pressure, including congressional pressure. FRC counsel Louis Caldwell later wrote of the "political pressure constantly exercised . . . in all manner of cases" by members of Congress.[21] Commission chairman Ira Robinson spoke of a request from a congressman who said he "would not take no for an answer." Chairman Robinson felt obliged to rule that letters from congressmen—although they influenced decisions—should not be entered in the record of any case "because we ought to admit in the record, which may go to the Court of Appeals of the District of Columbia, only those things which can be legitimately reviewed by the Court." Senator Dill seems to have been among those engaging in ex parte persuasion. At least, when Senator Couzens in a meeting of the Senate interstate commerce committee denounced congressmen for interceding with radio commissioners—almost as reprehensible, he thought, as telling a court "to do or not to do a certain thing"— Senator Dill demurred. Was there anything wrong with telling a commissioner, in connection with a pending case, "I happen to have the facts about the matter, and I should like to have you consider those facts?" Was this wrong? Senator Smith intervened; he was sure no congressman, however intent on serving constituents, "would disregard the public welfare." [22]

Throughout the first three years of the FRC the commissioners were kept in a state of uncertainty about their tenure. Their positions and the life of the commission were extended by Congress for short-term periods. This may have increased the effectiveness of congressional pressure.

The importance of congressional assistance in dealing with the FRC became notorious. *Radio Broadcast,* referring to the FRC as a "jellyfish commission," later wrote:

> All one must do, apparently, is gather unto himself a couple of Congressmen, visit the most weak-kneed commissioner available, make a few grand statements about service to the public, and some way, regardless of the general good of the listener, will be found to accommodate the pleading station.[23]

20. *Annual Report of the Federal Radio Commission* (1928), p. 155.
21. *Radio Broadcast,* March 1930.
22. *Commission on Communications,* pp. 177-9.
23. *Radio Broadcast,* March 1930.

The grand shuffles and shakedowns of 1927-28 won both praise and protest. Increased separations lessened interference. However, FRC chairman Ira Robinson felt obliged to dissociate himself from the reallocations, feeling they had been made with undue haste and insufficient study and favored the powerful stations.[24] Other protesters pointed out that of twenty-four clear channels created by the FRC, twenty-one had gone to network stations, with some authorized to use 50,000 watts. Was there need, asked Representative E. L. Davis of Tennessee, for chain stations to have such power when their programs now came from many different places?[25]

A number of powerful independent stations, including Dr. Brinkley's KFKB, fared well in the allocations. Its equipment was good and its schedule showed an array of educational talks and hymn-singers.

Virtually all stations operated by educational institutions received part-time assignments, in most cases confined to daytime hours, which many considered useless for adult education. The year 1928 was a bad one for educational stations. There had been few deaths among them in 1926 and 1927—eight in each year. But in 1928 twenty-three gave up; in 1929 thirteen more followed.[26]

The University of Arkansas's KFMQ, being forced to share time with a commercial station—which was given three-quarters of the hours including all night-time hours—felt "its arms, its legs, and its head" had been cut off, and gave up the ghost.[27]

Nebraska Wesleyan University's WCAJ, dating from 1922, had prided itself on holding to its assigned wave length during the chaos, in spite of wave pirates. It had continued to operate its authorized full time. In 1927 the FRC assigned it to 860 kc.;[28] then moved it to 790, sharing with KMMJ; then, in 1928, to 590, sharing with WOW, Omaha, which was given six-sevenths of the time. A hard struggle for the remaining one-seventh followed. WOW applied to the FRC for the full time; when this was denied, appealed to the District of Columbia Court of Appeals; when

24. *Ibid.* January 1929.
25. *Jurisdiction of Radio Commission*, pp. 40, 54. In most cases a clear channel accommodated two stations, widely separated, with one dominant. Thus WEAF, New York (50,000 watts), was on 610 kc., which also accommodated KGW, Portland, Ore. (1000 watts). *Annual Report of the Federal Radio Commission* (1928), p. 74
26. Frost, *Education's Own Stations*, p. 4.
27. *Ibid.* pp. 21-4.
28. The FRC began making assignments in *kilocycles* (frequency) instead of *meters* (wave length).

Graham McNamee interviews Babe Ruth, the Sultan of Swat, at Yankee Stadium.

NBC broadcasts the Kentucky Derby.

Herbert Hoover accepts presidential nomination.

NBC

Scanner with rotating disc, used by Ernst F. W. Alexanderson in tests at General Electric, 1928.

Smithsonian Institution

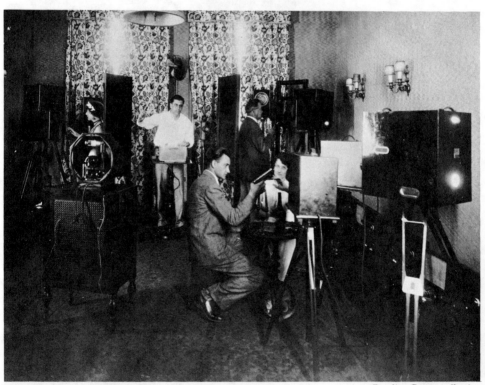

First televised drama: *The Queen's Messenger*, 1928.

Rosaline Greene collection

this action was lost, renewed its petition to the FRC. Each such hearing meant legal and travel costs for the Nebraska Wesleyan station. Its manager wrote despairingly to Commissioner Sykes:

> May I suggest that the commission made a technical blunder when WOW and WCAJ were ordered to share the same bed in 1928? This combination was neither sought nor desired by either party. WOW has always insisted on taking its six-sevenths of the bed in the middle, and now for a second time threatens to kill its smaller bedfellow. Rather than stand by while this murder is contemplated, cannot the commission make some needed changes in its room arrangements? [29]

Eventually, worn down by litigation, hearings, and travel costs, the University station sold out—to WOW. A number of other case histories followed this sequence.

The desire for full time for efficient network operation was one of the factors decimating the ranks of educational stations during 1927-28. Yet many were determined to survive. Looking back later, Orestes Caldwell would say: "We had to make some moves in a rather high-handed way . . . We took a lot of hearsay and I fear we did a lot of injustices." By 1929, however, "everything seemed to be in good shape." [30] That was also the year when the educational stations, alarmed by their thinning ranks, began to organize for a last-ditch fight. It would be bitter.

In a *Harvard Business Review* summary of the career of the FRC, E. Pendleton Herring would later write:

> . . . the point seems clear that the Federal Radio Commission has interpreted the concept of public interest so as to favor in actual practice one particular group. While talking in terms of the public interest, convenience and necessity the commission actually chose to further the ends of the commercial broadcasters. They form the substantive content of public interest as interpreted by the Commission. [31]

PLUCK AND LUCK

The Judson-Coats network venture had aspects of a Horatio Alger tale. At desperate moments a mysterious rich person would turn up.

There was Mrs. Christian Holmes, formerly of Cincinnati but now a

29. Frost, *Education's Own Stations*, pp. 237-42.
30. Caldwell, *Reminiscences*, pp. 16-19.
31. Herring, "Politics and Radio Regulation," *Harvard Business Review*, January 1935.

New York resident and staunch friend of the New York Philharmonic. Early in the saga of the new network she asked Arthur Judson how it was faring. He said, "Well, we are losing our shirts." Having heard details, she announced: "I'm a good sport! I want to come in. What will it cost me?" Judson felt obliged to urge her to save her money for the Philharmonic, but she insisted and was allowed to put up $6000 for travel expenses for Coats. This was only the start of her involvement. Other such occasions soon brought her investment to $29,500.[1]

Judson and his associates in United Independent Broadcasters did not really want to run a network. They wanted only to supply talent and programs. Early in 1927 they were looking resolutely for someone to take over the network operation. For a time there was interest at Atwater Kent.[2] Then Adolph Zukor of Paramount was reported ready to invest $80,000 if the network could be named Paramount Broadcasting System. There was talk of studios in the Paramount Theater on Times Square—possibly glass-enclosed—enticing the public into the theater. Possibly, it was thought, Times Square could be renamed Paramount Plaza.[3] The talks fell through. Bernarr Macfadden became interested, but advisers dissuaded him.[4] The Victor Talking Machine Company became interested, for good reasons. It had reserves in funds, but its own field was skidding toward oblivion. The need for decisive action was near. Talks were held in Camden and progressed rapidly, then suddenly halted.[5] The reason—another negotiation had taken its place, which would lead to the purchase of Victor by RCA.

The turn of events may have helped United Independent Broadcasters. The Columbia Phonograph Record Company—like Victor—had funds and a business that was trickling away. In April 1927, amid rumors of imminent deals between RCA and Victor, the Columbia Phonograph Record Company joined Judson and his associates in forming the Columbia Phonograph Broadcasting System, and provided $163,000 in funds. "The sum was probably arrived at," Judson recalled, "by the amount of money we needed." [6] The new corporation contracted with the Judson Radio Program Corporation to supply talent for ten hours of programming per week

1. Judson, *Reminiscences*, pp. 10-11.
2. Archer, *Big Business and Radio*, p. 305.
3. Barlow, *Reminiscences*, pp. 66-7.
4. Correspondence, William Sweets.
5. Judson, *Reminiscences*, p. 12.
6. *Ibid.* p. 14.

at about $10,000 per week.[7] The network could resell the programming to sponsors. The Judson unit thus became the programming division of the network.

During the following months the effort to find sponsors was pushed with almost total failure. Prospect after prospect, after hearing the full argument for going into radio, went ahead—with NBC. That seemed to guarantee prestige. As the September debut approached, only one sponsor had been found. The network start was postponed two weeks. Collapse seemed near.

Throughout these months, preparations for the premiere were under way. Here Judson was on firmer footing.

The programming he had contracted to supply was to include a concert orchestra, a dance orchestra, a singing group, and assorted soloists. Early in the spring Judson had talked with Howard Barlow about joining the proposed network as conductor of the concert orchestra.

At the age of ten in Mt. Carmel on the Wabash river in Illinois, Howard Barlow found a cracked cello in the attic of the Methodist Church where he was a choir boy, took it up and a few weeks later played an offertory solo in church—"O Du Mein Holder Abendstern" from *Tannhäuser*. On an uncle's farm he found an old E-flat alto bell-front horn and took that up and played it in the village band. His father got him a brass cornet from Sears, Roebuck at a bargain price so he took that up. Then he organized an orchestra. Later he went away to school and college and eventually Columbia University, and in 1926 was musical director of the Neighborhood Playhouse in lower Manhattan, where Judson took note of him and talked about the new network. Barlow said he could hardly leave the Neighborhood Playhouse for less than $15,000 a year. Unless he was worth $15,000 a year, Judson told Barlow, the network would not want him. That constituted the agreement. Judson, like Coats, was no penny-pincher with the money they hoped to find.[8]

Judson and Coats kept Barlow informed about the negotiations for backing. Finally came word that the Columbia Phonograph deal was set and the network would go forward. Howard Barlow was to head a twenty-three-piece concert orchestra, Donald Voorhees, a dance combination.[9]

7. *Ibid.* p. 15. Barlow, *Reminiscences*, p. 70.
8. Barlow, *Reminiscences*, pp. 6-7, 62.
9. *Ibid.* p. 70.

Each would be on the air five hours per week. The network by now had sixteen stations. The ten hours to be programmed each week would consist of two-hour periods on Monday, Wednesday, Friday, and Sunday evenings and another on Sunday afternoon.[10]

The first program over the Columbia Phonograph Broadcasting System, on the afternoon of September 18, 1927, was by the Barlow orchestra. Barlow had been told that it would be sponsored by the Berkey and Gay furniture company, so he had planned a woodsy program to be climaxed by "Tales From The Vienna Woods." Shortly before airtime he was told that the furniture deal had not materialized, but of course the woodsy theme remained. The second program was by Voorhees and included the group later known as Red Nichols and his Five Pennies.[11]

That night came an extraordinarily ambitious effort: the Deems Taylor-Edna St. Vincent Millay opera *The King's Henchman*, with Metropolitan Opera artists, and with Barlow conducting. It served notice that the network aimed high. Because of technical problems, the program began late. It was marred by widespread thunderstorms and also went on long beyond its scheduled time, to the annoyance of some radio columnists.

These first programs were produced from a new studio that WOR was "frantically" preparing for its role as network key station. The studio was not ready.[12] No control room was ready, and the first day's programs had to be monitored from the men's room, the only sound-proof space available.[13] There was no studio clock.

In this and succeeding programs, the positioning of musicians was to Barlow an agonizing process of trial and error. He tried conducting with earphones. When the control room was ready he tried conducting from there. Later he decided to conduct from the studio and leave balancing to others. To look after timing he got a young assistant known as "Kosty"—André Kostelanetz.[14]

One Friday there were no paychecks. For three weeks there were no paychecks. The network, it was learned, owed AT&T $40,000 in line charges; payment was due, and no funds were available. Columbia Phonograph Record Company declined to make further investments. The entrepreneurs huddled in crisis sessions. J. Andrew White is said to have

10. Isaac and Leon Levy, *Conversation*, p. 10.
11. Barlow, *Reminiscences*, p. 73.
12. Gambling, *Reminiscences*, pp. 14-15.
13. Barlow, *Reminiscences*, p. 77.
14. *Ibid.* p. 94.

phoned his Christian Science practitioner for advice. After an explanation, White was apparently asked how much was needed. He was heard saying: "Forty thousand . . . wait a minute, make it eighty thousand dollars. We can always use an extra forty." [15] Faith had results—through other channels. Judson sent a wireless to Mrs. Christian Holmes, who was aboard ship in mid-Atlantic, saying they needed "between forty and forty-five thousand dollars to pay the telephone bill." She wirelessed instructions to her office, which sent a check for $45,000.[16] But the Columbia Phonograph Record Company was pulling out. Without new backing, this would be the end anyway. Fortunately Isaac and Leon Levy of WCAU, Philadelphia, first affiliate of the network, were ready to help again. They talked to their Philadelphia friend Jerome H. Louchheim, a subway builder. He became interested and, with help from the Levy family, agreed to buy a controlling interest. When the time came for him to affix his signature to the contract, his attorney Ralph Colin thought it well to sound a warning. This network might be a bottomless pit: a hundred thousand now, a quarter of a million later. It might go on and on and on. That was true, Louchheim is reported to have said, "but after all it is my money." The initial payment by Louchheim and the Levy brothers was $135,000,[17] and the network became the Columbia Broadcasting System.

The brothers hardly knew what they had brought their friend into. Some sponsors turned up—Bromo-Seltzer, La Palina cigars, *True Story* magazine—but frightening deficits continued. More money was soon needed and additional stock was issued to Louchheim for additional transfusions of cash. Before long his investments approached half a million dollars. The brothers became deeply troubled about Louchheim's plight. "He and I," Isaac Levy recalled, "used to go to New York two or three times a week to see what we could do; I would get up in the morning and go and eat frogs' legs at his house at five o'clock in the morning and then go to New York. I didn't know what was going on." Then Louchheim broke his hip. Louchheim begged Isaac, "Get Leon to go to New York and assume the presidency of CBS." Leon declined, he liked Philadelphia.[18] What about the Paleys, though? The Paley family owned the Congress Cigar Company. Young William S. Paley, aged twenty-six, was an executive in the company. He had tried some radio advertising for La Palina

15. *Ibid.* p. 86.
16. Judson, *Reminiscences*, p. 16.
17. Archer, *Big Business and Radio*, pp. 314-15.
18. Isaac and Leon Levy, *Conversation*, pp. 9-10.

cigars, first on WCAU and then on CBS. The family had been surprised by the audience reaction and then by a startling sales increase. La Palina had suddenly doubled its sales.[19] There was another factor in the situation. Young William S. Paley was restless in Philadelphia, and ambitious. His family wanted to find a suitable opportunity for him.

In September 1928 the network acquired new capital and William S. Paley as president. "And," observed Isaac Levy later, he's made "a pretty decent living at it." [20] Paley almost at once renewed talks with Adolph Zukor, and Paramount-Publix became a 49 per cent partner in CBS in return for a block of Paramount stock, which at once strengthened the network's credit.

Mrs. Holmes, good sport, still held stock, which she is said to have sold eventually for some three million dollars.[21]

AIN'T DAT SUMPIN'?

The programs NBC and CBS sent throughout the United States in 1928 and 1929 were still largely musical. Many were "concerts," although dance music—it was all called "jazz" now—was on the increase. Along with these another element was seizing attention—drama.

The dramatic series pushed in various directions. Some mined traditional "period" material: *Great Moments in History, Biblical Dramas,* and the continuing *Eveready Hour,* all on NBC. These had an aura of respectability paralleling that of concert music. Other dramatic series exploited a native—and equally traditional—hayseed vein: *Real Folks* on NBC, *Main Street* sketches on CBS. More contemporary was *True Story* on CBS, sponsored by Macfadden Publications. Based on the magazine stories, neatly bowdlerized and dressed with strangely literate dialogue and philosophizing, the series was both lurid and respectable enough to be a smashing 1928-29 success. It exemplified the dictum of Peter Finley Dunne's Mr. Dooley: "The city of New York, Hennessy, sets the fashion of vice and starts the crusade against it." [1]

But all these were overshadowed by another series, in many respects a pioneering work, and considered by many the first classic of broadcasting.

19. Landry, *This Fascinating Radio Business,* p. 63.
20. Isaac and Leon Levy, *Conversation,* p. 10.
21. Judson, *Reminiscences,* pp. 19-20.
1. Dunne, *Mr. Dooley Remembers,* p. 288.

It became, according to some estimates,[2] the consuming delight of forty million people. It would influence dinner hours across the nation. It would involve the attention of Presidents. And it would pose a racial issue.

Robert J. Landry in *This Fascinating Radio Business* noted resemblances between the history of broadcasting and that of film. In each of these a crude toy became an industry; fierce patent struggles erupted; public acceptance skyrocketed; business combinations won domination; anonymous idols exploded into fame.[3] A further resemblance can be added. In each the first work that explored, with startling virtuosity, the possibilities of a new medium, and won unheard-of success financially and statistically, also raised tensions on the frontier of Negro-white relations.

There was little surface resemblance between D. W. Griffith's *Birth of a Nation* and Correll and Gosden's *Amos 'n' Andy*—their moods were different—but kinship is nevertheless clear.

Freeman Fisher Gosden (Amos) was, like D. W. Griffith, a product of southern heritage. His father had belonged to a group of Confederate raiders who fought on after Appomattox. The boy Freeman was born in Richmond, Va., in 1899. He was cared for by a Negro mammy in a household that also sheltered a Negro boy called Snowball. Freeman was close to Snowball, and later said many facets of *Amos 'n' Andy* were derived from Snowball. Freeman spent his youth in Richmond, except for a year in an Atlanta military school. Then he became the first Gosden in three generations to leave the South.[4] Regarded as a virtuoso in Negro dialect stories and banjo-playing, Gosden—after a stint on the road as tobacco salesman—landed with the Joe Bren Company, which made a business of staging local shows throughout the United States for lodges, churches, and clubs. Local talent was used; the Joe Bren Company supplied sketches, jokes, songs, costumes, and supervision. Freeman Gosden started traveling for Joe Bren, organizing reviews, minstrel shows, carnivals.

Charles J. Correll (Andy) was born in 1890 in Peoria, Illinois. He first joined his father in construction work but at night played the piano in a movie house, banging out "Hearts and Flowers" for Pearl White close-ups and a ragtime "Everybody's Doing It" for John Bunny comedies. Soft-shoe dancing was another of his talents. As a result of these abilities, he too was recruited by the Joe Bren Company. Gosden and Correll first traveled

2. Wylie, "Amos 'n' Andy—Loving Remembrance," *Television Quarterly*, Summer 1963.
3. Landry, *This Fascinating Radio Business*, pp. 217-18.
4. Correll and Gosden, *All About Amos 'n' Andy*, pp. 21-2.

separate routes but eventually worked and roomed together, and began to work up a blackface act. When they were promoted to the Chicago head-quarters, it gave them a chance to try out for WEBH in the Edgewater Beach Hotel. Still working for the Joe Bren Company, they began to broadcast weekly blackface routines, receiving free dinners.

Someone at the Chicago *Tribune* suggested they work up something like *Andy Gump,* transferring the comic strip form to radio. This led them first to the creation of *Sam 'n' Henry,* which landed them a paid spot on WGN and enabled them to leave Joe Bren. The series ran two years—586 five-a-week episodes. They expected renewal but, according to one ac-count, could find no one at the *Tribune* who could deal with them.[5] This allowed WMAQ at the Chicago *Daily News* to sign them, at $150 per week for each.[6] Because the title *Sam 'n' Henry* was owned by WGN the team became *Amos 'n' Andy.* Besides a raise, they won from WMAQ a concession of importance in the development of broadcasting economics. Correll and Gosden had the notion they would like to make recordings of their programs and sell them to other stations; this had been prevented by the WGN arrangement. WMAQ approved, provided the Chicago broad-casts were live. Each program was recorded in two five-minute parts at the Marsh studios in Chicago. The pioneering syndication—Correll and Gos-den called it a "chainless chain"—was handled by the Chicago *Daily News.* Starting early in 1928, it soon involved some thirty stations.[7] By 1929 *Amos 'n' Andy* were already widely celebrated. According to one account, Coolidge did not like to be disturbed at the White House while they were on the air.[8] Rand McNally decided to publish an *Amos 'n' Andy* autobiography, in which Correll and Gosden told about themselves and their characters. It was here that Gosden discussed Snowball, calling him the inspiration for Amos and to some extent other characters. The book included script excerpts illustrated with photographs in which Correll and Gosden, in burnt-cork make-up, gave an idea of how they visualized their creations. The book began:

QUESTION: Who are Amos 'n' Andy?
ANSWER: Freeman F. Gosden and Charles J. Correll.

5. Hedges, *Reminiscences,* p. 25.
6. Wylie, "Amos 'n' Andy—Loving Remembrance," *Television Quarterly,* Summer 1963.
7. Hedges, *Reminiscences,* p. 25.
8. Slate and Cook, *It Sounds Impossible,* p. 76.

QUESTION: Are they white or colored?
ANSWER: White.[9]

The radio characters were described as follows:

AMOS: Trusting, simple, unsophisticated. High and hesitating in voice. It's "Ain't dat sumpin'?" when he's happy or surprised, and "Awa, awa, awa," in the frequent moments when he's frightened or embarrassed. . . . Andy gives him credit for no brains but he's a hard, earnest worker and has a way of coming across with a real idea when ideas are most needed. He looks up to and depends on

ANDY: Domineering, a bit lazy, inclined to take credit for all of Amos' ideas and efforts. He's always "workin' on the books" or "restin' his brain," upon which (according to Andy) depends the success or failure of all the boys' joint enterprises. He'll browbeat Amos, belittle him, order him around, but let anyone else pick on the little one—then look out!

The boys hail from Atlanta and have come to the big city to make fame and fortune. After a year in Chicago they have to their credit one broken-down topless automobile, one business enterprise—the Fresh-Air Taxicab Company of America, Incorpulated—one desk (not paid for), one swivel chair for the president to rest in and think . . .[10]

In addition to the Fresh-Air Taxicab Company, the action revolved around a South Side rooming house and a brotherhood called the Mystic Knights of the Sea, presided over by a character called the Kingfish. An important early sequence involved the widow Parker, alias Snookems, and her breach-of-promise suit against Andy.

Correll and Gosden wrote every word. One typed while the other, often pacing, tried out dialogue, always in dialect. All speeches were put down as pronounced. "I'se regusted." "Recordin' to my figgers in de book . . ." "Splain dat to me." A script averaged 1500-2000 words and took ten minutes. There was no rehearsal before broadcast. Having thought the story through jointly, they felt rehearsal would reduce spontaneity. Under their method of working, neither could completely anticipate how the other would play a scene, and actual interaction resulted. Each occasionally ended a broadcast in tears. Gosden would say concerning Amos: "I feel so sorry for that poor ignorant fellow." [11]

They sat while broadcasting. Correll as Andy performed with furrowed brow and protruding lip. Gosden as Amos wore a vacant, naïve look. For

9. Correll and Gosden, *All About Amos 'n' Andy*, p. 13.
10. *Ibid.* pp. 43-4.
11. *Ibid.* pp. 53-4, 86, 114.

several years no other actors took part. In the widow Parker breach-of-promise episodes—in later years there was another breach-of-promise sequence—Correll played Andy, Attorney for the Defense, Judge, Policeman, Court Clerk; Gosden played Amos, Prosecuting Attorney, Bailiff, Kingfish, Consulting Attorney. Each actor changed his position, pitch, and volume for each character. Each could on occasion produce animal sounds. Women characters, though vividly real to the audience, appeared for some time only by reference; they were also illuminated by long phone conversations in which the women were not heard.

Correll and Gosden claimed not to depend on jokes, but repetitive gag lines were frequent. In a court sequence Andy was advised by his lawyer: "Now Brown, you can occasionally use the expression, 'I don't remember.' Don't make it noticeable, but occasionally say, 'I don't remember.'" The result was:

BAILIFF: Raise your right hand.
ANDY: I don't remembeh.
BAILIFF: Raise your right hand.
ANDY: Yessah, yessah.
BAILIFF: Do you solemnly swear that the evidence you are about to give in this case is the truth, the whole truth, and nothing but the truth, so help you God?
ANDY: I don't remembeh.
BAILIFF: Say "I do."
ANDY: I do.
BAILIFF: Sit down!
JUDGE (in distance): Attorney for the plaintiff will proceed with the cross examination.
ATTORNEY: Your name is Andrew Brown?
ANDY: I don't remembeh.

Word-distortion humor was often used. As Amos added up the day's receipts, Andy asked: "Wait a minute heah! Whut is you doin'? Is you mulsiflyin' or revidin'?" [12]

Correll and Gosden wrote that they made frequent contact with "colored folk" to keep the characters "true to life." They posed for publicity pictures making such contact. They felt their most important equipment for the series was "a thorough understanding of the colored race." [13]

The *Amos 'n' Andy* series broke new ground in several ways. It established syndication as a mechanism, even though recordings were still of

12. *Ibid.* pp. 67-8, 118.
13. *Ibid.* pp. 51-2.

doubtful quality and limited to five-minute lengths. The feasibility of the continued story was also overwhelmingly shown. A basic dilemma continuing for weeks, far from alienating listeners, enmeshed ever-widening rings of addicts. Throughout the breach-of-promise crises *Amos 'n' Andy*—echoing Dickens's success with this theme in the serialized *Pickwick Papers*—built audience frenzy and became mealtime and commuting train talk across the continent. All this would bring a flood of radio serials in succeeding years.

Two broadcasting triumphs, said John S. Cohen of the Atlanta *Journal* and its station WSB, did most to make radio a national medium: the 1924 Democratic convention and *Amos 'n' Andy*.[14]

By 1929 their fame had given birth to a daily *Amos 'n' Andy* comic strip syndicated by the Chicago *Daily News* and to *Amos 'n' Andy* phonograph records marketed by Victor, and NBC was ready to pay $100,000 a year for their services. They went on the network that summer, sponsored by Pepsodent. That fall *Amos 'n' Andy* sent hordes to radio shops; sales of radio sets and parts went from $650,550,000 in 1928 to $842,548,000 in 1929.[15] The program began on the network at a late hour but was soon shifted to 7:00 to 7:15 Eastern time, where it dominated all radio listening. In the spring, when daylight saving time began, some communities found themselves getting *Amos 'n' Andy* at 6 P.M. Crisis resulted. Forty factories in Charlotte, N.C., agreed to shift their closing time from 6:00 to 5:45 P.M.[16] When national telephone surveys began soon afterward, more than half of all those phoned were found listening to *Amos 'n' Andy*.[17]

During this staggering rise to fame, what had happened to Snowball? Repeated mention of Snowball in the 1929 autobiography suggests that he was on Gosden's mind. But the problem was not only Gosden's but the nation's.

In the 1920's the ghetto was well established and fortified. The Negro lived in his, the white man in his. Reasons and conditions differed, but the result was insulation. Except for Negro domestics, few crossed over. In New York white intellectuals taxied to Harlem to see Negro stars in nightclubs owned by white gangsters. Occasional Negro performers—musicians, dancers, actors—played "the white time." But when in that period Ethel Waters and other Negro girls went on tour in a musical—in "burnt-

14. Arnold, *Broadcast Advertising*, p. 226.
15. *Broadcasting*, 1939 Yearbook, p. 11.
16. Wallace, *The Development of Broadcasting in North Carolina*, p. 237.
17. Summers (ed.), *A Thirty-Year History of Programs*, p. 21.

cork" make-up—they had to be lodged at each stop in a brothel; no other place would take them.[18]

In the South the boy growing up with a Snowball was called on in puberty for that total repudiation—Faulkner wrote of this—seldom required of shielded northerners. It involved a deep sense of guilt that had to be combated and overlaid with endless fantasy: stories, jokes, burnt-cork comedy. In retrospect it is easy—at the time it was less easy—to see the stories and *Amos 'n' Andy* as part of the ghetto system. All of it was more readily accepted and maintained if one could hold onto this: "they" were lovely people, essentially happy people, ignorant and somewhat shiftless and lazy in a lovable, quaint way, not fitting in with higher levels of enterprise, better off where they were (the Fresh-Air Taxicab Company, Incorpulated), essentially happy, happy. The more one remembered Snowball, the more the fantasy was needed. It could make South Side poverty somehow charming and fitting. The nation needed the fantasy. It was a wall buttressed by decades of jokes, vaudeville sketches, cartoons, and joke books sold by millions of copies in 5&10¢ stores with titles like *Minstrel Jokes, Coon Jokes, Darky Jokes,* how-to-do books like *The Amateur Minstrel* and *Burnt Cork.*[19] So ingrained was all this that the idea of Negro objections to *Amos 'n' Andy* was at first received with disbelief. Was it not known that Negroes loved *Amos 'n' Andy?*

There was some truth in this, although statistics are scarce. The Negro writer William Branch remembered sitting in a family group roaring with laughter over *Amos 'n' Andy.* Those seemed very funny people. There was another memory: the father did not laugh. Only gradually the boy learned why. Those people were supposed to be "us." [20]

James Baldwin put this Negro experience vividly. At movies he always cheered wildly with others as heroes pursued and slaughtered Indians. Then he learned he was the Indian.

During the fantastic rise of *Amos 'n' Andy,* Secretary of Commerce Herbert Hoover was elected President of the United States. As he settled into the White House, *Amos 'n' Andy* led in program popularity. Presidential recognition followed in due course. At Hoover's invitation, Merlin Aylesworth brought the two men to the White House. Correll and Gosden told

18. Waters, *His Eye Is on the Sparrow,* p. 139.
19. Wehman Bros. publications sold throughout the 1910's and 1920's.
20. Interview, William Branch.

some of their best jokes. Hoover, in upright collar, warmed to the occasion and caused surprise by telling some himself—for more than an hour.[21]

It was not an accident that *Amos 'n' Andy* was a national triumph. It was virtually a national self-expression, a vivid amusement-park image of its time.

UPWARD

These same months saw frenzied bursts of competitive enterprise. With radio spiraling upward, there was also the conviction that television was almost ready.

Throughout 1928 Ernst F. W. Alexanderson at General Electric did daily television tests over experimental W2XAD. These led on September 11 to the first television drama production, the melodrama *The Queen's Messenger*, with sound elements over WGY. Three cameras were used; each was motionless. The viewer saw a 3″ × 4″ image.[1] Only close-ups were used. Later came an arresting science-fiction telecast dramatizing a guided-missile attack on New York City. This imaginative production gave the viewer a missile-eye view of New York, as the deadly weapon, electronically guided, approached its target. An aerial photo of New York, appearing on the television screen, came closer and closer and closer. Then an explosion, and the end of the program. A Royal Air Force visitor pronounced it one of the most interesting things he had seen in the United States "in its possibilities for future wars." [2]

These telecasts still used a rapidly revolving scanning wheel, with perforations arranged in a spiral pattern. RCA was also using such a system in New York over experimental 2XBS. AT&T in New York and Westinghouse in Pittsburgh also used it, as did John L. Baird in England. Parts for Baird receivers for home assembly were reported on sale at Selfridge's department store in London for the equivalent of $32 per set. Within five years, said Sarnoff, television would be "as much a part of our life" as radio had become. If used "to distribute miniature billboards into the home," said the New York *Telegram*, "its growth will be stifled at the outset." [3] The

21. Gross, *I Looked and Listened*, p. 155.
1. Weir, *Reminiscences*, p. 21.
2. Alexanderson, *Reminiscences*, p. 43.
3. *Radio Broadcast*, May 1928.

advent of television, said Lionel Barrymore, would "scrap theaters through-out the country." [4]

Throughout these developments there were reports of progress made by Vladimir Zworykin of Westinghouse in developing electronic, rather than mechanical, scanning. The sense that this would make mass acceptance imminent was behind countless moves. Paramount acquired 49 per cent of CBS in 1929 because, Zukor felt, television was at hand. A number of leading radio stations were applying for experimental television licenses.[5]

Meanwhile other developments caused a fever of speculative moves. The success of the Warner Brothers' partly talking film *The Jazz Singer*—premiered October 6, 1927—made 1928 a year of upheaval in Hollywood. Lisping and squeaking stars were fired, singers and playwrights frantically imported. A vast change-over of theaters and studios was under way. The crisis precipitated a New York crisis: the old struggle between AT&T and RCA, only recently smoothed in radio, was transplanted to a new arena. As the film world retooled for sound, AT&T's Western Electric, joining forces with Fox, gained acceptance of its sound-on-film system by Metro-Goldwyn-Mayer, Paramount, United Artists, Universal, and First National (which was presently taken over by the Warners). RCA and its principal owners, General Electric and Westinghouse, scrambled for pieces to pick up. Early in 1928 they formed RCA Photophone to exploit the old General Electric Pallophotophone process as a sound-on-film system. To secure it a market they joined forces with Joseph P. Kennedy (father of John Fitzgerald Kennedy) and his Film Booking Office and with the Keith-Albee-Orpheum chain of theaters to create—October 1928—Radio-Keith-Orpheum, or RKO. While equipping RKO theaters and studios, RCA Photophone also got its equipment accepted by Pathé (presently taken over by RKO), Mack Sennett, and other lesser film companies. A vast interlocking was developing; in the struggle, innumerable elements became valuable pawns. Music would rise in importance. RCA bought two music-publishing companies, Leo Feist, Inc. and Carl Fischer, Inc. (Aylesworth later told a Senate committee: "It is necessary for us to be in the music business to protect ourselves . . . the movies have bought most of the music houses . . . we have got to control the music situation. It is a simple business proposition with a little touch of sentiment in it." [6]) There

4. *Ibid.* August 1928.
5. *Ibid.* September 1929.
6. *Commission on Communications*, pp. 1711-13.

was also a much larger move. In March 1929, with the help of $32,000,000 advanced by GE and Westinghouse, RCA took over the Victor Talking Machine Company.[7] And in the bullish atmosphere RCA and General Motors formed General Motors Radio Corporation to exploit automobile radios.

Accompanying these feverish moves was a delirium of financial excitement such as the world had never known before. Wealth beyond dreams of avarice seemed implicit in each corporate maneuver. In the upward market spiral radio stocks—along with automobile and airplane stocks—were constantly in the vanguard.

Early in 1928 RCA stock was sold at 85¼. Then it began its astounding performance. On Saturday, March 3, it stood at 91½. On March 10 it *opened* at 107¾, closed at 120½. (Television rumors?) On March 12 it opened at 120½, closed at 138½. (Photophone news?) The next day it opened at 160—21½ points up. After a retreat, advance began again. By May it passed 200, then slipped early in June. By mid-June the skid stopped. (Hoover's nomination?) During the campaign the rise was resumed. ("We shall soon, with the help of God, be in sight of the day when poverty will be banished from this nation"—Hoover's acceptance over 107 NBC and CBS stations.) In November RCA stock touched 400. (Electoral college vote: Herbert Hoover 444, Alfred E. Smith 87.) On December 7, a moment of panic: RCA slipped 72 points. But confidence rallied. After a period of ups and downs, RCA began another steep climb. (Dismissal of Federal Trade Commission complaint? Formation of RKO? Zworykin? Color television patent? RCA purchase of Victor? *Amos 'n' Andy?* Debut of Rudy Vallee?) In mid-summer RCA stock reached 500 and pushed beyond. The stock was split: each share became five shares, each of which on September 3, 1929, stood at 101. It then edged up to 114¾. In eighteen months it had climbed over 600 per cent.[8]

The feeling was that almost everyone who was anything would move to a place like Jackson Heights, live a Nathaniel Hawthorne life with superheterodyne, television, electrical refrigerator, air conditioning, and other things available on installments, with a place in Florida for later. Automobile and airplane had made this plausible. The stock market had made it seem inevitable. Radio had done its share in building the dream and inflating the credit bubble.

7. Archer, *Big Business and Radio*, p. 345.
8. Allen, *Only Yesterday*, pp. 295-320.

When it burst—WALL STREET LAYS AN EGG, said *Variety*[9]—the confidence did not immediately vanish. Although RCA stock sagged to the 20's by November, statements of confidence were everywhere. The fundamental business condition of the country was sound, it was said. It became a radio incantation, in statement after statement by administration and business leaders. But paralysis took over. During 1930 income and employment dropped catastrophically. Building stopped. The following year one in four factory workers was jobless. Nine million savings accounts were lost. Breadlines stretched on and on.

Radio had been nurtured on war and, in prosperity, grown like a weed or a teenager. But the broadcasting industry entered the new period with internal tensions and conflicts unresolved. In these the panic would play a telling role.

9. *Variety*, October 30, 1929.

5 / PANIC

Things are in the saddle
And ride mankind.
RALPH WALDO EMERSON,
Ode

That a bottom would be reached and that this—in the nature of things—would bring an upward bounce, remained an article of faith through months of the Depression. That any interference with this aspect of nature could spell disaster and undermine character was implicit in many official pronouncements. But many people began to doubt there was a bottom, and were not sure what there would be to bounce.

The long deflation affected broadcasters notably at the local station. Some stations which had existed as publicity media now turned to the sale of time, but in many towns the advertising dollar was evaporating. Many a station lapsed into a barter operation. In Cedar Rapids a furniture store could not pay for its announcements over KWCR, so the station settled for a filing cabinet and other items. A restaurant paid its debts regularly with mealtickets.[1] Such arrangements were common. With many hotels three-quarters empty, scores of radio stations were invited to move into hotel space free of charge, in return for announcements.

All this affected station arrangements with staffs. When Kirk Knight joined WEXL, Royal Oak, Mich., as chief announcer in 1931, his salary for the first week was $5 in cash, a restaurant mealticket, and a bushel of potatoes.[2] In 1930 John E. Fetzer took over the station he had built for Emmanuel Missionary College and moved it to Kalamazoo, Mich., as WKZO. The college, which had spent $18,000 on new equipment in 1925-

1. Interview, Leo Cole.
2. Knight, *Reminiscences*, pp. 9-10. He became program manager, WWJ-TV.

26, had been required by the FRC in 1928 to show cause why it should exist. It had survived this challenge but had been squeezed into a daytime channel shared with two other stations. Now it decided to quit.[3] Fetzer bought the equipment for $5000 and went commercial. That year he lived on trade orders. His transmitter site was acquired from a cement-block maker for radio time. He built studios in the Burdick Hotel for radio time.[4]

At many stations the Depression increased station personnel. Some stations had numerous salesmen, all on commission basis without guarantee. In Toledo, WSPD, a shoestring enterprise, had seven salesmen. In the desperate quest for business they were authorized to give a week of free advertising.[5] In Detroit, WJR had fifteen nonsalaried salesmen.[6]

For a foothold many people worked months without salary. In Chicago, Ed Allen, joining the program staff of WAAF in November 1930, worked until March without pay, often ten hours a day and seven days a week. He then worked without pay for WJJD, WIND, and WSBC before landing a paying job with WGN.[7] In Columbia, Mo., when Roderick B. Cupp joined KFRU in 1933, he was paid in free lodging and mealtickets; for weeks he received no cash. Financial transactions sank to a miniature level. KFRU sold classified advertisements for 25¢ each.[8] KWCR, Cedar Rapids, sold announcements at 75¢. There were salaries of $4 and $5 per week.

The situation had curious effects on programming. Because the owners of WEXL, Royal Oak, could not afford a record library, they took up hillbillies. "We had more hillbillies than we had records." [9]

The scramble for business produced innovations. At WJR, Harry Bannister, one of its fifteen salesmen, was restricted to sales outside Detroit. He therefore arranged projects like *The Flint Hour*. In Flint, he persuaded the mayor, the fireman's band, the police quartet, a bank president, a minister or two, and miscellaneous other leaders to appear in a special Flint program over the Detroit station, scheduled some weeks in advance. Bus transportation was arranged. Then he pressed Flint merchants to buy announcements on the program. He applied the same for-

3. Frost, *Education's Own Stations*, pp. 88-9.
4. Fetzer, *Reminiscences*, p. 57.
5. Interview, Douglas Storer.
6. Bannister, *Reminiscences*, p. 5. He became general manager, WWJ.
7. Allen, *Reminiscences*, p. 2. He became president of WDOR, Sturgeon Bay, Wis.
8. Cupp, *Reminiscences*, p. 3. He became general manager of KOFO, Ottawa, Kan.
9. Knight, *Reminiscences*, p. 11.

mula in Pontiac, Lansing, and other nearby cities, sometimes clearing $60 in a week.[10]

In a number of cities smaller stations turned to foreign language programming and began to scratch a living—in merchandise and cash—from sponsorship by delicatessens, restaurants, and specialty products.

The barter economy led to some abuses. In Flint, the owners of WSPD dismissed the manager because he had accepted, in payment of time contracts, a car and a house for himself.[11]

At some stations, especially in larger cities, numbers of artists waited ceaselessly for possible employment. At KPO, San Francisco, the rate for actors was $5 per program. "The halls of 111 Sutter," the writer-director Carlton Morse later recalled, "were cluttered with humanity from early in the morning until midnight." If no work came, they went to the Morris Plan for loans, signing each other's notes.[12]

What the listener heard, throughout this time of travail, was increasing numbers of commercial announcements—at the network as well as the local level. They were also longer. In fact, the years 1929-32 were a period of almost spectacular retreat from previous standards, a retreat which can be clearly charted.

BUT FIRST

SENATOR DILL: But you do not put direct advertising into your programs?
AYLESWORTH: No . . . These clients neither describe their products or name its price but simply depend on the good-will that results from their contribution of good programs . . .[1]

These words, spoken in 1928, were perhaps even then a slight exaggeration. Within a year long announcements were heard.

George Washington Hill of the American Tobacco Company, one of the most determined of sponsors, was developing his theory that commercials should irritate. His agency, Lord & Thomas, did whatever was needed to please him. NBC may have demurred, but the commercials were broadcast. Undoubtedly listeners appreciated, *Radio Broadcast* observed, the jazz music which "punctuates the advertising announcements broadcast

10. Bannister, *Reminiscences*, pp. 5-6.
11. Interview, Douglas Storer.
12. Morse, *Interview*, pp. 5-6. He became creator of *One Man's Family*.
1. *Federal Radio Commissioners*, p. 219.

by the Lucky Strike people."[2] Hill also insisted on a loud, hard-driving style of performance, in commercials as in music.

In 1930 Aylesworth appeared again before a Senate committee.

AYLESWORTH: First . . . I am opposed to direct advertising on the air.
SENATOR DILL: And by direct advertising you mean what?
AYLESWORTH: I mean, stating prices . . .[3]

In 1931, although the air was crammed with loud, insistent announcements, NBC still did not mention prices and prided itself on decorum; it had long lists of taboo words.

As CBS fought for business, George Washington Hill found he could say what he wanted on CBS about his Cremo cigars: that they cost five cents and were not made with spit. "There is no spit in Cremo!" the announcer shouted. The next year William Paley was quoted as saying that the art of advertising by radio was developing rapidly. He added, like one tracing an aesthetic movement: "Our specific contribution toward this end is the permitting of price mention."[4]

Not long afterward President Aylesworth of NBC was telling his Advisory Council of distinguished citizens about a policy change:

> We believe that the interests of the listener, the client and the broadcaster are best served under our American system of broadcasting by frankly recognizing the part that each plays in its development. With this thought in mind, and after long consideration, the company has decided to alter its policy with reference to the mention of price in commercial announcements.[5]

The phrase "direct advertising," now completely drained of meaning, began to disappear from administrative prose.

According to Mark Woods, NBC treasurer at this time, there was constant effort by advertisers during the Depression to persuade the network to alter its policies. "And I would say that there were substantial revisions."[6]

George Washington Hill, one of those who led the successful pressure, is said to have been the inspiration for the sponsor portrayed in the novel *The Hucksters*, who contemptuously told his advertising agents: "All you

2. *Radio Broadcast*, June 1929.
3. *Commission on Communications*, p. 1705.
4. *Radio Art*, October 1, 1932.
5. *Broadcasting*, January 15, 1933.
6. Woods, *Reminiscences*, p. 62.

professional advertising men are scared to death of raping the public; I say the public likes it . . ." [7]

On December 29, 1932, observers on newspapers in various parts of the United States joined in gathering information on that day's broadcasts by 208 stations. According to the tabulated data, 2365 hours of broadcasting had 12,546 advertising interruptions. By now the "spot announcement" unrelated to programs was in full swing and accounted for about 40 per cent of the 12,546 interruptions. The total time devoted to news, education, lectures, and religion was "less than the amount of time absorbed by commercial sales talks." [8]

Behind the statistics was another story. When the networks were formed, almost all programs were developed and produced by network or station. There were exceptions, such as the *Eveready Hour*, produced by an advertising agency. By 1931 virtually all sponsored network programs were developed and produced by advertising agencies. Leading advertising agencies had built or were building radio departments. There was a drift of personnel from networks and stations to higher-paid positions as agency executives. Heads of advertising agency radio departments became an elite, besieged by time salesmen, producers, directors, and performing artists.

Behind this lay an economic story. By 1931 an hour over an NBC coast-to-coast network of fifty-odd stations cost the sponsor about $10,000. The advertising agency received from the network a 15 per cent commission, or $1500, for arranging this sale, and had minimal expenses in connection with it. The agency had established an additional commission. If it expended $6000 on program talent, it added 15 per cent, or $900, in billing the expenditure to the sponsor. Thus an advertising agency could earn $2400 on a single network hour, or $83,600 for a 39-week series, often involving the attention of only three or four agency employees. The developing wealth and power meant a flow of funds to the networks, which readily acquiesced. By 1932 network approval of agency-built programs was considered a formality. The shift to advertising agencies of control over the peak broadcasting hours would eventually become a social and political issue, but was at first taken for granted as a sensible, natural arrangement. The agencies were the conduit through which the money flowed.

7. Wakeman, *The Hucksters*, p. 24.
8. *American Broadcasting*, pp. 3, 11.

To the agencies, and the clients beyond them, networks and stations addressed a continual stream of promotional brochures, chronicling radio advertising successes. Typical was *The Story of WOR*, in which this Newark station with studios in New York City—"23.2 per cent of the nation's income tax returns are filed in the WOR area" [9]—listed 200 companies that had advertised over its facilities during an eighteen-month period. The brochure included the saga of "Uncle Don"—Donald Carney—one of a number of uncles sprouting across the continent. In 1930 a savings bank had made a thirteen-week contract with Uncle Don, who

> told his attentive radio nieces and nephews that, besides drinking milk and obeying their parents, they should save their pennies and deposit them in the little banks which the sponsor offered. He broadcast the names of those who started savings accounts, and awarded the titles of "Earnest Saver," "Earnest Saver, Jr.," and "Earnest Saver, Sr.," to the youngsters as their accounts grew.[10]

The bank, citing "most satisfactory results," renewed in 1931, 1932, 1933. Said WOR: "The reason for Uncle Don's unprecedented success may be summed up in one word—sincerity." [11]

If Uncle Don on WOR was becoming an oracle for the young, other sponsored oracles were looking after adults. The tastes of advertising agencies ran in different directions from those of Arthur Judson. While concert music was rapidly vanishing from sponsored periods, new arrivals included (1930) a CBS astrology series sponsored by Forhan's toothpaste. The listener sending in a Forhan's boxtop and date of birth, along with a letter about personal problems, was told by Evangeline Adams what the stars held for him. She read the most astonishing letters on the air; thousands of others were answered by mail. Perhaps as a countermove, Kolynos launched (1930) a numerology series with Edna Purdy Walsh over WMAQ, Chicago.[12] Over WMCA, New York, Bost toothpaste tried a success specialist, who offered his Balkin Success Charts in return for boxtops. The advertising agency for a nail polish selected Josef Ranald, palmist, for a WOR series, which soon drew 2000 letters per broadcast.[13] Tony Wons, breathing quietly an inch from the microphone, offering verses and advice on WLS, Chicago, became a soul mate to so many millions of women that

9. *The Story of WOR*, p. 31.
10. *Ibid.* p. 23.
11. *Ibid.* p. 28.
12. Caton, *Radio Station WMAQ*, p. 364.
13. *The Story of WOR*, p. 26.

he found himself on CBS philosophizing for the R. J. Reynolds Tobacco Company, which had become interested in women as an untapped cigarette market. Each day, with violin background, Wons spoke of the contentment to be derived from cellophane-wrapped Camels, "as fresh as the dew that dawn spills on a field of clover." [14] A similar phenomenon was Cheerio, who spoke to a background of canaries.

Perhaps the most remarkable of these phenomena was a man known on the air as The Voice of Experience, who advised on human-relations problems. He had broadcast over a number of different stations by 1932, when he landed at WOR, New York; a few months later he transferred to the CBS network under the sponsorship of Haley's M-O, Musterole, and other drug products which joined forces as Wasey Products in order to co-sponsor him. The Voice took care of from 10,000 to 20,000 letters per week by using Dr. Brinkley's system of numbered prescriptions. He found he could reduce most human problems to several dozen standard situations—eventually over a hundred—which were answered via printed leaflets. The most dramatic letters were winnowed for air use. They sometimes confessed to crime or sexual transgression, and asked for advice on moral dilemmas involved. Before giving such advice, he sometimes asked listeners for their comments. One problem is said to have elicited 28,000 letters.[15] Each day's mail brought desperate appeals for help. The Voice—his actual name, which was M. Sayle Taylor, was never used—sometimes mentioned that he had his own Investigation Bureau to check on these.

In time of deepening Depression, countless people seem to have turned to invisible radio voices as to salvation. Early in March 1933 a young woman who said she was sick and destitute wrote to the Voice of Experience:

> I lost my father in July, 1929, and then my husband in October, 1930, and now my mother is lying in Kings County Morgue with no prospect of burial because three of the ten days allotted to claim her body have gone by and I have been unable to raise any money. I have two brothers, but one is in jail and the other brother is a heavy drinker. I stay away from him because he acts crazy toward me when he gets drunk. He still suffers from shell shock after the World War. I have a sister in a mental institution, the same one where my father died. Tomorrow my landlord is going to put me out, because I am behind with my rent. I have no friends and nowhere to go. For God's sake

14. Erwin Wasey & Co. commercial announcement.
15. *Stranger Than Fiction*, p. xiii.

can you do something for me and please, if at all possible, take care of
the burial of my mother. I don't want her to have to go to Potter's
Field.[16]

The Voice told his listeners that Captain Hogkins and Lieutenant Peglow
of the Voice of Experience Investigation Bureau had looked into the case.
As they approached the room where the woman lived, they heard screams.
"As they opened the door, a strange sight greeted them. A woman, almost
completely nude, with her remaining undergarments torn to rags, was ly-
ing on the floor. Pinned helplessly against the wall, a rookie cop was
held in a jiu-jitsu grip by a man much bigger than he, in whose hand was
raised a dirk." The Voice reported that the investigators had rescued the
policeman, taken the woman to a hospital, and saved the mother from
Potter's Field. The assailant or "fiend," the woman's brother, was committed to an asylum.[17]

Sales of Haley's M-O are said to have jumped several hundred per cent
during the first month of its sponsorship of the Voice of Experience. By
1933 he said that two million people had turned to him with their personal
problems.[18]

The Voice of Experience series, like that of Evangeline Adams before it,
featured a continual series of offers involving boxtops. Merchandising
schemes were deluging the air in 1932.

In the magazine *Chain Store Management*, in the issue of June 1932, the
Kellogg Company asked its dealers:

Have you heard the Kellogg "Singing Lady" on the radio? If you
haven't—don't fail. For right now this program is one of the greatest
business-getters for the retail grocer in this country.

Just think of this: 14,000 people a day, from every state in the
Union, are sending tops of Kellogg packages to the Singing Lady for
her song book. Nearly 100,000 tops a week come into Battle Creek.

And many hundreds of thousands of children, fascinated by her
songs and stories, and helped by her counsel on food, are eating more
Kellogg cereals today than ever before. This entire program is pointed
to *increase consumption*—by suggesting Kellogg cereals, not only for
breakfast but for lunch, after school and the evening meal.

It is another evidence of the Kellogg policy to build business—and
it's building.[19]

16. *Ibid.* pp. 129-31.
17. *Ibid.* pp. 129-31.
18. *The Voice of Experience*, p. v.
19. Quoted, *Daytime Hours Sell*, p. 43.

Supplementing this information Hylan L. Hodgson, vice president of the N. W. Ayer advertising agency, told readers of the *National Broadcast Reporter* that thirty-eight women at the Kellogg plant in Battle Creek were devoting full time to answering Singing Lady mail and that "people are eating more Kellogg cereals than ever before." They were also consuming more Ovaltine. To get a picture of the heroine of *Little Orphan Annie,* 418,000 people sent the little folder from the Ovaltine can back to the Wander Company.[20]

The selling and merchandising atmosphere was noted at various times by leaders in government. To Senator Burton K. Wheeler the air had become a "pawnshop." [21] The Federal Radio Commission had, during its few years, mentioned the commercial tide on a number of occasions. The FRC generally took the view that advertising was an essential support. However, it had stated in 1928 that "such benefit as is derived by advertisers must be incidental and secondary to the interest of the public." [22]

On January 12, 1932, in a resolution introduced by Senator James Couzens, the Senate took note of "growing dissatisfaction with the present use of radio facilities," and asked the FRC a number of questions. Could advertising be limited to an announcement of sponsorship? Could it be restricted in length? Also, were educational needs adequately met? The resolution even asked about the "feasibility of government ownership and operation of broadcasting facilities." [23]

FRC chairman Charles McK. Saltzman, a retired major general who had joined the commission in 1929, answered with a long letter in which he sidestepped the question of government operation, and answered the others on the premise that the existing system would continue. His conclusions may be briefly summarized.

Limit advertising to an announcement of sponsorship? Not feasible. "Many products have several uses which must be described to be understood and appreciated."

Time limitations on commercial material? This would "result in a loss of revenue" and therefore curtail program service. Besides, the matter should be left to the broadcaster, who is "in a singularly favorable position to learn what the audience wants to hear." Also, since some stations were

20. *Ibid.* pp. 43, 77.
21. Payne, *Federal Communications Act,* p. 29.
22. *Annual Report of the Federal Radio Commission* (1928), pp. 169-70.
23. Resolution No. 129, 72nd Congress, 1st Session, 75. *Congressional Record,* pp. 1412-13.

spending more time on commercials than others were, any general restriction would "work inequitable results."

Above and beyond all this, the chairman saw reason for hope. "The situation should have its own cure within itself." People annoyed by an advertiser "can promptly eject him." In addition, program popularity surveys had been started and these could be expected to bring better programs.[24]

The chairman quoted several advertising men as supporting his views on proposed restrictions. Hill Blackett of Blackett, Sample & Hummert, which was producing *Little Orphan Annie* and other serials, said: "It is too early in the history of radio, in my opinion, to enact any such legislation. . . . If the matter is left to the public, I believe it will work itself out." [25]

What seemed to some a woeful deterioration was seen by others in quite different terms. In the face of a cataclysmic economic flood, a new industry was staying above water. It was even expanding, as many victims of disaster clung to it.

For several years following the crash, as adjacent businesses crumbled or collapsed, people and activities gravitated toward the broadcasting world.

Bruce Robertson was editing a travel magazine when the crash came. Immediately after Black Thursday almost all travel companies and steamship lines canceled their advertising. By November 1 his job had vanished. But he heard that a magazine called *Broadcast Advertising* was seeking an editor, and on December 1 he got the job. He remained with the magazine when it merged with *Broadcasting* two years later.[26]

In 1930 Jack and David Kapp realized their phonograph record store in Chicago could not survive. Jack went to New York for a job with Brunswick, leaving David to close up. David, because of his background in folk and race music, was hired by WJJD in Chicago to become its program director, and steered its schedule toward his specialties. He hired a struggling cowboy singer, Gene Autry, to do twelve programs a week—six in the morning, six in the afternoon—for $50 a week.[27]

In 1930 the Palace on Times Square, apex of the vaudeville world, closed for a change-over to talkies. As the Palace had symbolized vaude-

24. *Commercial Radio Advertising*, pp. 34-7.
25. *Ibid.* p. 167.
26. Robertson, *Recollections of the Radio Industry*, pp. 1-6.
27. Kapp, *Reminiscences*, p. 1980.

ville at the height of its glory, the occasion had the sound of a death rattle. Innumerable vaudeville performers, among them Jack Benny, drifted toward radio.

Abram Chasins, pianist and composer whose works had been played by the Philadelphia Orchestra under Stokowski and the New York Philharmonic under Toscanini, had $100,000 in securities when the Wall Street crash came. By 1931 he was wiped out. In 1933 he met William Paley, and this led to a series of Saturday afternoon programs in which Chasins, alone at the piano, played and analyzed passages, discussed form and structure, went over the fingering of difficult passages, mentioned errors in printed editions, and made interpretative suggestions. Uncompromising in level, the series became a weekly ritual for piano teachers and students.[28]

By 1930 the Brooklyn *Eagle*, victim of Depression and a devouring metropolis, faced a financial crisis. Its highest-paid and best-known employee, H. V. Kaltenborn, associate editor, received two weeks' notice. He was hired for $100 a week by CBS. It offered him for sponsorship, but for years had little success. However, he was kept on the air with weekly sustaining broadcasts.[29]

Throughout these years the networks were expanding their schedules. According to information supplied to the FRC, 33.8 per cent of the NBC schedule in 1931 was sponsored, 66.2 per cent unsponsored. Of the CBS schedule 21.94 per cent was sponsored, 78.06 per cent was unsponsored.[30] The sponsored programs were getting the best hours and the main attention from radio columns and fan magazines, but the income from the sponsored programs was supporting a growing spectrum of nonsponsored material. The network structure was beginning to shelter a surprising range of activities, some scarcely noticed but due to grow.

Among these, one of the most important looked to a wider world.

COME IN, WORLD

For years the laboratory tinkerers had been playing with the short waves. They knew it was possible to reach Australia—and beyond. But to what end?

Almost a century earlier Thoreau, learning that a magnetic telegraph

28. Chasins, *Reminiscences*, pp. 42-4.
29. Kaltenborn, *Reminiscences*, p. 166.
30. *Commercial Radio Advertising*, p. 15.

line would link Maine and Texas, had suggested that Maine and Texas might have nothing to communicate. For years the short-wave experimenters seemed intent on proving there was nothing to communicate.

To be sure, they had in 1929 short-waved messages from Schenectady to members of the Byrd Antarctic expedition, which included Malcolm Hanson of WHA, University of Wisconsin, as radio specialist. But many subsequent demonstrations were global tiddly-winks.

In June 1930, General Electric scientists sent a rendition of "I Love You Truly" around the world via short-wave pickups and rebroadcasts by Huizen, Netherlands; Bandung, Java; Sydney, Australia; Schenectady, New York. There WGY announced: "The music you are hearing has gone completely around the world." [1]

Later GE scientists placed a cat before a Schenectady microphone. In Sydney, Australia, a dog was brought to a microphone. In Schenectady the cat's tail was twisted and it howled. The dog in Australia, hearing it on a loudspeaker, backed up and barked. Ten thousand miles away, the cat's fur ruffled. It was the first transoceanic cat and dog fight. [2] It was followed by a radio bridge game between a team in New York and a team in Argentina. [3]

In another broadcast, celebrating Independence Day, a shot was sent around the world via the same route as "I Love You Truly." A revolutionary musket was used—at least, it was used in the publicity picture, held by the Governor of Massachusetts. For the broadcast it seemed safer for a technician to fire a sound-effects pistol. [4]

During these years more serious games were brewing. Amid world-wide crises, the United States was losing its sense of isolation. Headlines spoke of falling governments, riots, inflation, hunger. Only a few years before, President Calvin Coolidge had said in his 1925 inaugural, over a nation-wide hookup: "The physical configuration of the earth has separated us from all the Old World." Now that dream was over. Our troubles, President Hoover constantly suggested, had been brought on, or at least prolonged, by Europe's upheavals. Our prosperity had seemed our own, but not the catastrophe.

In January 1930, as an American delegation sailed on the *George Wash-*

1. Wagoner, *Reminiscences,* p. 17.
2. *Ibid.* p. 38.
3. Lang, *Reminiscences,* p. 24.
4. *Ibid.* p. 22.

ington for a five-power naval conference in London—hoping for a naval limitation treaty, reducing armament burdens—two radio newsmen went along: William Hard of NBC and Frederick William Wile of CBS. No such species of journalist had attended previous international meetings.

On January 21, at noon London time, the voice of King George V was heard by American listeners welcoming the delegates. It was 7 A.M. in New York, 4 A.M. in California. American network practice barred use of recordings for later broadcast as a "sort of hoax . . . on the listener," [5] although the British Broadcasting Corporation already used recordings for this purpose. Few Americans therefore heard the pickups of the conference opening, or even later reports by the two newsmen, generally scheduled at off-peak hours. But something important had been launched— more significant, in fact, than the naval limitation treaty, which would soon prove a scrap of paper.

The conference lasted too long for Frederick Wile; he had to go home. He asked another newsman, César Saerchinger, representing the New York *Post* and Philadelphia *Public Ledger,* to cover for him, which Saerchinger did. He gave reports and brought to the microphone conference participants including Henry L. Stimson, U. S. Secretary of State. When the conference ended, Saerchinger cabled CBS: JUST GETTING INTO MY STRIDE . . . HAVE PLAN TO SUBMIT. He sent details, with names like George Bernard Shaw, John Masefield, the Prince of Wales. It struck a spark. That summer Henry Bellows, former FRC member now turned CBS vice president, joined Saerchinger in a visit to Sir John Reith, director-general of the British Broadcasting Corporation. They discussed a working arrangement, involving regular use of BBC studios and facilities.

A fragment of dialogue from that meeting survives. Its participants represented two closely related cultures, which in the first decade of broadcasting had given birth to sharply contrasting systems. The BBC was fully committed to a system based on license fees levied on radio receivers. The revenue from the fees—or most of it—went to the operation of the BBC, which in January 1927 had become a public corporation. The revenue had proved sufficient to build an organization of technical excellence and with highly educated personnel. That it had a responsibility to help shape public tastes and interests was implicit in the BBC point of view. It considered it a duty to look far beyond momentary public tastes. This meant, in Sir

5. James, *Interview,* p. 11.

John's words, "an active faith that a supply of good things will create a demand for them, not waiting for the demand to express itself." [6] It was the job of BBC personnel to know what was good. The BBC carried no advertising.

To the men of the BBC the chaos of American radio seemed an extraordinary phenomenon. Travelers regularly reported on its extreme commercialism. The eruption of competing networks, vying for public events as well as advertising dollars, created a bizarre picture, totally unlike the more orderly BBC.

"What I'd like to know," said Sir John Reith to the CBS visitors, "is how you Americans can successfully worship God and Mammon at the same time." He did not, according to Saerchinger, insist on getting the recipe. [7]

The BBC-CBS agreement was followed by a long series of programs using BBC facilities, relayed by telephone cable or short-wave. Within a few months some thirty writers and statesmen spoke to American listeners. A few must be mentioned.

John Masefield said:

> In times past poetry was the delight of every member of the community. The poet sang or spoke to all and was listened to with rapture by all. Then came the printing press, which at first was thought to be of great benefit to poets. I think it has become a detriment to poetical art, though priceless as a distributor of knowledge. It has had this result—it has put away the poet from his public.

Perhaps, thought Masefield, radio could restore poetry to its place, able to "compete once again with the delights of the market place." [8] Such thoughts were to be echoed in later years by others on both sides of the Atlantic.

Then came George Bernard Shaw.

Saerchinger kept after Shaw for months. This seemed to puzzle as well as flatter Shaw. "I don't believe it's any good," he would say. "Anyway, your people wouldn't let me say what I please." Saerchinger expressed outraged pride. He assured Shaw that he could talk about anything. Shaw, who had had some censorship trouble with the BBC—it always insisted on an advance script—was skeptical about this. "Suppose I wanted to talk about Russia?" "Splendid!" said Saerchinger. Shaw chuckled. "We must

6. Quoted, Briggs, "Broadcasting and Society," *The Listener*, November 22, 1962.
7. Saerchinger, *Hello America!*, p. 17.
8. *Ibid.* pp. 35-6.

see about that." [9] A few months later he made a nine-day trip to the Soviet Union. On his return he was full of genial comments about the Russians. "You think you have them convicted of the most monstrous crimes; and you find the crimes are only very sensible arrangements." [10] There was no unemployment in Russia, he reported. Of course, he added, he reserved the right to criticize the Russians, when he felt like it. He then informed Saerchinger he was ready to broadcast.

On October 11, 1931, César Saerchinger escorted the great man to the studio—not asking for a script. Mrs. Shaw went along, and thought it well to warn Saerchinger. Shaw had rehearsed the talk carefully, and apparently she had been present. "It's very cheeky, you know." [11] Shaw greeted the United States in these words:

> Hello America! Hello, all my friends in America! How are all you dear old boobs who have been telling one another for a month that I have gone dotty about Russia? . . . Russia has the laugh on us. She has us fooled, beaten, shamed, shown up, outpointed, and all but knocked out. We have lectured her from the heights of our modern superiority and now we are calling on the mountains to hide our blushes in her presence. . . . Our agriculture is ruined and our industries collapsing under the weight of our own productiveness because we have not found out how to distribute our wealth as well as to produce it.

He twitted the United States because its President, famous for war relief, could not feed his own people in time of peace. Meanwhile, said Shaw, "the sun shines in Russia as on a country with which God is well pleased." He conceded that there was still poverty, ignorance, and dirt, but asserted: "These evils are retreating . . . as steadily as they are advancing upon us." Shaw found occasion for a broadcasting metaphor: Stalin's ship of state was the only one, he said, not "tapping out SOS on its wireless." [12]

The broadcast evoked outrage in the United States, and CBS gave time for reply to the Reverend Edmund A. Walsh, vice president of Georgetown University—presumably because Shaw, without proper credentials, had interpreted the divine attitude toward Russia. Father Walsh returned some pungent phrases, calling Shaw "the licensed charlatan of English letters." [13]

9. *Ibid.* pp. 56-7.
10. Henderson, *George Bernard Shaw*, p. 322.
11. Saerchinger, *Hello America!*, p. 58.
12. New York *Times*, October 12, 1931.
13. *Ibid.* October 19, 1931.

Radio had passed a test. Saerchinger had been upheld—Shaw had spoken freely. And he had been freely answered.

Earlier that year Benito Mussolini, via NBC, also spoke to the American people. The Hearst newspapers had commissioned the Duce to write a series of articles. To promote these the Hearst organization arranged the broadcast and offered it to NBC. Mussolini, to prepare for the day, had English lessons for several months but was not easily understood.

In the following months Mahatma Gandhi, Leon Trotsky, Pope Pius XI (CONTACT OLD GENTLEMAN DIRECT, were the cabled instructions from CBS to Saerchinger[14]), H. G. Wells, the Prince of Wales, and others spoke over American radio networks. From other continents similar short-wave and telephone pickups began, and multiplied rapidly.

These international broadcasts were only one part of spreading network activity. The year 1930, in which Saerchinger first put "European Director, Columbia Broadcasting System" on his stationery—no one had authorized it but it helped negotiations[15]—also found CBS organizing a series of programs for classroom use under the title *American School of the Air,* and inaugurating broadcasts of the New York Philharmonic under Toscanini, while NBC was serving farmers and the Department of Agriculture with the *National Farm and Home Hour,* broadcasting the Mormon Tabernacle Choir from Salt Lake City, offering adaptations of classic drama on *Radio Guild,* and continuing the Damrosch *Music Appreciation Hour*— heard, it was said, in 150,000 schools.[16]

By 1931 NBC had 1359 employees, exclusive of talent. That year, according to statistics supplied to the Federal Radio Commission, the NBC networks featured 256 special events, carried 159 incoming international programs from 34 points of origin, broadcast 28 appearances by the President, 37 by cabinet members, and 71 by U. S. Senators and Representatives. It also made a net profit of $2,325,229.

In 1931 CBS had 408 employees, featured 415 special events, carried 97 international programs from 19 points of origin, and broadcast 19 appearances by the President, 24 by cabinet members, and 65 by U. S. Senators and Representatives. And it made a net profit of $2,346,766.[17]

Under Paley, CBS quickly strengthened its position with station purchases. In January 1929, WABC (in later years WCBS) became its full-

14. Saerchinger, *Hello America!,* p. 73.
15. *Ibid.* p. 66.
16. *Report of the Advisory Committee on Education by Radio,* p. 70.
17. *Commercial Radio Advertising,* pp. 17-22. Archer, *Big Business and Radio,* p. 397.

Television audience: Ernst F. W. Alexanderson watches tests at home with family on a 3" x 4" screen, 1928.

New York Mayor "Jimmy" Walker faces CBS scanner, 1931.

Jenkins receiver with round screen, 1929.

"SPLAIN DAT TO ME"

Gosden and Correll at the microphone as Amos and Andy, *c.* 1928.

Amos 'n' Andy publicity photo of "the boys in
character."

Publicity photo showing Andy "too lazy even
to bait his own hook."

time key station. CBS then bought WBT, Charlotte; WCCO, Minneapolis; and later other stations. At the same time it solidified its operation through a new kind of contract with affiliates. By giving sustaining programs *free*, it won a concession: a firm option on the time of affiliates. CBS could now make a network sale to a national sponsor without consulting affiliates. It simply told them what period to clear of local programming. This control over station schedules—worked out by wheeler-dealer Sam Pickard, who stepped straight from the Federal Radio Commission into a CBS vice presidency—would later become a serious issue, but at first seemed merely a brilliant business coup. For carrying network sponsored programs, CBS reimbursed each affiliate by a negotiated formula, which depended on the station's bargaining power. In 1931 CBS could offer 79 stations coast to coast.[18] It also strengthened itself in other directions: under Arthur Judson it formed (1930) a subsidiary, Columbia Concerts Corporation. The growing CBS strength was symbolized by an extraordinary development. At the start of 1932 Paley and associates calmly bought back from Paramount its holdings of CBS stock, and gained complete control. Paramount was in trouble, CBS was not.

NBC, to keep its lead, would eventually remodel its station relations along lines developed by CBS, but in 1931 it still depended on clearances. Each of the NBC networks listed 61 stations coast to coast,[19] including many powerful stations. It also strengthened itself by means of station purchases—WENR and WMAQ, Chicago; WTAM, Cleveland, and others. And it expanded in other directions. Strengthening its artist bureau, headed by George Engles, it bought (1930) the booking activity of the Chicago Civic Opera Company; soon NBC had "the largest group of outstanding artists in the world under its management." [20]

At higher strata similar moves were in progress. David Sarnoff, who became President of RCA in January 1930, had already embarked on a bold move comparable to that by which Owen D. Young, a decade earlier, had created RCA. Having purchased Victor, and thus acquired for RCA large manufacturing facilities, Sarnoff proposed that GE and Westinghouse turn over to RCA their radio manufacturing activity and various plants. This "unification" would make their operation efficient and ready for any competition—as, for example, that of AT&T's Western Electric.

18. *Commercial Radio Advertising*, p. 26.
19. *Ibid.*
20. Woods, *Reminiscences*, p. 56.

GE and Westinghouse would be reimbursed via additional blocks of RCA stock—and, in the long run, larger revenues.

As Sarnoff assumed the RCA presidency—with Major General Harbord moving up to become chairman of the board—the unification plan was going forward. Then there came a jolting interruption. In May 1930, the U. S. Department of Justice brought an anti-trust suit against RCA, GE, Westinghouse, and AT&T. It demanded the dissolution of the 1919-21 patent agreements. It also demanded that the companies disentangle themselves from each other. The interlocking of directorates was to end.

To some, this action seemed beyond belief. Conferences were held with the Justice Department, which held to its point. Settlement without trial would require divorcement of the tangled companies. In place of the patent agreements there was to be an open patent pool.

A year went by. So intricate were the interrelationships that the problems seemed to defy solution. Fruitless meetings were held, one after another.

Finally, an eight-page letter, dated October 1, 1931, came from Owen D. Young to the Department of Justice. He called attention to the "unprecedented economic and industrial crisis" of the nation. Much of this was caused by "ruinous competition . . . destructive rivalry." [21] The action of the Justice Department, it was implied, would destroy what stability there was in the radio industry, and lead to further catastrophes.

There were further meetings and letters, but the Justice Department was not persuaded. AT&T moved to make peace with the Department of Justice. No longer holding RCA stock nor board membership, it could readily do so. Late in 1931, under the cancelation clause in the cross-licensing agreements, it served three years' notice of termination.

As RCA, GE, and Westinghouse faced their perilous decision, business conditions worsened. In September 1931, Britain went off the gold standard. Repercussions were felt throughout the world. During that month 305 American banks closed; during the next month, 522 closed. Adding to the sense of international disintegration, Japan began overrunning Manchuria.

If the Justice Department anti-trust suit were to go to trial and were lost by the defendants, the antimonopoly clauses in the Radio Act of 1927 would come into play. Radio licenses of incalculable value—KDKA, WJZ, WBZ, KYW, WEAF, WGY, KOA, KGO, WMAQ, WTAM—were imper-

21. Archer, *Big Business and Radio*, p. 358.

iled by the suit. If the defendants had hopes of a more lenient political climate, the news of the moment dispelled them.

As 1932 began, most estimates of unemployment in the United States stood at ten million or more. In every city countless stores stood boarded up, empty. The sound of riveting had almost vanished. People combed through city dumps. More than a million people were thought to be roaming from place to place, often sleeping in boxcars; along every railroad track campfires flickered. Bitterness increased. Farmers began to resist evictions with pitchforks and shotguns.

It was an election year. Both parties prepared for June conventions in Chicago. It would be President Hoover for the Republicans. Among the Democrats the name Franklin Delano Roosevelt was heard most often. What was known of his views was not reassuring to the patent allies.

Against this background GE, Westinghouse, and RCA sat down in 1932 to work out a divorcement plan to stave off trial. A date for trial had been set: November 15, 1932, a week after election.

As the rumblings of the election campaign built to a roar, there were long, innumerable GE-Westinghouse-RCA meetings.

GHOSTS

Did it all make sense? Why did the Department of Justice, after years of off-again-on-again hearings by various agencies, launch this suit in the depth of an economic slump? To many in the broadcasting industry, intent on other interests, the development was completely baffling. In Washington reasons seemed clearer. To those with memories or a taste for history, the answer was clear enough. In the annals of communication, monopoly had long been held one of the most corrupting of influences.

In the decades after the Civil War the Western Union Company, by buying, swallowing, or crushing smaller companies, achieved a monopoly position. By 1873 its wires reached into thirty-seven states and nine territories and comprised the only nation-wide web. It was a key to wealth and power in many ways. Representative Charles A. Sumner of California charged in 1875 that sudden changes in market prices were repeatedly withheld from San Francisco until insiders made a killing. Control of the flow of information netted vaster fortunes than the profits from telegraph service; and this, monopoly-priced, made fortunes by itself.[1]

1. Harlow, *Old Wires and New Waves*, pp. 333-4.

To break the monopoly power by creating an alternative channel, bills for a government telegraph service linking the nation's post offices were introduced in Congress in 1869, 1870, 1872, 1874, 1875, 1881, 1884, 1890. But Western Union could muster crushing opposition. It worked in close alliance with the old Associated Press, which used only Western Union. Newspapers aspiring to national or international coverage lived at the mercy of these allies. Newspapers backing postal telegraph proposals found their rates raised or service ended. Publishers, editors, reporters knew this topic was out of bounds.[2]

Press control was matched in importance by other persuasive pressures. Congressmen, as well as state legislators, received franks—free telegraph privileges—in apparently unlimited quantity. A Western Union official wrote to a New York politician shortly before a convention:

> Dear Mr. ————:
>
> I enclose another book of franks, of which I have extended the limits to cover all Western Union lines.
> I hope they may help you make a good nomination. Please use them freely on political messages, and telegraph me when you want a fresh supply.[3]

The company was equally generous with both major political parties: it took no undue risks. The company's affairs and prosperity, President Orton of Western Union informed his board of directors in 1873, were subject to governmental action at all levels, and the franks had saved revenue "many times the money value of the free service."[4]

The power exercised by Western Union was used with increasing ruthlessness when it came under control of Jay Gould. In the 1880's the fury aroused by Gould's machinations—via his hold over railroads, telegraph, press, politicians—found vent in song:

> We'll hang Jay Gould on a sour apple tree
> And bring to grief the plotters of a base monopoly![5]

After 1885 the growth of the AT&T web of wires ended Western Union's monopoly position and even permitted the rise of Postal Telegraph, a private company choosing a name that had become a sort of freedom banner.

2. *Ibid.* pp. 334, 338. John Wanamaker as Postmaster General under President Benjamin Harrison was among those who backed postal telegraph proposals.
3. *Ibid.* p. 337.
4. Western Union *Annual Report*, 1873. Quoted, *ibid.* p. 336.
5. *Ibid.* p. 405.

And the rise of United Press began to limit the power of the Associated Press.

These old battles were not quite forgotten in Washington; their echoes mingled curiously with new struggles.

The growing importance of networks in the field of news, their involvement in world-wide events and crucial issues, were welcomed by many. These could be seen as signs of growing maturity and responsibility. But they raised all the more compellingly the question: should the largest networks be controlled by the largest electrical companies, closely linked with mammoth utilities, who were among the most active lobbyists?

The generosity to President, congressmen, cabinet members, and other government officials—"worth," as NBC reported to the FRC in statistics for the year 1931, $2,047,200 "at regular rates" [6]—was welcomed. Reports on stewardship were surely needed in a democracy, and were a logical use of the air. But was there in this also something reminiscent of the Western Union franks? Did it likewise protect company revenues?

If fretful ghosts of yesterday were heard in an anti-monopoly chorus, so were living voices. A number of newspapers, staggered by the slump and radio inroads on advertising, were pressing the issue. So were RCA competitors. Month by month, smaller radio manufacturers were going into bankruptcy. Larger competitors were also being heard.

In 1930 B. J. Grigsby, president of the substantial Grigsby-Grunow, maker of Majestic radios, gave the Senate committee on interstate commerce an impassioned recital of the difficulties of competing with RCA. His company had entered radio manufacture in 1924, first making loudspeakers and other parts, later complete sets. In 1928 it had sought an RCA license. RCA was unwilling at that time to license more than twenty-five companies; Majestic entered the field by buying out a licensee who was on the point of collapse. Since then Majestic had paid RCA $5,302,879 in royalties. The RCA license did not tell the licensee what patents were covered. Perhaps this was because some patents were still in litigation. Majestic could not therefore know, said Grigsby, what it was buying for its five million dollars, other than immunity from suit by RCA. In fact, it did not believe it needed any patent of the patent group.

> But the radio combine had so terrorized the industry and the dealers and jobbers everywhere that they were afraid to handle what they called "unlicensed" sets. Our bankers said they would not finance us

6. *Commercial Radio Advertising*, p. 17.

unless we took out a license. They said they would not finance a patent fight against such a monopoly. . . . The merits of the patents were never examined by the bankers. The merits of the patents had nothing to do with it.[7]

The terrorizing referred to consisted of letters such as the following, sent to New York jobbers in December 1929:

Dear Sirs: We are advised that you are engaged in the manufacture, use, and sale of radio tubes which infringe each of the following United States Letters Patent, viz:

Arnold	1456528	Langmuir	1558437
Nicholson	1459412	Schottky	1537708
Langmuir (reissue)	15278	Seibt	1696103

. . . In behalf of our clients, the Radio Corporation of America, the American Telephone & Telegraph Co., and the General Electric Co., we hereby request that you refrain from further infringement of any of the above letters patent and that you account for all damages and all profit occasioned by reason of past infringements.

Yours very truly,
Fish, Richardson, & Neave[8]

Such letters, according to independent manufacturers, made jobbers afraid to handle anything but RCA-licensed equipment.

The RCA licenses required payment of a 7½ per cent royalty, based on wholesale costs. "No licensee," said Grigsby, "can long pay 7½% royalty to its competitor. Another grievance was the "tube-grab clause," so called because it required RCA licensees to buy RCA tubes and no others. Indignation over such issues helped foment the Justice Department suit, and also found expression in civil suits, which took RCA close to disaster.

The original tube patents of Fleming and De Forest, key elements in the formation of the patent alliance, had expired during the 1920's. To maintain their position the allies relied on later patents including those of Langmuir and Arnold, who had developed tubes with a more perfect vacuum. But in May 1931 the U. S. Supreme Court ruled that these refinements were not inventions and not patentable.[9]

A more serious threat was meanwhile developing. After expiration of the original patents, De Forest had re-entered tube manufacture, but his com-

7. *Commission on Communications*, pp. 1769-70.
8. *Commission on Communications*, p. 1870.
9. *De Forest* v. *General Electric*, 283 U.S. 664 (1931).

pany found RCA's tube-grab clause an obstacle to marketing, and went bankrupt. The receiver, Arthur D. Lord, sued RCA, charging that its practices violated the Clayton Act. The U. S. District Court in Delaware agreed, and its ruling was upheld on appeal.[10] Did this require the Federal Radio Commission to strip RCA of its broadcasting licenses, under the 1927 Radio Act? In 1931, as RCA station licenses came up for renewal, the FRC had to face this issue. Two commissioners felt that the law—Section 13[11]—required them to void the licenses. The three others disagreed, arguing that the monopolistic practices had involved equipment only, not "communication." By this 3-2 decision RCA retained its licenses. But under the combined onslaught of civil suit, injunction, and Justice Department action, an overhauling of RCA practices was under way. RCA began making its patents available to all, and reducing royalties; the tube-grab clause passed into oblivion. All this was still not enough. The unraveling of RCA-GE-Westinghouse had to begin. The deadline was near.

ARENA

The fear that the Radio Act of 1927 might be upset in court "before we would get a system going" affected—among others—Senator Clarence C. Dill, co-author of the law. As suits began and wound their way upward through appeal, he worried that "the judges might not know very much about this subject." He decided to get in touch with Chief Justice William Howard Taft of the U. S. Supreme Court.

. . . so I called him up on a Saturday morning at his home and I said, "I would like to come up and talk to you for a few minutes about a matter that I think is of some importance to you." "Well," he said, "Come on up." So I went up there, and he took me in his study, and he said, "What are you thinking about?" And I said, "Well, before I tell you, I want to say to you that I realize that I am going to discuss a case that is before the Court and—I have no interest in it personally, only the general public interest—and I, if I overstep my bounds, in the legislative body, talking to you as a judge, I want you to call my attention to it." And, "Well," he said, "I don't think the Court will be hurt in any way, and what is it?" [1]

10. *Lord* v. *RCA*, 24 F.(2nd) 565, affirmed 28 F.(2nd) 257.
11. See Appendix B, The Radio Act of 1927.
1. Dill, *Interview*, pp. 13-14.

The Senator told the Chief Justice about a particular case and hoped the Court would give it careful attention. "There's a lot of money invested and these people ought to know whether this law is a constitutional law." [2]

Ex-President Taft considered himself a final bulwark against dangerous and socialistic trends, which he saw even in the Hoover administration. During his term as Chief Justice, which ended in 1930, he was constantly conferring with lawmakers and making legislative suggestions, to an extent few of his predecessors would have felt proper. He apparently felt the crisis of the times demanded it. He now wondered whether radio was commerce. According to Senator Dill's recollection, Taft said: "We had the telegraph and the Court decided that was commerce . . . then the telephone came and that's been declared commerce . . . now if I'm to write a decision on this thing called radio, I'm afraid I'll have to get in touch with the occult."

The Chief Justice expressed the opinion that "if there is any way to avoid jurisdiction," the Court would do so. [3]

In several cases during the Taft chief justiceship and years immediately following, the U. S. Court of Appeals of the District of Columbia upheld the Federal Radio Commission, and the U. S. Supreme Court declined to review. These actions, strengthening the law, at the same time buttressed the position of the commissioners in office. Ironically, one of the litigants who contributed to this outcome and even pushed the FRC into a heroic stance and an important precedent, was the outrageous Dr. John R. Brinkley.

The FRC had several times renewed the license of KFKB, Milford, the voice of the goat-gland surgeon and drug peddler. But newspaper exposés and medical society pressure eventually brought a reconsideration. In 1930 the FRC held hearings, with testimony by Dr. Brinkley and his arch-foe, Dr. Morris Fishbein of the American Medical Association. When the FRC decided not to renew, Brinkley appealed to the U. S. Court of Appeals. A major issue: could the FRC, in its nonrenewal, base its action on statements made on the air by Brinkley? Was this not "censorship" such as the Radio Act of 1927 forbade? No, the Court decided. The FRC could consider past program content without committing "censorship." In fact, it must consider "the nature of the program broadcast" in order to assess

2. *Ibid.* p. 15. The Dill interview does not identify the case under discussion.
3. *Ibid.*

whether the public interest, convenience, or necessity had been served.[4] Thus the Brinkley case provided a significant precedent—which some broadcasters and even commissioners would, however, decline for decades to accept, in spite of additional court decisions of similar thrust.[5]

Defeat did not end the Brinkley saga. In 1930, the year of the FRC about-face, KFKB won the golden microphone of *Radio Digest* magazine as the most popular radio station in the nation, with 356,827 votes. It seemed to be what the public wanted even if it was not what some men in Washington felt was good for the public. As a further measure of public support, 183,278 Kansans that November cast write-in votes for Brinkley for governor of their state, against 217,171 for winner Harry Woodring (D.). The votes counted for Brinkley excluded thousands in which his name was misspelled or incomplete. With better spellers behind him, Brinkley would probably have won. The result persuaded him to seek a place on the ballot in the 1932 governorship race, and he began at once to make his plans. Meanwhile he obtained a radio station across the border in Mexico. Maintaining a telephone link from home, he was soon addressing the nation with a voice of 100,000 watts from XER, Mexico, and carrying on business without interruption.[6]

Among court cases which fortified the FRC, another must be mentioned. WNYC, New York City governmental station, was unhappy with its part-time, low-power assignment and brought suit. The U. S. Court of Appeals of the District of Columbia merely decided that the FRC had acted within its powers.[7] The Supreme Court, in a 1930 decision, declined to review. The case held special interest because the FRC had asserted that city government ownership did not give the station any special standing in regard to "the public interest, convenience, or necessity."[8]

Stations owned by other government units such as state colleges and universities found such an assertion ominous. They were drifting rapidly to the view that their hope of survival, if there was hope, lay not in the FRC but in political action. Meetings, resolutions, pamphlets, legislative

4. *KFKB Broadcasting Association* v. *Federal Radio Commission*, 47 F.(2nd)670, App. D.C.(1931).
5. See especially *Trinity Methodist Church South* v. *Federal Radio Commission*, 62 F.(2nd) 850, App. D.C. (1932).
6. Carson, *The Roguish World of Dr. Brinkley*, pp. 143-66.
7. *City of New York* v. *Federal Radio Commission*, 36 F.(2nd)117, App. D.C. (1929).
8. Nobel, *The Municipal Broadcasting System*, p. 13.

proposals, from 1929 on provided a crescendo of activity toward that end. Reflecting a rapidly changing political climate, the development took on an increasingly militant and even radical tone.

Throughout this period the ranks of stations owned by educational institutions thinned. Nine stations gave up in 1930 and others followed. In some cases the cause was the Depression. The Alabama Polytechnic Institute, a licensee since 1922, gave up "because of the tragic condition of state finances. Many school salaries were more than a year in arrears." The station was leased to, and then taken over by, commercial interests.[9]

But in other cases finance was not the issue. "For ten years," wrote Jerome Davis when the Connecticut State College station finally gave up, "this station has sought to secure the right to operate a more powerful station and one free from commercial interference. For ten years this college has continued to broadcast programs into whistle-ridden channels, vainly hoping that some provision would be made for state broadcasting needs." [10] Throughout this period its difficulties with regulatory authorities were truly staggering. Licensed full time by the Department of Commerce in 1923, it had its first shift in 1925. It operated at that time at 500 watts with call letters WCAC, Storrs. Then came a dizzying series of orders. In June 1927 the station was ordered by the FRC to share time with WDRC, Hartford; in August, shifted to 560 kc. to share time with WTIC, Hartford; in October 1928, shifted to 1330 kc. to share with WDRC; in January 1929, shifted to 600 kc. to share with WTIC, with power reduced to 250 watts; in January 1930, shifted to share with WGBS, New York instead of WTIC; in April, with WICC, Bridgeport instead of WGBS; in May, with WGBS instead of WICC; in March 1931, with WICC again. Under such circumstances, the college decided there was little chance of developing "a significant state educational project," and gave up.[11]

While Connecticut State College was shifted nine times, another educational station was shifted eight times, two others seven times, and four others six times.[12]

During this period, a commercial station sharing time with an educational station often petitioned the FRC for the full time. In such cases the

9. Frost, *Education's Own Stations*, pp. 12-13.
10. Tyler (ed.), *Radio as a Cultural Agency*, p. 4.
11. Frost, *Education's Own Stations*, pp. 71-2.
12. Tyler, *An Appraisal of Radio Broadcasting in the Land-Grant Colleges and State Universities*, p. 25.

FRC would set a hearing and invite both stations to send representatives. Survival seemed to require constant legal services and a budget for ceaseless travel to and from Washington. In February 1931, applications from commercial broadcasters who wanted to take over channels used by educators involved twenty-eight educational broadcasters in defensive action.[13] Some commercial broadcasters were attacking each other with equal persistence and ferocity, but this hardly comforted the educators.

Discouragement and anger over such developments brought organized action. The year 1929 saw meetings which led, in the following year, to the birth of the National Committee on Education by Radio, with financial backing from the Payne Fund. Mr. Joy Elmer Morgan of the National Education Association, editor of the NEA *Journal,* became chairman of the new organization.[14]

Its auspices hardly suggested radicalism. But Morgan announced as its first task: "Conservation . . . to save or to recover for the uses of education a fair share of the radio broadcasting frequencies." [15] The committee called for reallocation of channels, with 15 per cent set aside for governmental agencies or educational institutions chartered by them. This proposal, which found expression in 1931 in the Fess bill,[16] necessarily meant that many commercial broadcasters would lose channels. It was met with expressions of outrage. Commercial counterattack was inevitable and made the National Committee on Education by Radio a storm center of controversy.

The furor soon revolving about it provides a rich case study in Depression politics. The year 1930, when the National Committee took shape, also saw the birth of another organization, with a name so similar as to cause glorious confusion. Entitled the National Advisory Council on Radio in Education, it was provided with funds by John D. Rockefeller, Jr., and the Carnegie Corporation.

Obviously both organizations were dedicated to the educational use of radio. Some people applauded both without being sure which was which,

13. *Education on the Air* (1933), p. 41.
14. It included representation from: National Association of State Universities, National University Extension Association, National Catholic Education Association, American Council on Education, National Education Association, Jesuit Educational Association, National Council of State Superintendents, Association of Land-Grant Colleges and Universities, Association of College and University Broadcasting Stations.
15. *Education on the Air* (1931), p. 6.
16. S5589, 71st Congress (1931). S4, 72nd Congress (1932).

or how they might differ. But the two organizations had started from different premises, and the political cleavages of the time were to polarize them further.

The *Council* was dedicated to the proposition that commercial broadcasting gave ample shelter to educational needs, and that these could be safely left to commercial broadcasters. (The implication: educators did not need channels.) It flew the banner of co-operation. It cited the achievements of commercial broadcasting. It chose as its president Dr. Robert A. Millikan. Owen D. Young attended its first meeting. At this meeting, as recounted enthusiastically by Dr. Millikan—

> Owen D. Young . . . informed us that it was possible for any educational group which the Council might set up to obtain all the facilities for nationwide broadcasting that it could possibly use, without any expense whatever, the sole conditions being that the audience must be large and that the commercial companies which ˙furnish the facilities are to have nothing to do in any way, shape, or manner with the broadcasting program.[17]

A more generous proposal could hardly be imagined. NBC president Merlin Aylesworth was meanwhile proclaiming that the door was "wide open to those who would raise the level of national culture." NBC vice president John W. Elwood, following this generous lead, said the network had "all the place for education that education wants." [18]

Others considered such statements a maneuver to protect profitable channels. This view found expression in a meeting organized by the Department of the Interior. Here a "fact-finding committee" reported:

> There is widespread distrust among educators of commercial motives and "propaganda." The educational stations believe they are given the inferior positions on the broadcasting spectrum and in the allocation of hours. Commercial stations show a tendency to reduce educational programs to shorter and poorer periods as their time becomes more salable, and when they do offer educational programs it is usually in the endeavor to cultivate general good-will and create publicity, rather than build up a sound educational method . . ." [19]

Educators began to document these charges through case histories.[20] Their distrust was strengthened in 1931 and 1932 by a number of exposés of the

17. Tyler (ed.), *Radio as a Cultural Agency*, p. 112.
18. *Report of the Advisory Committee*, pp. 155, 230.
19. *Ibid.* p. 36.
20. *Ibid.* pp. 52-6.

private power industry and the work of Aylesworth on its behalf. These cast doubt on the sincerity of his interest in the educational process. Details soon found their way into broadcasting publications.

Throughout the 1920's the National Electric Light Association had aimed massive propaganda—subsidized textbooks, pamphlets, speakers— at schools and colleges to head off interest in public power projects. Samuel Insull had taken particular interest in the launching of this drive; Aylesworth had managed it. *The Public Pays* by Ernest Gruening (1931) documented it. The title derived from words spoken by Aylesworth: he had urged associates not to worry about the cost of the campaign because "the public pays." He meant, when it pays its electrical bill. Even more interesting was the advice Aylesworth gave to local power executives:

> I would advise any manager who lives in a community where there is a college to get the professor of economics . . . interested in your problems. Have him lecture on your subject to his classes. Once in a while it would pay you to take such men—getting $500 or $600 a year, or $1,000 perhaps—and give them a retainer of $100 or $200 a year for the privilege of letting you study and consult with them. For how in heaven's name can we do anything in the schools of the country with young people growing up if we have not first sold the idea of education to the college professor? [21]

The years 1932-33, during which economic conditions steadily worsened, saw a rising tide of political discussion and a swing to the left. The conviction that the economic order was due for sharp change appeared even among business leaders considered conservative. Among intellectuals it was a common assumption.

The violence with which the bonus marchers were dispersed in the summer of 1932 reflected a fear that a political turnover was about to begin.

Russia was constantly discussed. Lecturers on the subject were in demand. H. V. Kaltenborn, like George Bernard Shaw, spoke of recent Russian visits with warmth. As late as 1929 he had found Russians friendly, and eager to talk and debate.[22] At the same time revelations about American business leaders who had held positions of trust were fomenting the radical trend. Early in 1932 Samuel Insull, abandoning his eighty-five directorships, suddenly fled to Europe; indicted for embezzlement, he preferred not to return. Later the admissions of Charles E. Mitchell of the

21. Gruening, *The Public Pays*, p. 28. Tyler (ed.), *Radio as a Cultural Agency*, pp 112-13.
22. Kaltenborn, *Reminiscences*, pp. 140-41.

National City Bank concerning insider deals that had improperly bene-
fited bank officials—while others lost millions—shocked the American
public.[23] Trust in the business world, which had been at its highest in 1928,
reached a low in 1932-33.

Against this background the attack on commercial control of the broadcasting spectrum gathered momentum. The demands of the National
Committee on Education by Radio, modest as they were, at least called
for change, and attracted those who hoped for change.

To the *Council* the *Committee* seemed more and more a threat to the
established order.

To the *Committee* the *Council* seemed a tool of vested interests.

In May, 1932, the headline CANADIAN BROADCASTING TO BE NATIONAL-
IZED[24] encouraged the *Committee*. To our north, said the announcement,
the operation of high-powered stations would be reserved to government,
for educational and cultural purposes. There would also be private stations, but of low power, and advertising would be limited to 5 per cent of
the time.

The following month, Franklin Delano Roosevelt became the Democratic nominee for President. Already known as an enthusiast for public
power and conservation, his nomination encouraged those who looked for
change—and it frightened others.

President Hoover, as expected, was quickly renominated. At first confident, he gradually became an irritable, truculent prophet of doom. That
fall he was telling a nation-wide radio audience that if the Roosevelt program went into effect, "the grass will grow in the streets of a hundred
cities, a thousand towns." [25]

Roosevelt answered with equally strong attacks on "economic oli-
garchy." He spoke of public power projects as a yardstick "to prevent
extortion."

In the radical thrust of 1932-33, favorite villains included utilities, Wall
Street, monopolies, advertising.

To James Rorty, a vigorous pamphleteer of the time, who wrote in support of the *Committee* and spoke at one of its meetings, the villain was
advertising. He had himself been an advertising writer for one of the largest agencies until he suddenly found he had had enough. Now he dedi-

23. Schlesinger, *The Crisis of the Old Order,* p. 478.
24. *Broadcasting,* May 15, 1932.
25. New York *Times,* November 1, 1932.

cated himself to exposing what he considered its vicious effect, "something that a sane and vigorous people must reject in totality, on pain . . . of cultural death." [26]

Rorty, calling himself a socialist, wrote during the Depression years for *Harper's, New Republic, Nation, Freeman, New Freeman,* and *New Masses.* He later drew on much of this material for the book *Our Master's Voice.* More than any other writer, Rorty epitomized the intellectual anti-advertising animus of the time:

> The American apparatus of advertising is something unique in history and unique in the modern world; unique, fantastic, and fragile. . . . It is like a grotesque, smirking gargoyle set at the very top of America's skyscraping adventure in acquisition *ad infinitum.* The tower is tottering, but it probably will be some time before it falls. . . .
>
> The gargoyle's mouth is a loudspeaker, powered by the vested interest of a two-billion dollar industry, and back of that the vested interests of business as a whole, of industry, of finance. It is never silent, it drowns out all other voices, and it suffers no rebuke, for is it not the voice of America? That is its claim and to some extent it is a just claim. For at least two generations of Americans—the generations that grew up during the war and after—have listened to that voice as to an oracle. It has taught them how to live, what to be afraid of, what to be proud of, how to be beautiful, how to be loved, how to be envied, how to be successful.

To Rorty the earthly atmosphere was saturated with never-ending "jabberwocky" from hundreds of thousands of loudspeakers.

> Is it any wonder that the American population tends increasingly to speak, think, feel in terms of this jabberwocky? That the stimuli of art, science, religion are progressively expelled to the periphery of American life to become marginal values, cultivated by marginal people on marginal time?

He saw the unemployed as victims of a system of which the jabberwocky was a part. Burned clean of buying power, they could no longer "feed the machine," but were still assailed by the "electric breath of the jabberwock." Rorty summarized:

> An evening spent twiddling the dials of a radio set is indeed a profoundly educational experience for any student of the culture. America is too big to see itself. But radio has enabled America to hear itself.[27]

26. Tyler (ed.), *Radio as a Cultural Agency*, p. 33.
27. Rorty, *Our Master's Voice*, pp. 32-3, 70-72, 270.

As the election campaign of 1932 roared to a climax, there were round-the-clock meetings by representatives of RCA, GE, Westinghouse. During October they worked almost continuously. They were heading for approximately the same deadline as the candidates. To set aside the trial scheduled for November 15, they were to deliver to the U. S. Attorney General early that month a divorcement plan that could form the basis for a consent decree.

For the interests of GE, its president Gerard Swope carried the burden. The principal Westinghouse spokesman was Andrew W. Robertson, chairman of the board. For RCA it was David Sarnoff, president. In the marathon talks, specialists came and went.

With them sat Owen D. Young. He was chairman of the board of GE, creator of RCA, chairman of the NBC Advisory Council, and member of many other boards and committees. Somehow he was considered above the battle, a voice of impartial justice. His name was known throughout the world. In 1929-30, with assistance from Sarnoff, he had headed the international committee that developed the Young Plan—like the Dawes Plan, an attempt to save Germany from economic collapse and chaos.

Young was tired. Walter C. Evans, the KYW pioneer, who came to the talks to discuss the Westinghouse stations, gives a vivid picture:

> I distinctly recall Mr. Young slouched down in an armchair in the RCA board room with the appearance of being more than half asleep. When the controversy reached a complete impasse his eyes would open only a slight amount and he would suggest the compromise which solved the question.[1]

In this crisis David Sarnoff, with far-ranging grasp of detail and firmness for the RCA cause, emerged as a negotiator hardly less skillful than Young. RCA had been for much of its life a shell of an organization—a sales agent for others, and owned by others. Its ability to survive would depend on dispositions now made.

A crucial idea, the Sarnoff "unification," remained intact. RCA emerged with the radio manufacturing facilities. GE and Westinghouse would have the right to compete with RCA but, with Justice Department approval, agreed to defer such competition for at least two and a half years.

For yielding their facilities and their ownership rights in RCA and

1. Evans, *Reminiscences*, p. 50.

NBC, GE and Westinghouse would each receive RCA debentures. In addition GE would get real estate—an RCA-owned building on Lexington Avenue, New York, which at the moment was losing money. It became the General Electric Building.

By the end of October the divorce terms neared completion. GE and Westinghouse were to withdraw from the RCA and NBC boards. NBC would be a wholly owned subsidiary of RCA. GE and Westinghouse would retain their broadcasting stations, but NBC would manage them.

NBC would go ahead with a plan already widely discussed, of moving to a new complex of buildings being planned for mid-Manhattan. This vast Rockefeller project, for which blocks of brownstone buildings were being leveled, seemed to defy the Depression itself, and had caught the imagination of the public—which called it Radio City. To clinch the move, the Rockefeller interests made new concessions to RCA.

As election day approached, there were still unsolved questions concerning the extent of the RCA debt to GE and Westinghouse, and the value of debentures to be issued.

On November 8, Franklin Delano Roosevelt was elected President of the United States by an overwhelming majority of the electoral college vote.

In the Democratic flood there were few straws for Republicans to cling to. One was to be found in Kansas, where the governorship vote stood:[2]

Alfred M. Landon (R.)	278,581
Harry H. Woodring (D.)	272,944
John R. Brinkley	244,607

Because the Democratic vote was split between the incumbent Woodring and the radio sage, Dr. Brinkley, the victory went to Alfred M. Landon, who thus emerged as a Republican hope for 1936.

On November 10 there were day and night meetings of RCA, GE, Westinghouse officials, committees, subcommittees, and teams of attorneys. On November 11 their proposals were delivered to the Department of Justice. A few changes were needed. On Sunday, November 13, came a final RCA-GE-Westinghouse meeting, all day and far into the night.[3] The next day, a week's postponement of the trial was announced. On November 21 the consent decree was signed. The trial was canceled.

2. New York *Times*, November 10, 1932.
3. Archer, *Big Business and Radio*, p. 374.

Miraculously, RCA emerged as a strong and self-sufficient entity. No longer owned by others, it had its own destiny in hand. It owned two networks, broadcasting stations, manufacturing facilities, international and ship-to-shore communication facilities. It controlled a majority of clear-channel stations.

Now all roads led to the President-elect, Franklin D. Roosevelt. His supporters—they included very few among the leaders of broadcasting—would soon begin to split along new lines. For some supporters the primary task was economic recovery; for others, reform. For the latter, victory was not worth winning if it kept in control elements considered responsible for the catastrophe, and which—if left undisturbed—were considered certain to produce another cycle of boom and bust.

Around Roosevelt rumors swirled. There were lists of possible cabinet members. On a list considered for Secretary of State appeared the name Owen D. Young, veteran of many diplomatic encounters. The name was dropped—too much involvement with utilities.[4]

It was reported that Roosevelt favored a new commission to control telephone as well as broadcast communication. This meant a new law—perhaps a new shuffle, a new deal in radio frequencies. Champions of radio reform girded for battle. So did others. High cards were held by RCA with its two networks and CBS with its one. But power made them also targets and candidates for a possible scapegoat role. Of this they were well aware.

Some hurried housecleaning was going on. Fortune tellers of various kinds were disappearing from the air. Some of the more fraudulent nostrums were being dropped. Some people thought it was too little and too late. Levering Tyson, although prominent in the *Council* and a proponent of advertising-based broadcasting, felt that commercialism was "rampant." Unless the system reformed itself, he felt "nothing can save it."[5]

In the final months of 1932, economic conditions grew still worse. A report by Grace Abbott of the Children's Bureau warned that many children were being fed on as little as $2 per month.[6] Expectation of drastic action hung in the air.

That fall New York City police moved reluctantly to evict a colony of

4. Schlesinger, *The Crisis of the Old Order*, p. 468.
5. Tyson (ed.), *Radio and Education*, pp. 28-9.
6. Shannon, *The Great Depression*, p. 52.

derelicts living in shacks in Central Park. Near the obelisk they had built seventeen huts; most had beds and chairs and a few had carpets. In the center of the group was a shack made of fruit crates and egg crates, with a tattered American flag on top. It was a sort of community center and had a radio. The shack bore the sign "Radio City." [7]

The broadcasting industry that awaited the coming of a new administration was a vast and varied constellation, diffuse as the milky way, that by now included not only stations and networks but also—

Advertising agencies. They were producing almost all sponsored network programs. Scores of agencies had formed radio departments.

Independent producers. As subcontractors, a few such companies served agencies that did not have radio departments.

Transcription syndicates. Following up the early *Amos 'n' Andy* "chainless chain" success, they were trying to market recorded series —*Chandu the Magician* was one of them—for local use. They were valuable to sponsors whose distribution areas did not coincide with network areas.

Recording companies. To serve the syndicates, several companies operated facilities for the making of 16-inch discs, each side holding fifteen minutes. Western Electric had entered this field.

Script syndicates. A few firms were offering to local stations scripts for local use. Some were offered free for publicity purposes. *Time* magazine had been a pioneer in this, offering scripts called *News-Casting* as early as 1928.

Station representatives. Brokerage offices were springing up in New York and elsewhere, each selling time on behalf of a large list of local stations.

Merchandising services. A number of firms made a specialty of handling contests and premium offers.

Trade papers. They were becoming more specialized. *Broadcasting* was considered an unofficial voice of the National Association of

7. New York *Times,* September 22, 1932.

Broadcasters and closely reflected its views. *Variety* was supplementing alert reporting with meaningful program criticism and was virtually alone in this field. Late in 1932 it had moved Radio to second position, immediately following Pictures; only a few months earlier Radio had always appeared in the back of the issue after Vaudeville, Times Square, Sports, Legitimate, Literati, and Music. *Radio Broadcast*, without a clearly defined role, had expired.

Press agents. They were inundating trade papers, fan magazines, radio columns with material on behalf of stars, agencies, networks, stations.

Trade associations. The National Association of Broadcasters was in full swing. Still concerned about ASCAP, it was preparing to battle against government encroachment. Radio was also getting increasing attention from groups such as the Association of National Advertisers and the American Association of Advertising Agencies.

Unions. Unionization talk was barely beginning among actors, writers, and various groups of technicians. The well established American Federation of Musicians was preparing for moves in the radio field.

There were other phenomena. The traffic in licenses had produced some entrepreneurs owning numbers of stations. In the Midwest George Storer had sold his gas stations and bought radio stations: in Toledo, Wheeling, and Detroit. Buying and selling, he gradually strengthened and expanded his holdings into an empire. Others followed his example. These multiple-station owners had so far attracted little attention, but the phenomenon would soon raise issues.

There were other activities. After long planning the Cooperative Analysis of Broadcasting had been launched in 1930—the first national rating service, organized for the Association of National Advertisers by Archibald Crossley. Its task was "equivalent to determining the number of crickets chirping at any instant in a swamp on a foggy summer evening." [1] The CAB ratings or "Crossley ratings," based on telephone interviews with a small population sample, almost at once became a factor in program decisions. Many people believed they would improve programming.

Almost all forms of enterprise that would dominate radio and television in decades to come had taken shape.

1. *Radio Broadcast*, May 1928.

While many small stations were suffering from the Depression, a number of large stations were doing well. These included network stations in New York, Chicago, and Los Angeles but also large stations elsewhere. Some were burgeoning production centers. KPO (later KNBC, KNBR), San Francisco, bought by NBC in 1932, had some two hundred employees. During early network days scripts had often been sent by NBC in New York to be reperformed from KPO for the West Coast. (Talent costs were lower than wire costs.) Use of these scripts convinced many a San Francisco writer-director that he could do better. Among them Carlton Morse, inspired by John Galsworthy's *Forsyte Saga*, began in 1932 the series *One Man's Family*, which would last twenty-eight years.[2] WLW, Cincinnati, and WTAM, Cleveland, had similar concentrations of talent producing dramas, operas, revues. At WLW, actors were "scarcely aware that a Depression existed."[3] WTAM had found so many sponsors for its local productions that it gave NBC constant trouble over clearances; NBC bought the station in 1931 specifically to bring this problem under control.[4] Its studios continued to burst with activity. WWJ, Detroit, had become a busy drama center. Its staff writer Rex White often wrote 15 to 18 dramatic scripts a week ranging from dramatized want-ads to biographies of scientists, which were sponsored by a local dairy. Actors from disintegrating theatrical stock companies were available at $5 per performance. WWJ had become an NBC affiliate but for some time produced more plays locally than it received from NBC. A local production often brought a hundred or more local phone calls. However, "NBC programs kept coming faster and faster and there was less and less time for local shows."[5] WWJ made its first profit in 1930 and continued to be profitable, soon wiping out all accumulated deficits.[6] At WCCO, Minneapolis, "we made our first money in 1929 and we kept on increasing every year."[7] The station was bought by CBS in 1931 and remained active and profitable.

Among educational stations the most secure remained those operated by land-grant colleges and state universities as part of state educational systems. In 1933 there were twenty-four such stations. Their investment in equipment averaged $31,306.33. They operated on budgets averaging

2. Morse, *Interview*, p. 14.
3. Lyons, *Reminiscences*, p. 6.
4. Woods, *Reminiscences*, p. 77.
5. White, *Reminiscences*, pp. 8-17.
6. Ponting, *Reminiscences*, p. 10.
7. Gammons, *The Twin Cities Story*, p. 14.

$10,000 per year, but this did not include salaries paid by other university departments.[8] Although buffeted about the broadcast band, a number had won regional acceptance. Many gave particular attention to farm audiences. Of the twenty-four, only two had full-time licenses.

Twelve educational stations, while still operating on a nonprofit basis, had by 1933 begun to accept advertising.[9] Since the sale of advertising to defray costs was practised by scholarly journals, it seemed to many educational broadcasters an acceptable plan. But it at once brought demands from ASCAP and hostility from commercial stations.

The networks, like the larger stations, were successfully bucking the Depression. Revenues were edging down as 1933 began, but a profit margin remained. NBC had finished 1932 with a net profit of $1,050,113; CBS, with a net profit of $1,623,451.[10]

NBC with its powerful line-up of clear-channel stations still held the lead in prestige and ratings. But it did have problems. Of its two networks, the red was outstripping the blue. Even though NBC-blue had *Amos 'n' Andy*, most sponsors preferred NBC-red. Stemming from the AT&T chain, it was considered more commercial, whereas the blue retained a potted-palm aura. With sponsors preferring the red, the blue became a dumping ground for talks and other items which, it was felt, would be useful ammunition vis-à-vis Washington. The more this trend took hold, the more sponsors insisted on being scheduled on NBC-red. Eventually *Amos 'n' Andy* moved to NBC-red. While the process weakened NBC-blue, it also helped to protect the pre-eminence of NBC-red. NBC was clearly determined to hold its headstart. In 1932 it had begun to operate a television station from the Empire State Building—the half-empty skyscraper that had risen on the site of the old Waldorf-Astoria, scene of NBC's first broadcast. NBC was also preparing for the move to Radio City. Depression or no Depression, NBC was on the go.

So was CBS. It had proved shrewd in many ways. Two federal radio

8. Tyler, *An Appraisal of Radio Broadcasting in the Land-Grant Colleges and State Universities,* pp. 7, 96.
9. WRUF, Gainesville (University of Florida); WGST, Atlanta (Georgia School of Technology); KOOW, Chickasha (Oklahoma College for Women); KOB, Albuquerque (New Mexico College of Agriculture and Mechanic Arts); KFJM, Grand Forks (University of North Dakota); WESG, Ithaca, N.Y. (Cornell University); WHAZ, Troy, N.Y. (Rensselaer Polytechnic Institute); WJBU, Lewisburg, Pa. (Bucknell University); WEHC, Emory, Va. (Emory and Henry College); WJTL, Atlanta, Ga. (Oglethorpe University); WWL, New Orleans, La. (Loyola University); WHAD, Milwaukee, Wis. (Marquette University). *Fees for Radio Licenses,* p. 51.
10. Archer, *Big Business and Radio,* p. 397.

commissioners had become CBS vice presidents. Henry Bellows, who had been at Harvard with Franklin D. Roosevelt, was taking charge of CBS governmental relations. This was expected to give CBS an edge with the new administration, whereas NBC had been close to the outgoing regime. (NBC president Merlin Aylesworth had been quoted as saying he would leave the country if FDR were elected.)[11] Sam Pickard had stepped from the FRC into CBS to handle station relations. He jockeyed the FRC into decisions favorable to CBS outlets and strengthened the CBS line-up. His machinations in this work were tricky and were eventually aired in litigation,[12] but meanwhile CBS grew stronger. At the same time Paley, with a keen sense of popular tastes, had begun to build the fame of several little-known singers via daily broadcasts—including Kate Smith and Bing Crosby. The classically trained Howard Barlow had given Paley scathing reports on each of them,[13] but Paley knew better. While protecting its public-relations position with projects like the *American School of the Air*, CBS was pushing hard for a popular following.

As 1933 began, the networks were experiencing a vaudeville boom. The collapse of vaudeville and the slump in the theater had brought to radio a barrage of comedy and variety programs which now dominated the schedule. As 1933 began, Eddie Cantor (for Chase & Sanborn), having evicted *Amos 'n' Andy* from Crossley rating leadership, headed the NBC-red comedy roster, which also included Ed Wynn as the Fire Chief (Texaco), Jack Pearl in his Baron Munchhausen role (Lucky Strike), Charles Winninger in the *Showboat* (Maxwell House), Ken Murray as the Royal Vagabond (Royal gelatine), an Al Jolson series (Chevrolet), and Rudy Vallee's *Vallee Varieties* (Fleischman's yeast), which had replaced the Palace Theater as the prestige booking of vaudeville. NBC-blue had the Marx Brothers (Esso), while CBS had Jack Benny (Canada Dry), Fred Allen (Linit), Burns and Allen (Robert Burns cigars), Howard and Shelton (Chesterfield), and Stoopnagle and Budd (Pontiac).

The dominance of comedy and variety on the air at the lowest ebb of Depression seemed to some observers exactly what was needed. George Washington Hill of Lucky Strike was telling his public relations counselor,

---

11. Chicago *Tribune*, May 13, 1934. Quoted, *Congressional Record*, May 15, 1934, p. 8834.
12. Pickard, having made WOKO, Albany a CBS outlet, was rewarded with a partnership in the station. Because this fact was for years concealed in license-renewal applications, WOKO later lost its license. *FCC v. WOKO*, 329 U.S. 223.
13. Barlow, *Reminiscences*, p. 96.

Edward Bernays, that the nation could and should dance its way out of the Depression.[14] And President Hoover had told Rudy Vallee a few months earlier: "If you can sing a song that would make people forget their troubles and the Depression, I'll give you a medal." [15]

Meanwhile older geological layers of programming continued. Serials, many in comic-strip vein in emulation of *Amos 'n' Andy*, were numerous and still increasing at the start of 1933. Most of them originated in Chicago and New York. Most were at this time scheduled in evening or late-afternoon hours. NBC-red had *The Rise of the Goldbergs* (Pepsodent) at 7:45. NBC-blue had *Little Orphan Annie* (Ovaltine) at 5:45. CBS had *Skippy* (General Mills) at 5:30, *Just Plain Bill* (Kolynos) at 6:45, *Myrt and Marge* (Wrigley) at 7:00, *Buck Rogers in the Year 2433* (Kellogg) at 7:15.

A few were scheduled at other hours. NBC-blue had *Vic and Sade* (sustaining) at 9:30 A.M., *Clara Lu and Em* (Colgate) at 10:15 A.M., *Betty and Bob* (General Mills) at 3:00 P.M.; CBS had *Easy Aces* (Lavoris) at 10:15 P.M.

Among these, *Vic and Sade* had, in the industry, coteries of intense admirers. The series, written by Paul Rymer of Chicago, was praised for its understatement and quiet, authentic humor, but these qualities did not immediately win advertising support. The series also ignored the continued-story vogue, using independent episodes, slight but adroit. Its author was apparently devoid of the sadistic strain inherent in serial construction.

Easy Aces, written by the urbane Goodman Ace and featuring him and his wife, also had dedicated admirers. Its dialogue was often dazzling. Ace used a serialized construction but in fitful, zig-zag fashion. Having established a new sequence and involved his audience in its dilemma, he would promptly tire of it and, in a few minutes, dispose of the plot and launch a new one. He appeared to be congenitally at odds with the form he was using. He would in later years write for various radio and television comedians—at large salaries—and eventually become a *Saturday Review* columnist.

The Rise of the Goldbergs was both a critical and popular success. Some observers linked it with *Amos 'n' Andy* as a dramatization of minority-group life, but its relationship to its material was totally different. Implicit in *The Rise of the Goldbergs* was a sense of escape from old bondage. Its

14. Interview, Edward Bernays.
15. Schlesinger, *The Crisis of the Old Order*, p. 242.

older characters remembered another world, and were held by its beliefs and phobias. There had been a long journey and a Lower East Side sojourn, then emergence into a middle-class society. All this reflected personal experience. Gertrude Berg, its author, had written and directed entertainments at summer hotels; everyone said her work was amusing and she should "do something with it." The band leader Ben Bernie got her an appointment at WMCA, where she read some of her dialogue, with the result that she was paid $6 to do a Christmas cookie commercial in Yiddish for Con Edison:

> Eire freindliche gas and electrische company brengen alle menschen fun New York eine speciele reciepe far cookies far dem Yontevdiken seison . . .[16]

A sample script for a proposed series impressed William Rainey at NBC and resulted in a trial engagement, sustaining, at $75 a week, from which she was to pay her cast. On a week's notice, she faced the problem of going into mass production of scripts. The terror lasted only briefly. "I translated my life with my grandmother, my mother and father, my friends, the people I heard about, into the Goldbergs and began to relive it on the air." Sometimes she wrote—in longhand—in the main reading room at the 42d Street New York Public Library. People watched her making faces. Eventually Pepsodent decided to sponsor and stayed for three years; then Palmolive for two years; then Procter & Gamble, ten years.[17]

The Goldbergs—the title was shortened—made use of speech oddities but never with condescension:

MOLLY: Reading the paper, David?
DAVID: What else?
MOLLY: So read me.
DAVID: Listen: A gangster shot a man in the telephone booth and left him standing—
MOLLY: Yeah? What'll we have for supper, David?
DAVID: Whatever—
MOLLY: I thought maybe noodles—soft—it shouldn't be too hard for your new teeth.
DAVID: For me you don't have to bother.
MOLLY: For who else should I not bother? [18]

16. Berg, *Molly and Me*, p. 182.
17. *Ibid.* pp. 189-94.
18. *Ibid.* p. 204.

The Goldbergs reflected a group experience that Americans of many groups shared and could understand. It was a basic American experience: exodus, journey, settlement in a promised land. *Amos 'n' Andy* was something different: essentially, the ghetto-keeper's fantasy picture of the inside of the ghetto, which he preferred not to view closely. Tragically, this too reflected an experience shared by countless Americans—but in unrecognized fashion, masked by the fantasy.

Along with serials, half-hour dramas were coming in a rush. A mystery-and-crime cycle was beginning: *Eno Crime Club, Fu Manchu, Charlie Chan, Sherlock Holmes, The Shadow*. Romance and adventure were available: *First Nighter, Roses and Drums, Death Valley Days, Moonshine and Honeysuckle*.

The drama explosion was influencing advertising itself. The dramatized commercial had appeared. *Broadcasting* hailed the trend—"novel and effective . . . does not have a puff element" [19]—and reported Lucky Strike cigarettes, Blackstone cigars, and Chase & Sanborn coffee among pioneers in the technique. The singing commercial, a development of the theme song, was also in full flower:

> When you're feeling kinda blue
> And you wonder what to do,
> Che-e-ew Chiclets, and
> Chee-ee-eer up!
> When you've lost your appetite,
> Here's the way to set it right,
> Che-e-ew Chiclets, and
> Chee-ee-eer up! [20]

From none of this network programming would a visitor from another world have obtained even an inkling that it was addressed to a nation in the throes of economic calamity. The response of broadcast drama to the drama of the time was—at this moment—almost total rejection.

Not all wished to respond in this way. Walter Craig, a young New York writer-director, prepared six recordings of a series he hoped to sell. It was called *Ragamuffins* and dealt with boys living in a packing box in an empty lot at the edge of a great city. It had drama and humor and won enthusiastic comment from actors, writers, and directors. One of the boys was a Negro. Craig felt the idea was timely, and it seemed in the American

19. *Broadcasting*, February 1, 1932.
20. Chiclets commercial, Reis and Dunn, CBS.

tradition of *Huckleberry Finn*. He began taking it to advertising agencies. To his dismay, few even wanted to hear it. Executives were appalled at the very thought of such a series. Craig adjusted himself to realities, became a successful advertising agency producer, and eventually partner in the advertising agency Norman, Craig & Kummel, which would conduct a presidential campaign for Adlai Stevenson. *Ragamuffins* had died in 1933.

Those involved in radio entertainment production lived in a different world from those in news and special events. News reports came at various times: H. V. Kaltenborn at 6:00 P.M. Eastern time, Lowell Thomas at 6:45, Boake Carter at 7:45, Edwin C. Hill at 10:15. But the entertainers hardly knew them; there was almost no communication between the two groups.

In one startling exception drama and news met. Each Friday at 8:30 P.M., Eastern time, *The March of Time* erupted on CBS on behalf of *Time* magazine. Never had the rhetoric of words, of voice, of sound effects, of stirring music (Howard Barlow's concert orchestra) been fused so successfully on the air. It had started in 1931:

(*Orchestra—Fanfare*)

VOICE OF TIME: The March of Time . . .
(*Orchestra—"March of Time"*)
On a thousand fronts the history of the world moves swiftly forward—

(*At end of music*)
Tonight the Editors of TIME, the weekly newsmagazine, attempt a new kind of reporting of the news—the reenactment as clearly and dramatically as the medium of radio will permit, some memorable scenes from the news of the week—from the march of TIME!
(*Music*)[21]

Listeners began to make the acquaintance of such colorful impersonations as a fruity Huey Long, played by Jack Smart; a vainglorious Mussolini, played by Ted de Corsia; and (later) a quaint Eleanor Roosevelt, played by Jeannette Nolan, and a faintly superior FDR, by Bill Adams. In many cases it was not mimicry but invention: a plausible vocal image to go with faces seen in rotogravure sections. From the vantage of a later day it would seem wildly irresponsible and even illegal, but at the time it was a glorious game played with bravura by a brilliant company. In the course of a few years such actors as Orson Welles, Agnes Moorhead, Ray Collins,

21. *March of Time*, March 6, 1931, CBS.

Pedro de Cordoba, Porter Hall, Nancy Kelly, Arlene Francis, Kenneth Delmar, Arnold Moss, Paul Stewart, Juano Hernandez, Dwight Weist, John McIntire, and Billy Halop would portray hundreds of figures in the passing parade of history from Stalin to "nut-brown little Mahatma Gandhi."

With firm editorial control by Roy Larsen of *Time*, the series was produced by the advertising agency Batten, Barton, Durstine & Osborn under the supervision of Arthur Pryor, Jr., and was directed in its early months by Donald Stouffer and Thomas Harrington. Much of the early writing was by Fred Smith, formerly of WLW, who had proposed the idea for the series to Time, Inc.

Such was its success that the series would long be a point of reference. For decades producers would say, "Let's not have a *March of Time* voice-of-doom narrator." So indelibly did Westbrook van Voorhis, the third Voice of Time—he was preceded by Ted Husing and Harry Von Zell—impress himself on public consciousness that he would eventually seem a parody of himself, an amateur-hour impersonation of Van Voorhis.

The impact of the *March of Time*—and the vistas it opened—may have been among the factors that, in the closing months of 1932, sharpened the split between the newspaper world and the broadcasting world.

Although the networks carried news events and maintained an atmosphere of timeliness through current-events talks, they still had no news-gathering organizations. Commentators and newscasters drew on newspapers and wire services under informal understandings. It was astonishing that these had survived so long. As newspaper advertising shrank, a crisis approached. James G. Stahlman, publisher of the Nashville *Banner* and president of the Southern Newspaper Publishers Association, warned his colleagues: "Newspaper publishers had better wake up or newspapers will be nothing but a memory on a tablet at Radio City." [22] He urged publishers to exert political influence and gain control of the Federal Radio Commission.

The film industry was also becoming alarmed at the growing power of radio. In the closing weeks of 1932, according to *Variety*, all major studios —except RCA-controlled RKO—agreed to forbid all contract talent "from broadcasting under any circumstances." [23] As radio audiences grew, box-office returns were shrinking. Here, too, a struggle loomed.

22. *Radio Art*, November 1, 1932.
23. *Variety*, December 27, 1932.

Surrounded by disputes—involving motion pictures, newspapers, educators, ASCAP, unions, government—commercial broadcasters defended and attacked. It was a time of strong accusation and rebuttal via releases, brochures, books. The industry was by now so large that virtually anything could be proved.

With detailed documentation it could be shown that commercial broadcasting was venal, boorish, corrupt, tiresome. This was the picture that emerged from *American Broadcasting*, published early in 1933 by the Ventura Free Press. With equally detailed documentation it could be shown that commercial broadcasting was varied, educational, cultural, magnanimous. This was the picture that emerged from *Broadcasting in the United States*, published in 1933—in attractive format—by the National Association of Broadcasters.

The commercial spokesmen had an incomparable advantage. When they spoke of Walter Damrosch and his NBC *Music Appreciation Hour* or the CBS broadcasts of the New York Philharmonic, they were citing examples everyone knew or had heard of. Those who argued for something else—for reserved channels for education, for example—had no such advantage. No interconnection linked the educational stations of Wisconsin, Ohio, and Illinois. If programs were mentioned, they were programs not known to the country at large. Even in their own communities they were likely to be known to few, since most of these stations were daytime-only stations in crowded fringes of the dial. Thus protesting educators were in effect talking about an abstraction, an idea. Commercial broadcasters were talking about a reality that was becoming a part of the nation's daily life.

Perhaps because of this difficulty, argument often dealt with conditions —real or alleged—in other countries, especially England. No one knew much about broadcasting in England but it was a subject of constant discussion. For years travelers had brought tidbits of information. In 1925 a Midwestern broadcaster had been amazed by the technical excellence of British broadcasting, at which he could not help "marveling." Radio, he said, had become "a potent factor in the lives of the British people." He was surprised to find that all programs were rehearsed. The cross-fade, not yet established in the United States, was in regular use.[24] A later visitor, Dorothy Gordon, who had often sung folksongs over WEAF, was surprised to find that the British Broadcasting Corporation paid every per-

24. Fetzer, *Reminiscences*, pp. 24-6.

former, and paid the same to each.[25] Visitors from the world of journalism were less impressed. H. V. Kaltenborn and César Saerchinger found political discussion seriously inhibited and almost nonexistent. William Hard pointed out that Gandhi had been invited to address the American people by radio, but not the British people.[26] The National Association of Broadcasters quoted Winston Churchill as complaining that the BBC was trying to "*lull* . . . to *chloroform* . . . the British people into a state of apathy." [27] In 1931 Senator Clarence C. Dill made a European junket to observe broadcasting in a number of countries, and likewise found the BBC "stiff and bureaucratic." On returning, he expressed himself as well satisfied with broadcasting "by the American plan." But he did have reservations. He had found Britain, Germany, and Sweden far ahead of the United States in broadcasts to schools. And he mentioned that the commercialism of American radio was becoming excessive.[28] On such fragments of information, intense debates were mounted.

If American broadcasters knew little about other broadcasting systems, they knew almost as little about their own. To a surprising degree they were ignorant of its history, roots, legal foundations, and organization. So telling is the evidence of ignorance that one might almost suppose it to be the product of a conscious policy.

Ted Husing had been hired by Sarnoff himself in 1925 for WJZ and became a leading announcer of public events. Moving to CBS, he was the first Voice of Time, announced political conventions, and became the head of the CBS sports department. By 1935 he was sufficiently celebrated to write an autobiography, *Ten Years Before the Mike*, and to have it serialized in a magazine and published in book form. Husing offered the lay reader some explanations about radio. He described David Sarnoff as "the man to whom the Government had turned in its first attempts to control the growing anarchy of the air." [29] Did Husing believe this? Did no one bother to put him straight? Husing goes on, piling wonder on wonder.

> It seemed simpler for the Government to deal with a single head in the management of wave lengths, and when Herbert Hoover became Secretary of Commerce under President Harding he promoted the

25. Gordon, *Reminiscences*, p. 19.
26. *Broadcasting in the United States*, p. 109.
27. *Ibid.* p. 136.
28. Talk on NBC, June 13, 1931, in Arnold, *Broadcast Advertising*, Appendix D, pp. 220-21.
29. Husing, *Ten Years Before the Mike*, p. 14.

formation of the Radio Corporation of America. The intermediary between Government and Capital was David Sarnoff, and to him Secretary Hoover granted a monopoly of all radio wave lengths. So far as I know, that monopoly has never been revoked. I have a hunch that if Mr. Sarnoff wanted to, he could knock off the air every station that competes with his National Broadcasting Company. I'm going to ask him some day.[30]

The subject matter into which Husing was here plunging was seldom discussed by network leaders with any program personnel. This may have been less a policy of silence than of convenience. Everybody was busy.

But insulation from such problems may have served, or seemed to serve, a purpose. A young employee established in a network office as liaison with educators appearing on the *American School of the Air,* or ministers appearing on *National Radio Pulpit,* was in a position of service and magnanimity. He could believe in what he was doing. Would anything be gained by awareness of the extent to which his position might have been made possible by hard-fought patent wars, bitter struggles over channels, skillful and costly lobbying in Washington, windfall revenue from dubious drugs? The happily insulated compartments of network operation had a sheltering effect.

The radio world that awaited the new administration with trepidation— would it be recovery or reform?—had twelve years of program production behind it. Of those twelve years almost nothing remained. There had been few scripts, fewer recordings.

In these years artists had become conscious of radio as a distinct instrument of expression, likely to evolve its own forms—in drama, news, poetry. But the evolution of those forms had barely begun.

The industry had developed what was already known as the American system of broadcasting, which made the salesman the trustee of the public interest, with minimal supervision by a commission. Such a conception was not strange to the period that produced it. Business leadership as a form of stewardship was a favorite theme of Owen D. Young.

This system had never been formally adopted. There had never been a moment when Congress confronted the question: shall we have a nationwide broadcasting system financed by advertising? Rather, a plan tested by AT&T and at first hedged by patents, was later bequeathed to the National Broadcasting Company to be applied on a nation-wide basis.

30. *Ibid.* pp. 20-21. Each sentence in the passage includes at least one major error.

In the years since the birth of NBC, sponsorship had attracted huge funds to the broadcasting world and made possible its rapid growth. In the gold-rush atmosphere, a vast diversity of programs had been produced, with talent ranging from drug-peddling charlatans to symphony orchestras. In the process the system had won friends and vocal enemies. Friends or enemies, more than half the people in the nation had radios.

The gold-rush atmosphere had produced relentless struggles over channels, carried on under the eye of a laissez-faire commission. The struggles had involved commercial and political motives. The prediction that political use of radio would grow was increasingly heard.

In the course of the contest over channels, the once numerous educational stations had dwindled to a few dozen. These were preparing for battle; in Senate and House they were seeking friends.

The effects on American life of the rise of radio, and its commercialization, could not yet be assessed with any clarity. But effects vaguely sensed aroused strong feelings—hopeful and fearful—which would contribute to impending struggles for control. The struggles were heading for a climax in the new administration.

Meanwhile it was a war of words. To Joy Elmer Morgan and the *Committee*, the issue was commercial control over important aspects of education and national culture. Seeing this control as a slow but continuing corruption, he could say:

> There has never been in the entire history of the United States an example of mismanagement and lack of vision so colossal and far-reaching in its consequences as our turning over the radio channels almost exclusively into commercial hands.[31]

But there were also defenders. The American system was by now ringed with a trade press dedicated to its support. *Broadcasting* could be relied on to give commercial broadcasters—networks, stations, advertising agencies—the kind of editorial comment they relished, often written in hard-hitting, free-swinging style. As a number of educational stations vanished in 1932, *Broadcasting* said it showed they were "misfits in American broadcasting." Of Joy Elmer Morgan, *Broadcasting* said:

> How can Joy Elmer Morgan, professional reformer, and his group of misguided pedagogues, justify their silly demand . . . How can they have the audacity to oppose commercial broadcasting . . . ?[32]

31. *Harper's Magazine,* November 1931.
32. *Broadcasting,* January 15, 1933.

DEPRESSION

Rudy Vallee. A song to "make people forget their troubles and the Depression."

Ed Wynn as the Fire Chief. Comedians flocked to radio studios; audiences followed.

George Bernard Shaw (1931)—"Hello America!...How are all you dear old boobs...?"

CBS

William S. Paley: new CBS president at ribbon-cutting ceremony (1929) for new network home, 485 Madison Avenue.

CBS

Bing Crosby: he climbed with CBS.

Concerning the campaign for reserved channels—the "educational grab"—*Broadcasting* said:

> Education has been used as a cloak to cover many sins in this country and it may be that we shall be sentimental enough to permit the educational lobby to get away with this grab. But anyone who thinks it will increase the pleasure of listening to the radio is a sap.[33]

There were other lines of defense. Harold A. Lafount, the Utah manufacturer who had joined the Federal Radio Commission in November 1927, expressed himself in these words:

> Commercialism is the heart of broadcasting in the United States. What has education contributed to radio? Not one thing. What has commercialism contributed? Everything—the life blood of the industry.[34]

There were further lines of defense. Many congressmen, appearing regularly on commercial networks and stations, were closer to them than to the world of education.

But as the battle took shape, it changed. From laboratories—RCA's and others—an electronic system of television was emerging. The pieces were beginning to fit together. In 1933 the system seemed almost ready. As the battle lines formed, the stakes were mounting.

CHAT

The winter of 1932-33 saw a steady drift toward catastrophe. America's unemployed were estimated at twelve to fifteen million.

In January 1933, Hitler came to power in Germany. By hundreds of thousands the storm troops marched as Hitler watched in ecstasy. He began moves to control all media of communication.

In mid-February a banking crisis developed in Michigan. A panic of withdrawals closed all banks in the state. The spirit of panic spread to other states.

That month saw a mass movement toward Washington. Representatives of countless interests were at work. On February 20-21 the National Association of Broadcasters met in Washington. *Broadcasting* reported: "WAR PLANS" LAID TO PROTECT BROADCASTING. The story said the association had

33. *Ibid.* February 1, 1932.
34. Quoted, Tyler (ed.), *Radio as a Cultural Agency*, pp. 3-4.

developed plans to shield advertisers, agencies, and broadcasters from "attacks by unfriendly groups." [1]

By March 2 half the states were enacting or considering bank closings. By Saturday, March 4—inauguration day—the banking system of the entire nation was in paralysis. On a cloudy day, Franklin Delano Roosevelt made his inaugural address—carried by NBC and CBS networks.

Those who sought clues to the course of the new administration could find a diversity of them. The reform-minded heard words of a promising ring: "The money changers have fled from their high seats in the temple of our civilization!" Those looking for reassurance could find it also: "The only thing we have to fear is fear itself . . . The people of the United States have not failed." [2]

Eight days later, after a series of swift moves on the banking crisis, President Roosevelt was back on the air.

Until now the nation had heard him mainly addressing crowds—during the campaign and at the inauguration. In the campaign speeches, anxious to show that his crippled legs did not handicap him, he was inclined to strain for effect. The projection of vigor had seemed an end in itself. Now all that was over.

They heard a new FDR. It was not an "address." It was a chat, a fireside chat. Quietly, without a hint of anxiety, with utter clarity, he outlined steps being taken to deal with the crisis. He discussed where "we" were going, seeming to bring the nation into the thinking in the White House.

To Robert Sherwood—who would one day be writing fireside chats—it seemed like the talk of a friend or neighbor, who had figured out how to keep the mortgage from being foreclosed. [3]

Amid hopes—fears—resentments—FDR held the spotlight.

Somehow they had all been a part of it. William McKinley, telephone enthusiast, listening avidly at home over long-distance lines to the cheers of the convention nominating him for the presidency [4] . . . Theodore Roosevelt, whose program of naval expansion gave radio early nourishment . . . William Howard Taft, who fathered early efforts to bring order out of chaos . . . Woodrow Wilson, whose words traveled the kilocycles to distant lands . . . Warren G. Harding, symbol of the birth of

1. *Broadcasting*, March 1, 1933.
2. Roosevelt, *Selected Speeches*, pp. 90-95.
3. Sherwood, *Roosevelt and Hopkins*, V. 1, p. 52.
4. Casson, *The History of the Telephone*, pp. 201-2.

broadcasting . . . Calvin Coolidge, whose speeches marked the trail of an expanding chain . . . Herbert Hoover, first of the paternally reprimanding—but lenient—regulators . . . and now Franklin Delano Roosevelt, with a Crossley rating a sponsor would envy. He too would leave his mark on the medium.

APPENDIX A / CHRONOLOGY

1895 Guglielmo Marconi sends wireless messages on family estate.

1897 Marconi company formed in England.

1899 Marconi comes to United States to report *America's* Cup Race by wireless for New York *Herald;* forms American Marconi, demonstrates for army and navy.

1900 Weather Bureau employs Reginald A. Fessenden to test use of wireless.

1901 Marconi spans Atlantic with letter "S" in Morse code.

1902 Fessenden forms National Electric Signaling Company.
Lee de Forest forms De Forest Wireless Telegraph Company.

1904 De Forest demonstrates at St. Louis World's Fair.
John Ambrose Fleming in England develops glass-bulb detector.

1906 De Forest develops three-element Audion tube.
Use of various crystals as detectors demonstrated.
Fessenden broadcasts Christmas Eve program of music and readings.

1907 De Forest Radio Telephone Company begins broadcasts in New York.

1908 De Forest broadcasts from Eiffel Tower.

1909 S. S. *Republic* sinks after collision; most lives saved with help of wireless.

1910 De Forest presents opera broadcast with Enrico Caruso from stage of Metropolitan.

1912 News of *Titanic* disaster reaches United States through Marconi operator David Sarnoff.
Broadcasting licenses required by new law.

1913 AT&T begins purchase of De Forest patents.
Edwin H. Armstrong develops feedback circuit.

1915 AT&T long-distance service reaches San Francisco, using vacuum-tube amplifiers.

De Forest demonstrates radio at San Francisco World's Fair, receiving Herrold broadcasts from San Jose.

AMRAD organized at Medford Hillside, Mass.

Marconi negotiates with General Electric for purchase of Alexanderson alternators.

1916   De Forest broadcasts music and election returns in New York.

David Sarnoff urges American Marconi to market radio music box.

Court decision leaves neither AT&T nor Marconi interests in control of Audion; patent stalemate develops.

1917   After United States declaration of war on Germany, radio equipment—commercial and amateur—is sealed or taken over by navy.

Patent struggles shelved for war production, by government order.

1918   Alexanderson alternator broadcasts President Wilson's Fourteen Points throughout Europe from New Brunswick, N.J.

Alexanderson alternator plays role in peace negotiations.

Navy seeks permanent control of radio in the United States; rebuffed by Congress.

Marconi renews negotiation for Alexanderson alternators; navy officials urge American monopoly.

1919   GE forms Radio Corporation of America to take over assets of American Marconi.

Amateurs resume activity.

Vladimir Zworykin conducts television experiments at Westinghouse.

1920   AT&T becomes RCA partner; AT&T-GE-RCA cross-licensing agreement.

Amateur stations broadcasting in many parts of United States.

Detroit *News* station 8MK broadcasts primary and election returns.

Westinghouse buys Armstrong and Pupin patents.

Westinghouse station KDKA broadcasts election returns.

1921   WHA, WJZ, KYW, WBZ, and other stations broadcasting on announced schedules.

Westinghouse and United Fruit become RCA partners, join cross-licensing pact.

1922   More than 500 broadcasting stations licensed during year.

First Washington Radio Conference.

AT&T builds WBAY and WEAF, introduces "toll" broadcasting.

ASCAP demands royalties from radio stations for use of music.

WGY Players launch radio drama.

WGY and WJZ linked for World Series via telegraph line.

1923   Federal Trade Commission starts radio-monopoly investigation.

WEAF linked with WNAC, then WMAF and WJAR, via telephone lines.

Westinghouse pushes short-wave experiments as alternative to wire network.

WEAF signs ASCAP agreement.

NAB formed to resist ASCAP.

Second Washington Radio Conference.

Dr. John R. Brinkley starts KFKB.
Eveready Hour launched.
Radio helps locate kidnapped son of Alexanderson.
Plans for first coast-to-coast hookup halted by death of President Harding.
Opening of Congress broadcast for first time.
Zworykin demonstrates partly electronic television system.
1924 WEAF drops Kaltenborn under State Department pressure.
AT&T and "radio group" begin secret arbitration.
FTC files monopoly complaint against patent allies.
Broadcasts of political conventions spur set sales.
Third Washington Radio Conference.
Coolidge campaign speech on 26-station coast-to-coast hookup.
1925 RCA permits announcers to use names.
Fourth Washington Radio Conference.
Department of Commerce halts licensing, permits station sales; traffic in licenses develops.
Sale of time increasing.
Thirty-seven educational stations give up.
WGN broadcasts from Scopes trial.
1926 GE, Westinghouse, RCA organize National Broadcasting Company.
NBC buys WEAF for $1,000,000; contracts for use of AT&T wires.
Government defeat in *U.S.* v. *Zenith* leads to period of "wave piracy."
Arthur Judson, seeking NBC contract, forms Judson Radio Program Corporation.
1927 Two NBC networks, "red" and "blue," in operation.
"Silent Night" abandoned.
NBC moves headquarters to 711 Fifth Avenue.
Judson and others form Columbia Phonograph Broadcasting System—later CBS.
Farnsworth applies for patent on electronic television system.
Radio Act of 1927 passed; Federal Radio Commission formed.
Jazz Singer debut brings hasty conversion of film industry to sound.
1928 FRC shifts most stations, abolishes eighty-three.
Twenty-three educational stations give up.
William Paley takes over CBS.
GE presents *The Queen's Messenger*, first television drama, in Schenectady.
RKO formed by GE-Westinghouse-RCA and film interests.
1929 *Amos 'n' Andy* becomes NBC network series.
Paramount buys 49 per cent of CBS.
RCA buys Victor Talking Machine Company.
Wall Street boom—with spectacular rise of RCA stock—followed by crash.
1930 Collapse of vaudeville brings radio vaudeville era.

Start of "Crossley" ratings, based on telephone calls.

Naval conference broadcasts from London lead to further international programming.

David Sarnoff becomes RCA president.

United States anti-trust suit against RCA and patent allies.

FRC terminates Dr. Brinkley's license for KFKB.

1931   Increase in commercial announcements, contests, premiums, merchandising schemes.

Shaw, Mussolini, Pope Pius XI, Gandhi broadcast to United States.

AT&T withdraws from patent alliance.

Educators campaign for Fess bill, to reserve channels for education.

March of Time begins over CBS.

1932   GE-Westinghouse-RCA divorce plan brings consent decree, terminates anti-trust suit.

NBC becomes wholly owned RCA subsidiary.

Eddie Cantor takes lead in "Crossley" ratings.

NBC starts television station in Empire State Building.

Paley buys back Paramount holdings in CBS.

Radio City under construction.

Increased tension between radio and press, film.

1933   Banking crisis leads to first Fireside Chat.

APPENDIX B / LAWS

The Radio Act of 1912

Public Law No. 264, August 13, 1912, 62d Congress. An Act to regulate radio communication.

Be it enacted by the Senate and House of Representatives of the United States of America in Congress assembled,
That a person, company, or corporation within the jurisdiction of the United States shall not use or operate any apparatus for radio communication as a means of commercial intercourse among the several States, or with foreign nations, or upon any vessel of the United States engaged in interstate or foreign commerce, or for the transmission of radiograms or signals the effect of which extends beyond the jurisdiction of the State or Territory in which the same are made, or where interference would be caused thereby with the receipt of messages or signals from beyond the jurisdiction of the said State or Territory, except under and in accordance with a license, revocable for cause, in that behalf granted by the Secretary of Commerce and Labor upon application therefor; but nothing in this Act shall be construed to apply to the transmission and exchange of radiograms or signals between points situated in the same State: *Provided,* That the effect thereof shall not extend beyond the jurisdiction of the said State or interfere with the reception of radiograms or signals from beyond said jurisdiction; and a license shall not be required for the transmission or exchange of radiograms or signals by or on behalf of the Government of the United States, but every Government station on land or sea shall have special call letters designated and published in the list of radio stations of the United States by the Department of Commerce and Labor. Any person, company, or corporation that shall use or operate any apparatus for radio communication in violation of this section, or knowingly aid or abet an-

291

other person, company, or corporation in so doing, shall be deemed guilty of a misdemeanor, and on conviction thereof shall be punished by a fine not exceeding five hundred dollars, and the apparatus or device so unlawfully used and operated may be adjudged forfeited to the United States.

SEC. 2. That every such license shall be in such form as the Secretary of Commerce and Labor shall determine and shall contain the restrictions, pursuant to this Act, on and subject to which the license is granted; that every such license shall be issued only to citizens of the United States or Porto Rico or to a company incorporated under the laws of some State or Territory or of the United States or Porto Rico, and shall specify the ownership and location of the station in which said apparatus shall be used and other particulars for its identification and to enable its range to be estimated; shall state the purpose of the station, and, in case of a station in actual operation at the date of passage of this Act, shall contain the statement that satisfactory proof has been furnished that it was actually operating on the above-mentioned date; shall state the wave length or the wave lengths authorized for use by the station for the prevention of interference and the hours for which the station is licensed for work; and shall not be construed to authorize the use of any apparatus for radio communication in any other station than that specified. Every such license shall be subject to the regulations contained herein, and such regulations as may be established from time to time by authority of this act or subsequent acts and treaties of the United States. Every such license shall provide that the President of the United States in time of war or public peril or disaster may cause the closing of any station for radio communication and the removal therefrom of all radio apparatus, or may authorize the use or control of any such station or apparatus by any department of the Government, upon just compensation to the owners.

SEC. 3. That every such apparatus shall at all times while in use and operation as aforesaid be in charge or under the supervision of a person or persons licensed for that purpose by the Secretary of Commerce and Labor. Every person so licensed who in the operation of any radio apparatus shall fail to observe and obey regulations contained in or made pursuant to this act or subsequent acts or treaties of the United States, or any one of them, or who shall fail to enforce obedience thereto by an unlicensed person while serving under his supervision, in addition to the punishments and penalties herein prescribed, may suffer the suspension of the said license for a period to be fixed by the Secretary of Commerce and Labor not exceeding one year. It shall be unlawful to employ any unlicensed person or for any unlicensed person to serve in charge or in supervision of the use and operation of such apparatus, and any person violating this provision shall be guilty of a misdemeanor, and on conviction thereof shall be punished by a fine of not more than one hundred dollars or imprisonment for not more than two months; or both, in the discretion of the court, for each and every such offense: *Provided,* That in case of emergency the Secretary of Commerce and Labor may authorize a collector of customs to issue a temporary permit, in lieu of a license, to the operator on a vessel subject to the radio ship act of June twenty-fourth, nineteen hundred and ten.

SEC. 4. That for the purpose of preventing or minimizing interference with communication between stations in which such apparatus is operated, to facilitate radio communication, and to further the prompt receipt of distress signals, said private and commercial stations shall be subject to the regulations of this section. These regulations shall be enforced by the Secretary of Commerce and Labor through the collectors of customs and other officers of the Government as other regulations herein provided for.

The Secretary of Commerce and Labor may, in his discretion, waive the provisions of any or all of these regulations when no interference of the character above mentioned can ensue.

The Secretary of Commerce and Labor may grant special temporary licenses to stations actually engaged in conducting experiments for the development of the science of radio communication, or the apparatus pertaining thereto, to carry on special tests, using any amount of power or any wave lengths, at such hours and under such conditions as will insure the least interference with the sending or receipt of commercial or Government radiograms, of distress signals and radiograms, or with the work of other stations.

In these regulations the naval and military stations shall be understood to be stations on land.

REGULATIONS
NORMAL WAVE LENGTH

First. Every station shall be required to designate a certain definite wave length as the normal sending and receiving wave length of the station. This wave length shall not exceed six hundred meters or it shall exceed one thousand six hundred meters. Every coastal station open to general public service shall at all times be ready to receive messages of such wave lengths as are required by the Berlin convention. Every ship station, except as hereinafter provided, and every coast station open to general public service shall be prepared to use two sending wave lengths, one of three hundred meters and one of six hundred meters, as required by the international convention in force: *Provided,* That the Secretary of Commerce and Labor may, in his discretion, change the limit of wave length reservation made by regulations first and second to accord with any international agreement to which the United States is a party.

OTHER WAVE LENGTHS

Second. In addition to the normal sending wave length all stations, except as provided hereinafter in these regulations, may use other sending wave lengths: *Provided,* That they do not exceed six hundred meters or that they do exceed one thousand six hundred meters: *Provided further,* That the character of the waves emitted conforms to the requirements of regulations third and fourth following.

USE OF A "PURE WAVE"

Third. At all stations if the sending apparatus, to be referred to hereinafter as the "transmitter," is of such a character that the energy is radiated in two or more wave lengths, more or less sharply defined, as indicated by a sensitive wave meter, the energy in no one of the lesser waves shall exceed ten per centum of that in the greatest.

USE OF A "SHARP WAVE"

Fourth. At all stations the logarithmic decrement per complete oscillation in the wave trains emitted by the transmitter shall not exceed two-tenths, except when sending distress signals or signals and messages relating thereto.

USE OF "STANDARD DISTRESS WAVE"

Fifth. Every station on shipboard shall be prepared to send distress calls on the normal wave length designated by the international convention in force, except on vessels of small tonnage unable to have plants insuring that wave length.

SIGNAL OF DISTRESS

Sixth. The distress call used shall be the international signal of distress
. . . ⎯ ⎯ . . .

USE OF "BROAD INTERFERING WAVE" FOR DISTRESS SIGNALS

Seventh. When sending distress signals, the transmitter of a station on shipboard may be tuned in such a manner as to create a maximum of interference with a maximum of radiation.

DISTANCE REQUIREMENTS FOR DISTRESS SIGNALS

Eighth. Every station on shipboard, wherever practicable, shall be prepared to send distress signals of the character specified in regulations fifth and sixth with sufficient power to enable them to be received by day over sea a distance of one hundred nautical miles by a shipboard station equipped with apparatus for both sending and receiving equal in all essential particulars to that of the station first mentioned.

"RIGHT OF WAY" FOR DISTRESS SIGNALS

Ninth. All stations are required to give absolute priority to signals and radiograms relating to ships in distress; to cease all sending on hearing a distress signal; and, except when engaged in answering or aiding the ship in distress, to refrain from sending until all signals and radiograms relating thereto are completed.

REDUCED POWER FOR SHIPS NEAR A GOVERNMENT STATION

Tenth. No station on shipboard, when within fifteen nautical miles of a naval or military station, shall use a transformer input exceeding one kilowatt, nor, when within five nautical miles of such a station, a transformer input exceeding one-half kilowatt, except for sending signals of distress, or signals or radiograms relating thereto.

INTERCOMMUNICATION

Eleventh. Each shore station open to general public service between the coast and vessels at sea shall be bound to exchange radiograms with any similar shore station and with any ship station without distinction of the radio system adopted by such stations, respectively, and each station on shipboard shall be bound to exchange radiograms with any other station on shipboard without distinction of the radio systems adopted by each station, respectively.

It shall be the duty of each such shore station, during the hours it is in operation, to listen in at intervals of not less than fifteen minutes and for a period not less than two minutes, with the receiver tuned to receive messages of three hundred-meter wave lengths.

DIVISION OF TIME

Twelfth. At important seaports and at all other places where naval or military and private commercial shore stations operate in such close proximity that interference with the work of naval and military stations can not be avoided by the enforcement of the regulations contained in the foregoing regulations concerning wave lengths and character of signals emitted, such private or commercial shore stations as do interfere with the reception of signals by the naval and military stations concerned shall not use their transmitters during the first fifteen minutes of each hour, local standard time. The Secretary of Commerce and Labor may, on the recommendation of the department concerned, designate the station or stations which may be required to observe this division of time.

GOVERNMENT STATIONS TO OBSERVE DIVISION OF TIME

Thirteenth. The naval or military stations for which the abovementioned division of time may be established shall transmit signals or radiograms only during the first fifteen minutes of each hour, local standard time, except in case of signals or radiograms relating to vessels in distress, as hereinbefore provided.

USE OF UNNECESSARY POWER

Fourteenth. In all circumstances, except in case of signals or radiograms relating to vessels in distress, all stations shall use the minimum amount of energy necessary to carry out any communication desired.

GENERAL RESTRICTIONS ON PRIVATE STATIONS

Fifteenth. No private or commercial station not engaged in the transaction of bona fide commercial business by radio communication or in experimentation in connection with the development and manufacture of radio apparatus for commercial purposes shall use a transmitting wave length exceeding two hundred meters, or a transformer input exceeding one kilowatt, except by special authority of the Secretary of Commerce and Labor contained in the license of the station: *Provided,* That the owner or operator of a station of the character mentioned in this regulation shall not be liable for a violation of the requirements of the third or fourth regulations to the penalties of one hundred dollars or twenty-five dollars, respectively, provided in this section unless the person maintaining or operating such station shall have been notified in writing that the said transmitter has been found, upon tests conducted by the Government, to be so adjusted as to violate the said third and fourth regulations, and opportunity has been given to said owner or operator to adjust said transmitter in conformity with said regulations.

SPECIAL RESTRICTIONS IN THE VICINITIES OF GOVERNMENT STATIONS

Sixteenth. No station of the character mentioned in regulation fifteenth situated within five nautical miles of a naval or military station shall use a transmitting wave length exceeding two hundred meters or a transformer input exceeding one-half kilowatt.

SHIP STATIONS TO COMMUNICATE WITH NEAREST SHORE STATIONS

Seventeenth. In general, the shipboard stations shall transmit their radiograms to the nearest shore station. A sender on board a vessel shall, however, have the right to designate the shore station through which he desires to have his radiograms transmitted. If this can not be done, the wishes of the sender are to be complied with only if the transmission can be effected without interfering with the service of other stations.

LIMITATIONS FOR FUTURE INSTALLATIONS IN
VICINITIES OF GOVERNMENT STATIONS

Eighteenth. No station on shore not in actual operation at the date of the passage of this act shall be licensed for the transaction of commercial business by radio communication within fifteen nautical miles of the following naval or military stations, to wit: Arlington, Virginia; Key West, Florida; San Juan, Porto Rico; North Head and Tatoosh Island, Washington; San Diego, California; and those established or which may be established in Alaska and in the Canal Zone; and the head of the department having control of such Government stations shall, so far as is consistent with the transaction of governmental business, arrange for the transmission and receipt of commercial radiograms under the provisions of the Berlin convention of nineteen hundred and six and future international conventions or treaties to which the United States may be a party, at each of the stations above referred to, and shall fix the rates therefor, subject to control of such rates by Congress. At such stations and wherever and whenever shore stations open for general public business between the coast and vessels at sea under the provisions of the Berlin convention of nineteen hundred and six and future international conventions and treaties to which the United States may be a party shall not be so established as to insure a constant service day and night without interruption, and in all localities wherever or whenever such service shall not be maintained by a commercial shore station within one hundred nautical miles of a naval radio station, the Secretary of the Navy shall, so far as is consistent with the transaction of Government business, open naval radio stations to the general public business described above, and shall fix rates for such service, subject to control of such rates by Congress. The receipts from such radiograms shall be covered into the Treasury as miscellaneous receipts.

SECRECY OF MESSAGES

Nineteenth. No person or persons engaged in or having knowledge of the operation of any station or stations shall divulge or publish the contents of any messages transmitted or received by such station, except to the person or persons to whom the same may be directed, or their authorized agent, or to another station employed to forward such message to its destination, unless legally required so to do by the court of competent jurisdiction or other competent authority. Any person guilty of divulging or publishing any message, except as herein provided, shall, on conviction thereof, be punishable by a fine of not more than two hundred and fifty dollars or imprisonment for a period of not exceeding three months, or both fine and imprisonment, in the discretion of the court.

For violation of any of these regulations, subject to which a license under sections one and two of this act may be issued, the owner of the apparatus shall be liable to a penalty of one hundred dollars, which may be reduced or remitted by the Secretary of Commerce and Labor, and for repeated violations of any of such regulations the license may be revoked.

For violation of any of these regulations, except as provided in regulation nineteenth, subject to which a license under section three of this act may be issued, the operator shall be subject to a penalty of twenty-five dollars, which may be reduced or remitted by the Secretary of Commerce and Labor, and for repeated violations of any such regulations, the license shall be suspended or revoked.

SEC. 5. That every license granted under the provisions of this act for the operation or use of apparatus for radio communication shall prescribe that the operator thereof shall not willfully or maliciously interfere with any other radio communication. Such interference shall be deemed a misdemeanor, and upon conviction thereof the owner or operator, or both, shall be punishable by a fine of not to exceed five hundred dollars or imprisonment for not to exceed one year, or both.

SEC. 6. That the expression "radio communication" as used in this act means any system of electrical communication by telegraphy or telephony without the aid of any wire connecting the points from and at which the radiograms, signals, or other communications are sent or received.

SEC. 7. That a person, company, or corporation within the jurisdiction of the United States shall not knowingly utter or transmit, or cause to be uttered or transmitted, any false or fraudulent distress signal or call or false or fraudulent signal, call, or other radiogram of any kind. The penalty for so uttering or transmitting a false or fraudulent distress signal or call shall be a fine of not more than two thousand five hundred dollars or imprisonment for not more than five years, or both, in the discretion of the court, for each and every such offense, and the penalty for so uttering or transmitting, or causing to be uttered or transmitted, any other false or fraudulent signal, call, or other radiogram shall be a fine of not more than one thousand dollars or imprisonment for not more than two years, or both, in the discretion of the court, for each and every such offense.

SEC. 8. That a person, company, or corporation shall not use or operate any apparatus for radio communication on a foreign ship in territorial waters of the United States otherwise than in accordance with the provisions of sections four and seven of this act and so much of section five as imposes a penalty for interference. Save as aforesaid, nothing in this act shall apply to apparatus for radio communication on any foreign ship.

SEC. 9. That the trial of any offense under this act shall be in the district in which it is committed, or if the offense is committed upon the high seas or out of the jurisdiction of any particular State or district the trial shall be in the district where the offender may be found or into which he shall be first brought.

SEC. 10. That this act shall not apply to the Philippine Islands.

SEC. 11. That this act shall take effect and be in force on and after four months from its passage.

Approved, August 13, 1912.

Public Law No. 632, February 23, 1927, 69th Congress. An Act for the regulation of radio communications, and for other purposes.

Be it enacted by the Senate and House of Representatives of the United States of America in Congress assembled, That this Act is intended to regulate all forms of interstate and foreign radio transmissions and communications within the United States, its Territories and possessions; to maintain the control of the United States over all the channels of interstate and foreign radio transmission; and to provide for the use of such channels, but not the ownership thereof, by individuals, firms, or corporations, for limited periods of time, under licenses granted by Federal authority, and no such license shall be construed to create any right, beyond the terms, conditions, and periods of the license. That no person, firm, company, or corporation shall use or operate any apparatus for the transmission of energy or communications or signals by radio (a) from one place in any Territory or possession of the United States or in the District of Columbia to another place in the same Territory, possession or District; or (b) from any State, Territory, or possession of the United States, or from the District of Columbia to any other State, Territory, or possession of the United States; or (c) from any place in any State, Territory, or possession of the United States, or in the District of Columbia, to any place in any foreign country or to any vessel; or (d) within any State when the effects of such use extend beyond the borders of said State, or when interference is caused by such use or operation with the transmission of such energy, communications, or signals from within said State to any place beyond its borders, or from any place beyond its borders to any place within said State, or with the transmission or reception of such energy, communications, or signals from and/or to places beyond the borders of said State; or (e) upon any vessel of the United States; or (f) upon any aircraft or other mobile stations within the United States, except under and in accordance with this Act and with a license in that behalf granted under the provisions of this Act.

SEC. 2. For the purposes of this Act, the United States is divided into five zones, as follows: The first zone shall embrace the States of Maine, New Hampshire, Vermont, Massachusetts, Connecticut, Rhode Island, New York, New Jersey, Delaware, Maryland, the District of Columbia, Porto Rico, and the Virgin Islands; the second zone shall embrace the States of Pennsylvania, Virginia, West Virginia, Ohio, Michigan, and Kentucky; the third zone shall embrace the States of North Carolina, South Carolina, Georgia, Florida, Alabama, Tennessee, Mississippi, Arkansas, Louisiana, Texas, and Oklahoma; the fourth zone shall embrace the States of Indiana, Illinois, Wisconsin, Minnesota, North Dakota, South Dakota, Iowa, Nebraska, Kansas, and Missouri; and the fifth zone shall embrace the States of Montana, Idaho, Wyoming, Colorado, New Mexico, Arizona, Utah, Nevada, Washington, Oregon, California, the Territory of Hawaii, and Alaska.

SEC. 3. That a commission is hereby created and established to be known as the Federal Radio Commission, hereinafter referred to as the commission, which shall be composed of five commissioners appointed by the President, by and with the advice and consent of the Senate, and one of whom the President shall designate as chairman: *Provided*, That chairmen thereafter elected shall be chosen by the commission itself.

Each member of the commission shall be a citizen of the United States and an actual resident citizen of a State within the zone from which appointed at the time of said appointment. Not more than one commissioner shall be appointed from any zone. No member of the commission shall be financially interested in the manufacture or sale of radio apparatus or in the transmission or operation of radiotelegraphy, radio telephony, or radio broadcasting. Not more than three commissioners shall be members of the same political party.

The first commissioners shall be appointed for the terms of two, three, four, five, and six years, respectively, from the date of the taking effect of this Act, the term of each to be designated by the President, but their successors shall be appointed for terms of six years, except that any person chosen to fill a vacancy shall be appointed only for the unexpired term of the commissioner whom he shall succeed.

The first meeting of the commission shall be held in the city of Washington at such time and place as the chairman of the commission may fix. The commission shall convene thereafter at such times and places as a majority of the commission may determine, or upon call of the chairman thereof.

The commission may appoint a secretary, and such clerks, special counsel, experts, examiners, and other employees as it may from time to time find necessary for the proper performance of its duties and as from time to time may be appropriated for by Congress.

The commission shall have an official seal and shall annually make a full report of its operations to the Congress.

The members of the commission shall receive a compensation of $10,000 for the first year of their service, said year to date from the first meeting of said commission, and thereafter a compensation of $30 per day for each day's attendance upon sessions of the commission or while engaged upon work of the commission and while traveling to and from such sessions, and also their necessary traveling expenses.

SEC. 4. Except as otherwise provided in this Act, the commission, from time to time, as public convenience, interest, or necessity requires, shall—

(a) Classify radio stations;

(b) Prescribe the nature of the service to be rendered by each class of licensed stations and each station within any class;

(c) Assign bands of frequencies or wave lengths to the various classes of stations, and assign frequencies or wave lengths for each individual station and determine the power which each station shall use and the time during which it may operate;

(d) Determine the location of classes of stations or individual stations;

(e) Regulate the kind of apparatus to be used with respect to its external effects and the purity and sharpness of the emissions from each station and from the apparatus therein;

(f) Make such regulations not inconsistent with law as it may deem necessary to prevent interference between stations and to carry out the provisions of this Act: *Provided, however,* That changes in the wave lengths, authorized power, in the character of emitted signals, or in the times of operation of any station, shall not be made without the consent of the station licensee unless, in the judgment of the commission, such changes will promote public convenience or interest or will serve public necessity or the provisions of this Act will be more fully complied with;

(g) Have authority to establish areas or zones to be served by any station;

(h) Have authority to make special regulations applicable to radio stations engaged in chain broadcasting;

(i) Have authority to make general rules and regulations requiring stations to keep such records of programs, transmissions of energy, communications, or signals as it may deem desirable;

(j) Have authority to exclude from the requirements of any regulations in whole or in part any radio station upon railroad rolling stock, or to modify such regulations in its discretion;

(k) Have authority to hold hearings, summon witnesses, administer oaths, compel the production of books, documents, and papers and to make such investigations as may be necessary in the performance of its duties. The commission may make such expenditures (including expenditures for rent and personal services at the seat of government and elsewhere, for law books, periodicals, and books of reference, and for printing and binding) as may be necessary for the execution of the functions vested in the commission and, as from time to time may be appropriated for by Congress. All expenditures of the commission shall be allowed and paid upon the presentation of itemized vouchers therefor approved by the chairman.

SEC. 5. From and after one year after the first meeting of the commission created by this Act, all the powers and authority vested in the commission under the terms of this Act, except as to the revocation of licenses, shall be vested in and exercised by the Secretary of Commerce; except that thereafter the commission shall have power and jurisdiction to act upon and determine any and all matters brought before it under the terms of this section.

It shall also be the duty of the Secretary of Commerce—

(A) For and during a period of one year from the first meeting of the commission created by this Act, to immediately refer to the commission all applications for station licenses or for the renewal or modification of existing station licenses.

(B) From and after one year from the first meeting of the commission created by this Act, to refer to the commission for its action any application for a station license or for the renewal or modification of any existing station license as to the granting of which dispute, controversy, or conflict arises or against the granting of which protest is filed within ten days after the date of filing said application by any party in interest and any application as to which such reference is requested by the applicant at the time of filing said application.

(C) To prescribe the qualifications of station operators, to classify them according to the duties to be performed, to fix the forms of such licenses, and to issue them to such persons as he finds qualified.

(D) To suspend the license of any operator for a period not exceeding two years upon proof sufficient to satisfy him that the licensee (a) has violated any provision of any Act or treaty binding on the United States which the Secretary of Commerce or the commission is authorized by this Act to administer or by any regulation made by the commission or the Secretary of Commerce under any such Act or treaty; or (b) has failed to carry out the lawful orders of the master of the vessel on which he is employed; or (c) has willfully damaged or permitted radio apparatus to be damaged; or (d) has transmitted superfluous radio communications or signals or radio communications containing profane or obscene words or language; or (e) has willfully or maliciously interfered with any other radio communications or signals.

(E) To inspect all transmitting apparatus to ascertain whether in construction and operation it conforms to the requirements of this Act, the rules and regulations of the licensing authority, and the license under which it is constructed or operated.

(F) To report to the commission from time to time any violations of this Act, the rules, regulations, or orders of the commission, or of the terms or conditions of any license.

(G) To designate call letters of all stations.

(H) To cause to be published such call letters and such other announcements and data as in his judgment may be required for the efficient operation of radio stations subject to the jurisdiction of the United States and for the proper enforcement of this Act.

The Secretary may refer to the commission at any time any matter the determination of which is vested in him by the terms of this Act.

Any person, firm, company, or corporation, any State or political division thereof aggrieved or whose interests are adversely affected by any decision, determination, or regulation of the Secretary of Commerce may appeal therefrom to the commission by filing with the Secretary of Commerce notice of such appeal within thirty days after such decision or determination or promulgation of such regulation. All papers, documents, and other records pertaining to such application on file with the Secretary shall thereupon be transferred by him to the commission. The commission shall hear such appeal de novo under such rules and regulations as it may determine.

Decisions by the commission as to matters so appealed and as to all other matters over which it has jurisdiction shall be final, subject to the right of appeal herein given.

No station license shall be granted by the commission or the Secretary of Commerce until the applicant therefor shall have signed a waiver of any claim to the use of any particular frequency or wave length or of the ether as against the regulatory power of the United States because of the previous use of the same, whether by license or otherwise.

SEC. 6. Radio stations belonging to and operated by the United States shall not be subject to the provisions of sections 1, 4, and 5 of this Act. All such Government stations shall use such frequencies or wave lengths as shall be assigned to each or to each class by the President. All such stations, except stations on board naval and other Government vessels while at sea or beyond the limits of the continental United States, when transmitting any radio communication or signal other than a communication or signal relating to Government business shall conform to such rules and regulations designed to prevent interference with other radio stations and the rights of others as the licensing authority may prescribe. Upon proclamation by the President that there exists war or a threat of war or a state of public peril or disaster or other national emergency, or in order to preserve the neutrality of the United States, the President may suspend or amend, for such time as he may see fit, the rules and regulations applicable to any or all stations within the jurisdiction of the United States as prescribed by the licensing authority, and may cause the closing of any station for radio communication and the removal therefrom of its apparatus and equipment, or he may authorize the use or control of any such station and/or its apparatus and equipment by any department of the Government under such regulations as he may prescribe, upon just compensation to the owners. Radio stations on board vessels of the United States Shipping Board or the United States Shipping Board Emergency Fleet Corporation or the Inland and Coastwise Waterways Service shall be subject to the provisions of this Act.

SEC. 7. The President shall ascertain the just compensation for such use or control and certify the amount ascertained to Congress for appropriation and payment to the person entitled thereto. If the amount so certified is unsatisfactory to the person entitled thereto, such person shall be paid only 75 per centum of the amount and shall be entitled to sue the United States to recover such further sum as added to such payment of 75 per centum which will make such amount as will be just compensation for the use and control. Such suit shall be brought in the manner provided by paragraph 20 of section 24, or by section 145 of the Judicial Code, as amended.

SEC. 8. All stations owned and operated by the United States, except mobile stations of the Army of the United States, and all other stations on land and sea, shall have special call letters designated by the Secretary of Commerce.

Section 1 of this Act shall not apply to any person, firm, company, or corporation sending radio communications or signals on a foreign ship while the same is within the jurisdiction of the United States, but such communications or signals shall be transmitted only in accordance with such regulations designed to prevent interference as may be promulgated under the authority of this Act.

SEC. 9. The licensing authority, if public convenience, interest, or necessity will be served thereby, subject to the limitations of this Act, shall grant to any applicant therefor a station license provided for by this Act.

In considering applications for licenses and renewals of licenses, when and in so far as there is a demand for the same, the licensing authority shall make such a distribution of licenses, bands of frequency of wave lengths, periods of time for operation, and of power among the different States and communities as to give fair, efficient, and equitable radio service to each of the same.

No license granted for the operation of a broadcasting station shall be for a longer term than three years and no license so granted for any other class of station shall be for a longer term than five years, and any license granted may be revoked as hereinafter provided. Upon the expiration of any license, upon application therefor, a renewal of such license may be granted from time to time for a term of not to exceed three years in the case of broadcasting licenses and not to exceed five years in the case of other licenses.

No renewal of an existing station license shall be granted more than thirty days prior to the expiration of the original license.

SEC. 10. The licensing authority may grant station licenses only upon written application therefor addressed to it. All applications shall be filed with the Secretary of Commerce. All such applications shall set forth such facts as the licensing authority by regulation may prescribe as to the citizenship, character, and financial, technical, and other qualifications of the applicant to operate the station; the ownership and location of the proposed station and of the stations, if any, with which it is proposed to communicate; the frequencies or wave lengths and the power desired to be used; the hours of the day or other periods of time during which it is proposed to operate the station; the purposes for which the station is to be used; and such other information as it may require. The licensing authority at any time after the filing of such original application and during the term of any such license may require from an applicant or licensee further written statements of fact to enable it to determine whether such original application should be granted or denied or such license revoked. Such application and/or such statement of fact shall be signed by the applicant and/or licensee under oath or affirmation.

The licensing authority in granting any license for a station intended or used for commercial communication between the United States or any Territory or possession, continental or insular, subject to the jurisdiction of the United States, and any foreign country, may impose any terms, conditions, or restrictions authorized to be imposed with respect to submarine-cable licenses by section 2 of an Act entitled "An Act relating to the landing and the operation of submarine cables in the United States," approved May 24, 1921.

SEC. 11. If upon examination of any application for a station license or for the renewal or modification of a station license the licensing authority shall determine that public interest, convenience, or necessity would be served by the granting thereof, it shall authorize the issuance, renewal, or modification thereof in accordance with said finding. In the event the licensing authority upon examination of any such application does not reach such decision with respect thereto, it shall notify the applicant thereof, shall fix and give notice of a time and place for hearing thereon, and shall afford such applicant an opportunity to be heard under such rules and regulations as it may prescribe.

Such station licenses as the licensing authority may grant shall be in such general form as it may prescribe, but each license shall contain, in addition to other provisions, a statement of the following conditions to which such license shall be subject:

(A) The station license shall not vest in the licensee any right to operate the station nor any right in the use of the frequencies or wave length designated in the license beyond the term thereof nor in any other manner than authorized therein.

(B) Neither the license nor the right granted thereunder shall be assigned or otherwise transferred in violation of this Act.

(C) Every license issued under this Act shall be subject in terms to the right of use or control conferred by section 6 hereof.

In cases of emergency arising during the period of one year from and after the first meeting of the commission created hereby, or on applications filed during said time for temporary changes in terms of licenses when the commission is not in session and prompt action is deemed necessary, the Secretary of Commerce shall have authority to exercise the powers and duties of the commission, except as to revocation of licenses, but all such exercise of powers shall be promptly reported to the members of the commission, and any action by the Secretary authorized under this paragraph shall continue in force and have effect only until such time as the commission shall act thereon.

SEC. 14. Any station license shall be revocable by the commission for false after the granting thereof such license shall not be transferred in any manner, either voluntarily or involuntarily, to (a) any alien or the representative of any alien; (b) to any foreign government, or the representative thereof; (c) to any company, corporation, or association organized under the laws of any foreign government; (d) to any company, corporation, or association of which any officer or director is an alien, or of which more than one-fifth of the capital stock may be voted by aliens or their representatives or by a foreign government or representative thereof, or by any company, corporation, or association organized under the laws of a foreign country.

The station license required hereby, the frequencies or wave length or lengths authorized to be used by the licensee, and the rights therein granted shall not be transferred, assigned, or in any manner, either voluntarily or involuntarily, disposed of to any person, firm, company, or corporation without the consent in writing of the licensing authority.

SEC. 13. The licensing authority is hereby directed to refuse a station license and/or the permit hereinafter required for the construction of a station to any person, firm, company, or corporation, or any subsidiary thereof, which has been finally adjudged guilty by a Federal court of unlawfully monopolizing or attempting unlawfully to monopolize, after this Act takes effect, radio communication, directly or indirectly, through the control of the manufacture or sale of radio apparatus, through exclusive traffic arrangements, or by any other means or to have been using unfair methods of competition. The granting of a license shall not estop the United States or any person aggrieved from proceeding against such person, firm, company, or corporation for violating the law against unfair methods of competition or for a violation of the law against unlawful restraints and monopolies and/or combinations, contracts, or agreements in restraint of trade, or from instituting proceedings for the dissolution of such firm, company, or corporation.

SEC. 14. Any station license shall be revocable by the commission for false statements either in the application or in the statement of fact which may be required by section 10 hereof, or because of conditions revealed by such statements of fact as may be required from time to time which would warrant the licensing authority in refusing to grant a license on an original application, or for failure to operate substantially as set forth in the license, for violation of or failure to observe any of the restrictions and conditions of this Act, or of any regulation of the licensing authority authorized by this Act or by a treaty ratified by the United States, or whenever the Interstate Commerce Commission, or any other Federal body in the exercise of authority conferred upon it by law, shall find and shall certify to the commission that any licensee bound so to do, has failed to provide reasonable facilities for the transmission of radio communications, or that any licensee has made any unjust and unreasonable charge, or has been guilty of any discrimination, either as to charge or as to service or has made or prescribed any unjust and unreasonable classification, regulation, or practice with respect to the transmission of radio communications or service: *Provided,* That no such order of revocation shall take effect until thirty days' notice in writing thereof, stating the cause for the proposed revocation, has been given to the parties known by the commission to be interested in such license. Any person in interest aggrieved by said order may make written application to the commission at any time within said thirty days for a hearing upon such order, and upon the filing of such written application said order of revocation shall stand suspended until the conclusion of the hearing herein directed. Notice in writing of said hearing shall be given by the commission to all the parties known to it to be interested in such license twenty days prior to the time of said hearing. Said hearing shall be conducted under such rules and in such manner as the commission may prescribe. Upon the conclusion hereof the commission may affirm, modify, or revoke said orders of revocation.

SEC. 15. All laws of the United States relating to unlawful restraints and monopolies and to combinations, contracts, or agreements in restraint of trade are hereby declared to be applicable to the manufacture and sale of and to trade in radio apparatus and devices entering into or affecting interstate or foreign commerce and to interstate or foreign radio communications. Whenever in any suit, action, or proceeding, civil or criminal, brought under the provisions of any of said laws or in any proceedings brought to enforce or to review findings and orders of the Federal Trade Commission or other governmental agency in respect of any matters as to which said commission or other governmental agency is by law authorized to act, any licensee shall be found guilty of the violation of the provisions of such laws or any of them, the court, in addition to the penalties imposed by said laws, may adjudge, order, and/or decree that the license of such licensee shall, as of the date the decree or judgment becomes finally effective or as of such other date as the said decree shall fix, be revoked and that all rights under such license shall thereupon cease: *Provided, however,* That such licensee shall have the same right of appeal or review as is provided by law in respect of other decrees and judgments of said court.

SEC. 16. Any applicant for a construction permit, for a station license, or for the renewal or modification of an existing station license whose application is refused by the licensing authority shall have the right to appeal from said decision to the Court of Appeals of the District of Columbia; and any licensee whose license is revoked by the commission shall have the right to appeal from such decision of revocation to said Court of Appeals of the District of Columbia or to the district court of the United States in which the apparatus licensed is operated, by filing with said court, within twenty days after the decision complained of is effective, notice in writing of said appeal and of the reasons therefor.

The licensing authority from whose decision an appeal is taken shall be notified of said appeal by service upon it, prior to the filing thereof, of a certified copy of said appeal and of the reasons therefor. Within twenty days after the filing of said appeal the licensing authority shall file with the court the originals or certified copies of all papers and evidence presented to it upon the original application for a permit or license or in the hearing upon said order of revocation, and also a like copy of its decision thereon and a full statement in writing of the facts and the grounds for its decision as found and given by it. Within twenty days after the filing of said statement by the licensing authority either party may give notice to the court of his desire to adduce additional evidence. Said notice shall be in the form of a verified petition stating the nature and character of said additional evidence, and the court may thereupon order such evidence to be taken in such manner and upon such terms and conditions as it may deem proper.

At the earliest convenient time the court shall hear, review, and determine the appeal upon said record and evidence, and may alter or revise the decision appealed from and enter such judgment as to it may seem just. The revision by the court shall be confined to the points set forth in the reasons of appeal.

SEC. 17. After the passage of this Act no person, firm, company, or corporation now or hereafter directly or indirectly through any subsidiary, associated, or affiliated person, firm, company, corporation, or agent, or otherwise, in the business of transmitting and/or receiving for hire energy, communications, or signals by radio in accordance with the terms of the license issued under this Act, shall by purchase, lease, construction, or otherwise, directly or indirectly, acquire, own, control, or operate any cable or wire telegraph or telephone line or system between any place in any State, Territory, or possession of the United States or in the District of Columbia, and any place in any foreign country, or shall acquire, own, or control any part of the stock or other capital share of any interest in the physical property and/or other assets of any such cable, wire, telegraph, or telephone line or system, if in either case the purpose is and/or the effect thereof may be to substantially lessen competition or to restrain commerce between any place in any State, Territory, or possession of the United States or in the District of Columbia and any place in any foreign country, or unlawfully to create monopoly in any line of commerce; nor shall any person, firm, company, or corporation now or hereafter engaged directly or indirectly through any subsidiary, associated, or affiliated person, company, corporation, or agent, or otherwise, in the business of transmitting and/or receiving for hire messages by any cable, wire, telegraph, or telephone line or system (a) between any place in any State, Territory, or possession of the United States or in the District of Columbia, and any place in any other State, Territory, or possession of the United States; or (b) between any place in any State, Territory, or possession of the United States, or the District of Columbia, and any place in any foreign country, by purchase, lease, construction, or otherwise, directly or indirectly acquire, own, control, or operate any station or the apparatus therein, or any system for transmitting and/or receiving radio communications or signals between any place in any State, Territory, or possession of the United States or in the District of Columbia, and any place in any foreign country, or shall acquire, own, or control any part of the stock or other capital share or any interest in the physical property and/or other assets of any such radio station, apparatus, or system, if in either case the purpose is and/or the effect thereof may be to substantially lessen competition or to restrain commerce between any place in any State, Territory, or possession of the United States or in the District of Columbia, and any place in any foreign country, or unlawfully to create monopoly in any line of commerce.

SEC. 18. If any licensee shall permit any person who is a legally qualified candidate for any public office to use a broadcasting station, he shall afford equal opportunities to all other such candidates for that office in the use of such broadcasting station, and the licensing authority shall make rules and regulations to carry this provision into effect: *Provided,* That such licensee shall have no power of censorship over the material broadcast under the provisions of this paragraph. No obligation is hereby imposed upon any licensee to allow the use of its station by any such candidate.

SEC. 19. All matter broadcast by any radio station for which service, money, or any other valuable consideration is directly or indirectly paid, or promised to or charged or accepted by, the station so broadcasting, from any person, firm, company, or corporation, shall, at the time the same is so broadcast, be announced as paid for or furnished, as the case may be, by such person, firm, company, or corporation.

SEC. 20. The actual operation of all transmitting apparatus in any radio station for which a station license is required by this Act shall be carried on only by a person holding an operator's license issued hereunder. No person shall operate any such apparatus in such station except under and in accordance with an operator's license issued to him by the Secretary of Commerce.

SEC. 21. No license shall be issued under the authority of this Act for the operation of any station the construction of which is begun or is continued after this Act takes effect, unless a permit for its construction has been granted by the licensing authority upon written application therefor. The licensing authority may grant such permit if public convenience, interest, or necessity will be served by the construction of the station. This application shall set forth such facts as the licensing authority by regulation may prescribe as to the citizenship, character, and the financial, technical, and other ability of the applicant to construct and operate the station, the ownership and location of the proposed station and of the station or stations with which it is proposed to communicate, the frequencies and wave length or wave lengths desired to be used, the hours of the day or other periods of time during which it is proposed to operate the station, the purpose for which the station is to be used, the type of transmitting apparatus to be used, the power to be used, the date upon which the station is expected to be completed and in operation, and such other information as the licensing authority may require. Such application shall be signed by the applicant under oath or affirmation.

Such permit for construction shall show specifically the earliest and latest dates between which the actual operation of such station is expected to begin, and shall provide that said permit will be automatically forfeited if the station is not ready for operation within the time specified or within such further time as the licensing authority may allow, unless prevented by causes not under the control of the grantee. The rights under any such permit shall not be assigned or otherwise transferred to any person, firm, company, or corporation without the approval of the licensing authority. A permit for construction shall not be required for Government stations, amateur stations, or stations upon mobile vessels, railroad rolling stock, or aircraft. Upon the completion of any station for the construction or continued construction for which a permit has been granted, and upon it being made to appear to the licensing authority that all the terms, conditions, and obligations set forth in the application and permit have been fully met, and that no cause or circumstance arising or first coming to the knowledge of the licensing authority since the granting of the permit would, in the judgment of the licensing authority, make the operation of such station against the public interest, the licensing authority shall issue a license to the lawful holder of said permit for the operation of said station. Said license shall conform generally to the terms of said permit.

SEC. 22. The licensing authority is authorized to designate from time to time radio stations the communications or signals of which, in its opinion, are liable to interfere with the transmission or reception of distress signals of ships. Such stations are required to keep a licensed radio operator listening in on the wave lengths designated for signals of distress and radio communications relating thereto during the entire period the transmitter of such station is in operation.

SEC. 23. Every radio station on shipboard shall be equipped to transmit radio communications or signals of distress on the frequency or wave length specified by the licensing authority, with apparatus capable of transmitting and receiving messages over a distance of at least one hundred miles by day or night. When sending radio communications or signals of distress and radio communications relating thereto the transmitting set may be adjusted in such a manner as to produce a maximum of radiation irrespective of the amount of interference which may thus be caused.

All radio stations, including Government stations and stations on board foreign vessels when within the territorial waters of the United States, shall give absolute priority to radio communications or signals relating to ships in distress; shall cease all sending on frequencies or wave lengths which will interfere with hearing a radio communication or signal of distress, and, except when engaged in answering or aiding the ship in distress, shall refrain from sending any radio communications or signals until there is assurance that no interference will be caused with the radio communications or signals relating thereto, and shall assist the vessel in distress, so far as possible, by complying with its instructions.

SEC. 24. Every shore station open to general public service between the coast and vessels at sea shall be bound to exchange radio communications or signals with any ship station without distinction as to radio systems or instruments adopted by such stations, respectively, and each station on shipboard shall be bound to exchange radio communications or signals with any other station on shipboard without distinction as to radio systems or instruments adopted by each station.

SEC. 25. At all places where Government and private or commercial radio stations on land operate in such close proximity that interference with the work of Government stations can not be avoided when they are operating simultaneously such private or commercial stations as do interfere with the transmission or reception of radio communications or signals by the Government stations concerned shall not use their transmitters during the first fifteen minutes of each hour, local standard time.

The Government stations for which the above-mentioned division of time is established shall transmit radio communications or signals only during the first fifteen minutes of each hour, local standard time, except in case of signals or radio communications relating to vessels in distress and vessel requests for information as to course, location, or compass direction.

SEC. 26. In all circumstances, except in case of radio communications or signals relating to vessels in distress, all radio stations, including those owned and operated by the United States, shall use the minimum amount of power necessary to carry out the communication desired.

SEC. 27. No person receiving or assisting in receiving any radio communication shall divulge or publish the contents, substance, purport, effect, or meaning thereof except through authorized channels of transmission or reception to any person other than the addressee, his agent, or attorney, or to a telephone, telegraph, cable, or radio station employed or authorized to forward such radio communication to its destination, or to proper accounting or distributing officers of the various communicating centers over which the radio communication may be passed, or to the master of a ship under whom he is serving, or in response to a subpoena issued by a court of competent jurisdiction, or on demand of other lawful authority; and no person not being authorized by the sender shall intercept any message and divulge or publish the contents, substance, purport, effect, or meaning of such intercepted message to any person; and no person not being entitled thereto shall receive or assist in receiving any radio communication and use the same or any information therein contained for his own benefit or for the benefit of another not entitled thereto; and no person having received such intercepted radio communication or having become acquainted with the contents, substance, purport, effect, or meaning of the same or any part thereof, knowing that such information was so obtained, shall divulge or publish the contents, substance, purport, effect, or meaning of the same or any part thereof, or use the same or any information therein contained for his own benefit or for the benefit of another not entitled thereto: *Provided,* That this section shall not apply to the receiving, divulging, publishing, or utilizing the contents of any radio communication broadcasted or transmitted by amateurs or others for the use of the general public or relating to ships in distress.

SEC. 28. No person, firm, company, or corporation within the jurisdiction of the United States shall knowingly utter or transmit, or cause to be uttered or transmitted, any false or fraudulent signal of distress, or communication relating thereto, nor shall any broadcasting station rebroadcast the program or any part thereof of another broadcasting station without the express authority of the originating station.

SEC. 29. Nothing in this Act shall be understood or construed to give the licensing authority the power of censorship over the radio communications or signals transmitted by any radio station, and no regulation or condition shall be promulgated or fixed by the licensing authority which shall interfere with the right of free speech by means of radio communications. No person within the jurisdiction of the United States shall utter any obscene, indecent, or profane language by means of radio communication.

SEC. 30. The Secretary of the Navy is hereby authorized unless restrained by international agreement, under the terms and conditions and at rates prescribed by him, which rates shall be just and reasonable, and which, upon complaint, shall be subject to review and revision by the Interstate Commerce

Commission, to use all radio stations and apparatus, wherever located, owned by the United States and under the control of the Navy Department (a) for the reception and transmission of press messages offered by any newspaper published in the United States, its Territories or possessions, or published by citizens of the United States in foreign countries, or by any press association of the United States, and (b) for the reception and transmission of private commercial messages between ships, between ship and shore, between localities in Alaska and between Alaska and the continental United States: *Provided,* That the rates fixed for the reception and transmission of all such messages, other than press messages between the Pacific coast of the United States, Hawaii, Alaska, the Philippine Islands, and the Orient, and between the United States and the Virgin Islands, shall not be less than the rates charged by privately owned and operated stations for like messages and service: *Provided further,* That the right to use such stations for any of the purposes named in this section shall terminate and cease as between any countries or localities or between any locality and privately operated ships whenever privately owned and operated stations are capable of meeting the normal communication requirements between such countries or localities or between any locality and privately operated ships, and the licensing authority shall have notified the Secretary of the Navy thereof.

SEC. 31. The expression "radio communication" or "radio communications" wherever used in this Act means any intelligence, message, signal, power, pictures, or communication of any nature transferred by electrical energy from one point to another without the aid of any wire connecting the points from and at which the electrical energy is sent or received and any system by means of which such transfer of energy is effected.

SEC. 32. Any person, firm, company, or corporation failing or refusing to observe or violating any rule, regulation, restriction, or condition made or imposed by the licensing authority under the authority of this Act or of any international radio convention or treaty ratified or adhered to by the United States, in addition to any other penalties provided by law, upon conviction thereof by a court of competent jurisdiction, shall be punished by a fine of not more than $500 for each and every offense.

SEC. 33. Any person, firm, company, or corporation who shall violate any provision of this Act, or shall knowingly make any false oath or affirmation in any affidavit required or authorized by this Act, or shall knowingly swear falsely to a material matter in any hearing authorized by this Act, upon conviction thereof in any court of competent jurisdiction shall be punished by a fine of not more than $5,000 or by imprisonment for a term of not more than five years or both for each and every such offense.

SEC. 34. The trial of any offense under this Act shall be in the district in which it is committed; or if the offense is committed upon the high seas, or out of the jurisdiction of any particular State or district, the trial shall be in the district where the offender may be found or into which he shall be first brought.

SEC. 35. This Act shall not apply to the Philippine Islands or to the Canal Zone. In international radio matters the Philippine Islands and the Canal Zone shall be represented by the Secretary of State.

SEC. 36. The licensing authority is authorized to designate any officer or employee of any other department of the Government on duty in any Territory or possession of the United States other than the Philippine Islands and the Canal Zone, to render therein such services in connection with the administration of the radio laws of the United States as such authority may prescribe: *Provided*, That such designation shall be approved by the head of the department in which such person is employed.

SEC. 37. The unexpended balance of the moneys appropriated in the item for "wireless communication laws," under the caption "Bureau of Navigation" in Title III of the Act entitled "An Act making appropriations for the Departments of State and Justice and for the judiciary, and for the Departments of Commerce and Labor, for the fiscal year ending June 30, 1927, and for other purposes," approved April 29, 1926, and the appropriation for the same purposes for the fiscal year ending June 30, 1928, shall be available both for expenditures incurred in the administration of this Act and for expenditures for the purposes specified in such items. There is hereby authorized to be appropriated for each fiscal year such sums as may be necessary for the administration of this Act and for the purposes specified in such item.

SEC. 38. If any provision of this Act or the application thereof to any person, firm, company, or corporation, or to any circumstances, is held invalid, the remainder of the Act and the application of such provision to other persons, firms, companies, or corporations, or to other circumstances, shall not be affected thereby.

SEC. 39. The Act entitled "An Act to regulate radio communication," approved August 13, 1912, the joint resolution to authorize the operation of Government-owned radio stations for the general public, and for other purposes, approved June 5, 1920, as amended, and the joint resolution entitled "Joint resolution limiting the time for which licenses for radio transmission may be granted, and for other purposes," approved December 8, 1926, are hereby repealed.

Such repeal, however, shall not affect any act done or any right accrued or any suit or proceeding had or commenced in any civil cause prior to said repeal, but all liabilities under said laws shall continue and may be enforced in the same manner as if committed; and all penalties, forfeitures, or liabilities incurred prior to taking effect hereof, under any law embraced in, changed, modified, or repealed by this Act, may be prosecuted and punished in the same manner and with the same effect as if this Act had not been passed.

Nothing in this section shall be construed as authorizing any person now using or operating any apparatus for the transmission of radio energy or radio communications or signals to continue such use except under and in accordance with this Act and with a license granted in accordance with the authority hereinbefore conferred.

The March of Time: in Studio 1, CBS, 1931.

The Voice of Time—or "voice of doom"—
Westbrook Van Voorhis.

"Time . . . marches on!"

1933

RCA

Marconi (at right) and heir apparent,
David Sarnoff. A tour of RCA facilities.

"World's largest radio studio" nears
completion. Studio 8H, NBC, Radio
City. Seen from observation booth.

NBC

SEC. 40. This Act shall take effect and be in force upon its passage and approval, except that for and during a period of sixty days after such approval no holder of a license or an extension thereof issued by the Secretary of Commerce under said Act of August 13, 1912, shall be subject to the penalties provided herein for operating a station without the license herein required.

SEC. 41. This Act may be referred to and cited as the Radio Act of 1927.

Approved, February 23, 1927.

BIBLIOGRAPHY

Collections. Manuscript collections have proved of special value. Collections are identified in the bibliography by letter, as follows:

(C) Columbia University Oral History Collection, New York.
(D) Detroit Historical Museum, Detroit.
(M) Mass Communications History Center of the Wisconsin Historical Society, Madison.
(N) National Broadcasting Company Library, New York.
(P) Broadcast Pioneers History Project, New York.
(S) Smithsonian Institution, Radioana Collection, Washington.

Alexanderson, Ernst Frederick Werner. Reminiscences, 1951. Unpublished. (C)
Allen, Ed. Reminiscences, 1963. Unpublished. (C)
Allen, Frederick Lewis. Only Yesterday: an informal history of the nineteen-twenties. New York and London, Harper, 1951.
American Broadcasting: an analytical study of one day's output of 206 commercial radio stations including program contents and advertising interruptions. Ventura (Cal.), Ventura Free Press, 1933.
Anderson, Robert Gordon. See McNamee, Graham, in collaboration with—
Annual Report of the Federal Radio Commission. 1st report, 1927; 2nd, 1927-28, etc. Washington, Government Printing Office, 1927, etc.
Archer, Gleason L. Big Business and Radio. New York, American Historical Company, 1939.
Archer, Gleason L. History of Radio: to 1926. New York, American Historical Society, 1938.
Arnold, Frank A. Broadcast Advertising: the fourth dimension. New York, John Wiley, 1931.

Baker, Ray Stannard. Woodrow Wilson and World Settlement. 3v. Garden City (N.Y.), Doubleday, Page, 1922.

Baker, Walter Ransom Gail. Reminiscences, 1950. Unpublished. (C)

Baldwin, James. Notes of a Native Son. New York, Bantam, 1964.

Banning, William Peck. Commercial Broadcasting Pioneer: the WEAF experiment 1922-1926. Cambridge, Harvard University Press, 1946.

Bannister, Harry Ray. Reminiscences, 1951. Unpublished. (C)

Barlow, Howard. Reminiscences, 1951. Unpublished. (C)

Barnes, Patrick Henry. Reminiscences, 1951. Unpublished. (C)

Barnett, Joseph M. Reminiscences, 1951. Unpublished. (C)

Barton, Bruce. The Man Nobody Knows. Indianapolis, Bobbs-Merrill, 1924.

Berg, Cherney. See Berg, Gertrude, with—

Berg, Gertrude, with Cherney Berg. Molly and Me. New York, McGraw-Hill, 1961.

Berle, Adolf A., Jr., and Gardiner C. Means. The Modern Corporation and Private Property. New York, Macmillan, 1932, 1948.

Bernays, Edward L. Biography of an Idea: memoirs of a public relations counsel. New York, Simon and Schuster, 1965.

Bliven, Bruce. "How Radio Is Remaking Our World," Century, June 1924.

Bosler, Gustave A. Reminiscences, 1950. Unpublished. (C)

Bouck, Zeh. Making a Living in Radio. New York and London, McGraw-Hill, 1935.

Bragdon, Everett L. Reminiscences, 1950. Unpublished. (C)

Briggs, Asa. The Birth of Broadcasting: the history of broadcasting in the United Kingdom, v. 1. London, Oxford University Press, 1961.

Briggs, Asa. "Broadcasting and Society." The Listener, November 22, 1962.

Brindze, Ruth. Not To Be Broadcast: the truth about radio. New York, Vanguard Press, 1937.

Broadcasting. Washington, semimonthly, then weekly, 1931—

Broadcasting yearbooks. Washington, 1935, etc.

Broadcasting in the United States. Washington, National Association of Broadcasters, 1933.

Brokenshire, Norman. This Is Norman Brokenshire: an unvarnished self-portrait. New York, David McKay, 1954.

Brown, William Wilbur, Reminiscences, 1951. Unpublished. (C)

Bryson, Lyman Lloyd. Reminiscences, 1951. Unpublished. (C)

Caldwell, Orestes Hampton. Reminiscences, 1951. Unpublished. (C)

Cappa, Joseph D. Interview by Gordon B. Greb, 1959. Unpublished. (C)

Carlin, Phillips. Reminiscences, 1951. Unpublished. (C)

Carneal, Georgette. A Conqueror of Space: an authorized biography of the life and work of Lee de Forest. New York, Horace Liveright, 1930.

Carson, Gerald. The Roguish World of Doctor Brinkley. New York, Holt, Rinehart & Winston, 1960.

Casson, Herbert N. The History of the Telephone. Chicago, A. C. McClurg, 1910.

Caton, Chester F. Radio Station WMAQ: a history of its independent years, 1922-1931. Ph.D. dissertation. Evanston, Northwestern University, 1951. Unpublished.

Chafee, Zechariah, Jr. Freedom of Speech and Press. New York, Freedom Agenda, 1955.

Chafee, Zechariah, Jr. Government and Mass Communications: a report from the Commission on Freedom of the Press. 2 v. Chicago, University of Chicago Press, 1947.

Chase, Francis, Jr. Sound and Fury: an informal history of broadcasting. New York, Harper, 1942.

Chasins, Abram. Reminiscences, 1950. Unpublished. (C)

Chester, Giraud. The Radio Commentaries of H. V. Kaltenborn: a case study in persuasion. Ph.D. dissertation. Madison, University of Wisconsin, 1947. Unpublished.

Chicago Tribune Radio Book: a listener's handbook. Chicago, Chicago Tribune, 1925.

Clark, George H. The Formation of RCA. Unpublished. (S)

Clark, Thomas Edward. Papers. Unpublished. (D)

Clark, Thomas Edward. Reminiscences, 1951. Unpublished. (C)

Commercial Radio Advertising: a letter from the chairman of the Federal Radio Commission in response to Senate resolution 129, 72nd Congress. Senate document 137, 72nd Congress, 1st session. Washington, Government Printing Office, 1932.

Commission on Communications: hearings before the committee on interstate commerce, U. S. Senate, 71st Congress, 1929-30, on S. 6. Washington, Government Printing Office, 1930.

Cook, Joe. See Slate, Sam, and—

Correll, Charles J., and Freeman F. Gosden. All About Amos 'n' Andy. New York, Rand McNally, 1929.

Cowan, Thomas H. Reminiscences, 1950, 1951. Unpublished. (C)

Crookes, William C. "Some Possibilities in Electricity." Fortnightly Review, February 1, 1892.

Crosby, Bing, as told to Pete Martin. Call Me Lucky. New York, Simon and Schuster, 1953.

Crosley, Powel, Jr. Simplicity of Radio: the blue book of radio. Cincinnati, Crosley Publishing Company, 1924.

Cupp, Roderick B. Reminiscences, 1963. Unpublished. (C)

David Sarnoff: biographical sketch. New York, Radio Corporation of America, 1945. (N)

Davies, Edward A., and Jim Tisdale. Philadelphia's Pioneer Voice. Conversation recorded September 2, 1964, at WVCH, Chester, Pa. Unpublished. (P)

Davis, H. P. "The Early History of Broadcasting in the United States," in The Radio Industry. Chicago and New York, A. W. Shaw, 1928.

Daytime Hours Sell. New York, National Broadcasting Company, 1933.

De Forest, Lee. Father of Radio: the autobiography of Lee de Forest. Chi-
    cago, Wilcox and Follett, 1950.
De Forest, Lee. Interview by Gordon B. Greb, 1959. Unpublished. (C)
Dill, Clarence C. Interview by Ed Craney recorded in Butte, Mont., 1964. Un-
    published. (P)
Dill, Clarence C. Talk over NBC, June 13, 1931, in Arnold, Frank A. Broadcast
    Advertising: the fourth dimension. New York, John Wiley, 1931.
Dr. Conrad and His Work. Westinghouse press release, June 27, 1942. (M)
Dunham, Edwin L. This Is the AMRAD Story. Article including texts of in-
    terviews with Harold J. Power and others recorded in 1964. Unpub-
    lished. (P)
Dunlap, Orrin E., Jr. Marconi: the man and his wireless. New York, Macmil-
    lan, 1937.
Dunlap, Orrin E., Jr. Radio and Television Almanac. New York, Harper, 1951.
Dunlap, Orrin E., Jr. The Story of Radio. New York, Dial Press, 1935.
Dunne, Philip. Mr. Dooley Remembers: the informal memoirs of Finley Peter
    Dunne. Boston, Little, Brown & Co., 1963.
Education on the Air. Columbus (O.), Institute for Education by Radio, an-
    nual, 1930-
Electrical Engineer. New York, weekly, 1882-99.
Empire of the Air. Ventura (Cal.), Ventura Free Press, 1932.
Espenschied, Lloyd. Recollections of the Radio Industry, 1963. Unpublished.
    (C)
Evans, Walter Chew. Reminiscences, 1950, 1951. Unpublished. (C)
Federal Radio Commission. For annual reports see Annual Report of the Fed-
    eral Radio Commission. See also Commercial Radio Advertising.
Federal Radio Commissioners: hearing before the committee on interstate com-
    merce, U. S. Senate, 70th Congress, 1st session, on the confirmation of
    the federal radio commissioners, January 6-February 6, 1928. Wash-
    ington, Government Printing Office, 1928.
Federal Trade Commission. See Report of the Federal Trade Commission on
    the Radio Industry.
Fees for Radio Licenses: hearings before a subcommittee of the committee on
    interstate commerce, U. S. Senate, 72nd Congress, 2nd session. Washing-
    ton, Government Printing Office, 1933.
Felix, Edgar H. Reminiscences, 1962. Unpublished. (C)
Fessenden, Helen M. Fessenden: builder of tomorrows. New York, Coward-
    McCann, 1940.
Fetzer, John Earl. Reminiscences, 1950. Unpublished. (C)
Friedrich, Carl J., with Jeannette Sayre Smith. Radio Broadcasting and Higher
    Education. Cambridge (Mass.), Studies in the Control of Radio, 1942.
From Crystal to Color: WFBM. Indianapolis, the WFBM Stations, 1964.
Frost, S. E., Jr. Education's Own Stations: the history of broadcast licenses
    issued to educational institutions. Chicago, University of Chicago Press,
    1937.

Frost, S. E., Jr. Is American Radio Democratic? Chicago, University of Chicago Press, 1937.

Gambling, John. Reminiscences, 1951. Unpublished. (C)

Gammons, Earl. The Twin Cities Story, 1964. Unpublished. (P)

Gentlemen, Be Seated. New York, National Broadcasting Company, 1930.

Goldsmith, Alfred N. Interview by William S. Hedges, 1964. Unpublished. (P)

Goldsmith, Alfred N., and Austin C. Lescarboura. This Thing Called Broadcasting. New York, Henry Holt, 1930.

Gordon, Dorothy. Reminiscences, 1951. Unpublished. (C)

Gosden, Freeman F. See Correll, Charles J., and—

Government Control of Radio Communication: hearings before the committee on merchant marine and fisheries, U. S. House of Representatives, 65th Congress, 3rd session, December 12-19, 1918. Washington, Government Printing Office, 1919.

Greb, Gordon B. "The Golden Anniversary of Broadcasting," Journal of Broadcasting, Winter 1958-59.

Greb, Gordon B. Interviews. See Cappa, Joseph D.; De Forest, Lee; Hart, Fred J.; Smith, Ira D.; True, Sybil M.

Green, Abel, and Joe Laurie, Jr. Show Biz: from vaude to video. New York, Henry Holt, 1951.

Greene, Rosaline. Reminiscences, 1951. Unpublished. (C)

Gross, Ben. I Looked and Listened: informal recollections of radio and TV. New York, Random House, 1954.

Gruening, Ernest. The Public Pays: a study of power propaganda. New York, Vanguard Press, 1931, 1964.

Gunzendorfer, Wilton. Reminiscences, 1960. Unpublished. (C)

Guy, Raymond Frederick. Reminiscences, 1951. Unpublished. (C)

Hager, Kolin. Reminiscences, 1960. Unpublished. (C)

Hanson, Malcolm P. Papers, 1906-47. Unpublished. (M)

Harkness, William E. Reminiscences, 1951. Unpublished. (C)

Harlow, Alvin F. Old Wires and New Waves: the history of the telegraph, telephone and wireless. New York, Appleton-Century, 1936.

Harris, Credo Fitch. Microphone Memoirs: of the horse and buggy days of radio. Indianapolis and New York, Bobbs-Merrill, 1937.

Hart, Fred J. Interview over KCBS, San Francisco by Gordon B. Greb, 1962. Unpublished. (C)

Hart, Herschell. Reminiscences, 1951. Unpublished. (C)

Hawkins, Laurence Ashley. Reminiscences, 1951. Unpublished. (C)

Hedges, William S. Reminiscences, 1951. Unpublished. (C)

Hedges, William S. See Goldsmith, Alfred N., Interview by—

Henderson, Archibald. George Bernard Shaw: man of the century. New York, Appleton-Century-Crofts, 1956.

Herring, E. Pendleton. Federal Commissioners: a study of their careers and qualifications. Cambridge, Harvard University Press, 1936.

Herring, E. Pendleton. "Politics and Radio Regulation," Harvard Business Review, January 1935.

Hill, Frank Ernest. Listen and Learn: fifteen years of adult education on the air. New York, American Association for Adult Education, 1937.

Hill, Frank Ernest. Tune in for Education: eleven years of education by radio. New York, National Committee on Education by Radio, 1942.

History of Communications-Electronics in the United States Navy. Prepared by Captain L. S. Howeth, USN (retired) under the auspices of the Bureau of Ships and Office of Naval History. Washington, Government Printing Office, 1963.

Hoins, Jack. The History of WABC, 1946. Unpublished. (N)

Holland, Lawrence LaMotte. Reminiscences, 1951. Unpublished. (C)

Hollywood Quarterly. Berkeley and Los Angeles, University of California Press, quarterly, 1945-51.

Hoover, Herbert. The Memoirs of Herbert Hoover: the cabinet and the presidency, 1920-1933. New York, Macmillan, 1952.

Hoover, Herbert. Reminiscences, 1950. Unpublished. (C)

Horn, C. W. Address: broadcast over KDKA January 3, 1923. Unpublished. (M)

Howeth, L. S. See History of Communications-Electronics in the United States Navy.

Hull, Albert Wallace. Reminiscences, 1950, 1951. Unpublished. (C)

Husing, Ted. Ten Years before the Mike. New York, Farrar & Rinehart, 1935.

Innis, Harold A. The Bias of Communication. Toronto, University of Toronto Press, 1951.

Innis, Harold A. Empire and Communications. Oxford, Clarendon Press, 1950.

James, E. P. H. Interview, 1963. Unpublished. (C)

Janis, Eddie. Reminiscences, 1960. Unpublished. (C)

Judson, Arthur. Reminiscences, 1950. Unpublished. (C)

Johnson, James L. Address to Kentucky Broadcasters Association, May 18, 1961. Unpublished.

Jome, Hiram L. Economics of the Radio Industry. Chicago and New York, A. W. Shaw, 1925.

Journal of Broadcasting. Los Angeles, Association for Professional Broadcasting Education, quarterly, 1956-

Jurisdiction of Radio Commission: hearings before the committee on the merchant marine and fisheries, U. S. House of Representatives, 70th Congress, 1st session, January 26-February 14, 1928. Washington, Government Printing Office, 1928.

Kaland, William J. Interview, 1963. Unpublished. (C)

Kapp, David. Reminiscences, 1959. Unpublished. (C)

Kaltenborn, H. V. Papers. Unpublished. (M)

Kaltenborn, H. V. Reminiscences, 1950. Unpublished. (C)

Kintner, S. H. Address: delivered over KDKA December 20, 1922; also broadcast over WJZ, KYW, WBZ. Unpublished. (M)

Knight, Kirk. Reminiscences, 1951. Unpublished. (C)

KNX-CBS Radio: continuity, growth and creativity. Los Angeles, KNX, 1961. Unpublished.

Landry, Robert J. This Fascinating Radio Business. Indianapolis and New York, Bobbs-Merrill, 1946.

Landry, Robert J. Who, What, Why Is Radio? New York, George W. Stewart, 1942.

Lang, Chester Henry. Reminiscences, 1951. Unpublished. (C)

Lasker, Albert Davis. Reminiscences, 1950. Unpublished. (C)

Laurie, Joe, Jr. See Green, Abel, and—

Lescarboura, Austin C. See Goldsmith, Alfred N., and—

Lessing, Lawrence. Man of High Fidelity: Edwin Howard Armstrong. Philadelphia and New York, Lippincott, 1956.

Levy, I. D., and Leon Levy. Conversation: text of recording, ca. 1964. Unpublished. (P)

Lichtenfield, Leon. Interview, 1963. Unpublished. (C)

Lichty, Lawrence W. The Nation's Station: a history of radio station WLW. Ph.D. dissertation. Columbus, Ohio State University, 1964. Unpublished.

Lichty, Lawrence W. A Study of the Careers and Qualifications of the Members of the Federal Radio Commission and the Federal Communications Commission, 1927-1961. Master's essay. Columbus, Ohio State University, 1961. Unpublished.

Linton, Bruce A. A History of Chicago Radio Station Programming 1921-1931: with emphasis on stations WMAQ and WGN. Ph.D. dissertation. Evanston (Ill.), Northwestern University, 1954. Unpublished.

The Listener. London, British Broadcasting Corporation, weekly, 1930-

Little, Donald G. Reminiscences, 1951. Unpublished. (C)

Love, Edgar J. Reminiscences, 1951. Unpublished. (C)

Lyons, Eugene. David Sarnoff—a biography. New York, Harper, 1966.

Lyons, Ruth. Reminiscences, 1959. Unpublished. (C)

Making Pep and Sparkle Typify a Ginger Ale. New York, National Broadcasting Company, 1929.

Manning, Stanley Rutter. Reminiscences, 1951. Unpublished. (C)

Marconi, Degna. My Father, Marconi. New York, McGraw-Hill, 1962.

Martin, Pete. See Crosby, Bing, as told to—

McCarty, Harold B. "WHA, Wisconsin's Radio Pioneer," in Wisconsin Blue Book 1937. Madison, State of Wisconsin, 1938.

McLuhan, Marshall. The Gutenberg Galaxy. Toronto, University of Toronto Press, 1962.

McMahon, Robert S. For so-called "McMahon Report" see Regulation of Broadcasting.

McNamee, Graham, in collaboration with Robert Gordon Anderson. You're On the Air. New York and London, Harper, 1926.

Means, Gardiner C. See Berle, Adolf A., Jr., and—

Memorandum of Minutes: of the advisory council of the National Broadcasting Company. Annual meetings, 1927, etc. New York, National Broadcasting Company, 1928, etc.

Mills, John. A Fugue in Cycles and Bells. New York, Van Nostrand, 1935.

Morris, Lloyd. Not So Long Ago. New York, Random House, 1949.

Morse, Carlton. Interview, 1963. Unpublished. (C)

Newby, Ray. Interview by Gordon B. Greb, 1959. Unpublished. (C)

Nobel, Milton. The Municipal Broadcasting System: its history, organization and activities. Master's essay. New York, City College of New York, 1953. Unpublished.

Patt, John F. Reminiscences, 1960. Unpublished. (C)

Payne, George Henry. The Federal Communications Act: lecture at Harvard University Graduate School of Business Administration, May 14, 1935. New York, Ritz Tower, 1935.

Plant, Elton M. Reminiscences, 1951. Unpublished. (C)

Ponting, Herbert. Reminiscences, 1951. Unpublished. (C)

Popenoe, Charles B. WJZ. Undated, unpublished. (N)

Power, Harold J. See Dunham, Edwin L., This Is the AMRAD Story.

Quarterly of Film, Radio and Television. Berkeley and Los Angeles. University of California Press, quarterly, 1951-57.

QST. Hartford (Conn.), American Radio Relay League, monthly, 1915-

Radio Age. Chicago, monthly, 1923-28.

Radio Annual. New York, Radio Daily, annual, 1938-

Radio Art. New York, semimonthly, then quarterly, 1932-39.

Radio as a Cultural Agency. See Tyler, Tracy (ed.).

Radio Broadcast. Garden City (N.Y.), Doubleday, Page, monthly, 1922-30.

Radio Control: hearings before the committee on interstate commerce, U. S. Senate, 69th Congress, 1st session, January 8-March 2, 1926. Washington, Government Printing Office, 1926.

Radio Daily. New York, daily, 1937-

Radio Dealer. New York, monthly, 1922-28.

Radio Digest. Chicago, irregularly, 1922-33.

Radio Drama Prize Competition. Schenectady (N.Y.), WGY, 1923.

Radio Enters the Home. New York, Radio Corporation of America, 1922.

Radio Guide. New York, monthly, 1925-26. Also weekly, 1931-

The Radio Industry: the story of its development as told by leaders of the industry to the students of the Graduate School of Business Administration, George F. Baker Foundation, Harvard University. Chicago and New York, A. W. Shaw, 1928.

Radio Retailing. New York, McGraw-Hill, monthly, 1925-39.

Radio Service Bulletin. Washington, U. S. Department of Commerce, monthly, 1915-34; Federal Communications Commission, 1934-

Radio Stars. New York, Dell Publishing Company, 1932-38.

Radio Today. New York, monthly, 1935-36.

Radio World. New York, weekly, 1922.

Radovsky, M. Alexander Popov: inventor of radio. Moscow, Foreign Languages Publishing House, 1957.

Rafetto, Michael. Interview, 1963. Unpublished. (C)

Regulation of Broadcasting: half a century of government regulation of broadcasting and the need for further legislative action. Study for the committee on interstate and foreign commerce, U. S. House of Representatives, 85th Congress, 2nd session (The "McMahon Report"). Washington, Government Printing Office, 1958.

Report of the Advisory Committee on Education by Radio, U. S. Department of the Interior. Columbus (O.), F. J. Heer Printing Company, 1930.

Report of the Federal Trade Commission on the Radio Industry: in response to House resolution 548, 67th Congress, 4th session. Submitted December 1, 1923. Washington, Government Printing Office, 1924.

Rhodes, Frederick Leland. Beginnings of Telephony. New York, Harper, 1929.

Richards, Ronald P. "Montana's Pioneer Radio Stations: a Hobby Becomes an Industry," Montana Journalism Review, Spring 1963.

Robertson, Bruce. Recollections of the Radio Industry, 1963. Unpublished. (C)

Robinson, Otis E. Interview, 1963. Unpublished. (C)

Robinson, Thomas Porter. Radio Networks and the Federal Government. New York, Columbia University Press, 1943.

Roosevelt, Franklin D. Selected Speeches, Messages, Press Conferences, and Letters. New York, Rinehart, 1957.

Rorty, James. "The Impending Radio War," Harper's Magazine, November 1931.

Rorty, James. Order on the Air! New York, John Day, 1934.

Rorty, James. Our Master's Voice: advertising. New York, John Day, 1934.

Saerchinger, César. Hello America! radio adventures in Europe. Boston, Houghton Mifflin, 1938.

Saltzman, Charles McKinley. See Commercial Radio Advertising.

Samuels, Charles. See Waters, Ethel, with—

Sarnoff, David. "Development of the Radio Art and Radio Industry Since 1920," in The Radio Industry. Chicago and New York, A. W. Shaw, 1928.

Sarnoff, David. See also title David Sarnoff.

Saudek, Robert. "Program Coming in Fine, Please Play Japanese Sandman," American Heritage, August 1965.

Schairer, Otto S. Patent Policies of the Radio Corporation of America. New York, RCA Institutes Technical Press, 1939.

Schlesinger, Arthur M., Jr. The Coming of the New Deal. Boston, Houghton Mifflin, 1959.

Schlesinger, Arthur M., Jr. The Crisis of the Old Order. Boston, Houghton Mifflin, 1957.

Schmeckebier, Laurence F. The Federal Radio Commission: its history, activities and organization. Washington, Brookings Institution, 1932.

Schramm, Wilbur (ed.). Mass Communications. Urbana, University of Illinois Press, 1949.

BIBLIOGRAPHY

Schubert, Paul. The Electric Word: the rise of radio. New York, Macmillan, 1928.

Scripps, William Edmund. Reminiscences, 1951. Unpublished. (C)

Seldes, Gilbert. The Public Arts. New York, Simon and Schuster, 1956.

Shannon, David A. (ed.). The Great Depression. New York, Prentice-Hall, 1960.

Sherwood, Robert E. Roosevelt and Hopkins: an intimate history. 2v. New York, Harper, 1950.

Shurick, E. P. J. The First Quarter-Century of American Broadcasting. Kansas City, Midland Publishing Company, 1946.

Slate, Sam J., and Joe Cook. It Sounds Impossible. New York, Macmillan, 1963.

Smith, Gene. When the Cheering Stopped: the last years of Woodrow Wilson. New York, William Morrow, 1964.

Smith, Ira D. Interview by Gordon B. Greb over KCBS, San Francisco, 1962. Unpublished. (C)

Smith, Jeannette Sayre. See Friedrich, Carl J., with—

Sowell, F. C. Reminiscences, 1951. Unpublished. (C)

Standard Book of Reference. Medford (Mass.), American Radio and Research Corporation, 1924.

Stearns, Marshall W. The Story of Jazz. New York, Oxford University Press, 1956.

Stokes, George M. A Public Service Program History of Radio Station WFAA-820, Dallas, Texas. Ph.D. dissertation. Evanston (Ill.), Northwestern University, 1954. (Unpublished.)

The Story of WOR. Newark, Bamberger Broadcasting Service, 1934.

Stranger than Fiction ("by the Voice of Experience"). New York, Dodd, Mead, 1934.

Summers, Harrison B. (ed.), A Thirty-Year History of Programs Carried on National Radio Networks in the United States, 1926-1956. Columbus, Ohio State University, 1958.

Tarbell, Ida M. Owen D. Young: a new type of industrial leader. New York, Macmillan, 1932.

Tebbel, John. David Sarnoff: putting electrons to work. Chicago, New York, and London, Encyclopedia Britannica Press, 1963.

Television. New York, Experimental Publishing Company, 1927-?

Television Quarterly. Syracuse (N.Y.), National Academy of Television Arts and Sciences, quarterly, 1962-

Tisdale, Jim. See Davies, Edward A., and—

True, Sybil M. Interview by Gordon B. Greb, 1959. Unpublished. (C)

Tull, Charles J. Father Coughlin and the New Deal. Syracuse, Syracuse University Press, 1965.

Tyler, Tracy F. An Appraisal of Radio Broadcasting in the Land-Grant Colleges and State Universities. Washington, National Committee on Education by Radio, 1933.

Tyler, Tracy F. (ed.). Radio as a Cultural Agency: proceedings of a national conference on the use of radio as a cultural agency in a democracy. Washington, D.C., National Committee on Education by Radio, 1934.

Tyson, Edwin Lloyd. Reminiscences, 1951. Unpublished. (C)

Tyson, Levering (ed.). Radio and Education. Chicago, University of Chicago Press, 1933.

Ulanov, Barry, The Incredible Crosby. New York and Toronto. Whittlesey House, 1948.

United States Department of Commerce. See Radio Service Bulletin.

United States Department of the Interior. See Report of the Advisory Committee on Education by Radio.

United States House of Representatives, committee on interstate and foreign commerce. See Regulation of Broadcasting.

United States House of Representatives, committee on merchant marine and fisheries. See following titles: Government Control of Radio Communication; Jurisdiction of Radio Commission.

United States Senate, committee on interstate commerce. See following titles: Commission on Communications; Federal Radio Commissioners; Fees for Radio Licenses; Radio Control.

Variety. New York, weekly, 1905-

Variety Radio Directory. New York, Variety, annual, 1937-41.

The Voice of Experience. New York, Dodd, Mead, 1933. See also Stranger than Fiction ("by the Voice of Experience").

Wagoner, Clyde D. Reminiscences, 1950. Unpublished. (C)

Wakeman, Frederic. The Hucksters. New York, Rinehart, 1946.

Wallace, Wesley Herndon. The Development of Broadcasting in North Carolina, 1922-1948. Ph.D. dissertation. Durham (N.C.), Duke University, 1962. Unpublished.

Waters, Ethel, with Charles Samuels. His Eye Is on the Sparrow. Garden City (N.Y.), Doubleday, 1951.

Webster, Bethuel M., Jr. Our Stake in the Ether. Washington, American Academy of Air Law, 1931.

Weir, Irving Reid. Reminiscences, 1951. Unpublished. (C)

Western Electrician. Chicago, monthly, 1887-1908.

Whalen, Grover A. Reminiscences, 1951. Unpublished. (C)

White, Llewellyn. The American Radio: a report on the broadcasting industry in the United States from the Commission on Freedom of the Press. Chicago, University of Chicago Press, 1947.

White, Paul W. News on the Air. New York, Harcourt, Brace, 1947.

White, Rex G. Reminiscences, 1951. Unpublished. (C)

White, William C. Reminiscences, 1951. Unpublished. (C)

Wile, Frederic William. News Is Where You Find It: forty years' reporting at home and abroad. Indianapolis and New York, Bobbs-Merrill, 1939.

Wireless Age. New York, Marconi, monthly, 1913-19; RCA, 1919-25.

Wisconsin Blue Book, 1937. Madison, State of Wisconsin, 1938.

WJZ Log, 1923-26, in NBC Papers. Unpublished. (M)

WWJ—the Detroit News. Detroit, Detroit News, 1922.

Woods, Mark. Reminiscences, 1951. Unpublished. (C)

Wylie, Max. "Amos 'n' Andy—Loving Remembrance," Television Quarterly, Summer 1963.

Young, Otis B. "The Real Beginning of Radio," Saturday Review, March 7, 1964.

The Zenith Story: a history from 1919. Chicago, Zenith Corporation, 1955.

Zworykin, Vladimir K. "The Early Days," Television Quarterly, November 1962.

INDEX

329

64, 93, 99, 169–70, 271; hostility of film industry, 278
Los Angeles *Examiner*, 99n.
Los Angeles *Times*, 170
Louchheim, Jerome H., 223
Louisville *Courier-Journal*, 92
Love, Edgar S., 32–3, 210
Loyola University, New Orleans, 32n., 37, 98n.
Lucky Strike cigarettes, 158, 202, 237–8, 273, 276

Macfadden, Bernarr, 167–8, 220
Macfarland, Charles F., 204–5
Macy, R. C., store, 113
Magnavox radio, 255
Main Street Sketches, 224
Majestic radio, 255
Manning, Stanley R., 29–30
March of Time, radio series, 277–8; photographs, Plate 15
Marconi, Guglielmo, invention of wireless, 9–12; early recognition, 12–15; formation and rise of American Marconi, 15–16, 42–3, 76; friction with U. S. Navy Department, 16–18; receives transatlantic signal, 20; patent disputes, 42, 47; interest in alternator, 49, 57; disguised aboard ship, 50; interest in short waves, 152; photographs, Plates 1, 16
Marietta College, 98n.
Marshall radio, 163
Marx Brothers, 273
Masefield, John, 247–8
Massachusetts Institute of Technology, 152
Maxim, Hiram Percy, 54–6, 94
Maxwell House Hour, 191
Mayo, Mary, 45
McAdoo, William G., 149
McClelland, George F., 113, 188
McDonald, Eugene F., 180, 189
McIntire, John, 278
McKinley, William, 23, 284
McLean, Angus Wilton, 210
McNamee, Graham, 149, 165–6, 180, 194; photograph, Plate 9
McPherson, Aimee Semple, 179–80
Melco Supreme radio, 163
merchandising, 240–44, 268–9
Mercury radio, 163
Merrill (Wisc.) *Advocate*, 139
Metro-Goldwyn-Mayer, 232
Metropolitan Opera, 1910 broadcast, 27

Mexico, Brinkley broadcasts from, 259
Meyers, Sidney, 45
microphone, problems and experiments, 62, 86, 89, 136; *see also* Plates 1-10, 12-15
Millay, Edna St. Vincent, 222
Miller, Elam, 191n.
Millikan, Robert A., 262
Millikin University, 98n.
Mills, E. C., 120
Mineralava, 113
Minnesota, University of, 98n.
Missouri, University of, 98n.
Mitchell, Charles E., 263–4
monopoly, over cables by Britain, 12, 15, 50; Western Union monopoly period, 43, 253–4; U. S. Navy Department proposes radio communication monopoly, 52–5; RCA monopoly charter proposed by Owen D. Young, 59; FTC investigation of monopoly charges, 117, 161–2, 184, 201; monopoly clauses in Radio Act of 1927, 198, 257; U. S. Department of Justice suit against patent allies, 252–3, 257, 266–7
Montgomery Ward, 202; early receiver, Plate 7
Moonshine and Honeysuckle, radio drama series, 276
Moorhead, Agnes, 277
Morgan, Anne, 81
Morgan, Joy Elmer, 261, 282
Morgan, J. P., 35–6
Mormon Tabernacle Choir, 250
Morrow, Dwight, 204
Morse, Carlton, 237, 271
Moss, Arnold, 278
Mound City Blue Blowers, 129
Mullen, Frank, 192
Murray, Ken, 273
music, pioneer broadcasts of, 20, 25–7, 30, 34, 36, 45–6, 52, 61–4, 67–8, 89; "radio music box" proposal, 78–80; status and fees of musical artists, 87, 112, 127–8, 131–5, 193, 222; issue of music royalty fees, 119–21, 194, 200; during 1920's, emphasis on "potted palm music," 125–35, 191; beginnings of jazz, 128–31; music as unsponsored "public service," 205, 250, 279
Music Appreciation Hour, 205, 250, 279
Mussolini, broadcast to United States, 250; portrayed by De Corsia, 277

181–8; disputes with licensees, 201, 255–7; formation of National Broadcasting Company, 184–8; of RKO, 232–3; television experimentation, 231, 272, 283; purchase of Victor, 233, 251; U. S. Department of Justice anti-trust suit, 252–3, 257; consent decree, 266–9; plans for Radio City, 267, 269, 272; photographs, Plates 9, 12, 13, 16
Radio Dealer, periodical, 102, 107
Radio Digest, periodical, 172
Radio Guild, radio drama series, 250
Radio-Keith-Orpheum, 232–3, 278
radio music box, Sarnoff proposal, 78–80
Radio Retailing, periodical, 212–14
Radio World, periodical, 102
Radiola radio, 91, 162
Ragamuffins, transcriptions, 276–7
Ranald, Josef, 240
Randall, Vischer A., 110–11
Rankin advertising agency, 113
rating, *see* Crossley rating
RCA, *see* Radio Corporation of America
Readers' Guide to Periodical Literature, 103
Real Folks, radio drama series, 224
receivers, production of, 71–2, 82–3, 91, 114–17, 125, 154, 160–63, 187; patent disputes over, 82–3, 115–17, 160–61, 183–4, 255–7; photographs, Plates 7, 8, 11
recordings, use of, 153, 226, 228–9, 247, 269; attitudes toward, 247; *see also* phonograph records
red network, *see* National Broadcasting Company
Reith, Sir John, 247–8
religious broadcasting, 4, 103–4, 265; stations licensed to religious groups, 35, 99, 122, 174, 179–80; religious programs on other stations, 71, 170, 205, 250, 281; on commercial basis, 176
Report of the Federal Trade Commission on the Radio Industry, 161
Revelers, The, 86
Reynolds, R. J., tobacco company, 241
Rice, E. W., 79, 135
Rice, Martin P.
Richmond (Va.) *Times Dispatch*, 99n.
Rickard, Tex, 80–81
Rise of the Goldbergs, 274–6
Rivoli Theater, 153
RKO, *see* Radio-Keith-Orpheum

Robertson, Andrew W., 266
Robertson, Bruce, 244
Robinson, Carson, 133
Robinson, Henry M., 204
Robinson, Ira, 215, 217–18
Rochester (N. Y.) *Times Union*, 99n.
Rockefeller, John D., Jr., 261
Rockefeller Center, *see* Radio City
Rogers, Will, 148, 159, 190
Rolfe, B. A., 190
Roosevelt, Franklin D., as Assistant Secretary of the Navy, 47–8, 57–8; sponsor, Dempsey-Carpentier fight broadcast, 81; presidential candidate and President-elect, 253, 264, 267–8, 273; as President, 284–5
Roosevelt, Theodore, 20–21, 284
Root, Elihu, 204–6
Rorty, James, 264–5
Rosenberg, L. H., 69
Rosenwald, Julius, 204
Roses and Drums, radio drama series, 276
Ross, Samuel, 109
Rothapfel, S. L. (Rothafel), *see* Roxy
Roxy, 113, 180
Ruffo, Titta, 191
Russia, radio and television experimentation, 10, 14; effects of Revolution on United States, 56, 83, 90; Kaltenborn broadcast on U. S.-Russian relations, 139–41; broadcast by Shaw on Soviet visit, 248–50; interest during Depression, 263
Rymer, Paul, 274

Saerchinger, César, 247–50, 280
St. Joseph's College, Philadelphia, 32n., 98n.
St. Louis, 1904 exposition, 24
St. Louis *Post Dispatch*, 99n.
St. Louis University, 32n., 98n.
St. Martin's College, Lacey, Wash., 98n.
Saltzman, Charles McK., 243–4
Sam 'n' Henry, 226
San Francisco, 1915 exposition, 35, 44, 46; as broadcasting center, 93, 146, 174, 207; during Depression, 237, 271
San Jose, Calif., early broadcasting, 34–5
Sandburg, Carl, 130
Sarnoff, David, *Titanic* disaster, 43, 77; with RCA, 61, 74, 79–83, 115, 123, 151–2, 184–5, 193–4, 231, 251–2, 280–81; early life, 75–6; with Amer-